Justice in the Risk Society

Challenging and Re-affirming Justice in Late Modernity

Barbara Hudson

SAGE Publications
London • Thousand Oaks • New Delhi

First published 2003

SAGE Publications Ltd
6 Bonhill Street
London EC2A 4PU

SAGE Publications Inc
2455 Teller Road
Thousand Oaks, California 91320

SAGE Publications India Pvt Ltd
B-42, Panchsheel Enclave
Post Box 4109
New Delhi 100 017

British Library Cataloguing in Publication data

A catalogue record for this book is available from the British Library

ISBN 0-7619 6159 3
      0-7619 6160 7

Library of Congress control number available

Typeset by C&M Digitals (P) Ltd, Chennai, India
Printed in Great Britain by Athenaeum Press, Gateshead

In memory of my father, Frederick Groves Leigh, a good
man who cared about justice

Contents

Acknowledgements

This book has taken an inordinately long time to write, and I wish to thank Gillian Stern and her colleagues at Sage for their patience. There are always tales that could be told about why books take so long, but with this book there are two principal causes of delay. The first is that I didn't want *not* to be writing it: so much of my work is about things I dislike – race discrimination in punishment, for example – and it was good to be writing something positive and idealistic, what justice should and could be like. The second reason is that each chapter engaged with vast bodies of literature, and at times I felt both intimidated and overwhelmed. I am therefore extremely grateful to David Garland, for his wise words at an 'author meets readers panel' at the British Criminology Conference in July 2002: 'A book should know its questions and try to answer them, not try to answer all possible questions.' Thanks David, that got me out of the trees and into the wood!

Lots of people have helped me develop the ideas in the book. Andrew Ashworth, Andrew von Hirsch and Antony Duff have been important throughout, and the arguments and debates we have had have helped sharpen my thinking at various points. My own 'risk society' was a group of criminologists who write influentially and insightfully about risk: Kelly Hannah-Moffat, Pat O'Malley, Jonathan Simon, Kevin Stenson and Richard Sparks have provided good ideas and good company. Stan Cohen's work is inspirational as always; Kathy Daly, Joe Sim and Phil Scraton have provided debate, encouragement and friendship whenever I've needed it. Colleagues and students at the University of Central Lancashire have questioned, argued and encouraged: Gaynor Bramhall, Helen Codd, Michael Salter and David Scott have been the most supportive and understanding colleagues one could wish for. Heather Scott has been a far better friend than I deserve.

Finally, my love and thanks to Harry, for your patience, sharing laughter, pouring gin and tonic when required, and all kinds of good things.

Introduction

This book was prompted by concern that 'justice' is very much under threat in the 'risk society'. In contemporary western societies adherence to long-held principles of justice is endangered by excessive concern with safety: fear of crime and fear of terrorism are rational fears, but are heightened to the point where they overwhelm our care for liberty and justice. Contemporary Britain furnishes plenty of examples of fears overwhelming concern for justice: policy proposals about sex offenders and persons diagnosed with serious personality disorders; restrictions on asylum seekers' rights to move freely about the country and to receive welfare benefits; detention without trial of suspected terrorists, are just a few that spring to mind. Less serious threats are also being responded to with scant regard for justice: proposals to admit hearsay evidence in trials; unregulated extension of CCTV systems; proliferation of 'gated' communities, are examples. The idea that 'it is better for ten guilty persons to go free than for one innocent person to be convicted' is seen as naïve and 'soft' on criminals; the 'beyond reasonable doubt' standard of proof is regarded as inconvenient and outmoded. Readers can no doubt think of many examples of developments in the name of safety which have raised questions for them about the balance to be struck between freedom and safety, justice and risk.

Western societies seem to be becoming much more concerned with rights and justice abroad than at home. While we sacrifice liberty to safety, and compromise justice through our strategies to control risk in our own countries, we refuse trade and aid, and threaten or (maybe, by the time this book is published) actually wage war in the name of justice and human rights. While we disregard the rights of offenders and other risky people here, dividing people into those (potential victims) who *deserve* rights and those (potential offenders) who don't, we condemn rights abuses in other countries, and the arguments of their governments that incarcerating dissidents and other 'enemies' is necessary for public safety are dismissed. Some of the practices western democracies are currently pursuing in the name of public safety would be condemned by us if they were happening in another country.

Around the time I was beginning to plan this book, I gave a lecture in Budapest. One of the other speakers, a forensic psychiatrist, was explaining the idea of the Serious Personality Disorder incarceration. The translator repeatedly asked the speaker to repeat her words: she could not believe she was interpreting correctly, that it was proposed in democratic, rights-regarding England and Wales to imprison people indefinitely who had not committed any offence, on the grounds that they could be dangerous. We should, perhaps, all be Hungarians in our own country!

Liberal legal theorists such as Andrew Ashworth and Andrew von Hirsch, and liberal criminologists like Rod Morgan, have challenged many of these recent developments that are so worrying from the point of view of justice; their counterparts in other countries have similarly challenged innovations there which disregard justice. These powerfully argued, impeccably reasoned challenges, however, have not been successful in stemming the tide of risk-oriented, justice-careless policy shifts. The most prominent example is the demise of the 1991 Criminal Justice Act. This was based very firmly on liberal justice principles of proportionality, consistency and fairness; its introduction was accompanied by an unprecedented amount of training of criminal justice professionals and explanations of its principles to the public through the media, and it was heralded as the legislation to set the principles of criminal justice for decades to come. Within six months, however, it was being undermined in the courts and by politicians, and from 1993 onwards a series of Acts and amendments – and sentencing practice itself – reflected less concern with justice and more concern with public protection.

While this story has been told by many writers, I wanted to explore the question of whether liberal theories of justice were not so much inadequately defended, but were in themselves inadequate to meet the challenges of risk politics. This meant looking at the two primary branches of liberalism: deontological liberalism and Utilitarianism. Deontological theories are theories which inquire not into the nature and essence of goodness, but into the nature of ethical duty. They put forward no ideas about the 'good life', but look at what it is to behave according to principles of justice. Deontological liberals do not seek to promote substantive goods, such as happiness or welfare, but to delineate regulatory principles, such as equal respect, fairness and consistency so as to create a social framework in which individuals can pursue their own ideas about the good life without interference from others. These values are clearly behind the main principles of the 1991 Criminal Justice Act.

Utilitarianism seeks to promote the good of all members of society, and defines this good as happiness, or absence of pain. The problem with Utilitarianism is that it does not offer adequate protection of each individual citizen against encroachments in the name of the good of society as a whole, or of the majority. In criminal justice terms, the rights of offenders to proportionate punishment cannot be guaranteed against the good of crime prevention in the wider society. Criminal justice systems in actual societies necessarily balance these two liberal models, and most analysts of the demise of the 1991 Criminal Justice Act feel that it was too preoccupied with its internal goals (fairness and consistency), and not enough concerned with the utilitarian goal of public safety (Bottoms, 1995). Rebalancing, towards greater public protection during the early 1990s was, therefore, scarcely surprising.

Beyond pendulum swings within the criminal justice response to routine crimes, however, could be detected moves which raised questions about the adequacy of liberal theory in any version to deal with the challenges of risk. People's estrangement from each other; their unwillingness to pay taxes for public services; the demands being made by feminists and by minority ethnic and religious groups; hostility towards foreigners; terrorism and threats of terrorism: these new orders of risk and claims to justice seem to be beyond the scope of liberalism's repertoire of theory and politics. I wanted to explore challenges to established ideas and institutions of justice that were coming from beyond liberalism. The most powerful challenges are those of communitarianism, feminism, and postmodernism.

Part I of the book – 'Challenging Liberal Justice' – opens with an outline and analysis of liberal moral philosophy and political theory, explaining the tensions between the two branches of liberalism, and then discusses liberal approaches to punishment and to security. This is followed by chapters on the politics of risk and safety; the communitarian challenge; and the critiques of liberalism advanced by liberal and post-structuralist feminists.

The critiques of liberal theories and practices of justice explored in Part I are powerful and persuasive. The chapter on risk shows how vulnerable the ideal of justice can be in face of heightened populist and political demand for safety from dangers (real or imagined) posed by other people. We see in our everyday lives how difficult it can be to achieve a balance between promoting security and respecting justice. Issues such as the penetration of CCTV systems – their location; whether private individuals as well as public bodies should be able to install cameras; who should have access to the films; camera footage's status as evidence; who, if anyone, has a right to object if cameras are sited in residential areas and other privatised space – make us think about the requirements of safety but also raise questions about the right to privacy. Measures put in place to strengthen prevention of terrorism post-11 September 2001; tighter border controls, detention and other measures to restrict illegal immigration, and the pros and cons of compulsory identity cards make us think about the balance between freedom and safety, for ourselves as well as for those we think may threaten us. These questions not only provoke different responses in different people, but they provoke different responses in the same people at different times: we are all supportive of greater restriction in the immediate aftermath of a terrorist attack or a particularly outrageous crime.

The difficulty of thinking through these issues reveals at least two deficiencies in liberalism as a guide to practical actions. First of all, liberalism provides the principle that restriction on freedom is to be allowed only in the cause of prevention of harm, but this principle gives us no firm guidance about how to balance harm and freedom. Secondly, it can provide little help in drawing the boundaries of justice: who is included in, and who is excluded by the social contract. Liberalism has not solved the problems of relationships between different cultures and nations, and it has not solved the problems posed by radical pluralism within liberal societies.

Utilitarian liberalism cannot guarantee the rights of individuals or minorities against majority opinions. This is particularly significant in present times when the clamorous politics of risk and safety drowns out the voices of those who seek to defend the rights of unpopular or unorthodox persons or groups, whether or not these persons or groups pose any real danger. Deontological versions of liberalism attempt to solve this problem by doing away with the promotion of good: in order to prevent any one person being sacrificed to the general or majoritarian good, pursuit of the good must be given up. What this leaves is an approach to justice which is devoid of substantive ethical content, so that doing justice entails – only – following justly decided procedures. The price of seeing all persons as being owed equal justice is to substitute a fictitious, abstract, identical 'person of reason' for the real, individual, flesh-and-blood moral citizen.

Just as Utilitarian liberalism resolves the problem of the relation of individual to society by dissolving the notion of the individual in the idea of the general good, deontological liberalism resolves the same problem by dissolving society, abstracting the individual from her social context. Communitarian critiques are directed at this aspect of liberalism. They are undoubtedly correct in objecting to this abstraction of individual from context, and any reconstruction of justice must take the relationship of individual to society much more seriously than traditional liberalism has done.

This is especially the case with criminal justice. The essence of crime is that it is a wrong against society as well as a harm against another individual. As Duff (1996) has insisted in his communitarian approach to punishment, assessment of harm does not capture the whole meaning of a crime; we are offended by crime because it offends a community's shared sense of right and wrong, not just because it is a harm done by one person to another. In Durkheimian terms, while the sense of crime as an offence against God might have disappeared from most sections of modern secularised societies, there remains the sense that when society's moral boundaries have been transgressed, justice requires blaming commensurate with the wrongness of the crime as well as recompense for the harm suffered by individual victims.

Communitarians, then, are on firm ground when arguing for the replacement of the Kantian 'unencumbered self' with a 'situated self'. However, they thereby return us to the utilitarian dilemma of how to protect the individual against community majoritarianism. In many ways, communitarianism appears as a new form of utilitarianism, with its emphasis on the general good rather than on individual freedoms. As well as the problem of toleration of a moderate range of diversity envisaged by liberal founding fathers such as Locke and Mill, however, contemporary consciousness recognises a much deeper and wider spectrum of difference. Feminist and post-structuralist writers challenge the potential repressiveness of communitarianism, and also its failure to move beyond Kantian liberalism's *logic of identity* which formulates principles of justice deriving from the qualities that all humans have in common (the ability to reason; the desire to pursue their own ends). In fact, it can be argued that communitarianism adds a political logic of identity to the philosophical logic of identity of deontological liberalism, because contemporary communities are groupings of 'people like us', to be defended against people who are not 'like us'.

Feminists and post-structuralists pose challenges that go beyond the tolerance of a diversity of views and beliefs about the good life and the rules necessary to organise society according to principles of justice. They locate diversity in the idea of the human subject herself. Gender, race, the contingencies of individual biographies mean that there cannot be a single subjectivity; the logic of identity is an illogic. Whether difference is taken to be so central to human being, and identity so contingent on the flux of relationships and experiences that no categories can be stabilised, or whether there are some categories of identity which do reflect commonalities of experience and are therefore useful as a basis for developing ideas and institutions of justice (categories such as gender, race, religion, class, nationality) is a matter of debate, but feminists and postmodernists are agreed that there can be no single voice of all humankind, no *legislating reason* which can lay down rules to which we can all, rationally, accede.

Theories and practices of justice are found wanting because they do not meet the political challenges of our times and also because they are founded on unsatisfactory philosophical grounds (Matravers, 2000; Norrie, 2000). Nonetheless, all the critical perspectives discussed in Part I recognise the need for some sort of universalistic ideal of justice. No one denies that societies and communities should treat their citizens justly; that social institutions should dispense the goods within their domain justly, be these 'goods' education, health and welfare, or punishment and safety. No one disputes that recognising a practice or a distribution as unjust is reason for changing it; no one disputes that there should be mechanisms and institutions for remedying injustice between citizens and between government and citizen. The task is, then, to develop ideas about justice which can meet the challenges of the times – both political and theoretical.

Part II – 'Reaffirming justice' – engages with some ideas and practices that have emerged which can be regarded either as resources for reconstructing theories and institutions of justice, or as glimpses of new forms of justice in theory and practice. Chapter 5 looks at the work of Jurgen Habermas, whose writing addresses questions of truth and justice, rights, and the constitutional challenges posed by the rise of the 'security state'. Habermas has developed a model of *discursive* justice, which is drawn upon by feminist political philosophers including Seyla Benhabib and Iris Young, whose work is discussed in Chapter 4. Habermas's early work reflects the concerns of the Frankfurt School of German critical theorists, but in his later work he has set himself the task of reworking Kantian Enlightenment ideas to meet the conditions and challenges posed by contemporary society. He lays down rules of discourse which, he argues, can reconcile competing claims, and which are necessary if decisions are to reflect the concerns of justice as well as those of instrumental effectiveness. Habermas's latest work takes account of criticisms made by feminists of his earlier writings, and although he concedes a great deal to them, he does not answer all their objections. Habermas has disputed vigorously with postmodernists, especially Foucault, Lyotard and Derrida, whom he sees as representing a new 'conservative irrationalism' in their rejection of Enlightenment categories of reason and subjectivity.

Chapter 6 examines the work of 'affirmative postmodernists': Lyotard, Derrida and Bauman. They mount a powerful case that liberalism's exclusions and omissions from the circle of rights and justice are not accidental, but are entailed by the very categories of thought and language in which liberalism assembles its philosophy and politics. Unlike Habermas, they do not see the impetus of discourse as being towards intersubjective agreement, but towards domination. Who is excluded, who is marginalised, who is repressed, are the questions they say should be raised against systems of law and ideas of justice. These postmodernists do not put forward any new models of justice, but they adopt Levinas's ethics of *alterity* as the starting-point for justice. This is an ethics which, if it can be incorporated into a practice of justice, can go beyond liberalism's limit of doing justice to people like ourselves, because the ethics of alterity insists that our responsibility to others is prior to, and does not depend on, our being able to understand them.

Postmodern approaches go beyond discursive justice towards a more radical *reflective justice*. Reflective justice involves making judgments based on the individual case, a judgment which looks at the individual case in the light of more universal aspirations to justice, rather than applying general rules to particular cases (Ferrara, 1999). Law's usual relationship between the general and the particular (that particular cases should be fitted into the categories of general rules) is reversed in reflective justice: individual judgments look to universal horizons rather than to general rules.

The final chapter looks at restorative justice as the mode of contemporary justice which comes closest to the ideal of discursiveness. Its progressive potential is acknowledged, but it is criticised for its failure to develop a fully *relational* perspective. Legal philosophers who do develop relational theories of justice (Duff and Norrie) are discussed, and relationalism is commended as a possible way to avoid the extremes of either Kantian individualism or communitarian repressiveness.

The chapter, and the book, closes with a reflection on human rights. Although communitarianism, feminism and postmodernism are critical of some aspects of liberalism's construction of rights, they nonetheless remain attached to the idea of rights. Questions about the conditionality or inalienability of rights are discussed, and it is the book's conclusion that some rights must be regarded as inalienable, while others may be suspended only in extreme circumstances and with properly argued justification. Discursive justice, it is argued, reaches its limits at the edge of communities who share the same basic moral principles or who can at least make themselves comprehensible to each other; beyond sympathy and beyond comprehension only rights can guard against injustice.

Discursive justice, relational justice, reflective justice and rights-regarding justice are very much work-in-progress perspectives, and although much has been done within them, none has reached the level of sophistication and influence of, for example, liberal social contract theory which has been diversified into its Utilitarian and Kantian traditions and been so influential among western theorists and institution-builders. These new perspectives are, however, beginning to influence ideas about policy and practice in criminal justice and may point the way towards avoidance of throwing the baby of regard for individual liberty and universal respect out with the bathwater of insufficient regard to the self–society relationship and misguided conceptions of identical, essentialist human subjectivity. Doing justice in the risk society may mean rethinking liberalism (Bellamy, 2000); the rethinking, however, needs to be radical.

As well as wishing to make a substantive, albeit modest, contribution to rethinking justice, the book was prompted by a wish to bring this range of political and legal philosophical writing on justice to the attention of criminologists and penologists. I am concerned that not only has society at large lost a sense of justice, but penology and criminology have lost interest in justice too. The criminology of control and sociology of punishment have been enriched by utilising a range of social theory – risk society, governmentality – and by drawing on the ideas of a range of writers such as Foucault, Bauman, Beck, Bataille and others who write on the boundaries of sociology and philosophy. These perspectives have been deployed to produce analytically rich descriptions of what is going on in late-modern societies in relation to crime, control and punishment. What criminology and penology have lost touch with, however, is work aimed at normative reconstruction of law and penality. Penology seems content to be descriptive or instrumental: it does not appear to see its endeavour as an aspiration to justice. It is not surprising that Stan Cohen described himself as having 'stopped doing criminology' in favour of 'doing human rights' (Cohen, 1993). Theoretical books on punishment seem to stop – chronologically and conceptually – with Foucault, who, as I argue, gives us complex descriptions of punishment, but little by way of inspiration or signposts towards justice.

The book, therefore, is intended to introduce students, academics and professionals involved in criminology and penology to work being produced in parallel disciplines that aim to reconstruct theories and institutions of justice Each chapter deals with work that is in itself the subject of large bodies of literature, and I make no claims to comprehensive coverage of liberalism, risk, communitarianism, feminism, Habermas's work, postmodernism, restorative justice, relational justice or human rights. I only discuss aspects of these theories and bodies of work which are relevant to my topic of challenges to, and reaffirmations of, justice in the risk society. My hope is that I might kindle some spark of concern for the problems facing justice, and some inspiration to come to its defence.

Part I
Challenging Liberal Justice

1

Justice in the Liberal Tradition

In this chapter, I will look at theories of justice that have underpinned the development of the rules and institutions of justice in modern western societies. I will proceed first, by examining the general political-philosophical ideas and concepts in the area of justice in the modernist era, and then by looking at the perspectives on punishment which are linked with these philosophical theories. I will conclude the chapter by discussing liberalism's concerns with *security*, highlighting certain issues which are, I believe, posing threats to justice in the *risk society*.

By 'modernist era', I mean the period from the seventeenth century to the late twentieth century. This was the period which saw the development of modernism in most areas of western European life. In the sphere of government, it was the time of change from absolutist to constitutional government; in the sphere of the economy, it saw the ending of feudalism and the development of capitalism, with the transition from a predominantly agrarian to a predominantly industrial economy; in the sphere of religion, it saw the ending of the monopolistic influence of the Roman Catholic church and the rise of Protestantism and then of secularism; in terms of demographics it saw the shift of populations from the country to the towns and cities. The period saw the consolidation of the nation-state as the main political entity, and it saw the rise and fall of some nation-states, the movement of national boundaries, the rise and fall of dynasties; it saw changes in the form of families and changes in the roles of males and females; it saw the establishment of state-financed police services and of penal codes and systems of punishment; it saw developments in people's understandings of the extent of the world and the nature of the universe. These far-reaching developments not surprisingly stimulated much activity in political, moral and legal philosophy – the fields at whose intersection we find *justice*.

Although there are many different and competing theories and concepts in the philosophy of the era, these do have distinctiveness and coherence, such that different schools of thought can reasonably be seen as variants within a tradition, as different ways of institutionalising the same values and beliefs. The various theories are differently nuanced balances between the values and the states-of-being given importance in the tradition, and they are different interpretations or ways of securing those values and states of being. This modernist tradition began with what came to be known as the Enlightenment, and then developed into modern liberalism. Into the twenty-first century, our most influential theories of justice are liberal formulations of Enlightenment themes and values.

This modernist tradition begins with seventeenth-century theories of natural rights exemplified in the work of John Locke; progresses through ideas on the grounding of principles of morality and justice propounded by high Enlightenment philosophers, most notably Immanuel Kant, and culminates in the social contract Utilitarian liberalism of John Stuart Mill.[1] In the second half of the twentieth century, these theories were revitalised for changed times by latter-day liberal theorists such as John Rawls (1972) and Robert Nozick (1974). In turn, the implications of liberalism in their original and revised versions for law and morality have been questioned and elaborated by Dworkin (1978, 1986a), Raz (1986) and others.

What makes it plausible to read these divergent writings as comprising one tradition is that there has been no wholesale repudiation of their most fundamental tenets – constitutionally limited government; individualism; equality of freedom and respect – through successive generations of liberal thinkers. Rather, the tradition has developed through writers on the one hand addressing philosophical problems raised by, or left unresolved by, previous formulations, and on the other hand, foregrounding different questions raised within the tradition, according to political, moral and social circumstances at different times. But whatever challenges have been made to these philosophical keystones, there has always been a response from a recognisably liberal perspective.

The earliest phase of the nascent Enlightenment-liberal tradition is concerned first and foremost with questions of the limits of political power and the extent of political obligation. Early Enlightenment, pre-liberal works were produced at a time of emergent challenges to the autocratic monarchies of Europe, and a decline in adherence to the doctrine of the divine right of kings. Hobbes's great work, *Leviathan*, for example, was first published in 1651, two years after the execution of Charles I. John Locke was born ten years before the outbreak of the English Civil War, the son of a lawyer who fought on the side of the Parliamentary party. Locke underwent periods of exile during the Restoration period, finally returning to England in 1689 after the expulsion of James II and the accession of William of Orange, whose supporters he had associated with in Holland. His best known political works, the *Two Treatises of Civil Government*, were written in defence of the 'Glorious Revolution' of 1688 which ended the Stuart era. Although Hobbes and Locke differed in their ideas on the strength of the duty of subjects to obey the sovereign (Hobbes positing absolute duty and Locke duty conditional on the sovereign governing in accordance with the rights of subjects), both locate the basis of sovereign power and the duty of obedience in the self-interest of subjects, rather than in the divine status of the ruler. This idea of *social contract*, of political power arising from the agreement of individuals to cede some of their freedom in return for the security offered by the institution of state power, is one of the main foundations of modernism. It has been subject to many different formulations, but it has not yet been effectively or decisively displaced.

The next key theme in the development of the Enlightenment-liberal tradition was the search for the source or measure of justice. If it has been accepted that power was to be justly established, that it was to be exercised justly over subjects, and to arbitrate justly between subjects, in what did justice consist, what did it mean to act justly? Although Hobbes and Locke had broken with the doctrine of the sovereign as the earthly representative of God, they did not advance on seeing justice and virtue as reflections of the divine will and temperament; they produced no new theories on the source and nature of justice. For Kant and for Mill, who formulated what continue to be the two great streams of post-Enlightenment liberalism, God's will (or even existence) was not directly demonstrable, and the source of value must therefore be found in human beings themselves and their empirical situations. Kant located *rightness* in human capacities, whilst Mill argued that *goodness* lies in human desires. These two approaches, the deontological and the Utilitarian, are the main branches of modern liberalism, and as such they are manifested in the major theories of punishment.

In the twentieth century, the primary concerns of liberalism turned once again to political rather than moral philosophy. With constitutional government securely established, the most pressing issues of justice for liberal democracies in the past century have been to do with the distribution of material and social goods. In the west at least, challenges to liberalism have come not from religion but from socialism and communism, which have charged that liberalism's attachment to property rights and to limited government have together legitimised excessive inequalities in life-chances and in degrees of wealth. Liberalism has responded by developing ideas which would set principled limits to inequalities (Rawls) or would justify existing inequalities (Nozick). The political embodiment of these ideas is seen in the welfare-liberalism of Roosevelt's New Deal in the USA after the depression of the late 1920s and early 1930s, and the west European social democracies, vying with the minimal-state ideologies of conservative libertarianism and neo-liberalism.

The other great challenge to which liberalism has responded is pluralism. Liberalism was, of course, founded in circumstances of emerging religious pluralism and political difference, but the degrees of difference between Catholics and Protestants within the same Christian religion, and between proponents of different degrees of constitutionalism, were not of the same order as the overlapping and highly charged pluralisms of religion, race, ethnicity, sexuality and value systems that we recognise as the inevitable character of contemporary societies. Locke's denunciation of religious persecution falls far short of Mill's positive evaluation of diversity of character, and even further short of the centrality of pluralism in the ideas of Rawls. And for many critics, even this recognition of pluralism does not go far enough. What is a common thread throughout the liberal tradition, however, is the definitional connectedness of the very concepts of pluralism and justice. Liberals are united in their advocacy of *anti-majoritarianism*: they see that it is as important to protect minorities against the tyranny of the majority, as it is to protect subjects against the tyranny of the sovereign.

What follows is by no means a comprehensive exposition of the liberal tradition. There is a large body of literature devoted to the tradition as a whole, and to each of the authors and themes located within it.[2] I will briefly sketch some of the main themes, indicating the areas of agreement and disagreement between the different strands within the liberal tradition which have bearing on the topic of justice. The principles which are particularly vulnerable to the politics of risk and safety, and to feminist, communitarian and postmodern critiques, will be drawn to the reader's attention.

The emergence of the liberal agenda

John Locke is sometimes regarded as the first Whig theorist, a pre-Enlightenment thinker whose work influenced Enlightenment philosophers; sometimes as the founding father of the Enlightenment. Wherever the boundaries of the Enlightenment are placed, however, there is no doubt that his *Letters concerning Toleration* (1689–92), *Two Treatises of Government* (1690) and *Essay Concerning Human Understanding* (1694) had a profound impact on the subsequent flowering of Enlightenment thought (Williams, 1999: 5). His writings concerned key Enlightenment-liberal themes: the sources and limitations of knowledge in human experience in the world; the wrongness of religious persecution even to eradicate a belief one firmly holds to be mistaken; and the contractarian vision of a society of citizens governed by laws founded on respect for equal freedoms.

Locke sees knowledge as springing from experience; and experience, for him, consists of two elements, sensation and reflection. Although writing at the time of declining belief in divine authority, Locke was not seeking to repudiate religious truth itself, but the idea of truth and knowledge as immediately revealed and not subject to interpretation or indeed to construction in the light of human experience. Writing at a time of the growth of the continental hermeneutic tradition of producing competing interpretations of religious texts (Palmer, 1969: 34–5), and directly affected by political movements clustered around the religious schisms of Reformation and Restoration, it would be surprising if Locke's ideas were not as they were. He saw all knowledge as formed through the twin filters of experience of external phenomena and mental introspection:

All those sublime thoughts which tower above the clouds, and reach as high as heaven itself, take their rise and footing here; in all that great extent wherein the mind wanders in those remote speculations it stirs not one foot beyond those ideas which sense or reflection have offered for its contemplation. (*Essay Concerning Human Understanding*, Book II, Chapter 1, Section 24)

More than anything, however, Locke's dispute was with the theory of *innate ideas*, which had wide currency in his time (O'Connor, 1964: 207). According to this theory, some items of knowledge are not acquired through experience but exist *a priori*, that is they are present in the mind prior to experience. This theory had its antecedents in Plato and Augustine, and it surfaces in various guises from time to time. Locke examined two kinds of knowledge claimed as 'innate': self-evident logical principles, and moral rules. Logical principles, he argued, only seem self-evident through processes of rigorous mental analysis; moral rules, even if they seem to have universal assent, are nonetheless rooted in experience. If they are universal, this must be because of some commonality of human experience.

Criticisms of Locke's theory of knowledge, as with other parts of his philosophical corpus, centre mainly on his somewhat muddled and inadequate argumentation rather than on the truth or otherwise of his propositions themselves. What was important for the future development of the liberal tradition, was the way in which he directed attention to the operation of human capacities for reflection in empirical situations, as the source of knowledge and judgment. This quality of reflective experience remains the source of principles and values of justice throughout the modernist liberal tradition.

The human capacity for reflection means that members of a society are able to contrast their actual experience of life in that society with the imaginary experience of life in a hypothetical society, or in a hypothetical state of being outside all society. Locke depicted the freedoms that persons would have in a pre-social *state of nature*: freedom to act as one wishes; freedom to dispose of one's property unhindered; freedom to repel or exact vengeance upon those who impinged on one's actions or property. He claimed these primary freedoms associated with a state of nature as *natural rights*, arguing that people associate in societies in order best to protect those natural rights. The just society is therefore one which secures natural rights, and its use of coercive power and infringement of liberty is justified only to the extent that these are necessary to secure natural rights.

For Locke, legitimation of state power comes from 'tacit consent' in a (hypothetical) foundational social contract whereby members of a society agree to stop short of harming the life, liberty and property of others in the exercise of their own freedom, and to hand over to the state the role of punishing infringements of the laws enacted to uphold these rights and freedoms. They thus accept a measure of curtailment of freedom to act in pursuit of their self-interest, including curtailment of freedom to seek retribution or to deter further encroachments on their life, liberty or possessions.

Natural rights, and the freedoms and limitations they imply, provide the standards of right and wrong, justice and injustice, and are prior to any particular regime. It is the duty of those in power as well as those over whom power is exercised to uphold these standards. Locke's ideal state of affairs was the *civil society*, the society of free men [sic], equal under the rule of law, bound together by no common purpose but sharing a respect for each other's rights (Gray, 1995: 13).

It follows from Locke's conception of natural rights and the narrow limits to legitimate power to interfere with subjects' freedom of action, that he would be opposed to any attempts to impose uniformity of belief or custom. The form of his conception of natural rights also meant that he cast his views on religious tolerance in negative rather than positive terms: diversity is an outcome of lack of interference with people's worship, rather than a good in itself. He did not propose a duty to promote diversity – for according to him it is not the state's role to promote anything – but he deplored religious persecution as unwarranted interference with freedom. In his *Letter on Toleration* he argued that coercion – the means by which state power produces its effects – cannot change belief. Religious persecution can produce conformist religious behaviour, but cannot produce that which it seeks – a change in religious faith. Religion is mainly a matter of belief, so religious persecution is irrational. Locke looked to the motives and efficacy of the persecutors, not to the effects on the persecuted (Mendus, 1989: 28).

While Locke did not advance to a full theory of pluralism, he did open an important portal towards the idea of acceptance of freedom to pursue a variety of beliefs and value systems. Similarly, while he did not develop a full theory of rights, he took important steps in that direction.

Like his theory of knowledge, Locke's ideas on rights and toleration are criticised less for their substance than for his failure to theorise them adequately. He neither generalised from religious difference to other forms of difference, nor made a clear argument for religious tolerance as a special case. Likewise, he did not offer substantial explanation of why the state of nature would engender the rights he specifies, rather than engendering more or different rights. While his right of equal freedom under the law has been more or less uncontentiously incorporated into the liberal perspective, his ideas about property rights have proved more problematic.

Again, some of the difficulty with Locke's ideas comes from deficiencies of argument, rather than from the propositions themselves. It has been objected that a Lockean approach to property legitimates what are – to someone nurtured in twentieth-century western welfare liberalism at least – unconscionable levels of inequality. This objection arises most urgently when one has in mind contemporary formulations of entitlement theories such as that put forward by Nozick (1974), according to which natural rights allow for only *minimal state* governance. In particular, no redistributive taxation could be justified (Pettit, 1980: 85). Two Lockean ideas compromise a straightforward understanding of his theory as allowing for unlimited inequalities and giving undue emphasis to uninterrupted enjoyment and free disposal of property. These are the meaning he gives to 'property', and what Nozick refers to as his 'proviso' concerning the acquisition and deployment of property (Nozick, 1974: 175–82).

For Locke, 'property' refers to life and liberty as well as to material possessions, and it is to protect their rights in this broadly conceived 'property' that people come together in societies. Individuals relinquish the state of nature and co-operate 'for the mutual preservation of their lives, liberties and estates, which I call by the general name – property' (*Two Treatises of Government*: 180)

Free disposal of one's property is thus equivalent to inviolability of life and liberty, and the conditions under which it can be suspended would not seem unreasonable to most liberals. What is confusing is this inclusion of what we would generally take to be very different categories of things and qualities that can be possessed and enjoyed, under the common label 'property'. The 'proviso' provides some glimmer of differentiation between property rights in one's own body and in other material things. It stipulates that property rights in hitherto unowned things can be acquired through the 'mingling of one's labour, joining it to something that is one's own', 'at least where there is enough, and as good left in common for others' (*Two Treatises*, Section 27). The proviso offers a criterion of justice in property-holding when the principle of property is extended from one's own body to things externi to it. Ownership of one's own body cannot be deleterious to anyone else, but for other goods (including liberty) one person's gain may be someone else's loss.

Although Locke's idea of property may seem perversely wide, one advantage it offers is that it does subject forms of property such as land, goods and wealth to the principle of equal and compatible freedom, alongside life and liberty. Although it is, of course, by no means an egalitarian, full-blown principle of distribution, it provides some limit to inequality, and suggests that external property entitlements should not be immune to challenge by standards of justice.

Locke's work introduced most of the themes of contemporary liberalism: equal freedom; the social contract; limits to governmental power; rights and the just society; tolerance and diversity; distribution of property; derivation of knowledge and values from experience. His formulation of these ideas has been contested in the centuries that have followed, but the least we can concede is that he set the agenda for the liberal tradition.

The morality of reason

Enlightenment moral philosophy is a *post-conventional* ethics. By post-conventional, what is meant is that moral values are espoused, and moral decisions made, through individual choice and reflection. Moral rules are no longer fulfilled merely by following convention, whether these conventions are laid down by religious or secular authorities. If religious ethical codes such as the Ten Commandments are followed, this is because those who follow them choose to do so; similarly, law is not obeyed automatically – one has choice in whether or not to obey the law in general and in the particular, although knowledge of sanctions consequent upon disobedience may well become part of the decision-making process.

Important Enlightenment themes were, therefore, formulation of the essential principles of post-conventional morality, description of the procedures and sources whence those principles would be derived, and identifying the basis of the authority invested in those principles and procedures.

A consequence of this post-conventional stance was that autonomy was more highly valued than making the 'right' choice on any particular occasion: the fact that some course of action was chosen freely, upon reflection, was more important than the outcome of the reflection. Voltaire's well-known aphorism of deploring a choice but defending to the death the chooser's right to make it exemplifies the Enlightenment spirit.

Enlightenment, then, is a moral/intellectual coming of age; it is an acceptance of responsibility for knowledge and morality rather than following tradition for its own sake. As Kant, the pre-eminent Enlightenment thinker, puts it in his essay *An Answer to the Question: What is Enlightenment?*, in 1784:

> Enlightenment is man's emergence from his self-incurred immaturity. Immaturity is the inability to use one's own understanding without the guidance of another. This immaturity is self-incurred if its cause is not lack of understanding, but lack of resolution and courage to use it without the guidance of another. The motto of the Enlightenment is therefore: *Sapere aude!* Have courage to use your own understanding! (Kant, 1784, quoted in Williams, 1999: 2)

Kant is not advocating a radical relativism in which each person makes up their own moral code, their own idea of justice; nor is he arguing against the existence of God: what he is claiming is that moral law is law which a rational being would – and must – adopt for herself. This rational endorsement by the individual is a continuing and central idea in liberal theory, through to Rawls and beyond into the discursive philosophies of Habermas and other contemporary theorists.[3] A *sine qua non* of modernism is this reflexive individualism in which each person, if not their own moral author, is their own moral authority.

Immanuel Kant was through-and-through a German academic, schooled in the German rationalist tradition; his innovativeness lay in bringing this together with the developing British empiricist movement. Like Locke and Hume, Kant attached great weight to human experience as the source of knowledge and understanding, but he did not see these as the sole sources.

10

He distinguished theoretical reason, which is subject to confirmation by sense experience, from *a priori* categorical reason, which precedes experience. The categories of reason, he argues, organise the way in which we perceive the world.

The principles of justice, according to Kant, are therefore derivable from the categories of reason, rather than from any conditions of life in an actual society, or in a hypothetical natural state. Justice, he says, is a property of relations between people; it concerns the exercise of will among people; and it is concerned with the possibility and freedom of the exercise of will rather than the content or aim of that exercise of will. These conditions distinguish justice from other moral ideas such as virtue (which is something to do with the actor herself and may be exhibited in purely private conduct); they also distinguish justice from benevolence or charity (which though exercised towards other people, involve their desires or well-being rather than their free exercise of will). The conditions also establish justice as a form of moral rationality, as distinct from instrumental rationality which is deployed to bring about effects desired by the agent for herself.

Kant argues that is in the nature of reason that it is something that is actively exercised, and that the outcome of the exercise of reason is the formation of will. Only will formed by free exercise of reason can be described as moral: will formed in response to any form of coercion will be prudential or conventional, and since justice is a moral category, justice must be predicated on the free exercise of will. Since justice is concerned with free exercise of will in relationship with other people, it follows that the freedom involved must be of a relational quality. Justice is thus a state of relationships which brings about equilibrium in the free exercise of wills of all participants in the relational environment:

> Justice is therefore the aggregate of those conditions under which the will of one person can be conjoined with the will of another in accordance with a universal idea of freedom... Every action is just [right] that in itself or its maxim is such that the freedom of the will of each can consist with the freedom of everyone in accordance with a universal law. (Kant, 1996: 151)

Freedom of the will is thus a – perhaps the – crucial concept in Kant's theory of justice, and is posited in the *Critique of Pure Reason*, first published in 1781. Developing the idea further in the *Critique of Practical Reason* (1788), he argues that freedom of will is not something that can be proved theoretically, but that it is presupposed by our conception of morality, and that it is implicated in our acceptance of any moral law (Acton, 1970: 44–52).

The universal law to which Kant refers is that of equal freedom for all human beings – which is the fundamental maxim of classical liberalism, and which marks a clear departure from pre-Enlightenment philosophies. This law is fundamental to Kant's system of moral philosophy because it is essential for the realisation of his two elements of a universal law: treat all persons as ends and never as means, and act only in such a way that you could will your acts to be universalised. The first element comes from our recognition of human freedom as consisting in the capacity to determine ends for oneself; the second element is linked to the demand for equality, and also to the logical conditions of possibility of moral rules. So, to take the example which Kant uses, as do other moral philosophers, it would be irrational to break a promise because if everyone broke promises, the practice of promising would collapse, so that there would no longer be the opportunity to break promises. A promise and its acceptance marks a relationship of trust between promiser and promisee; in a society where no promises were kept, a promise would cease to be interpreted as a statement of intent of future action and therefore promises would no longer be sought or offered.

Kant's rule of universalizability – the categorical imperative as it is known – and the rule of treating people as end and never as means, imply two essential characteristics of morality. First, morality is unconditional, the logic of universalizability means that there can be no exceptions; secondly, its content is based on an ethic of equal respect, all people are to be treated as ends, as I am an end to myself. *All* persons are to be respected in their self-determination, on *all* occasions.

The structure of this derivation of morality and thence of principles of justice demonstrate, among other things, Kant's distinctive innovation in philosophical reasoning. His argument moves from the nature of moral life – the kinds of moral rules humans make between themselves, and the processes involved in making moral decisions – to the presuppositions involved in moral ideas and processes. Equal freedom, then, is not a prescription produced by morality, or a description of a just society, but a *condition of possibility* of justice. What he is saying here is that if we do not recognise other people as equal to ourselves and deserving of both respect and freedom, then our treatment of them will be motivated by instrumentalism and domination – the desire to make them act in our interests, rather than the recognition of our responsibility to enable them to advance their own interests. Justice is a way of remedying inequalities in freedom – of securing freedom from domination – therefore it necessarily rests upon the presumption that equal freedom is the fundamental precept of justice. Kant's focus on 'conditions of possibility' of concepts, processes and principles is his innovatory mode of 'critical' philosophy, and it begins a tradition of critical philosophy which is continued by Habermas in the present time.

Kant also introduced into theories of justice an important separation between the *right* and the *good*, the distinction between acting justly and acting from desire. Again, Kant reasons back from general human thought processes to first principles, rather than the other way round. He argues that we commonly experience the tension between duty and desire – we often have a sense that we ought to do something we don't really want to do, or ought not to do something that we do want to do. Morality, therefore, cannot be a matter of fulfilling desire, and justice must therefore be something other than promoting what is generally desired, or desired by a majority of people. Acting justly is therefore a matter of doing right, rather than bringing about good.

Clearly, Kant's importance in the liberal tradition can hardly be overestimated. He set forward the main principles and ideas of one of the two major streams of liberal thought, and his ideas have been seminally influential on current theories of distributive and punitive justice directly, and also as reformulated by more recent liberal philosophers such as Rawls (Murphy, 1987). Later chapters will raise questions about the appropriateness of his ideas of justice in the present day, and will also engage with contemporary theorists who wish to retain much that they believe continues to be of value in the Kantian branch of the liberal tradition, while addressing some aspects which are perceived to be inadequate in present social, political and intellectual contexts.

The greatest good

For Kant, the root of morality is in the reasoning *subject*; for Bentham, Mill and the Utilitarian philosophy they established, it is in the *object* of reason. For Utilitarians, morality is to be found not in how reason proceeds, but in what the reasoning subject desires. This return to the object of desire rather than the desiring subject was not a return to the pre-Enlightenment tradition of seeing the good as some supra-natural quality external to persons, which humans should strive to incorporate into their mode of being. The good, for Utilitarians, is what people themselves value; what is worthy, is that which people seek to promote. Rather than finding the right and the good in *a priori* principles, Utilitarians find the good and the right in empirical generalisations. What people desire, and seek to promote for themselves and those they care about, is their happiness. Right action, therefore, is action which promotes happiness; a just society is a society which produces happiness for its members. If happiness is desirable, then it should be maximised: the best society is that which produces the greatest happiness for the greatest number of people.

This single-criterion standard of the right, the good and the just gives Utilitarianism what Pettit describes as its 'attractive simplicity':

> The just social charter is required, not to meet obscure metaphysical constraints such as natural rights represent, but merely to ensure that more happiness is brought about by the charter than would be realised by any alternative. (Pettit, 1980: 111)

Bentham laid the foundations of Utilitarianism in his *Introduction to the Principles of Morals and Legislation*, first published in 1789, building his theory on the human impulses to pursue pleasure and avoid pain as the basis of rules of conduct. He defines the good for each individual as the securing of a maximum of pleasurable experiences and a minimum of painful experiences, a balance which he calls 'happiness'.

This hedonistic generalisation serves Bentham as an account of *motivation; morality* is action which promotes the happiness of others. But without some sort of theory of moral reasoning such as that offered by Kant, there is no bridge between the motivation of pursuing one's own happiness and the morality of promoting the happiness of others, and of the generality of people. For Utilitarians this bridge is provided by the laws and institutions of state: laws provide a prudential reason (avoiding the pain of sanctions) for stopping short of causing misery to others through pursuit of one's own happiness; social institutions should be arranged so as to produce a maximum of happiness optimally distributed between the generality of people.

The simplicity of this early Benthamite Utilitarianism may indeed be attractive, but it oversimplifies some important issues. One is how to prioritise pleasures; another is how to balance the pleasures of some against the pains of others. The first question of which pleasures, which forms of happiness, the just society should promote, has led to various formulations, which generally fall under the heading of justice as welfare, the satisfaction of needs; or justice as self-actualisation, the freedom and ability to follow one's own ends. The second question, balancing the pleasures of some against the pains of others, is the crucial issue for justice in the risk society. It raises the problem of the relationship of social utility to individual rights.

Bentham's down-to-earth empiricism had no difficulty with rights, famously dismissing the idea of natural rights as 'nonsense on stilts'. For John Stuart Mill, however, rights could not so easily be dismissed, and one of the important threads in his works *On Liberty* (1859) and *Utilitarianism* (1861) is that of trying to show that rights can be derived from the principle of utility, and thence that justice can be reconciled with Utilitarianism.

In *On Liberty* Mill makes a powerful case that liberty is essential for human flourishing. He argues for freedom of thought and freedom of action as the basic conditions of well-being and happiness. Mill moves from Locke's narrow defence of religious tolerance to proposing diversity of ideas and character as necessary for individual and social advance. Suppression of false ideas, he says, is as injurious to society as is suppression of true ideas: only through the interplay of ideas can truth be established and embraced with confidence. Diversity of character is necessary to provide a range of choices (his argument here is similar to contemporary ideas about the desirability of a range of role models), and also to demonstrate the consequences of bad character (he gives the example of the way people shun the company of drunks, an idea familiar in everyday discourse now in the notion of the 'pub bore').

The high value Mill places on liberty leads to his principle of harm: that the only reason for which liberty in any person may justly be curtailed is to prevent harm to others. Neither the advancement of the general good nor the prospect of self-harm is, according to Mill, sufficient grounds for restriction of liberty. The proper response to an agent doing or contemplating behaviour which might result in self-harm is, he would suggest, advice rather than coerced restraint; except in the case of harm to others, his arguments for the importance of freedom to society in general as well as to individuals imply that any restriction of liberty is likely to be inimical rather than beneficial to general welfare.

Mill's views on liberty and his harm principle represent a considerable advance on Bentham's 'felicific calculus', the simple aggregating of benefits and harms which gives no sense of individuals as separate, and entitled to Kantian respect as ends rather than as means to the general good. Nonetheless, Mill's attempts to bring together individual rights to freedom and the principle of utility as maximisation of general welfare are generally thought unsuccessful (Gray, 1995: 51). The problem is that freedom can only be guaranteed if liberty and general welfare do indeed, as he suggests, coincide. Protection of liberty is therefore contingent on liberty being what individuals value most, on it being the highest good to the majority of people. If this is not the case – and there is strong empirical evidence that people do not always maintain a strong conscious commitment to freedom – then liberty is precarious. Liberty can only be guaranteed if it has value of an *a priori* nature, which is precisely what Utilitarians want to deny.

This is a profound difficulty for Mill, because it is not in the qualities or states which are accorded value that he differs from Kant and other non-Utilitarian liberals, or in the priority which he believes the principles of justice derived from these values should be accorded, but in the grounding of those values and principles. He returns to this problem of the relationship between justice and utility in *Utilitarianism*:

> While I dispute the pretensions of any theory which sets up an imaginary standard of justice not grounded on utility, I account the justice which is grounded on utility to be the chief part, and incomparably the most sacred and binding part, of all morality. Justice is a name for certain classes of moral rules, which concern the essentials of human well-being more nearly, and are therefore of more absolute obligation, than any other rules for the guidance of life... (Mill, 1861, quoted in Westphal, 1996: 173)

Mill brings these rules of justice grounded on utility together with the concept of rights by arguing that we recognise the primacy of rules of justice because they imply rights residing in the individual. The further step he takes is to derive rights from *security*. Security is, he says, the most basic, general utility. Without security in ownership of one's life and property, one cannot be said to possess liberty, and one cannot pursue one's own version of happiness.

Security is, therefore, the one non-substitutable good and thus a society which seeks to promote happiness is bound to afford to everyone the universal elements of security as basic rights. Security is, Mill explains,

> to everyone's feelings, the most vital of all interests. All other earthly benefits are needed by one person, not needed by another; and many of them can, if necessary, be cheerfully forgone, or replaced by something else; but security no human being can possibly do without; on it we depend for all our immunity from evil, and for the whole value of all and every good, beyond the passing moment, since nothing but the gratification of the instant could be of any worth to us, if we could be deprived of everything the next instant by whoever was momentarily stronger than ourselves. (ibid.: 168)

Without doubt, Mill was concerned to guarantee individual liberty against the wishes of other citizens as well as against oppressive governments. In *On Liberty*, he says that social convention is as significant a source of coercion as governmental tyranny; with the coming of democracy, he might well have expected it to become the most significant form of oppression. He inveighs against the Chinese practice of foot-binding, which to him epitomised everything that was to be feared in the suppression of individuality by the 'despotism of custom' (Mendus, 1989: 49). It incorporated the stunting of natural growth, both physical and moral, and the dreariness of a society where the imposition of uniformity stifled the emergence of variety or excitement.

Because of this strong abhorrence of the tyranny of imposed uniformity, Mill would, no doubt, have expected his work to be deployed on the side of liberal opponents of the tyranny of 'grand plan' political theories such as communism. He would surely have endorsed Isaiah Berlin's championing of value pluralism against any 'final solution' of the resolution of conflict between competing ideals and values. Mill's own writing is very close to Berlin's warning that it is the idea that there is one best set of values, one best form of social organisation, one best way of ordering human affairs, that 'more than any other, is responsible for the slaughter of individuals on the altars of the greatest historical ideals' (Berlin, 1969: 167). Mill would surely be horrified if he could have known that in the twentieth century Utilitarianism was cited as an anti-libertarian tendency alongside communism, that it is a philosophy which contemporary liberals such as Rawls are ranged against.

This staunch liberal thrust of Mill's writing on the tyranny of public opinion, echoing Montesquieu's (1989) concern with democracy as the 'tyranny of the averages' prompts some commentators to make a distinction between *rule-Utilitarianism* and *act-Utilitarianism*. With act-Utilitarianism, the losses and benefits to happiness/welfare are calculated for each action, and such an approach clearly could not yield any authoritative charter of stabilised individual rights. Rule-Utilitarianism, on the other hand, generates a set of rule-governed institutions and practices designed to promote general well-being.

Once these are in existence, right action consists of following these rules, rather than calculating utility afresh for each action.

An example that is often used to illustrate the difference between these two forms of Utilitarianism is that act-Utilitarianism could not forbid punishment of the innocent, inflicted for reasons of deterrence. If it is desired to send very powerful messages condemning a certain form of behaviour, then what matters is that broadcast media publicise the sentences being given; the deterrent effect will still be realised if the person sentenced in the case was actually innocent. The important message is that this sort of behaviour attracts this sort of punishment. The answer suggested by Rawls (1972) and others is to appeal to rule-Utilitarianism. A society would institute a criminal justice system in which punishing the innocent would be against the rules, because a system would have no deterrent effect if it did not convey the message that the sure way in which people could avoid punishment was by refraining from crime. Punishing those known to be innocent would therefore be against the rules of criminal proceedings, since knowledge that the rules were sometimes circumvented would lead to loss of confidence in the system.

To punish someone without conviction might be against the rules of the criminal justice system, but as Duff suggests, a judge might pronounce guilt whilst actually believing the person to be innocent (Duff, 1986: 163; Matravers, 2000: 17–21). Another example which comes to mind is that of police 'planting' evidence where they think that a person is guilty but cannot find enough properly obtained evidence to secure a conviction, or where they think the suspect is innocent this time, but has got away with crimes on previous occasions, 'noble cause corruption', as it is often called. The distinction between act- and rule-Utilitarianism, in other words, might be difficult to sustain in individual cases of rule application.

This argument could, of course, be made against any rule-generating philosophy: there is never any guarantee that each individual action will live up to the principles incorporated in the rules. It can plausibly be argued that rule-Utilitarianism would yield institutions designed to maximise liberty, a system of rights to guarantee basic security, and a distribution system that ensures a reasonable supply of goods to all. Since rule-Utilitarianism is concerned with institutions and rules for a whole society with the objective of promoting the desires of members of society as defined by themselves, it has a strong egalitarian and democratic thrust.

The real difficulty with Utilitarianism that remains even with rule-Utilitarianism, is the *contingency* of liberty, and of individual rights. Protection of these values is contingent upon the self-interest of happiness-seeking persons being enlightened. These values will only be inscribed into the rules and institutions of a society if people really do desire freedom and security rather than more immediate or ephemeral goods, and protection of freedom and rights is also contingent upon people being sufficiently enlightened to recognise that their self-interest is bound up with the interests of others. If these conditions are not met, then the formula that a just society protects the happiness of the 'aggregate' of persons – a formula endorsed by Mill as well as Bentham – would mean that the interests of (some) individuals may be sacrificed for those of the majority population or the society as a whole. Mill certainly believed in a general capacity for enlightened self-interest, but he offers no proof of its generality or of its dependability, so that in his theory individual rights and liberties have a degree of contingency that is unacceptable to most contemporary liberals.

Even if enlightened self-interest, rather than the narrow interests of those with power and influence, is the basis on which people establish social institutions, Utilitarianism has important pragmatic deficiencies from the point of view of justice. These arise because of the inadequacy of the specification of the concept of harm, and the minimalism of the rights defined. Taken together, these defects produce the effect that a very small degree of probable harm could justify a large restriction on freedom. They also mean that there is nothing to mitigate very large degrees of inequality in distribution; if very unequal distribution, either of goods or of freedoms, would produce the greatest aggregate happiness, then Utilitarianism would recommend very unequal distribution.

Fairness and impartiality

As the twentieth century progressed, deontological liberalism seemed to yield to state activism (Gray, 1995: 36). The liberal ideal of limited government based on individual rights gave way to various forms of enhanced state power, harnessed to different visions of human good. Counterposed to socialism and Fascism, with their ideas of the perfect society, was western European welfare statism, and in the USA the interventionist economics of the New Deal. The response to the economic depression of the 1930s and the Second World War in the 1940s was the promise of state-delivered power, prosperity and welfare. Utilitarianism, in one form or another, seemed to have triumphed. Although not without powerful defenders such as Popper (1945) and Berlin (1969), deontological liberalism seemed to be in defeat, to have run its intellectual and political course.

In the 1970s, Kantian liberalism revived. Theoretically, the standard-bearer of this revival has been John Rawls, whose formulation of *justice as fairness* has become perhaps the key reference point of contemporary liberalism. Rawls's A *Theory of Justice* (1972) aims to provide a critique of Utilitarianism and to develop a persuasive alternative to it. He sets his sights against all forms of Utilitarianism, but sees the essential doctrine most clearly and accessibly delineated by Sidgwick (1907):

> The main idea is that society is rightly ordered, and therefore just, when its major institutions are arranged so as to achieve the greatest

net balance of satisfaction summed over all the individuals belonging to it. (Rawls, 1972: 22)

In Rawls's much-quoted phrase, this summative approach does not take seriously the 'distinction between persons' (ibid.: 27). The available mechanisms for distribution of goods and rights for Utilitarianism are the 'big brother' method, where a single legislator presumes to know what will generate happiness for most, or the democratic majoritarian method, where those preferences with the most votes will be supported and minority preferences will be rejected. For Rawls, this means that the objection raised against Mill, that only if all people desire the same thing – equal liberty of all over all other things – can everyone be sure that their interests will be respected, makes Utilitarianism in general unacceptable.

Rawls starts from the assumption that in post-conventional society people will *not* have the same preferences. Where there is a plurality of ideas of the good, the task for justice is not to maximise the good, but to regulate relationships between different versions of the good. Instead of the Utilitarians' arithmetical answer to the problem of the choice between preferences – each person to count for one and only one – Rawls's solution is *impartialism*: the rules of a just society are impartial between competing ideas of the good. Justice as impartiality does not tell us what goods we should pursue (self-development, self-determinism, righteousness, freedom from pain or want), nor what the good society should provide (welfare, security, religious tolerance or strict conformity, diversity, racial purity, adherence to tradition are some 'goods' that different societies have espoused from time to time), but sets the 'ground rules' for pursuit of any vision of the good:

> justice as impartiality is not designed to tell us how to live. It addresses itself to a different but equally important question: how are we to live *together*, given that we have different ideas about how to live? (Barry, 1995: 77, emphasis in the original)

Rawls returns to Kant's location of the sources of morality in the reasoning subject rather than in what is desired by the subject. He brings Kant's ideas of the *a priori* authority of reason together with the political philosophy of social contract theory, to develop his political theory of justice. Thus Kantian essentialism as regards reason is joined with the political question of how to limit pursuit of self-interest in favour of social co-operation. In brief, Rawls turns to Kantian transcendent reason to solve the Utilitarian problem of the loss of individual rights in the name of a general good, and the democratic problem of majoritarian disregard or suppression of minority views and interests. He returns to Kant's emphasis on the *process* of deriving moral principles over the *outcomes* of procedures to determine the good. The right is again prioritised over the good, and the key question in setting up the basic structures of a just society is, 'What processes could ensure that choices made would be those of reason rather than of self-interest?' Kant's abstract moral criterion of universalizability – his categorical imperative – is transposed into a formula for establishing principles of justice for actual political societies.

Rawls is not concerned with all possible societies, but with those characterised by what he calls 'circumstances of justice'. These circumstances of justice are those familiar from social contract theory: social co-operation is feasible and desirable; social co-operation is not inevitable because divergence of self-interests arising from plurality of ideas of the good means that co-operation will involve some sacrifice of individual self-interest.[4]

In order to arrive at truly impartial decisions, decisions to which all members of a society could agree, which are the product of reason rather than self-regard, which deal fairly with all preferences, Rawls prescribes that people should contemplate foundational decisions by mentally placing themselves behind a *veil of ignorance* about their actual present and probable future position in society. This obviously has family resemblances with older contractarian concepts of the state of nature; the difference is that Rawls does not ask people to imagine themselves prior to society, but to be in a society and potentially occupying any possible position within it. Although Rawls of course realises that everyone is cognisant of their present social position and has ideas about their likely future position, he suggests that it is possible to put on the veil of ignorance and make choices as if in this pre-cognisant *original position.*

Choosing from this original position, Rawls argues, is the only way to achieve fairness to all, and to protect the position of the worst-off. For example, in considering whether to have a system of redistributive taxation, if we know ourselves to be wealthy we would be against such a system; if we are aware of ourselves as poor we would favour it, with high rates of taxation on the rich: only if we did not know our economic status would we think about a system being fair to all. Furthermore, if we have no idea of our actual position, we will have to envisage the possibility that we might be in the worst-off position: institutions which protect the worst-off are therefore the rational choice.

Rawls allows his decision-makers elementary knowledge of the circumstances and basic values of their society. They will have understanding that their society is restricted by some degree of scarcity; that human beings value freedom and that they desire to pursue their own self-determined interests. This elementary knowledge means that there is held in common what Rawls describes as a 'thin theory' of the good. People share concern for what he calls primary goods – liberty, opportunity, self-respect, food and shelter. Justice is concerned with the distribution of these goods.

It is important to the theory that the choosers have no knowledge which would enable them to calculate the probability of being in one social position rather than another. Lack of probability data dictates that the distribution that will be chosen is the *maximin*, the best of the worst outcomes: Rawls believes that his choosers will guarantee against the possibility of being in the worst-off position rather than gambling on being in one of the better-off positions.

Rawls believes two principles of justice would emerge from reflective deliberations under these conditions, one governing the distribution of rights and liberties, and the second governing the distribution of income and wealth, status and power. The first set of goods would be distributed according to an equal liberty principle:

> each person is to have an equal right to the most extensive basic liberty compatible with a similar liberty for others.

The second set is to be governed by the rule that social inequalities are to be arranged so that they are both (a) reasonably expected to be to everyone's advantage, and (b) attached to positions and offices open to all (1972: 60).

The equal liberties principle is incorporated, in some way, in all formulations of liberalism; what distinguishes Rawls's version from the Utilitarians' is that it is not contingent on liberty being a good desired by an aggregate or majority of persons, and that it is accorded inviolable priority over the second principle. Rawls's second principle of justice, the principle for the distribution of social and material inequalities, is distinctive in that since it specifies that the benefits of inequalities are to be for all, those in the worst-off position are to be protected. He therefore proposes his *difference principle*, that social and economic inequalities are only justifiable to the extent that they are to the benefit of the least advantaged (1972: 14–15).

As well as positing this principle as being the rational choice from the maximin position, Rawls defends the difference principle on two other grounds. The first is prudential: no-one could be expected to agree to co-operate unless such co-operation would be to their advantage, so the distribution must be favourable to the least well-off, those who are gaining least from co-operation. Secondly, he argues that inheritance of talent, wealth, educational opportunity or ambition is fortunate rather than earned, so it can yield no deserved advantage and should therefore be used for the benefit of all.

These two principles address the main problems of earlier theories. Natural rights theory offers no guarantee against very unequal distributions and no promise of redressing the injustice of earlier distributions; Utilitarian theory fails to offer adequate guarantees of individual rights. Rawls's *Theory of Justice* combines the essential wisdom of Kantian approaches, that justice is a set of principles for enabling impartial resolution of conflicts between the ends of self-determining persons, and the insight of Utilitarianism, that the satisfaction of human wants, rather than the implementation of abstract, mystical principles, is what the just society should promote.

An aspect of his theory that has been emphasised by subsequent writers is its capacity to deal with the problem of *external preferences* (that is, preferences which are external to the exercise of reason in the original position). In spite of Mill's attention to the question of diversity, Utilitarianism generally fails to deal adequately with the possibility that some people's preferences will not be supported, because not enough people vote for them. But the problem of external preferences is, in our times, perhaps even more significant: some people's pleasure might consist in visiting hardship on others. Persecution or restriction of rights of sexual or racial minorities, for example, are prime examples of external preferences:

> Assume that racial prejudice is so widespread in a community that laws enacted specifically for the purpose of putting the despised race at a disadvantage would satisfy the preferences of most people overall ... Pure utilitarianism (and pure majoritarianism) would then endorse these laws because they are laws that a legislature weighing the preferences of all citizens equally, with no regard to the character or source of these preferences, would enact. If a judge accepts the pure utilitarian account of treating people as equals, then he must conclude that in these circumstances laws deliberately designed to put blacks at an economic disadvantage... treat blacks as equals. He cannot rely on equality or on any egalitarian theory of democracy to condemn such laws.
>
> We know, however, that such laws do not treat blacks as equals. On what theory of equality must we then be relying? (Dworkin, 1986a: 65)

Dworkin is pointing out here that the Utilitarian dilemma of the sacrifice of individual liberties to the general good, the problem of the contingency of equal maximum liberty being promoted only if it is a majority preference, calls into question not only the issue of the priority of good over right, but also what is meant by 'equality'. As Dworkin demonstrates, equality of preferences, with equality defined as each one to count as one and one only, does not offer the safeguards against discriminatory laws that our sense of equal justice seems to demand: only an understanding of equality as equal rights will suffice.

Dworkin regards Rawls's Kantian theory as advancing a long way towards providing a necessarily robust grounding for the inviolability of individual liberty. He has concerned himself with the application of the principle of equal liberty and the priority of rights over expediency or general welfare concerns in actual legal-political issues such as minority rights. Dworkin commends a rights-based rather than a rule-based approach to law, saying that rights are 'trump cards' held by individuals, which allow resistance to decisions even when made by legitimate authorities, following properly constituted rules (ibid.: 198). He is thereby extending the Rawlsian approach from the establishment of basic principles and structures to actual functioning institutions and their decision-making.

Another advantage that Rawls's theory offers is that his 'difference principle' provides a rational approach to the limitation of inequalities. Without this or a similar principle, we are forced to choose between Lockean entitlement theory, which legitimates all inequalities so long as they arise from lawful disposal of lawfully held assets; or a rigid egalitarianism such as that all must have the same, or all must have only what they need. The Lockean approach offends our sense of solidarity by allowing some to starve while others have unlimited wealth; both versions of the second approach offend our sense of the rightness of people being at liberty to enjoy that which they have legitimately earned. Even Nozick, who advocates a Lockean minimal state and is against intervention to achieve any particular pattern of distribution, supports Rawls's difference principle as a rough guide to measuring and remedying past injustices in bestowing new property entitlements (Nozick, 1974: 230–1).

Contemporary liberals have suggested modifications or developments of Rawls's theory, and have pointed out some deficiencies. Dworkin argues that Rawls does not take seriously enough the possibility of conflict between the ideals of liberty and equality; it has been held that he does not provide sufficient evidence for his list of primary goods, and that he fails to demonstrate convincingly that decision-makers would be pessimistic maximin-ers rather than optimists or gamblers (Matravers, 2000). These deficiencies notwithstanding, his theory has been acknowledged as the most successful and authoritative recent formulation of liberalism. As Gray summarises, in spite of 'some empirical difficulties', 'It is in the development of this contractarian method that the most promising solution of liberalism's foundational questions is to be found' (Gray, 1995: 55).

Liberalism and punishment

All forms of liberalism mandate the punishment of offenders. Because of the value liberalism ascribes to free pursuit of one's chosen ends, however, it follows that for liberals, punishment should be subject to principled limits, and that it should be for legitimate purposes. The two streams of liberalism – Kantian deontologism and Utilitarianism – are associated with two approaches to punishment: retributivism and consequentialism. There is an extensive literature on punishment theory; for my present purposes I will concentrate only on those features of the two approaches which are important for the main issues dealt with in this book.[5]

Both deontological and consequentialist approaches to punishment share the same fundamental aim, which is to deter harmful or undesirable behaviour (Hart, 1968; von Hirsch, 1993). This is almost a truth-by-definition, since punishment is always, whatever else it may or may not be, a negative sanction invoked by proscribed behaviour (Hudson, 1996). The essential question is not what punishment is for, but by what justification is the deliberate infliction of pain or hardship a proper means to pursue this aim of deterring harmful behaviour. It is on this version of the 'why punish?' question that the two approaches diverge: consequentialism looks forward to future preventable harms; retributivism looks backwards to harms already enacted. Consequentialism argues that offenders *need* punishment to reduce the likelihood that they will offend again; retributivists argue that they *deserve* punishment because of crimes they have already committed. Consequentialists argue that communities need the imposition of punishment on offenders to deter potential offenders and prevent future crime; retributivists argue that communities need punishment to be inflicted on offenders to restore the balance of benefits and harms in the society and to remedy the damage that has been done to its moral boundaries. Both perspectives agree that the existence of a system of punishments is necessary to dissuade potential offenders (all of us) from transgressive acts and to assure potential victims (any of us) that any encroachment on their well-being is taken seriously. Both agree that to ensure the limitation of self-interest in favour of respect for each other's liberty and property, positive sanctions in the form of benefits from such social co-operation need to be complemented by negative sanctions in the form of 'hard treatment' for transgression. This general argument for the necessity of a system of punishment is what Rawls describes as the *assurance* justification for coercion: it provides an assurance that rules will be enforced (Rawls, 1972: 315).

Consequentialist theories of punishment

Consequentialism faces up to the fact that once a crime has been committed, punishment is an additional pain. It is therefore only justified if the good consequences it brings about outweigh this extra, intentional pain. The good achieved by punishment is prevention of future crime; for consequentialists, punishment is only justified if the total amount of crime reduction it brings about through individual and general deterrence is greater than the extra burden of punitive hard treatment. Although this might warrant draconian punishments to maximise deterrence, the fact that the pain of punishment is immediate and certain but the alleviation of potential pain through deterrence is uncertain, leads most consequentialists to call for moderate punishments. Braithwaite and Pettit (1990), who have led a contemporary revival of principled consequentialism, advocate *decrementalism*, systematic lowering of penalties until crime rates begin to show rises which can be demonstrably linked to penal deflation.

A system of penalties commensurate with the harm done by the offence would satisfy most consequentialists. Jeremy Bentham advocated a penal system that was moderate by the standards of his times, as did the other 'founding father' of modern penal science, Cesare Beccaria. Both insisted that punishment was tyrannous if imposed for any purpose other than promoting general happiness; it was in fact the penologist Beccaria who first used the phrase which is often taken to sum up Utilitarian philosophy by arguing that laws should be evaluated by whether or not they conduce to 'the greatest happiness shared among the greater number' (1999: 441), rather than Bentham as is usually supposed.

Beccaria, in his great work *On Crimes and Punishments*, first published in 1764, uses the harm principle to determine which acts should be classified as crimes and insists that no punishments should be inflicted before a conviction beyond doubt has been obtained through a fair trial, based on evidence rather than on (forced) confession. He argues forcefully against torture and the death penalty, and equally forcefully in favour of proportionality in punishments.

The section of his work which emphasises the due process rights of fair trial and proof beyond doubt, together with emphasising certainty and proportionality, often leads to Beccaria being considered a 'classicist' rather than a consequentialist in penal philosophy.[6] His writing, however, exemplifies the distinction between Utilitarians and deontological liberals, which lies not in the principles that they espouse but in the derivation of those principles.

Beccaria advocated proportionate penalties not as a matter of moral principle, but as a matter of deterrent utility, arguing that severe and inhuman penalties reduce crimes less effectively than more moderate sanctions:

> The harsher the punishment and the worse the evil he faces, the more anxious the criminal is to avoid it, and it makes him commit other crimes to escape the punishment of the first... As punishments become harsher, human souls which, like fluids, find their level from their surroundings, become hardened and the ever lively power of the emotions brings it about that, after a hundred years of cruel tortures, the wheel only causes as much fear as prison previously did. If a punishment is to serve its purpose, it is enough that the harm of punishment should outweigh the good which the criminal can derive from the crime, and into the calculation of this balance, we must add the unerringness of the punishment and the loss of the good produced by the crime. Anything more than this is superfluous and, therefore, tyrannous. (ibid.: 455)

If it could be shown that harsh, disproportionate penalties do reduce crime effectively, then Beccaria and other consequentialists would have no reason to oppose them. Indeed Bentham, in a posthumously published article, questioned Beccaria's argument against torture. Saying that utility should not be overridden by sentiment, he suggests that if torture could make someone do something which it was overwhelmingly in the public interest to have done, then there is no harm. Bentham even suggests that the justification for torture in such a case would be greater than the justification for punishment, because with the purpose of deterrence or reformation in punishment there is the possibility either that this may not be brought about or that more punishment may be used than is necessary. But with torture, as soon as the result is achieved the torment stops (Morgan, 2000: 186–7).

In our own times, we see penalties becoming harsher on just this basis: that it is believed that they are effective in reducing crime. Arguments about the connection between enhanced punishments and crime rates are conducted in mathematical terms, with rival calculations of the number of crimes 'saved' by increases in levels of imprisonment the main point of contention (Zimring and Hawkins, 1995).[7]

As well as crime reduction, there is another contribution to the general happiness claimed for punishment. People gain satisfaction from offenders being punished. This expressive aspect of punishment has been somewhat neglected in most accounts of the justification of punishment, but penal practice cannot be understood without it (Garland, 1990). Punishment is a cultural phenomenon, expressing society's commitment to its moral standards in ways that are consistent with the wider culture of the society, but it is also a source of individual gratification. Popular support for the death penalty and for long prison sentences and austere, inhumane prison regimes persists in spite of dissemination of information on their ineffectiveness in crime reduction; these 'life-trashing' punishments are *enjoyed* by their supporters quite apart from any belief in their instrumental efficacy (Simon, 2001).

Vengeance in punishment is a vent for individual feelings, as can be seen when relatives of a murder victim want to witness the killer's execution, or when they oppose a murderer's release even after he or she has served a long sentence. At times these individual sentiments are widely shared, there is a popular outpouring or shared moment of national consciousness, often after some widely publicized, horrific acts.[8] Vengeance is also a strong cultural theme, the subject of countless western and crime films and novels, and so it would be surprising not to find it present in punishment (Murphy, 2000: 132–3). The cultural presence of vengeance and its apparent near-universality in the human psyche mean that it is easily roused. Vengeance seems to be providing a populist underpinning of increasing severity of punishments in the 1990s and into the present century (Sarat, 1997). Consequentialism would have no basis for calling for limits to vengeance, other than lack of public support.

Consequentialist punishment theories, scarcely surprisingly, incorporate the strengths and weaknesses of the Utilitarianism from which they are derived (Matravers, 2000). Any limitations on the distribution and nature of punishment are entirely contingent on the preferences of the majority. Even the requirement that those to be punished should be properly convicted is subject to people's regard for due process conventions. Walker poses the question mentioned earlier of whether, for purposes of deterrence of potential offenders, it matters whether someone on whom sentence is passed is actually guilty: what is important is that potential criminals can see a certain level of punishment attaching to the crime (Walker, 1991: Chapter 11). He quotes the usual consequentialist answer to this objection in terms of rule-Utilitarianism, that punishing the innocent, or punishing without demonstrably sound conviction, would weaken confidence in the criminal justice system. This would mean, among other things, that threat of punishment would cease to deter, since deterrence rests not just on fear of punishment but on confidence in being able to avoid punishment by refraining from crime.

As Walker says, this may well be true in an open, democratic society, but it is not true in a closed one. Even in an open society, protection of the innocent depends on an effective appeals system and is, as we see in our own time, subject to balance in the rules of evidence that protect the innocent as well as convict the guilty.

Again, in our own times we see little public resistance to weakening of conventions such as the right to silence, double jeopardy (people cannot be tried twice for the same offence) and the right to jury trial; and we see the connection between high-profile cases where there is public demand for someone to be caught and punished, and conviction of the innocent.

Proportionate penalties; punishment only of the guilty; fair trials; high standards of proof, cannot be guaranteed by consequentialism. It may be supposed that rule-Utilitarians, such as Bentham is sometimes held to have been, may well have thought such standards important (Kelly, 1990). The Utilitarian problem of contingency arises in this context: the importance of due process is not secured as a basic principle; under consequentialist penalties it is contingent on particular policy-makers believing in its importance.

The strength of consequentialism is its placing at the heart of matters of criminal justice the demand that punishment, like other social institutions, should be justified by its contribution to human welfare. Even if the existence of a system of punishments generally contributes to welfare, there is nothing sacrosanct about it which prescribes its application in every individual case including those where it serves no useful purpose. Consequentialism recognises punishment for what it is: the deliberate infliction of pain, which as such is inevitably morally problematic, at best a 'necessary evil'.

Liberal retributivist approaches

Utilitarian, consequentialist theories look to the effects of punishment on future potential crime for both general justification and principles of distribution. Modern retributivist theorists separate general justification from distribution of punishment. Like consequentialists, they see that the reason for having a system of punishments is to make people obey the law – whether they express this in penological terms as deterring crime or in more contractarian terms as the limitations on pursuit of self-interest inherent in social co-operation. A system of punishment supplies a prudential reason for complying with laws. Retributivists, like Utilitarians, see that the moral claims associated with membership of a co-operative, contract-based society will not be sufficient to bind all people, all the time, to legality, and that there will be times when the self-interested temptation to unco-operative activity will be hard to resist. When they consider distribution of punishment, however, retributivists take the Kantian turn, basing distributive principles on the moral status of offenders themselves, not on the community of potential victims.

The key principle of retributive theories, then, is that offenders should be punished for crimes they have (actually, already) committed and to the extent that they deserve to be punished. This principle offers a guarantee against punishment of the innocent, and it decrees that punishments should be commensurate with the crimes for which they are imposed. It does not, however, as retributivists themselves point out, define what is to count as commensurate punishment: commensurate retributivism might be interpreted as exact equivalence of punishment to crime (an eye for an eye, a life for a life), but in contemporary versions commensurability is most often interpreted as proportionality, the most severe penalties for the most serious crimes (von Hirsch, 1976, 1993). The scale and nature of penalties (whether death or life imprisonment, for example, is the most severe penalty available) will depend on the culture and sensibilities of the society in which the penal system exists (Garland, 1990; Spierenburg, 1984).

These distributive principles, modern retributivists claim, are necessary for systems of punishment to conform to the principles of justice specified by deontological liberals. Retributivism in distribution fulfils the Kantian 'golden rule' of treating people only as ends and never as means, and of incorporating rules that rational people would choose to be universalised. Rational free-choosers would choose to have some system of enforcement of the rules they establish: willing the existence of rules implies willing that they be upheld. Punishment of an offender as an example to others, or to protect society against something she might do, uses the offender as means; punishment without sound conviction of guilt is something people would not rationally endorse because it would mean that for any individual, avoidance of punishment would not be within their own power. Only if punishment follows conviction for a crime already committed can there be any certainty of avoiding punishment through restraint from crime.

Modern retributivists seek to incorporate the values of liberalism – equal liberty, fairness, impartiality – into penal systems. They insist that the rights which are central to all forms of liberalism, whether described as natural rights, prerequisites of equal liberty, the essential conditions of happiness, or a particular set of primary goods, should be central to criminal justice as they are to all basic institutions of the just society. Due process rights should not be compromised or suspended for reasons of utility; behaviour should not be the subject of criminal law unless it is harmful to others.

Contemporary liberal philosophical writing, however, with its emphasis on distributive justice, offers little guidance on punishment. Rawls assumes that penal justice is retributive justice, but offers only a few paragraphs on the matter. He puts forward what might, in his own terms, be called a 'thin theory' of deterrence, explaining that

the purpose of the criminal law is to uphold basic natural duties, those which forbid us to injure other persons in their life and limb, or to deprive them of their liberty and property, and punishments are designed to serve this end. (Rawls, 1972: 314)

Rawls points out that punishments are not 'a scheme of taxes and burdens' (ibid.: 314–5), and yet one of the most prevalent interpretations of contractarian retributivism is that it sees punishment primarily as a device to restore a proper balance of social benefits and burdens. The criminal, on this account, has claimed a benefit unfairly, and has refused to accept a legitimately imposed burden or restraint. Benefits in this context are not just benefits of income or property not legally owned or earned, but include benefits in terms of some sort of emotional gratification or removal of inconvenience gained by committing violent crime; the burden or restraint is that of acting within the limits imposed on self-interest by law. Punishment removes the benefit, and/or imposes a burden to counterbalance a benefit already unfairly enjoyed. At the same time, punishment assures the law-abiding that unfair advantages will not be allowed to stand, that 'free-loaders' on the social contract will not prosper (Matravers, 2000: 52–72).

As Duff (1986, 1996) has objected, this account does not capture the full moral essence of crime and punishment. Not only is the moral meaning of crime not exhausted by a refusal of the restraints of law, but the moral meaning of punishment is not exhausted by redressing the balance of advantage and constraint. Most of us do not kill, rape or steal because our consciences are repelled by the nature of the behaviour; we do not refrain merely because of boundaries imposed by law. Similarly, there is a difference between punishment according to criminal law, and reparation paid by offenders to victims or to the community generally. Crimes are *bad* as well as unfair actions, and the key difference between punishment and taxes or compensation is that punishment conveys a message of blame, or *censure*.

Just as criminal laws are statements of societies' moral bounds (the expressive element of law), so punishments are pronouncements of the wrongness of criminal acts (the communicative aspect of punishment). A form of retributivism which either stresses the aspect of punishment which is the communication of censure (von Hirsch, 1993) or which sees the whole of punishment as an act of communication (Duff, 1986, 1996) has emerged and enjoys considerable influence. Whereas, however, distribution-of-benefits and burdens explanations have difficulty in accommodating the censure element of punishment, communicative theories have plausibly to account for the hard treatment aspect. With benefits-and-burdens theories the question is, 'Why punishment and not reparation?' With communicative theories the question is, 'Why is a stern lecture from a judge not sufficient?'

Von Hirsch sees the harsh treatment as a prudential supplement to the censure, not as censure itself. An attraction of his formulation is that, he claims, it has an inbuilt thrust towards moderate punishments because otherwise the prudential element would be so strong that the censuring message would be lost: people would refrain from crime because they were afraid of the hard treatment rather than because they were persuaded by the moral message. Duff's formulation is more thoroughly communicative in that although he also endorses the idea of hard treatment as a prudential reason for obeying the law, he proposes the hard treatment itself as a moral expression; the harsh treatment of punishment has penitential character and status.

Both Duff's and von Hirsch's penal communications are different in a significant way to the 'expressive element' in punishment as described in the section on consequentialism, above. The expressive vengeance there is an expression of sentiment by or on behalf of victims with no sense of responsibility towards the offender; the communication in these contemporary retributive theories is addressed to the offender, as rational moral agent. Von Hirsch's censure addresses the offender as a member of society operating on the same sort of motivational system as the non-offender, reminding her of the costs of criminal behaviour as well as the moral rules of the society. Duff's communication seeks to reintegrate the offender as a member of the moral community, affording her the opportunity to re-adopt and affirm its moral rules and principles by accepting the wrongness of the crime.

Rawls's brief remarks on retributive justice seem to me to pose a difficulty which I do not as yet see adequately dealt with by subsequent desert theorists (a term frequently applied to contemporary retributivists). This is that although in connection with the distribution of goods Rawls argues that talents, characteristics and opportunities are acquired through fortune and therefore the results of their employment cannot be associated with the idea of desert, he does not offer the same possibility for the distribution of legitimate and illegitimate opportunities, personal and social characteristics implicated in criminality. Referring to 'acts proscribed by penal statutes', he states simplistically that 'propensity to commit such acts is a mark of bad character' (1972: 315). The question then is, to what extent are we responsible for our characters? If our characters are formed by factors (genetic predisposition) and events (our upbringing and life-chances) which are not the result of our own choices, then can character be used as the basis for culpability and therefore for punishment?

Modern retributivists and consequentialists have some difficulties with this question of character and responsibility (Norrie, 2000: 127–41). For desert theory, the question of character is problematic because to admit it as a causal factor in crime denies the Kantian link of crime (and therefore desert) to pure-and-simple freely willed choice. If we don't choose our characters, how can we be held to blame for crimes resulting from acting 'in character'? Consequentialism has less difficulty: if crime is in character, this has to be taken into account in assessing dangerousness and likelihood of reoffending. Lacey concedes the Kantian objection to considering character in deciding penalties, but argues that because of the social functions of law (public protection and deterrence of anti-social behaviour) it is impossible to discount character and rely entirely on freedom of choice. She asks us to think about the 'irascible, thoughtless or stupid person' who runs a 'systematically higher chance' of committing crimes than someone with a better-ordered disposition. While acknowledging that 'however dispositions are constructed, most of us would agree that many of their features are either totally or practically impossible to change and moreover not voluntarily acquired', criminal justice must 'deal with us as we are' (Lacey, 1988: 67). The paradox in Rawlsian liberalism remains unsolved, however. If we are not to be praised for possession of those characteristics which facilitate our doing well in society, why should we be held to blame for those characteristics which predispose us to do badly?

The usual solution for criminal justice is to hold to a theory of free choice in establishing the offender as blameworthy, and to consider character only in the context of assessing the likelihood of reoffending, not as a mitigation or excuse. For me, this is a central weakness of modern retributivism in relation to responsibility: it relies upon too narrow and untheorised a concept of desert (Hudson, 1999, 2000). It assumes too readily that crime is a matter of freely willed choice, and it pays insufficient attention to the differences in circumstances under which choices are made. Offences being committed in situations of drastic limitations on choice, whether arising through severe economic disadvantage; perception of powerlessness such as abused women may experience in relation to their abusers; or denial of membership of the co-operative group such as is endured by refugees and asylum seekers, raise difficult questions for retributive theories of justice. Ignoring them, or allowing them insufficient scope and influence in calculations of culpability, means that contemporary retributivism does not amount to a desert theory proper, but simplifies to a 'harm done' theory. This means, of course, that the calculus of punishment is not actually the desert of the offender to be punished, but only that of the wrong done to the victim and community. Such an approach thus fails in its Kantian aspiration to derive the distribution of punishment from the moral desert of the criminal.

Whether circumstances of severely restricted choice to achieve generally desired primary goods (food, shelter, status, pleasure) make for reduced or zero culpability depending on the degree of choice restriction, as on my own analyses of the question (1999, 2000); whether they destabilise the legitimacy of the power to punish (Duff, 1998a; Murphy, 1973); or whether the proper description of 'coercive protection' by states against people committing illegal acts in such circumstances is not properly called 'punishment' (Matravers, 2000: 266–7), the situation of extreme inequalities in the distribution of choices and opportunities poses strong challenges to liberal regimes of punishment as well as to theories of justice.[9]

Modern retributivism, like consequentialism, faces up to the fact that punishment is deliberate infliction of suffering on an individual by the state, something which in most circumstances we would think of as wrong. Retributivism's answer to this 'evil necessity' is to see that it must be subject to principled limitation. Whilst retributivists can say that a punishment system is necessary to enforce the terms of the social contract, they are on less solid ground with the question of whether in individual cases punishment is justifiable if it has no crime reduction utility. Consequentialism seems to be on stronger ground on questions of justification, and retributivism on questions of limitations against punishment of the innocent, and punishment for possible rather than actual crimes.

Actual penal systems in liberal societies combine both consequentialist and retributivist features. Penal theorists have made various suggestions for combining features, one of the most well known being Norval Morris's 'limited retributivism', which suggests that punishment should normally be proportionate to the seriousness of the offence committed, unless there are particularly strong indications of future dangerousness of the criminal (Morris, 1982: Chapter 5). Whatever compromises and hybrids are proposed (Hudson, 1996: Chapter 3), the question of the tension between retributive and consequentialist, due process and crime control concerns is perpetual, and the balance to be struck between them changes from time to time and place to place (Packer, 1969). Some consequentialists have tried to secure proper concern for deontological principles of justice by making the 'good' to be promoted entail a relational concept of liberty: Braithwaite and Pettit's 'dominion' is an important contemporary example (Braithwaite and Pettit, 1990). They claim that because this concept relates to capacities held by each individual, it escapes the subsuming of individual freedom in general welfare that other consequentialist approaches entail. Coming from the opposite pole, most contemporary retributivists accept that there is a place for the *content* of penal sanctions to be designed to reduce the likelihood of reoffending, as long as the *amount* of punishment is determined by desert constraints.[10]

Threats to security

At the core of liberalism, security is located as the 'most fundamental good', the one 'unsubstitutable' good, on which freedom depends. Security in one's person and possessions is the precondition of freedom. At this point, then, it is helpful to recapitulate some specifically liberal interests in security, and to summarise the kinds of threats which are envisaged in liberal writings.

Liberal commitment to equal liberty means that if security is the precondition of freedom, then security is due equally to all. For social contract liberalism, the promise of security is the reason each person gives up a measure of freedom, so security is owed equally to each citizen; for other liberalisms, security is the good which all persons value equally, so again it is owed equally to all. The nature of security is that it is a public good; security must, then, be organised as a public good. That is to say, its provision and distribution must be organised in such a way that no one person's security reduces the security of others.

Michael Walzer (1983) who, as we shall see in Chapter 3, shares many of the communitarian critiques of liberalism, nonetheless holds to the liberal values of freedom and equality, and to liberals' concern for these values to be reflected in societies' patterns of distributions. He contests Rawls's attempt to formulate one principle of distribution for all types of goods, but proposes his own principle of distribution that in many respects tries to secure the same aims as Rawls, which is that distribution should be governed by principles of fairness and not by the power and advantages of individuals in the society.

Walzer advocates an idea of *complex equality* which, against Rawls, rests on the belief that there cannot be one sole principle of distribution for every kind of good. The key is to guard against *domination* of the distribution of any good by mechanisms that do not properly reflect the nature of that good. In capitalist democracies, the danger is of domination of distributions by money; in communist or one-party states domination may be through membership of a political elite. Distribution of a public good should not be dominated by money, but by a principle intrinsic to the nature of the good: so the distribution of education should be determined by desire and ability to benefit, with each person receiving as much education as they are able to absorb; distribution of healthcare should be according to each person's state of health/ill-health. While we may take issue with some of the details of Walzer's theory, the general principle is clear, that public goods should be distributed according to the nature of the good, not the power of demand.

Recognition of the public nature of security as a good has led to the shaping of modern democracies as they have developed in nation-states in the nineteenth and twentieth centuries. Security of borders was to be achieved through national armed forces; security of person and property within the territory was to be achieved through a national police force and national system of criminal justice; security against plague and infectious diseases was achieved through the creation of public health systems; and the welfare state principle of securing freedom of all from poverty, illness and ignorance led to the creation of the national health service, social security and universal free education.

Liberalism recognises two principal threats to provision of security as a public good. One is that security will change from being a public good to a *club good*; the second is the problem of *free riders* (Hope, 2000). A club good is one that is only available to members, and it is therefore a distribution that tends towards domination by money (or political patronage or whatever the domination factor is in the society in question). Only those who join the club (by paying the fee, by being a member of the party, etc.) will receive the good. We can see the public goods/club goods tension in trends towards greater use of private health and education, and in affluent housing estates and apartment blocks where residents pay together for security measures, whereas defenders of the public provision tradition argue for universal provision and try to stem the tide of privatisation.

Proponents of privatisation and neighbourhood/community provision are generally more preoccupied with the free-rider problem. They fear that people will take advantage of the goods provided without making any contribution, whether through working and paying taxes and insurance contributions, or through keeping to the rules of society. Free-rider arguments are often invoked in disputes about membership, for example about immigrant workers or refugees receiving benefits and enjoying the advantages of living in advanced western countries. In criminal justice terms, offenders are free riders in the sense that they benefit from the majority law-abiding population keeping to the rules of the society and not impinging on the security of the offenders' person and property, but they do not accept their responsibility for showing similar respect for the security of others.

The idea of free riders provides something of a bridge between the twin liberal concepts of public goods and individual responsibility. Basic goods are to be provided on the public distributive principle that no-one's possession of the good should deprive anyone else of their proper share of the good. At the same, time, liberalism rests on the idea of individual responsibility, and in terms of provision of security everyone is expected to take care not to fall prey to the risks identified (O'Malley, 2000). People are expected to avoid poverty and ignorance by working hard in education and employment; to avoid illness by maintaining standards of hygiene, having vaccinations, eating healthily and avoiding excess alcohol – we see campaigns to persuade us to stop smoking, watch our cholesterol intake, monitor our weight and blood pressure, and avoid unsafe neighbourhoods.

Liberal governance is also preoccupied by the threat posed by *dangerous persons*. With the rise of modern constitutional states, the threat mostly feared was that of dangerous classes: classes of people who threatened political and social rebellion, and who threatened the inculcation of modern virtues of thrift, hard work and the settled life. The eighteenth and nineteenth centuries saw regular eruptions of protest and violence, in some cases local and minor, but in other cases more cataclysmic. The French Revolution at the end of the eighteenth century was followed by further regime-changing revolts in 1830, 1848 and 1870. A wave of revolutions spread across many European countries in 1848; in England there were movements such as Chartistm and the Anti-Corn Law League, with events including the 'Peterloo' massacres in Manchester making the ruling elite fearful of political upheaval. As well as this political fervour, the 'dangerous classes' represented a threat to the values of modern industrialism. Vagrancy, thievery, excessive drinking and general lawlessness and thuggery challenged the ideal of the responsible, hard-working citizen of the modern state.

As the new political, industrial and social forms of modernity became embedded, attention turned from dangerous 'classes' to dangerous sub-groups and individuals. Foucault (1977) shows how the modernist penal system provided a political economy of illegality, constituting and differentiating deviant identities into those that could be tolerated or reformed, and those that must be repressed and incapacitated. The working classes were induced to lose sympathy with those among them who defied the laws and the work ethic, and thereby legitimated government powers to discipline and punish those who did not obey the rules of the modern industrial state. The poor were divided into the 'rough and respectable', the 'deserving and undeserving', and the old solidarities of the powerless 'us' against the powerful 'them' were dissolved.

'Dangerousness' became a label that attached to individuals as well as to classes and sub-groups. The dangerous offender became identified as the persistent offender who is not legally insane, but because of his (usually male) proclivities posed greater risk than the person who committed occasional crimes. Criminological science developed primarily as a way to separate the 'corrigible' from the 'incorrigible', with early criminologists such as Lombroso and Ferri devising typographies to identify the 'born', the 'insane' and the 'force of circumstances' criminal. This form of criminology is, of course, very active and influential today, and has been the mainstay of the discipline throughout its existence. 'Habitual criminals' (they are usually known as 'persistent' criminals today) offended liberal society in two ways: they were 'beyond law' in that they constantly flouted legality, and they were 'beyond governance' in that they evaded the structures of identification and classification, surveillance and discipline by changing names, changing addresses, and evading public records and systems of control (Pratt, 2000a).

Since the inception of modern penal systems there have been special penal laws to protect society from dangerous and habitual (persistent) offenders (Pratt, 1998). What has changed is the scope of these laws – mainly whether they covered only offences against the person or whether they included offences against property – and the levels of support for such laws. As we have noted in earlier sections, liberal lawyers and philosophers have always had a 'bad conscience' about penalising people because of things they might do in the future or because of their characters and proclivities, and the passage of such laws is usually accompanied by attempts to clarify the definitions. A common worry is that the risk posed by people classified as dangerous is future and speculative, but the deprivation they face is real and immediate. The criteria of 'clear and present danger' are often proposed in liberal democracies, but operation of the criteria is difficult and the assessment can never be certain. Because of such anxieties, protection from danger legislation has tended to be at the margins of penal systems (Pratt, 2000a).

Similar worries affect measures to protect liberal societies from threats posed by people who are thought dangerous because of political as well as criminal potential behaviour. Internment of suspected enemies and suspected terrorists is usually controversial, and although regularly used in liberal societies, it is generally instigated as a temporary measure (though 'temporary' can last for many years). Internment usually takes place in times of war or other unrest, and merges the categories of internal and external threats. One of the problems with internment (as with other forms of protective detention) is that evidence can be difficult to obtain and assess, and so standards of proof required for criminal convictions are often dispensed with (such as with the 'Diplock courts' in Northern Ireland), Like 'dangerous offender' legislation, internment and other forms of protection against suspected 'enemies' are at the margins of law, often on a murky border between criminal law and national security regulations where they lack transparency and accountability and barely respect the liberal ideals of due process protections, and separation of governing powers.

External threats are recognised as reasons for interference with the freedoms of others, and most liberal societies have armed forces to protect against these threats, as well as allowing powers of internment and arrest of suspected agents, terrorists and others who might represent danger. Modern liberalism has seen the rise of international law and conventions such as respect for the sovereignty of other states, non-aggression pacts, and the establishment of international bodies to try to resolve international conflicts without recourse to war. The League of Nations formed after the First World War, the United Nations formed after the Second World War, and regional bodies such as NATO (the North Atlantic Treaty Organisation) and the Organisation of African Unity have tried to secure the rule of law between nations. When war does take place, there are agreements such as the Geneva Convention which govern treatment of enemy prisoners. These bodies and conventions have not been as effective in preventing and regulating conflict as their founders hoped, and there are difficulties about conflicts between principles of national sovereignty and the right to intervene to protect citizens' human rights; nonetheless these developments do show that liberal ideals have gained hold in thinking about threats posed by outsiders as well as those posed by insiders. It is with threats posed by insiders and those wishing to be insiders, however, that this book is mostly concerned.

Conclusion

We have seen that all versions of liberalism value liberty and equality, and that most versions incorporate as fundamental the principle of equal liberty: the maximum possible amount of freedom compatible with the equal freedom of all. Should liberty and equality conflict, the conservative strand of the liberal tradition values liberty more highly than equality, whereas the welfare or egalitarian strand values equality more highly than liberty. Among contemporary liberals, Hayek (1960) and Nozick (1974) represent the conservative strand and Rawls (1972) and Dworkin (1978) represent the egalitarian strand. Modern liberalism continues to be divided into two strands: Utilitarianism with its derivation of morality from the things people value, and deontologism which derives moral principles from the quality of human rationality that makes the choices. Liberalism values impartiality. Utilitarianism is impartial between persons, with each to count as one and only one; deonotological theories are impartial between different ideas of the good.

Liberalism as a political-philosophical tradition has established the idea of rights as the practical enactment of equal liberty, and of the concomitant idea of limited government power. As the liberal tradition has developed, successive writers have examined how securely rights and freedom are established in earlier formulations. Contemporary liberalism has tried to strengthen the defence of freedom offered by Utilitarians – although there are some critics of contemporary contractarianism who argue that Mill's defence of freedom is every bit as robust as Rawls's (Gray, 1983; Riley, 1998). The liberal ideals of equality, freedom and security are important values for humans living in societies, and there is little doubt that liberal societies – though they may be far from perfect – have seen significant advances towards freedom from tyranny and freedom to determine one's own life and goals. These are considerable gains for people, and to most citizens of liberal societies, seem to be worth defending.

This brief review of theories of justice in the liberal tradition shows that there are some inherent tensions in liberalism, tensions which cannot be resolved without the surrender of important values and insights. The main tension, we have seen, is between utility and rights. Another is between generality and particularity. For example, there may be occasions when rules made for the general run of situations, such as freedom of expression, may seem better suspended; in criminal cases, there is inevitably some loss to justice to an individual in applying rules made for the generality of instances, to which a particular case will only approximate, rather than correspond exactly. These questions have, of course, been addressed within contemporary liberalism, most rigorously by Dworkin (1978; 1986a).

Liberals have considered these questions and have made progress, but there are newer challenges. Many arise from the depth of difference in contemporary societies, with population movements making for cultural and religious differences of a degree unimagined by earlier writers on tolerance and diversity, and also new consciousness of differences, for example, between the standpoints of males and females. The perennial problems of liberalism must, therefore, be reviewed in the light of a radical, fissured pluralism that calls into question even the 'thin theory' of the good, and of understandings held in common, on which Rawls's theory rests.

Reflexive awareness of difference has made liberalism sensitive to attack from feminists, postmodernists and communitarians: these perspectives question the universalism of the process of reason as posited by deontological liberals, and the elements of the good posited by Utilitarians. Reasoning processes and ideas about fundamental goods and liberty may be derived from modern western experience, and, moreover, from white, male western experience, and from the sorts of communities in which liberals live, rather than from any sort of universal fundamentals of human nature.

These issues of rights and utility, difference and identity, universalism and community-derived particularity, together pose what I suggest is the key question for liberal theories of justice: that of membership and exclusion. Who is to be included in the community of justice, and whom is the just community to defend itself against? The following chapters will examine some of these contemporary challenges to liberal theories of justice, and will then turn to the possibilities of stronger and more adequate conceptions of the necessary elements of justice which could stand against them.

The principal categories of threats with which liberalism is concerned – conversion of public goods into private or club goods, free riders and dangerous persons – will be reconsidered at various points during the book, and questions will be raised about how they are perceived and responded to at different times and in different theories.

Notes

[1]The editions of classic Enlightenment and liberal texts on which I have drawn for this chapter are: Bentham, (1970) *An Introduction to the Principles of Morals and Legislation*, Hobbes (1991) *Leviathan*, Hume, David (1957) *An Enquiry Concerning the Principles of Morals*, ed. CW Hendel, Oxford University Press and (1978) *A Treatise of Human Nature*; I. Kant (1965a, 1965b) *The Metaphysical Elements of Justice*, and *Critique of Practical Reason*; Locke (1967) *Two Treatises of Government*, Lazlett; Mill, John Stuart (1969) *Utilitarianism* and (1977) *On Liberty*, in *Collected Works of John Stuart Mill*, 163–71. At some points in the text, dates of original publication of the works are given; where quotations are made from works in reproduction, the citation is to the reproduction.

[2]See for example Barry (1973); Damico (1986); Gray (1995); Gutman (1980); Hobhouse (1964); Pettit (1980); Sen and Williams (1982); Shapiro (1986).

[3]Habermas's work is discussed in Chapter 5, below.

[4]In seeing that co-operation may well require some sacrifice of self-interest, Rawls is setting himself against the philosophical tradition of *intuitionism*. This tradition is associated first of all with Hume's *Treatises of Human Nature* (first published 1739 and 1740) Although Hume sees all knowledge and judgment as emanating from experience he says that experience is interpreted intuitively, rather than through exercise of reason, arguing that children, animals and others without or with as yet undeveloped capacities for formal reasoning, can nevertheless learn from experience. In his subsequent *Enquiry Concerning Human Understanding* (1955, first published 1758) and *Enquiry Concerning the Principles of Morals* (1957), he extends his intuitionism into moral reasoning, and says that one of the things that informs moral decision-making is an innate sentiment of moral benevolence, an intuitive sympathy for human misery. On this account, our instinctive benevolence would mean that acting justly towards another would be what we wanted to do, so there would be no sacrifice involved. In insisting on the use of reason to establish principles of justice and just institutions, Rawls is concerned with twentieth century developments of intuitionism in relation to justice as described by Barry (1965). The intuitionist approach to justice is characterised as suggesting that in any situation of conflict between principles or choice of principles, the right choice will be that which intuitively fits best with the chooser's sense of justice. Rawls mentions Moore (1903), Pritchard (1949) and Ross (1930) as important contributors to this approach (1972: 34–40).

[5]See, for example, Hart (1968); Hudson (1987, 1996); Matravers (2000); von Hirsch (1976, 1985, 1993); Walker (1991).

[6]See, for example, Cavadino and Dignan (1997): 45–6.

[7]There is a mathematical construct, the *lamda*, a measure of the crime rate of an individual offender, which is used as the basis of estimates of the crimes saved by long, incapacitative prison sentences for those identified as persistent offenders. Use of such a measure is subject to mathematical, criminological and moral objections (Zimring and Hawkins, 1995: Chapters 2 and 3).

[8]Examples in the USA include the Megan Kanka and Polly Klaas cases, which led to the introduction of 'Megan's Law', on community notification of the whereabouts of sexual offenders and the California 'three-strikes' legislation respectively; in England the Sarah Payne case led to calls for the introduction of an equivalent to 'Megan's Law', while hostility to the release of Myra Hindley persisted despite her having served a long prison term and being judged no longer a danger to the public. Following her death in 2002, newspaper headlines and public demonstrations showed how strong the vengeful mood remained despite her being beyond any possibility of causing further harm. (These issues are discussed more fully in the following chapter.)

[9]This issue is discussed further in Chapter 7, below.

[10]Rotman (1990) offers a good account of rehabilitation in desert-determined determinate sentences.

2
Risk and the Politics of Safety: Justice Endangered

We saw in the previous chapter that the primary tension in the liberal political-philosophical tradition is that between security and liberty. While liberty is what humans most desire, security of person and property is the necessary condition for liberty to be realised. Without security, liberty is ephemeral and transitory – it amounts only to momentary glimpses, not the continuing, dependable freedom to plan a life course and implement chosen actions. The two goals are thus bound together: Mill describes security as the 'one non-substitutable good'; Rawls prescribes 'the most extensive basic liberty' as his first principle of justice. The social contract is essentially a trade-off between liberty and security: renouncement of some measure of liberty for secure protection against predatory acts by others. But how much liberty should be traded for what level of security? This is the key question for liberal theories and practices of justice.

Liberalism has engaged with this tension by proposing its defining principle of equal liberty, and by developing rules, concepts and institutions that operationalise this basic tenet of liberalism. The *equality* of liberty is what brings about the balancing of liberty and security, and this is why, as Dworkin argues, if liberals care about freedom, they must care about equality (1986a: 205–13). A key rule for institutionalising maximum equal liberty is the harm principle – that the only legitimate purpose for which liberty can be curtailed is prevention of harm to others. The key concept for operationalising maximum equal liberty is the concept of rights – all members of a society hold basic rights which guarantee their freedoms. Liberal theorists have, however, been vague in their specification of what is to count as harm, and how potential harms and present liberties are to be equated. They have also been vague on questions of competing or conflicting rights and the equilibrium to be maintained between rights to liberty and rights to security.

Like liberal theories of justice in the general sense, liberal criminal justice systems have relied on checks and balances and on the good conscience of legislators and interpreters (Bauman, 1987). Just as liberty and the interests of minorities in liberal societies generally have been contingent on the enlightenment of the majority population, so humanity and reasonableness in punitive justice have been dependent on moderation in public and political opinion.

The tension between liberty and security is articulated in criminal justice in the idea of a balance between crime control objectives and due process rights (Packer, 1969). All criminal justice systems are (definitionally) instituted to deter crime and to restrain criminals. Whether these crimes are in the form of direct encroachments on the property of others, or in the form of free-loading, claiming benefits from society but not abiding by the rules for the distribution of those benefits, liberal societies have affirmed the necessity for and legitimacy of systems of punitive sanctions consequent upon those crimes. But as we have seen, liberal societies have acknowledged that their most cherished principles dictate that the right to punish should be tempered by respect for the liberty and dignity of the criminal. This is because the criminal, though a transgressor, is presumed to share the basic human capacities for reason and for sympathetic understanding of the suffering of others.

Although, then, all liberal societies punish offenders, they nonetheless recognise offenders as citizens with rights. Punishment in modern societies is, indeed, a system of suspension of rights rather than a system of exercise of power upon the body through torture and mutilation (Foucault, 1977).[1] The balance between pursuit of crime control constraints, and maintenance of principled limits on punishment, is essentially a calculation of what rights, for how long, and with what justification, are to be suspended in the interests of security. This calculation changes from time to time and place to place. While the balance is constantly shifting and is inherently unstable, there is a fear in some quarters that present developments, at least in the USA and UK, represent a change of such magnitude that it is not exaggerating to talk of a new 'master pattern' (Cohen, 1985) emerging in these societies' engagement with crime. There has, indeed, been a claim that a 'new penology' emphasising control of risk has replaced the 'old penology', which is concerned with the moral state of the offender (Feeley and Simon, 1992). Others see the shift as less profound, or less coherent, suggesting either dual modes of crime control (Garland, 1996), or a plethora of responses to crime and the threat of crime so 'volatile and contradictory' (O'Malley, 1999) that they are difficult to characterise.

What accounts of recent changes in crime control strategies have in common is that they see a significant shift in the balances between crime control and due process; between inclusionary (keeping offenders in the community) and exclusionary (banishing them, to other territories or to segregative institutions) penal techniques; between 'normalising' (making the deviant more like the normal citizen) and managing (not seeking to change the deviant, but restricting his/her possibilities of movement and action so as to minimise the threat to the normal population) strategies; between individualising (responding to the needs and circumstances of the individual offender) and aggregating (controlling groups or categories of offenders and potential offenders), to use some of the current criminological terms.[2] These changes are all in the direction of identifying offenders according to the degree of risk of reoffending they pose rather than addressing them as rational moral agents. In terms of liberalism's most highly valued goods, the changes in control strategies that occurred at the end of the 20th century and continue into the twenty-first century represent a heightened concern for security at the expense of concern for liberty.

Social theorists have identified this contemporary era (approximately the last thirty years) as *late modernity*, a characterisation which sees it as clearly rooted in modernism and therefore containing many continuities with earlier modernist eras, but undergoing important transformations which make it recognisable as a different stage of social development. 'Late' has connotations of being departed, being aged (perhaps beyond its sell-by date), but not something completely different. 'Late modernity' has been described as

> the social, economic and cultural configuration brought into being by the confluence of a number of interlinked developments. These include (i) the transformative dynamic of capitalist production and exchange (the emergence of mass consumerism, globalization, the restructuring of the labour market, the new insecurity of employment); (ii) the secular changes in the structure of families and households (the movement of women into the paid labour force, the increased rates of divorce and family breakdown, the decreasing size of the average household; the coming of the teenager as a separate and often unsupervised age grade); (iii) changes in social ecology and demography (the stretching of time and space brought about by cars, suburbs, commuting, information technology); (iv) the social impact of electronic mass media (the generalization of expectations and fears; the reduced importance of localized corporatist cultures, changes in the conditions of political speech) and, (v) the democratization of social and cultural life (the 'desubordination' of lower class and minority groups, shifts in power ratios between men and women; the questioning of authority, the rise of moral individualism.) (Garland and Sparks, 2000: 199)

Most analytical accounts of changing patterns in crime control locate the roots of the shift they describe in certain conditions and consequences of late modernity: in particular, the mutation of political liberalism into contemporary neo-liberalism, and the emergence of late-modern preoccupation with risk (Bottoms, 1995; Garland, 1996; O'Malley, 1999; Sullivan, 2001 *inter alia*). Neo-liberalism, it seems, has abandoned mature liberalism's philosophical egalitarianism and its political concern for principled limits to inequalities in distribution; risk society has abandoned mature contractarianism's commitment to 'take rights seriously' (Dworkin, 1978) and so to accept principled limits to the promotion of security. The outcome is that:

> It is now possible to contend that we live in a 'risk society' ... There is a drift in the public agenda away from economic inequality to the

distribution and control of risks. The values of the unsafe society displace those of the unequal society. (Ericson and Carriere, 1994: 102–3)

In this chapter I examine some significant features of contemporary society's engagement with risk, and the consequences of this for, and reflection in, penal strategies. I will conclude the chapter by pointing out some of the principles of traditional liberal ideals of justice which are endangered by these transitions in societal response to risk.

The 'risk society' thesis

The richest, longest-lived, best-protected, most resourceful civilization, with the highest degree of insight into its own technology, is on the way to becoming the most frightened. (Wildavsky, 1979: 32)

Justice as security is both goal and legitimation for governance in modern liberal democracies so its negative counterpart, risk, is both target and legitimation of criminal justice. Security is, as Mill says and as few would disagree, a good, and it is the good which governmental power is charged with achieving (Foucault, 1991). Risk is something undesired which may happen, and criminal justice is charged with managing the risk of crime. Risk is central to law and order policies, and it is hardly surprising, then, that the *risk society* perspective developed in writings by Beck and Giddens has been drawn on by criminal justice writers seeking to understand recent developments in penality and social control (Beck, 1992; Beck et al., 1994; Bottoms, 1995; Giddens, 1990; O'Malley, 1999, 2001; Hope and Sparks, 2000; Stenson and Sullivan, 2001 *inter alia*).

'Risk society' analyses of contemporary life suggest that risk has become a central, generalized preoccupation, to the extent that it is configuring contemporary institutions and contemporary consciousness. Beck argues that the modernist optimistic idea that science and rational government can deliver security, prosperity and general welfare has been replaced by a pessimistic awareness of the ills brought about by the scientific-rational endeavour to deliver a planned, safe, opportunity-rich society. We can see what he means clearly if we just imagine our immediate associations with words like 'industry': earlier generations would think in terms of employment, higher than previously dreamed of levels of earnings, inventions that would reduce human drudgery; today we are more likely to think first of pollution, environmental accidents, structural unemployment, damage to family life, etc. In other words, we now think of the negatives – the risks – associated with the possibilities of modernity, rather than the benefits. In Beck's terms, our individual consciousness and our social organisation are dominated by the distribution of ills rather than the distribution of goods. Risk society means that risk-thinking has become not only pervasive but also routinised: it is part of the everyday thinking processes of individuals in their private and organisational lives. For those concerned with governance (at any level), it means the centring of everyday practices on 'bringing possible future undesired events into calculations in the present, making their avoidance the central object of decision-making processes, and administering individuals, institutions, expertise and resources in the service of that ambition' (Rose, 2000: 332).

Beck and Giddens point to the way in which the reflexivity of modernism – the ability of modernism to think for itself and about itself – which we recognise as the keynote of Enlightenment, induces critical attention to the problems caused by modernity itself. The expectation of mastery of the social and natural environment which is the hallmark of modernism (the 'meliorism', the belief that bad conditions will be ameliorated, which Gray, 1995 describes as one of the defining characteristics of liberalism) demands that risks will be recognised and countered. Risk society theory explains how this expectation engenders expectations of safety and security that can never be satisfied. Put together with modernity's characteristic questioning of authoritative belief systems, this insatiability of demand for security engenders growing distrust of expert knowledge. The distance from nature which is the situation of the citizens of modernity necessitates an ever-increasing dependency on expert knowledge, but at the same time the critical reflexivity of modernity's mentalities means that confidence in such knowledge tends to decline rather than increase. Mistrust of experts and their knowledge systems means that events such as the sinking of the *Titanic*, the crash of Concorde, the BSE outbreak and the foot-and-mouth epidemic appear not just as tragic for their victims, but as hubristic, mocking the over-ambitiousness of modernity. And of course criminal justice 'experts' and practitioners also attract their share of this mistrust. Reports of failures of parole assessments when a released offender commits a further crime; crime rate increases in spite of strenuous government activism in law and order spheres; perceived over-leniency of sentencing in some cases or miscarriages of justice in others: these appear as general failures of penal treatments, of courts and of the whole political-professional criminal justice complex.

Beck, Giddens and other risk society theorists also emphasise the individualisation of modern life, with the progressive loss of tradition and social bonds as parameters for structuring identity and life courses. This means that as citizens of modernity, as well as distrusting our expert professionals, we find it difficult to trust our fellow citizens. No longer able to depend upon solidarity, we come to anticipate threat from one another. The threat we fear most from each other is the threat of crime. In these circumstances of atomistic individualism fear of crime is, hardly surprisingly, an ever-present accompaniment to daily life. Fear of crime is an amalgam of hostility towards those whom government-sponsored social science has constructed as threats, but it also expresses a more generalised fear of strangers (Merry, 1981). With the breakdown of solidarity, we want our crime strategies to be constructed

Important! – use

defensively and repressively. We want those who threaten us excluded from our immediate environment, and thus from any possibility of inadvertent contact, both before and after the crime, the risk event.

Risk and criminal justice

A reflection of the 'risk society thesis' in criminal justice theory is the proposition that a 'new penology', with risk as its key motif, emerged in the last quarter of the twentieth century (Feeley and Simon, 1994). This new penology is distinguished from 'old penology' by three shifts:

- shifts in discursive themes;
- shifts in the targets of penal strategies;
- shifts in penal techniques.

Penal discourse is said to have replaced the old penology concern with morality and the apportionment of guilt with a new emphasis on risk and safety; strategies are targeted at aggregates, at people as members of certain groups rather than as individuals; actuarial, geographic and electronic techniques (statistically based risk assessment; mapping crime patterns and emphasis on hot-spots and unsafe places; use of closed circuit television and many different kinds of electronic security devices; following people's movements through and across computerised databases) have replaced social work and individual psychology.   benewable

Whilst risk society theory is a plausible account of life in modernity, and while new penology brings to our attention important features of late-modern crime control, these accounts beg the question of what is new in all this.[3] Furthermore, although the risk society/new penology paradigm may be able to account for the apparent increasing predominance of risk assessment in criminal justice, and of risk avoidance measures in our daily individual and collective life, it cannot, at first glance, throw much light on the turn that seems to have taken place from justice to vengeance, from due process to gloves-off crime control. Risk is, after all, an inescapable part of the human condition. It is also, as we have seen, the basic ingredient of social co-operation: the social contract is that individuals cede some of their freedom to governments in return for a greater level of security than they could provide for themselves. Risk reduction is what social co-operation is for; it is the 'what's in it', for each of us. Provision of security – risk management, in other words – is thus the central focus of governance, as Foucault, among the most influential contemporary theorists of risk society and late-modern governance, makes particularly clear in his *Two Lectures* (Foucault, 1991).

Risk management is also a fundamental, virtually definitionally entailed feature of criminal justice. The whole point of criminalisation backed by penal sanctions is to make crime less likely: to reduce the risk of crime. As

45

Clear and Cadora (2001) point out, to criticize, or see as novel, criminal justice concern with risk is misguided, amounting almost to a category error. The crux, according to them, is that in the latest crime control developments, risk *management* has given way to risk *control*.

Criminal justice is about risk management in the sense that though risks might not be able to be eliminated, they can be kept within reasonable levels, and can be reduced where they can be anticipated. This essentially means that risks must be balanced: the risk to the public of being victimised must be balanced against the risk to offenders (actual and potential) of undeserved restriction of liberty or other form of deprivation.

We are all of us, obviously, both potential victims and potential offenders, at risk therefore both of undeserved burdens of punishment and at risk of harm by our fellows. The traditional balance of risk has been to protect non-offenders from undeserved punishment first and foremost; but once someone is convicted and becomes an actual as well as a potential offender, then the balance swings in favour of the potential victim (Bottoms and Brownsword, 1983; Walker, 1991). Parole, early release, protective sentencing provisions, confinement in open or closed prisons, and life sentences are all devices to manage the risk posed by actual offenders of committing further offences, by making decisions about confinement and release subject to risk assessment.

For actual offenders, this risk assessment has generally been carried out on an individual basis, by prison governors, and by the Parole Board or its equivalent in other jurisdictions, as have been the various forms of risk assessment carried out by probation and social services in their court reports recommending custodial or non-custodial sentences, or when selecting programmes for offenders on community supervision orders, placements for community service orders, etc. Aggregate risk reduction policies have been targeted at potential rather than actual offenders and victims: policing tactics, for example, are based on patterns of crime; on area patterns of residence and use of space, and on social-demographic composition of areas.

Recent legislation and policy initiatives, however, move towards risk assessments for (assumed) actual offenders which are based on aggregates, on group characteristics rather than on knowledge of the individual about whom the assessment is made. Jonathan Simon makes this point in relation to the violent and sexual offender legislation introduced in the USA in the 1990s, particularly the 1994 Kansas Sexually Violent Predators Act and Megan's Law, the 1994 New Jersey sex offender legislation. Both of these Acts, or Acts very similar, have subsequently been adopted by other states:

> in place of old penology's concern with individuals, and like Kansas' Sexually Violent Offenders Act, Megan's Law names a subpopulation or category of persons as its target. The statute defined its target as 'sex offenders ... offenders who commit other predatory acts against children ... and ... persons who prey on others as a result of mental illness.' The logic of the classification is one based on statistical evidence

about recidivism rather than on clinical judgments about individual
proclivities. (Simon, 1998: 9)

In the UK, sexual offender notification schemes require sexual offenders to
register their addresses with police, and subject them to monitoring by police
and probation services. Such schemes have existed in several areas from the
mid-1980s, but were implemented nation-wide with the Sex Offenders Act
1997. The Act has been interpreted as a requirement not just that police hold
a register, but that probation actively 'manage' the risk posed by such offenders (Kemshall and Maguire, 2002). Public reaction to the death of Sarah Payne
in summer 2000 took the form of demand for a 'Sarah's Law', similar to
Megan's Law, which would give not only police and concerned professionals
but also parents the right to notification if a sex offender should move into
their neighbourhood. Political and professional opposition to the proposal
was not on the grounds of intrusiveness, rights to privacy, full restoration of
rights once an offence has been 'paid' for by due punishment, or similar principled concern, but was expressed solely in terms of the likelihood of sex
offenders 'going to ground', changing their identities, moving frequently, and
otherwise evading existing controls. Existing and proposed sex offender provisions do not apply only to individuals released early from prison or community sentences, but to most sexual offenders, whether or not they have
served their imposed penalty in full.

The rationale for the severe sentences, and supervision continuing long
after release – 'penal marking', as Garland (2000: 350) calls it – is that sex
offenders can never be 'cured'. Research evidence for this belief is by no
means conclusive; on the contrary, such evidence as there is points to a lower
rate of reconviction for sex offenders than for perpetrators of more routine
offences such as burglary and theft. One authoritative recent study found a
reconviction rate after six years of below 10 per cent of serious sex offenders convicted of another sexual offence, and about one in four within six
years convicted of another sexual offence among the small group who had
committed offences against children not in their own family (Hood et al.,
2002). Nevertheless, belief in the incurability and unreformability of sex
offenders remains widespread among professionals, politicians and the
public. With other types of offending, such as theft and burglary, it has generally been believed that crime rates fall with age, but with sex offending
there is a general belief that sex offenders continue throughout their lives: the
'dirty old man' is a professional as well as a public stereotype. So entrenched
is this belief that any evidence that reconviction rates are low for sex offenders compared to other types of offenders tends to be taken as demonstrating
that conviction is an inaccurate representation of reoffending (Marshall,
1997). Thus the very fact of a low level of reoffending is taken as confirmation of the stereotype: sex offenders do not stop offending, but they grow
increasingly crafty and proficient at avoiding prosecution. Whether this is

true or not is impossible to ascertain on the research evidence available, but it is a belief which feeds into popular, political and professional views.[4] One consequence of this is that provisions introduced to apply to convicted offenders are gradually being extended to cover all those who have been charged, or arrested on suspicion of sex offending.

Risk of reoffending factors associated with routine crimes such as burglary have been found to be to do with family size and income; employment record; incarceration as a juvenile; other family members' involvement in crime; drug use; and delinquent friends (Farrington, 1997; Gendreau et al., 1996). 'Risk score' instruments based on such factors can be and are used in individual assessments of offenders serving proportionate sentences, and in helping probation officers and prison staff in selecting suitable rehabilitative programmes for offenders, for example. But they can also be used in actuarial, aggregated penal schemes such that a certain type of sentence, level of intensity of community supervision or early release availability is prescribed according to risk score:

> Every offender in Britain is to be given a computer-generated score that will tell the courts before they are sentenced how likely they are to reoffend and what danger they pose to the public ... The punishment would no longer fit the crime, but the criminal ... The system, developed by the Home Office, gives an offender a computerised score based on factors including unemployment, literacy, family circumstances, lifestyle, history, who he or she has mixed with and educational background ... (Travis, 2000)

These new risk strategies are not, then, making clinical judgments that a particular offender is likely to reoffend, but actuarial judgments that this person possesses the characteristics associated with reoffending. These characteristics – risk factors – may be personal/social, or they may be derived from more or less well founded beliefs about the type of offence concerned.

With this actuarial, collective approach to risk assessment, the old problem of 'false positives' disappears. This is the difficulty that predictions of likelihood of reoffending offer two possibilities of wrong predictions: the false negative, when someone who is not predicted to reoffend does; and the false positive, when someone who is predicted to reoffend does not (or would not, if given the chance). While the potential victim wants to be protected against false negatives, the potential offender has an equally strong interest in protection against being a false positive. False negatives are readily apparent: if someone reoffends whilst on parole, there is generally a public outcry, whereas a false positive usually has little chance to demonstrate the wrongness of the prediction, because a positive prediction usually means being locked away. For that reason, it is important to build safeguards into penal systems to protect people from being false positives; the best protection is to make sentences proportionate to offences which have already been committed, and the false positive possibility has usually been considered one of the strongest arguments in favour of desert-based penal systems (Hudson, 1996; von Hirsch, 1985; Walker, 1991). With the new, actuarial justice, the 'truth' of an assessment lies in correctly identifying the factors, not in whether an individual really would or would not reoffend. There could be statistical errors (adding risk factor scores up wrongly) or clerical errors (ticking the wrong boxes) but no substantive falsity errors. People are correctly identified as risks if they possess the factors specified, if they 'display whatever characteristics the specialists responsible for the definition of preventive policy have constituted as risk factors' (Castel, 1991: 285). There need be no verification of predictions in actual behaviour.

In jurisdictions where risk assessment has been most thoroughly embraced as a penal technique, there have been transitions from clinical to actuarial assessments, and perhaps back again. In the USA, the simple factorial assessments of the 1980s used in the 'selective incapacitation' models proposed by the Rand Corporation and others (Zimring and Hawkins, 1995) have been augmented by some factors taken from clinical perspectives. 'Static' actuarial risk assessments overpredict, since many people possess the deprivation indicators that are used as factors indicating likely reoffending. Furthermore, because they use factors that cannot be changed (social background, employment history), they give little scope for reformative work with offenders. The new 'dynamic' factors include attitudes such as remorse, empathy with victims, and acceptance of responsibility for one's actions, and combinations of static and dynamic factors are widely used to predict risk of reoffending. Unlike the earlier actuarial assessments, they demonstrate areas that can be worked on, thus constituting a 'transformative' rather than 'fixed' risk subject for penal intervention (Hannah-Moffat, 2002). This type of actuarial/clinical hybrid risk assessment was first used widely in the Canadian penal system, but has now been adopted in the USA and the UK.

Proponents of these new risk instruments claim that they get over the problems of the earlier actuarial models concerning false positives and using characteristics of populations to make predictions about individuals (Hare, 2002). To the extent that they still incorporate factors such as employment, substance abuse, educational levels and criminal records of family members, however, these techniques continue to use actuarial assessments as though they were clinical assessments, that is, they are using descriptions of the characteristics of populations of offenders to predict the likelihood of reoffending of individual offenders.

The new legislation, policy, practices and general control culture that emerged in the 1990s and continue in the 2000s, then, demonstrate not only a greater concern with risk at the expense of due process and the principle of proportionality in punishment, but more than anything signify a shift from risk management to risk control. Clear and Cadora explain the difference between the two strategies:

Risk management

The use of managerial techniques to deal with risk recognises the uncertainty associated with risk situations. The intent is not to eliminate risk, but to manage error by marginal improvements in program assignment ... The recognition is that even among lower risk offenders there will be failures, but risk management approaches recognize the costs of false positives as well as false negatives, and offender assignments are made in order to minimize the joint costs of these errors. Unlike risk control, risk management approaches accept the inevitability of error, and this is dealt with by an attempt to shift errors into more acceptable settings and toward marginally reduced levels.

Risk control

This strategy attempts to exert controls on the risk in order to prevent the recurrence of a new crime. These methods are defined by the relationship between the external agent and the target of control; the former uses penal methods to eliminate the choices of the latter... Risk control strategies have as their purpose to take power over situations of risk in an offender's life such that the offender may not engage in crimes. Their primary intent is thus containment, not change ... (Clear and Cadora, 2001: 59)

As Clear and Cadora argue with regard to the United States, even small evidence of risk seems to generate an overwhelming response. They cite the 'three strikes' legislation in California and other states, where, as they say, life sentences following a third conviction means that any possibility of a fourth felony offence results in life imprisonment without any possibility of parole (ibid: 58). In England and Wales as in the US, sex offender legislation and popular campaigns exemplify this intolerance of risk, as does the proposed (at the time of writing) Serious Personality Disorder legislation. Under this legislation, persons diagnosed with a serious personality disorder who cannot be detained under existing mental health legislation because of the 'untreatability' of the disorder, can be incarcerated for life, even without conviction for a criminal offence. Although the number of people killed or seriously injured by persons with serious personality disorders is very small (such persons are far more likely to kill or injure themselves than others), two cases in particular have prompted the demand for new powers to enforce treatment. The case of Anthony Clunes, who killed John Zito, led to a move for enforceable community treatment; the case of Michael Stone, convicted of the murders of Lyn and Megan Russell, and the attempted murder of Josie Russell, prompted the proposed provision for incarceration, until such time 'if ever, that the risk they posed was minimised' (Paul Boateng, Home Office Minister, reported in The *Guardian*, 2000).[5]

Risk, blame and the end of solidarity

As Clear and Cadora say, the important issue is not whether risk matters in penal practice, but how it matters. It does seem that changes in strategies towards crime reflect not a new concern with risk, but a new orientation towards it. The risk society thesis needs to be supplemented by other insights which can help us understand the connection between risk consciousness, harsh punishments, and the decline in adherence to due process rights.

Mary Douglas's cultural-anthropological studies of risk are illuminating in relation to changing ways of apprehending risk, and for understanding the connection between societies' orientations to risk and their institutions for dealing with crime and justice. Where Beck and Giddens discuss social and cultural phenomena in terms of risk, Douglas discusses risk in terms of social and cultural phenomena (Crook, 1999). Instead of proposing new levels of preoccupation with risk, she takes risk as her constant and investigates different sociocultural traditions of explaining and dealing with it. The reality of risk, she explains, is not at issue: dangers, both modern and pre-modern, are all too horribly apparent: what is at issue and what demands examination, is the way in which risks are politicised (Douglas, 1992: 29). Douglas argues that social institutions including law and criminal justice systems correspond in considerable measure not only to the risks that the society sees as important to manage or control, but also to the society's explanations of the source of those risks, and to its attribution of responsibility for those risks (Douglas, 1992; Douglas and Wildavsky, 1982).

Douglas looks at different societies and examines whether they attribute risks to the victims themselves (for example a miscarriage may be attributed to a woman drinking alcohol during pregnancy), to individual miscreants, to rulers or to outsiders. She observes that in an individualist culture, the weak are going to be held to blame for the ills that befall them, giving examples from the Great Plague to poverty in more recent times. Cultural debates about risk, Douglas contends, are inevitably about inculpating those designated as 'the other side' (the poor, foreigners, unbelievers, deviants) and exonerating one's own side from blame – we can certainly see this today in the way that criminals are held wholly to blame, and factors such as structural unemployment, lack of provision for drug treatment outside the criminal justice system, and similar factors linked to the actions and inactions of governing elites, are dismissed as causes of crime.

Douglas argues that a society's patterns of laying blame for risk will have considerable influence on the nature of its justice system (this is Clear and Cadora's 'how it matters' issue). She says that contemporary late-modern society is one in which risk-posing is almost always attributed to specific individuals; not just risk of crime, but risks of all kinds:

> Of the different types of blaming system we can find in tribal society, the one we are in now is almost ready to treat every death as chargeable to someone's account, every accident as caused by someone's criminal negligence, every sickness a threatened prosecution. Whose fault? is the first question. (Douglas, 1992: 15–16)

Douglas gives the example of the Sherpas as a 'no-blame' society. Bad events are followed by various kinds of compensation, but not by blame-laying. Although there are systems of no-fault compensation in some spheres of social life, the much more dominant characteristic is the relentless apportioning of blame. Our litigious, compensation- and prosecution-seeking society no longer attributes risk to providence, or the gods, or ignorance of the rules of physics or psychology, but to the wrongdoing of an individual, whether by design or neglect. Plane, train or coach crashes result in the search for a culprit (or scapegoat) – the pilot, the driver, the maintenance engineer, the traffic controller. Epidemics must have a source in human fault; deaths in hospital are due to malpractice or medical negligence; efforts to prosecute follow disasters such as deaths at football stadia. So although there may be nothing new about fearful consciousness of risk, there is something new about the placing of responsibility for risk so unequivocally on individuals.

Although societies have always sought to protect themselves against danger, the level of prosecutions of those identified as the source of danger seems newly heightened. Giddens has taken up this theme himself in more recent writings, pointing out that a 'risk society' is not necessarily more hazardous than other forms of society, but it is a society in which hazards are no longer taken as coming from God or as inherent in a world which cannot be changed (Giddens, 1999). Risk society is a new social form in that it signifies, he explains, a new relationship between risk, responsibility for risk, and the decisions taken by people and governments.

If we ask ourselves what is the difference between the ancients sacrificing animals, children or young women to appease the gods, and preventive incarceration today, one key difference is surely that the ceremonies of old, cruel though they may have been, were not blaming ceremonies. They were appeals to providence; they were ceremonies that accepted the inevitability of danger: they were, in fact, risk management ceremonies, attempting to achieve small improvements in the riskiness of life, rather than risk control ceremonies, which the ancients would have regarded as necessarily in vain. Today's risk ceremonies are rituals not of appeasement, but of *censure* (von Hirsch, 1993).

There is nothing new in focusing policy on risk and safety; neither is there anything new in the aggregated approach to crime control. Law and order strategies have always been concerned above all with minimising the risks posed by the 'dangerous classes' (Pearson, 1983 *inter alia*). There is also nothing new in targeting persistence: the persistent offender has always been criminology's privileged object. The project of positivist criminology is centred on the search for reliable methods of sorting the hardened criminal from the one-time unfortunate, the corrigible from the incorrigible, and the contemporary terminology of high-risk/low-risk is a variation on an old theme, not a new motif (Cohen, 1985; Pratt, 1996).

The persistent offender is the privileged object of criminology in that he is the object-of-knowledge which defines the discipline; the object-of-knowledge produced by penal techniques (Foucault, 1977; Pasquino, 1991). The routine persistent offender is the object-of-knowledge unique to criminology/penology: the insane offender is the province of psychiatry, and the reluctant offender pressured by circumstances is the province of social policy (Pratt, 1995). And although the specific techniques in use may be new, there is nothing new about strategies for control of crime and promotion of public safety using the most up-to-date techniques and disciplines available. Categorising offenders in terms of riskiness is nothing new either. What is new, perhaps, is the joining together of the actuarial, probabilistic language of risk and the moral language of blame.

Risk, insurance and governmentality

If there is nothing new in governments' trying to manage risk and promote security; if there is nothing new in the enlistment of available knowledges in crime control, what is new, at least in modernity, is the pursuance of crime control and public safety objectives in a context of such risk intolerance and such a culture of individual blame. The common element in the most influential accounts of late-modern crime control strategies and other risk-associated policy spheres is the idea of a retreat from *the social*. A crucial part of Beck's and Giddens's 'risk society' formulation is their emphasis on the individualism of contemporary western societies. The reflexivity which they note is a defining constituent of Enlightenment, as was noted in the section on Kant in the preceding chapter. Reflexivity is a constituent of liberalism *per se*, and is not just an ingredient of contemporary neo-liberalism; individualism and individual responsibility are also central to liberalism. If anything is new, and characteristic of late modernism/neo-liberalism, it is the *defensive* individualism that that has replaced traditional solidarity as the dominant trait in late-modern identity.

The 'risk society' thesis defines the new social form not merely as a society which is preoccupied with risk avoidance and control, but as one which 'increasingly governs its problems in terms of discourses and technologies of risk' (O'Malley, 1998: xi). Risk society commentaries on aspects of social life and social policy thus draw on another current perspective which is in many ways complementary to the Beck/Giddens work: the *governmentality* approach, which looks at the exercise of power in contemporary times (Burchell et al., 1991; Miller and Rose, 1990; Rose, 1996a *inter alia*). This perspective shares many of the themes of Beck and Giddens and of neo-liberal philosophers like Nozick: withdrawal of support for state activism; unwillingness to contribute to the welfare of others. These works show that in many policy spheres there has been a retreat from government-led, collective approaches to risk management and the provision of welfare and security.

Contemporary developments, therefore, mark not just exaggerated concern with risk, or mistrust of experts (though both of those things are demonstrably involved), but also, crucially, show a retreat from approaching risk as something to be shared between members of a society; they mark a retreat from seeing the causes of risk as social and the best source of protection as social. This movement is so pronounced that it has been remarked upon as *the death of the social* (Rose, 1996b). The 'discourses and technologies of risk' to which O'Malley refers, and the new discourses and techniques identified as constitutive of a new penology, are above all, those of *insurance*. However, while many theorists of contemporary social-political life have commented on the rise of insurance as the template for dealing with the eventualities of life (Ewald, 1991; Simon, 1987), what is new and significant is not so much the rise of risk insurance and its spread to ever more spheres of life, but the move from social insurance to private insurance, the move from the welfare state to *private prudentialism* (O'Malley, 1992).

The significant change is not from some unspecified, untheorised welfare state towards an insurance society, but specifically from collective forms of insurance (national health insurance, state pensions for the elderly) towards private insurance schemes (private pensions, private health insurance). This private insurance is supplemented by smaller collectivities of individuals who come together in transitory groups for specific purposes (residents in neighbourhood watch schemes; traders in a shopping mall sharing the costs of security patrols and cameras; 'friends' of a hospital raising money for specialist equipment; lobbyists for or against a proposed road scheme). These groups only exist insofar as they are seen to further an interest members hold as individuals.

It is not the risk concern that is new here. As was mentioned in the previous chapter, modern society has always been a society where an increasing range of risks are dealt with through social forms of prevention: this acceptance of responsibility for public protection across the various areas of social life is a defining characteristic of modern liberal societies. Since prevention can never be complete, preventive programmes have been complemented by insurance against the ills that nonetheless occur. Public health programmes (clean water, drainage, immunisation, food hygiene regulations) have reduced the risk of disease; industry, increased productivity, birth control and health care have raised prosperity among working people; state armed forces and police services have curbed external and internal threats to body and property. These systems are mirrored by the universal insurance systems of the modern welfare state which protect those who in spite of all the improvements of modernity, are still vulnerable to disease, poverty or violence, whether through economic recession, war, old age, ill-health or crime. To use the language of risk, these systems depend on the understanding of risk as a shared condition; we understand ourselves as at any time vulnerable to these risks.

In recent years, these social insurance systems have declined. Part of the reason may be the very success of modernity: the modernist promise of risk control has been so successfully sold that many of us feel we are immune to the traditional shared dangers and therefore do not need to buy into social insurance systems. Collective risks are, for many in the affluent western nations at least, too far in the past to have any influence on the way we lead our lives: public health and immunisation programmes have removed some of the scourges of old such as cholera, typhoid and polio; wars no longer involve whole nations but (again for western affluent nations) are waged by small professional armies, watched by the rest of us as virtual-reality computer games. Decades of prosperity and expanded opportunity from the 1950s onwards meant that by the time 'restructuring' meant unemployment for many of our fellow citizens, the idea that there was work for anyone who could get it was entrenched, to the detriment of sympathy for those without employment. Similarly, for most of us, decades without ourselves or our loved ones being killed or injured in war have reduced empathy with refugees from today's conflicts.

Putting together this ability of many of us to distance ourselves from the possibility of risky events, the individualism of modernity and the reflexivity which contributes to a mistrust of expert systems, we have a situation understandably unfavourable for the maintenance of collective welfare and security systems. The individualism of modernity means that we care less and less about our fellow beings; the reflexivity of modernity means that we distrust governments and professionals; the distance from many forms of risk encourages a hyper-attention to those risks which are readily perceptible, which are proximate and from which government protection is demonstrably unlikely. The risks from our fellow citizens are more readily appreciable than the risks from beyond the streets; we are in a low-war and low-mortality society, but a high-crime society.

Rather than having a stable solidarity with each other as fellow members of a society, we have an aggressive individualism, punctuated by outbreaks of volatile, frenetic compassion or volatile quasi-solidarity built around hostility to dangerous or unfamiliar outsiders. Excessive demonstrations following the death of Princess Diana, and generous but short-term responses to natural disasters are examples of the former tendency; hostility to asylum seekers, particularly Muslim or Romany asylum seekers, exemplifies the latter.

This transitory solidarity has been described as 'new tribalism' (Maffesoli, 1996). It is different from earlier forms of solidarity in that associations are self-chosen rather than ascribed by birth, and in that its defining trait is less its loyalty to co-members than its hostility to outsiders. Football affiliation is a good example of new tribalism. Although many football supporters follow their local club, and allegiance is handed down through the generations, increasingly people choose their team, often choosing the most famous or most successful team at the time they begin to be interested in football, or the one that is shown most often on their televisions, or because of well-known glamorous stars (Manchester United is reputed to have more fans outside the country than in it). Fans not only support their own team but gain solidarity from 'hating' other teams (again, 'we hate Manchester United' is a frequently heard chant). At international level, too, bursts of intense patriotic affiliation break out during competitions such as the World Cup, and against particular 'enemies' (in England's case, Germany and Argentina).

Whatever the complex of causes of this decline of solidarity and social connectedness, the individualistic minimal-statism of contemporary neo-liberalism has resonated with the temper of contemporary times more than the welfare liberalism of the mid-twentieth century. If it were true at the mid-century that liberalism had given way to state activism, the reverse is true now: the minimal state entitlement liberalism of Nozick and Hayek has had more influence on recent economic and social policy than the welfare liber-alism of Rawls.

The governmentality perspective, with its 'death of the social' thesis, has gen-erally been held to be suggestive for criminal justice, but less readily applica-ble here than to fields such as health, education or social security. One of the main grounds for this reservation is that there is more state activism rather than less in the field of crime, and, moreover, there are constant popular demands for ever more action (Garland, 1997; Hudson, 1998a, 2001; Stenson, 1999). The governmentality thesis is obviously plausible in relation to much social policy, where private and neighbourhood action is substituted for state action; in the field of penal policy, state action has vastly expanded. Furthermore, there is ongoing public demand for more, not less, public expenditure. What seems to have happened is, not a rolling back of the state, but a transference of state activity from social policy to penal policy (Stenson, 1998).

It is important to notice that those who identify less collective action and more private action are talking about the *social*, whereas those talking about more central, repressive powers are talking about the *state*. The two terms are by no means synonymous, and misunderstandings can arise if they are taken as such.

'Social/society' refers to the sense of fellow membership, of community, of solidarity and belonging together; 'the state' is the formal organization of power. While the ideal of the modern liberal state is that it should derive from and represent society, this is not always the case, but whether it is the case in any particular territory or not, the two terms refer to different material, cog-nitive and affective entities. With this distinction in mind, it is not surprising that a diminishing sense of the social should lead to demands for strength-ening of the state. If society cannot be relied upon, what we are left with is the state to defend us each against the other, and to defend us together with those we do recognise as fellow members against those we define as outsiders. What we see today is a narrowing of the bounds of sociality to those most obviously 'like us' – whether through kinship or lifestyle. We are indeed experiencing a new Leviathan, where a strong state is demanded to protect each against all.

Our social institutions and even the physical design of our towns and cities (Body-Gendrot, 2000; Davis, 1990; Sennett, 1992) reflect this sense of wanting strong defences against enemies and strangers. Spaces are increasingly segregated into zones such as retail, leisure, business and residential, with the effect that it is easy to spot the out-of-place stranger. Commercial as well as residential buildings and developments have courtyards and atriums – internal space, looking inwards rather than outwards. More and more, spaces are designed and managed so as to minimize the chances of encounters with strangers.

Crook (1999: 164), drawing on all these approaches – risk society thesis, cultural anthropology and the governmentality perspective – argues that what we are seeing is a shifting balance between three different orders of risk management that are jostling together in this late-modern era:

- *modern ordering* which operates at the level of national societies through differentiated, rationalised and organised institutions and through technologies of mass communication. The exemplary modern institutions are those of the state and the market;
- *hyper-reflexive ordering* which is global in scope and which operates through networks of highly reflexive individuals rather than stable institutions. It is dependent on computerised communications, and engages individuals in selected, shifting coalitions of interest;
- *neo-traditional ordering* which operates as intense group solidarity, such as that associated with ethnic, religious or lifestyle groups. The intensity of solidarity with the group is matched by intensity of antagonism towards outsiders.

We can see that what is omitted from this typology is the traditional idea of the social, the civil society. There is nothing between the self-chosen, often temporary intensities of individual and group ordering and that of the formal state with its powers of repression.

Risk and sovereignty

Considering the differences and similarities between the approach to motor insurance, industrial accidents, credit card management etc., and the systems dealing with social security and other risk systems that deal with the poor, Simon contrasts the anonymising, non-blaming, routinising approach to the riskiness of affluence to the punitive, stigmatising, demeaning approach to the riskiness of poverty:

> Outside the circle of affluence in America, the rationality of risk becomes attenuated. Harsher, more old-fashioned forms of security management, including police and prisons, become more central. Yet increasingly these harsher methods are directed by the same actuarial methods that operate the soft machine of access channelling. Prison sentences, levels of parole supervision, and access to public benefits are more and more coming to be distributed through methods of risk assessment. Yet, at the level of ritual, the poor are exposed in their daily lives to a much more punitive and stigmatizing set of social practices than the rest of us. The poor, locked out of the access and security channels of insurance and credit, remain a constant reminder that capitalism cannot achieve the rationality of risk in its fullest sense. As an odd reward for their suffering, the poor remain the last sovereign subjects left to carry the economic and moral burden of their circumstances. (Simon, 1987: 78)

This passage shows the fit of risk thinking and new right politics: risk systems are operating within a particular political context and it is the 'how risk matters' that reveals what is new and what is significant for the liberal ideal of justice, rather than risk consciousness in itself. Simon's description is entirely consistent with authoritarian populism's strategy of blaming the victims of poverty for both the risks that they face and the risks that they pose. He describes the way in which the management systems developed to deal with the misadventures and transgressions of the affluent are democratic, non-discriminatory, and govern access to numerous social goods – motoring, healthcare, consumer credit, home ownership. Risks such as defaulting on mortgages, needing frequent and expensive healthcare and overspending on credit cards are managed through insurance rather than eliminated by restriction or repression. Most of us are willing to share the risks posed by those who are similarly situated to ourselves through paying insurance premiums, bank charges and the like, which cover risks.

The essential point about these benign, democratic systems is that at the point of entry to them, people are not already identified as either risk posers or risk bearers. When I take out car insurance, there is no way of knowing whether I will be harmed by another road user or will myself cause harm to another; similarly, if I take out private health insurance, there is no knowing whether I will pay contributions for many years without needing to claim, or whether I will draw on the fund regularly. Actuarial tables indicate the statistical likelihood of my being a risk poser and so affect the level of premium, but this is not in any way a personalised prediction and so carries no censure. The fact is that these systems do not differentiate between risk bearers or risk posers; they do not assume that an individual is either one or the other, but that most of us will be both, sometimes bearing the risks of others and sometimes causing harms that others must indemnify us against.

The poor, excluded by their poverty from such systems, come into contact with risk systems at points where they are already identified as risk posers, as drawers upon systems rather than contributors to them. They enter the social security system at assistance points rather than taxation/contribution points; and they enter the criminal justice system as offenders, or sometimes as victims who bear some responsibility for their victimisation (being vulnerable to assault through unrespectable, rackety lifestyles; being vulnerable to property crime through living in 'bad' areas, in badly secured homes).

Simon argues that the difference between the treatment of the poor and of the affluent demonstrates the limits of the 'rationality of risk'. He says that an alternative rationality, *sovereignty*, governs those areas of life where risk rationality is not yet established (1987: 78–83). He cites the power to make war and the power to punish as the two prime examples of sovereign power.

Although war and punishment certainly are examples of sovereign power, I think the distinction between risk and sovereignty is slightly overdrawn. Sovereignty is the establishment of power recognised as legitimate – within a territory; over a population. But risk management is precisely the reason that people yield sovereign power; risk is the legitimating impulse for sovereignty. Sovereignty is made manifest in a system of laws codifying risks and remedies, delimiting powers and rights of sovereign and subject in relation to those risks and remedies.

The difference between treatment of the riskiness of affluence and that of the riskiness of poverty reveals, not the boundary between risk and sovereignty, but the boundary between risk management and risk control. Risk management is an acceptance of risk, a pooling of risk amongst people who see themselves as a group of some sort; risk control is a refusal of risk, and it is the response to risks posed by people we do not associate ourselves with. Indeed, we should recognise here that the very notion of risk tends to have bad or good connotations according to the status of the person to whom it is attached. The penal risk assessment instruments mentioned earlier include 'risk-taking behaviour' as among the indices of likely reoffending, yet as O'Malley reminds us, risk-taking is an essential, applauded quality, necessary for economic growth (O'Malley, 2000). Of course the risk-taking he has in mind is that undertaken by the affluent – investing in stocks and shares, starting businesses, opting for the venture of private business rather than the security of public service.

Simon describes risk systems for the poor, and with Feeley he shows the poor as an identified aggregate – the underclass – risk practices in respect of whom are likened to those used by the Israelis to control the Palestinians within the occupied territories of Gaza and the West Bank (Feeley and Simon, 1994). As Rose puts it, contemporary risk strategies can be divided into roughly two kinds, 'those that seek to regulate conduct by enmeshing individuals within circuits of inclusion and those that seek to act upon pathologies through ... circuits of exclusion' (Rose, 2000: 324). This inclusion/exclusion division corresponds very closely to my division of risk management and risk control systems.

The boundary between risk management and risk control thus reveals the limits of sociality: the borderline between the social and the state. We organise our risk practices according to whom we collaborate with and whom we defend against. We join with neighbours in neighbourhood watch schemes; we join with fellow traders, residents and local councillors to install CCTV schemes: these are then targeted against the poor and unconventional (Norris et al., 1998). Similarly, we welcome business exchanges and tourism from some foreigners and erect legal and physical barriers to prevent the entry of others; we enter into pacts with some countries to protect against incursion by others; the underclass become aliens within our own borders, posing risks to be controlled rather than managed. Our risk strategies plainly do not produce safety: all the hazards we fear most – crime, asylum-seeking, pollution, accidents – occur ever more frequently, and some we thought we had conquered – epidemics, diseases such as tuberculosis and malaria, economic depression – return.

Risk society theory, cultural studies of risk and blame, new right politics and the rationalities of governance all contribute to an understanding of the way in which risk matters in contemporary western democracies. They reveal how the demand for safety is insatiable; they show how risk knowledge engenders appreciation of the necessarily elusive quality of security (Short, 1990). They show how we come to distrust experts and each other, and how we blame and refuse to share the burdens of danger. Risk practices may seem irrational if viewed in terms of their efficacy for enhancing security; they make sense if they are viewed as techniques for expressing resentment as well as for promoting safety (Sagoff, 1982).

Explaining the move from risk management to risk control

I have argued that what took place at the end of the twentieth century was a move from risk management to risk control. The accounts of risk and of crime control strategies I have drawn on illustrate this move, and show some of the deeper, structural features in the evolution of late-modern societies that it represents. These accounts show that the potential for risk control is embedded in the conditions of existence of modernity itself.[6] Nonetheless, the question arises of why the move from risk management to risk control happened, and moreover, why it happened when it did. Why did strategies in relation to the risk of crime move from risk management to risk control? Why was professional management of risks, with the core task being that of balancing risks to offenders of undue punishment and to potential victims of avoidable victimisation, displaced in favour of new strategies in which public and political demand for unrealistic levels of safety give rise to ever-increasing levels of repression and exclusion of those identified as risky? Why, in other words, did 'penal rationalism' give way to 'populist punitiveness'? (Bottoms, 1995).

Garland discusses the role of the professional elites, traditional supporters of due process and proportionality, and of correction rather than exclusion, in criminal justice. He considers why they have embraced, or at the very least, not vigorously resisted, the new penal imperative, 'that the public be protected and its sentiments be expressed' (2000: 350) He emphasizes two factors which have played a significant role in forming the stance taken by professionals towards crime control. These are the bypassing of professional groups as policy-making becomes a more direct response to public demand, and the fact that middle-class professionals are no longer isolated from crime and disorder.

The first of these factors, the bypassing of professional groups, was part of the agenda of the new right politics that triumphed in the English-speaking world in the 1980s. This new right politics has also been cited as the best explanation for why the shift in control strategies occurred when it did by O'Malley (1999, 2001), who however, like Garland, is careful to avoid the reductionism of single-factor explanations. Despite this methodological caution, O'Malley and other analysts suggest that the politics of the 1980s undoubtedly were of great significance in this context. New right politics combined a neo-liberal agenda which sought to restrict progressive taxation and to curb welfare spending, with an authoritarian agenda which increased regulation and repression of the poor, the criminal and the unconventional. Right-wing governments of the 1980s and 1990s were neo-liberal with regard to public spending, but by no means libertarian with regard to public morals.

Punitive populism is, in this account, an element of a more general strategy of 'authoritarian populism', to bring about a regime under which 'the market is to be free; the people are to be disciplined' (Hall, 1980: 5). During the 1980s, explanations for this project were largely in terms of the failings of capitalism to deliver prosperity to all the people. To retain legitimacy, capitalism had to project phenomena such as mass unemployment as failings of the people, not of the system. Its first tactic was to identify a range of groups – strikers, especially striking miners; single parents; new age travellers; scroungers and benefit fraudsters; anti-nuclear campaigners – as 'enemies within', who were to blame for economic recession and whom 'respectable people' needed to be defended against (Hall, 1980; Scraton, 1987). With hindsight, and with the insights learned from the more recent writings on control, we can see this as a clear stage in the entrenchment of *categorical suspicion*, such that people are regarded as criminal not because of their behaviour but because of the groups to which they belong (Marx, 1988).

As well as legitimising failure to deliver jobs and prosperity to everyone, this strategy of identifying groups who were 'to blame' for society's as well as their own troubles legitimised the scaling down of welfare spending. 'Underclass' ideology proposed a social group equivalent to the old 'lumpenproletariat' or

61

the rough poor, who were feckless and work-shy, and who would remain unemployed even in an economic upturn because they were unemployable, and had rendered themselves unemployable through truancy, followed by undisciplined post-school lifestyles. These unemployables were, it was claimed, perfectly content to live without work, content to subsist on welfare benefits topped up by the proceeds of crime (Murray, 1984).

Again, one can well ask what is new in this. There is nothing new in using crime control to divide the poor from the poorest, the respectable poor from the rough poor, the docile from the dissident. Foucault (1977) suggested that modern penality is a political economy of crime, not aimed at reducing crime but at producing the delinquent as object of knowledge; showing the non-criminal whom it is they should fear and should organise defences against; showing what crimes are tolerable and what are intolerable; changing popular perceptions of routine illegalities from understandable and forgivable survival behaviours to reprehensible predatory evils. Underclass theory, then, is just the latest in a long line of 'dangerous classes' criminologies (Morris, 1994).

What was new was neo-liberal economic doctrine. As well as the 'legitimation crisis' explanation, the idea of the 'free economy and the strong state' (Gamble, 1988) is consistent not only with the shift from expert to populist influence on policy-making, but also with the shift from concern with the risk of unemployment and economic recession to the heightened preoccupation with fear of crime. Whilst the 'authoritarian populism' framework in law and order commentaries gives prominence to authoritarian social/penal policies, this political economy framework focuses on the consequences of new right economics, stressing the 'markets must be free' part of the agenda. Neo-liberal economic orthodoxy insists that 'markets must decide'; it proscribes any interference with market forces to regulate levels of employment or to enhance welfare. If governments cannot pursue activism in the economic sphere, but nevertheless wish to project themselves as strong, then they must select some other sphere for activism. Crime fulfils this requirement perfectly, fitting the late-modernist mood of fear of strangers, and the late-modernist mode of laying blame for risk on individuals.

The new right agenda of authoritarian populism, combining neo-liberal public spending reductions with legitimating promotion of the criminal, the dissident and the unconventional as the source of society's problems, was pursued through a vigorous process of persuasion. In the UK during the early 1980s Keith Joseph and his Centre for Policy Studies targeted the people who influence the thinking of the nation (Sim, 2000: 321). He and his colleagues met with media barons, academics, and also the leaders of the very professions whose influence he was determined to reduce, astutely realising that even those who might be thought to be most opposed to new right thinking would be flattered to be invited to dine at the fashionable restaurants favoured by those in power.[7] In the USA, a similar new right agenda was promoted by the Heritage Foundation in the 1980s (Carrington, 1983). In the 1990s, this agenda was robustly championed and raised to new levels of populist punitiveness in the 1990s by Attorney-General William Barr (Greene, 1998).

Another new element was the penetration of the mass media. This meant that the ideological campaign targeted at the liberal professionals was supplemented by an appeal to the groups from whom those selected as 'enemies within' sprang. The reach of the media is now so extensive and intensive that even the neighbours of the underclass criminals, those who share their circumstances and might be expected to take a 'there but for the grace of God ...' attitude, learn what to think about them from tabloids and from television rather than from commonality of experience. The success of this ideological project fanned public intolerance of even routine, non-violent crime and stimulated virulent demands for action.

While similarly anxious to avoid reductionist explanations, it seems clear that the new right project has been successful in becoming hegemonic. Populist authoritarianism is now the widespread way of thinking about crime and disorder in, at least, the Anglo-North American world. One outcome of this is that whatever their traditional beliefs and instincts, New Labour and the US Democrats could not but continue with the same strategies towards crime and public safety. By the time the Bush/Major era gave way to that of Clinton/Blair, new right thinking had become the consensual start-point for law and order politics (Melossi, 2000: 308). In part, this was a matter of politics. In the US, the loss of support for Dukakis in the 1988 presidential election following his liberal stance in commenting on the Willy Horton case, (in which a white woman was brutally raped by William Horton, a black man on weekend leave in the final months of a prison sentence for a 1974 murder) showed Bill Clinton and the Democrats that being seen as 'soft' (or even mildly liberal) on crime was a huge political disadvantage (Sasson, 2000). As governor of Arkansas Clinton vigorously enforced the death penalty, and in the 1992 election he 'talked tough' on crime. By the 1997 election, 'new' Labour had learned the same lesson. Throughout the 1980s it was clear that 'law and order' was an issue on which Conservatives were ahead. A new, tough agenda was developed, and a virtually bipartisan approach to crime control was pursued.[8] The spate of ever more punitive and repressive measures started by the Conservatives in the mid-1990s continued unchanged under the Labour government in the late 1990s (Brownlee, 1998; Leacock and Sparks, 2002). It remains in full flood in the early 2000s.

There are material as well as ideological stimuli for this increasingly repressive control of crime. The economic recovery of the 1990s was a recovery in profits and dividends, not a recovery of jobs. Unemployment rates have fallen, it is true, but in the US especially, unemployment rates would be higher if the people in prison were on the labour market. In some of the 'rust belt' cities where old manufacturing industries have declined, imprisonment rates among young adults have risen dramatically. Mass imprisonment has followed mass unemployment.[9] Those who bear the brunt of this are black males in the impoverished urban areas. Prison and ghetto merge as prisons are filled with black inmates, leading to organisation of prison wings along race and ethnic lines, with African-American, Hispanic and other categories form-ing distinctive prison subcultures; at the same time the black ghettos become more like prisons, policed and controlled coercively and militaristically, with no regard for the rights and dignity of inhabitants (Wacquant, 2001).

Another material aspect to the continuation of tough-on-crime policies is that crime control is – if anything is – the replacement industry for those old extraction and manufacturing industries that have disappeared (Christie, 1993). Prison building is now discussed in somewhat surreal economic terms. States in the USA bid against each other to become the location for a new federal maximum security prison; within states, counties bid against each other to have new correctional facilities, in both cases because of the jobs prisons bring. In the UK, proposals to moor a prison ship off the Dorset coast, and to turn a former holiday camp in Morecambe, Lancashire into a prison, were debated in similar terms – the pros were the coming of jobs, the cons were the possible putting off of tourists. A map showing the new prisons looks very much like a map of closed coal-mines.[10] There is an economic demand as well as an ideological demand for crime control.

With the more interventionist Democrat/New Labour governments, and with a softening of new right economic doctrines generally, inner-city regen-eration provides another economic stimulus to crime control. Neo-liberal eco-nomic ideas persist, in that governments still resist directly providing jobs or funding industry, but they have found a new arena for activism in persuad-ing businesses to come into the towns and cities. They seek to provide attrac-tive business environments to encourage global investment, and safe towns and malls to encourage people to shop and conduct their transactions. Crime control is at the centre of the packaging of these attractive commercial environ-ments, and the provision of safety is the task allotted to governments:

> To focus locally on the 'safe environment'; and everything it punitively entails, is exactly what the 'market forces', by now global and so extraterritorial, want the nation-state governments to do (effectively barring them from doing anything else). In the world of global finances, state governments are allotted the role of little else than oversized police precincts; the quantity and quality of the policemen on the beat, efficiency displayed in sweeping the streets clean of beggars, pesterers and pilferers, and the tightness of the jail walls loom large among the factors of 'investors' confidence', and so among the items calculated when the decisions to invest or cut the losses and run are made. To excel in the job of precinct policemen is the best (perhaps the only) thing state government may do to cajole the nomadic capital into investing in its subjects' welfare. (Bauman, 2001: 216)

The hegemonic success of the stigmatising tough-on-crime ideological project has been complemented by another success: that of the safety lobby itself. A changing coalition of left-of-centre politicians trying to reclaim the law and order issue from the right; academics and other researchers concerned with policy relevance; police, local councils and various agencies all anxious to establish or re-establish public confidence, has created a resonant community safety agenda (Crawford, 1997). This agenda emphasizes the effects of crime on the respectable poor, who are less defended by private security devices and property insurance than the rich; on the elderly and women who fear to walk the streets; and of course on children, vulnerable to sexual predators. This has constituted a group of potential victims seen as vulnerable and powerless, and has correspondingly constituted offenders – any offenders, even those who in other times might have been seen as inadequate, deprived or in some way needy – as predators undeserving of sympathy.

The powerful construction of communities as groups of potential victims has been an important part of the way in which professional groups (especially probation officers and juvenile justice workers) have adopted the pursuit of community safety as their goal even at the expense of traditional concern with the rights of offenders. Their identification with victims and potential victims as the underdogs allows them to move from risk management, which seeks to balance the rights of victims and offenders, to risk control, which accepts the zero-sum approach that the rights of some may be forfeit to protect the rights of others, whilst still retaining their sense of being liberal champions of the powerless.

Identification with the safety agenda is also enhanced by the conditions of life in high-crime societies (Garland, 2000). Risk of criminal victimization remains very unevenly distributed, and most professionals live in relatively 'safe' areas, with far less risk of burglary, car crime or robbery than the residents of less favoured neighbourhoods. Nonetheless, professionals are less insulated from the daily possibilities of victimization both at home and at work than in lower-crime periods, and many will have occasional experiences of being victims; even without actual victimization they will share anxieties about the safety of themselves, children and other loved ones with like-minded crime-fearing citizens. Just as suspect people do not have to (actually) commit crimes to be identified as criminal, nor do respectable people have to experience crime to identify themselves as (potential) victims. Ordinary citizens – criminal justice professionals among them – join in the daily experience of (potential) victimization through their daily routines of setting burglar alarms when they leave for work, activating car alarms when they park outside their offices, glimpsing themselves on CCTV when they do their midday shopping and entering PIN codes to withdraw cash to pay for their evening's sustenance and entertainment. And in the contemporary culture of risk-mongering and exclusion of the risky, the professional along with everyone else mediates her stance towards offenders through representations of the criminal as the producer of evil, the 'monstruum, the monstrosity, far removed from any common experience and hence from the possibility of empathy' (Melossi, 2000: 300).

If they can no longer distance themselves from fear of crime, professionals can distance themselves from the repressive aspects of risk control policies by the use of benevolent-sounding euphemisms. One of the criticisms of the rehabilitative schemes of the 1970s and 1980s was of the use of a language of care and treatment for what were experienced as punitive, repressive practices by those on whom they were inflicted. 'Care orders' on young people meant that they were placed under the control of local authorities, and could be left at home under supervision, or removed to an institution, as the local authority saw fit; juvenile incarceration was 'borstal training'. Indeterminate rehabilitative sentences added the anxiety of not knowing the release date and feeling that the date was decided according to the whim of prison administrators, to the normal pains of imprisonment (American Friends Service Committee, 1972). As critics of the time pointed out, these 'for-your-own-good' penalties allowed levels of restriction of liberty and intrusiveness that could be grossly disproportionate to the actions (sometimes the anticipated actions of 'pre-delinquents' rather than the actual actions of adjudicated delinquents) that provoked them, and they may well have seemed inordinate if freely acknowledged as punishment or repression (Cohen, 1979, 1985; Hudson, 1987; von Hirsch, 1976). The due process reform movement of the 1980s called for plain speaking as well as for proportionate sanctions.

Contemporary risk control innovations have brought a return of the euphemistic tendency in corrections. New probation and prison programmes talk of effective 'treatments', and levels of supervision, control and programme participation for offenders – allocated by risk assessment – are measured in 'dosages'. This reintroduction of the so-called medical model of rehabilitation is accompanied by the reintroduction of the educational language of reformism, with the content of punitive sanctions designated as 'courses', available both voluntarily and coercively.

Douglas has suggested that the attractiveness of risk as a 'forensic resource' is at least partly attributable to the moral neutrality, the scientificity, of its language. Developing a theme from earlier work with Wildavsky, she argues that the language of risk plays the same role in contemporary society as stigma and taboo in pre-modern societies (Douglas, 1966). The morally neutral scientific, actuarial terminology of risk disguises the condemnatory pariahdom created by the classifications. Persistent offenders, especially sex offenders, become the new lepers: diseased, incurable, unable to control outbreaks, themselves to blame for whatever privations society imposes upon them. The fact that so many persistent offenders turn out to have come from hopeless, deprived backgrounds, the fact that so many sex offenders turn out to have been abused themselves, does nothing to allay blame and arouse sympathy: rather it serves to reinforce the image of sex offending and other detested forms of criminality as contagious and untreatable. Whilst the flat neutrality of risk language lulls the professionals, the unambiguously stigmatising moral charge of the categorisations connects with public resentment.

Risk and justice

The new systems of risk control violate some of the fundamental tenets of due process. The principles of no punishment without conviction, and proportionality of punishment to harm done, are set aside by the new technologies of risk. They are breached by allocating penalties on the basis of risk of reoffending, where punishment is being imposed as much for what offenders may do in the future as for what they have done in the past; they are breached in the treating of suspects in the same way as convicted offenders. Whilst occasionally the departure from established principles of justice becomes starkly clear, as in the Severe Personality Disorder proposals in the UK, more often it is blurred as the departures are brought about through changes in parole regulations; through emphasis on previous offending rather than risk of future offending; by introducing preventive imprisonment through extension of life sentences or whole-life tariffs (or determinate tariffs which are longer than life sentences, such as the 25 years without parole standard in California and other states, which is much longer than the 'tariff' period of most European life sentences), rather than using the old terminology of indeterminate sentences and preventive detention. The fudged language and the harsh public-political mood mean that there is no public opposition to these movements. There is very little professional opposition, either. As Tonry puts it, 'just about everyone' has been 'socialized by the ethos of our time' into thinking that the public protection arguments for risk-oriented preventive detention and severity of criminal justice policies are self-evident, and all-important (2001: 171).

Removing those who may do us harm is thought so all-important that adherence to the idea that punishment should only follow conviction under a 'beyond reasonable doubt' standard is greatly reduced. This was dramatically made clear in the O.J. Simpson case, when many people regarded his acquittal as a 'perverse' jury decision.[11] Most (white, at least) Americans and observers around the world thought that Simpson committed the murders of his ex-wife and her friend, and appeared to think that even if the prosecution case was unsatisfactory, the jury should nevertheless have convicted. However over-theatrical the representations about the forensic evidence, the political views of the vital police witness and other aspects of the trial, when the police officer who had allegedly found the damaging bloodspots and other forensic evidence 'took the fifth', i.e. claimed constitutional protection against self-incrimination by refusing to say whether he had lied in answering questions about whether he had genuinely found the evidence at the crime scene or had subsequently planted it, then surely an acquittal was the only possible verdict under a 'beyond reasonable doubt' standard. Rather than being held to be an important principle, the 'beyond reasonable' doubt standard is more often seen now as an inconvenient 'legal mantra' (Dershowitz, 1997: 128). Rather than being seen as a crucial protection against punishment of the innocent, it is more often seen as an obstacle to punishment of the guilty, with the result that once suspected, people now tend to be presumed guilty.

A similar tendency is apparent in the UK, and the contrast between the acquittal of Simpson in the criminal trial and the success of the relatives of victims in gaining punitive damages in civil proceedings, was drawn on following the failure to obtain convictions against any of the supposed killers of the student Stephen Lawrence. After an inquest failed to be followed by criminal prosecution of the young men widely believed to be the killers, a private prosecution was mounted against three of them. In both countries, the 'failures' of criminal proceedings resulted in calls to move more generally from a 'beyond reasonable doubt' to a 'probable cause' standard of proof – but no doubt with criminal law penalties following 'convictions' on the lower standard. Unlike the O.J. Simpson case, in the Stephen Lawrence case the private prosecution case also failed, and this acquittal meant that even if further evidence could be discovered, the suspects could not be retried. An official inquiry into the incident, the Macpherson Report, criticised police procedures, but one of its recommendations was for the revocation of the provision against double jeopardy: the rule that no-one can be retried after being acquitted for the offence in question. Police handling of the case was undoubtedly flawed, particularly it seems because stereotypes of black young men led them to see Stephen as part of 'the trouble' at first, rather than treating him straight-forwardly as a victim and his friend as a credible eyewitness. Nevertheless, wide-spread support for repealing the double jeopardy provisions has to be seen as yet another worrying index of the lack of commitment to due process and lack of concern with the rights of suspected persons not to be pursued beyond acquittal on a 'beyond reasonable doubt' standard of proof.

Another manifestation of the tendency to want someone to be 'put away' rather than maintaining the 'beyond reasonable doubt' standard, is the way in which all too often the quashing of convictions in miscarriages of justice cases leave a 'no smoke without fire' opinion that the person concerned probably did do it even though the conviction may be unsafe, and where successful appeals against conviction, or acquittals, often fail to lead to the case in question being reopened. Unsafe convictions, appeals, and the general reduction in adherence to the presumption of innocence and the importance of 'beyond reasonable doubt' have led to more private prosecutions; changes in rules of disclosure to the advantage of the prosecution; changes in the import of the right to silence, again to the advantage of the prosecution; proposals to end the double jeopardy rule for some cases and some types of evidence; proposals to remove the right to jury trial for some medium-serious offence types, and a general tendency to dilute the distinction between the suspect and the convicted offender.

At the margins of criminal justice, in the wider control system, the distinction between suspect and offender has been erased altogether for some sorts of people. The surveillance gaze operates on the basis of suspicion, but categorical suspicion can have consequences beyond (mere) surveillance. People can be and are excluded from shopping malls, made subject to curfews, coercively recruited to behavioural programmes, all because of who they are and what they look like. This exclusion by stereotyping is compounded by the fact that delinquency is being 'defined up'. 'Zero tolerance' policing; local authority action under Crime and Disorder legislation; and neighbourhood demands for action are directed at certain types of people whatever they are doing.

Surveillance, repression and exclusion are directed at *incivilities* such as raucous behaviour, begging or loitering. The distinction between illegal and unpleasant behaviour, crime and nuisance, delinquency and disorderliness is being eroded. This is a distinction that was thought to be of great importance as the defence against 'net-widening' (extending the control network to those who had not committed offences) and 'net-strengthening' (imposing increasing amounts of control and surveillance on the same people) only a couple of decades ago (Austin and Krisberg, 1981; Cohen, 1979, 1985). Young people, especially economically and socially marginalized young people, are regarded with fear, hostility and suspicion; they are perceived as dangerous, intimidating – risky:

> Their committing an offence is a matter of secondary importance to those parts of society that define what deviance is ... What is important is their perceived probability of being dangerous and this can be associated with completely legal behaviour, like that of adolescents gathering together at the entrances of buildings in which they live. Such behaviour is a major cause of fear of crime even though it is open to observation. It is almost as though poor young people should pretend that there is a job waiting for them in the morning and go to bed early, and children from the housing estates should 'keep out of trouble' by staying indoors as if they had departed on a language exchange scheme abroad. (Lianos with Douglas, 2000: 263)

These developments show a lack of concern with the rights and civil liberties of those caught in the net of punishment and control. Politicians and professionals asked about these matters usually dismiss them by saying that it is the rights and liberties of potential victims with which they are concerned. Two points are illustrated by such responses. First, a 'zero-sum' mentality has become entrenched, where it is thought that increases in rights for some (victims and potential victims) must mean a diminution or denial of rights of others (offenders and potential offenders). Moreover, it is assumed that anything that *helps* victims, and contributes to public safety in general, must *hurt* offenders and the general community of the lawless and uncivil (Zimring, 2001: 163–4). The other element of this zero-sum approach to rights is the coupling of rights and responsibilities. In a culture where risks are attributed to (ir)responsible individuals, a corresponding stance on rights is hardly surprising (Giddens, 1999). Risks are posed by individual malefaction; rights must be earned through individual propriety. People who actively pose risks to others, on this view, cannot expect to be protected from any correlative risks of surveillance, punishment or exclusion because their rights (to privacy, due process, freedom of movement, etc.) have not been earned and are therefore forfeit.[12]

Risk society and liberal security concerns

Towards the end of the last chapter, I summarised the principal concerns that liberalism has had about security: its equal distribution as a public good; defence against free riders; defence against dangerous persons; external threats. At various points in this chapter I have hinted that the demand for security is insatiable, that its heightened pursuit is making the citizens of late modernity more fearful and more suspicious, and it is destroying bonds of solidarity which may well be necessary for our well-being and social functioning. It is now time to bring together these policies and practices that have emerged and proliferated in response to the politics of safety and ask about their consequences for liberal interests in security.

Liberal-egalitarian fears about the distribution of security are undoubtedly being realised in that it is turning from a public good to a 'club good' and to a private good. The 'death of the social', the hyper-individualism and distrust of state provision are important elements in the social-political context in which security is being demanded. Looking at the supply of security rather than just the demand, however, we see that in the market society, security has become 'commodified' (Zedner, 2000). This is turning it into a commodity like any other, and it is accordingly becoming dominated by the market mechanism of commodity exchange: money. 'Security' is a state of mind, a state of relationships, but it is also a series of commodities to be bought and sold. Security is the gadgetry of alarms and cameras; it is security personnel, secure locations, secure transportation and secure communications. These commodities are bought and sold privately, and they are bought and sold by and to groups and associations. Security is bought and sold by the private and corporate dollar rather than provided by public expenditure.

This commodification of security has led to magnified inequalities of distribution (Hope, 2000). While it is of course true that the rich have always been able to provide more protection for themselves than the poor, what is worrying about the present era is that the availability of security commodities has arisen alongside the withdrawal of state security provision. The state has not merely acquiesced in this commodification, it has actively encouraged citizens to take responsibility for their own security provision through its twin strategies of 'responsibilisation' of private individuals and devolving of security functions in public spaces to local authority and business partnerships (Garland, 1996; Crawford, 1997). This has resulted in inequalities in security not merely between rich and poor, but also between young and old, male and female.[13]

Feminist criminologists and others have pointed out that the distribution of security has been patterned very much on male ideas of risk and threat. The work of Stanko and Walklate in the UK and their counterparts elsewhere has shown that community safety campaigns and provisions concentrate on theft and robbery of businesses, car crime and other street crime, and concentrate almost exclusively on 'stranger danger', whereas women and children are most at risk in their own homes, and from people they know (Stanko, 1990, 1997, 2000; Walklate, 1997; Johnson and Sacco, 1995; Madriz, 1997).

Women's safety has been dealt with almost entirely by strategies of individual responsibilisation. They are bombarded with advice on avoidance of dark places, of being out alone at night, of wearing provocative clothing, and they are prime marketing targets for personal security devices (Stanko, 2000). What is far less common is consultation with women about their security needs, or public provision taking account of their descriptions of their fears and experiences of danger.

There is also racial inequality in security provision. It has been held for many years that white neighbourhoods are over-protected and under-policed, in that the criminal activities that take place behind close doors in affluent white neighbourhoods go undetected, whereas the street crime of poor – especially poor black – neighbourhoods is vigorously prosecuted while residents are inadequately protected against racial violence and other dangers (Bowling, 1999; Keith, 1991). Crime and disorder legislation and zero-tolerance policing campaigns treat young black people as 'the problem', whereas crime surveys repeatedly find that they are the group with the highest rates of victimization (Mirrlees-Black et al., 1996).

Similar stories can be told about security as a 'club good'. Early studies of situational crime prevention measures such as neighbourhood and shopping precinct CCTV schemes reported 'displacement' of crime from locations that had schemes to those that didn't; from well-protected areas to those where residents or businesses had not formed security partnerships (Hesseling, 1994; Pease, 2002). Business and shopping areas were better protected than residential areas; affluent residential areas were better protected than poorer ones, and these inequalities in security distribution were reflected in rates of car crime, burglary and theft. Studies of crime prevention effectiveness only began to show reduced rates of displacement and greater all-round effectiveness when local authorities began to fund CCTV and other crime prevention schemes in residential and commercial neighbourhoods where residents and traders had not funded, and could not afford to fund, their own schemes. In other words, inequalities – though still existing – could only be ameliorated by reintroducing a degree of public provision.

The threat of free riders has been responded to vigorously, but again the response has been extremely unequal. Campaigns against people 'sponging off the state' have targeted the poor, restricting access to benefits or making the tests stiffer for the unemployed, for young homeless people or for lone parents, for example. Differences in the response to benefit fraud and to tax evasion illustrate that social attitudes towards the former are that such people are frauds and scroungers, but towards the latter there is an attitude of 'everybody does it, you're a fool if you don't' (Cook, 1989). There have been aggressive campaigns about single mothers 'married to the state', but concerns about mis-selling of endowment policies and suspension by companies of their contributions to pension funds have been aired on the financial pages of the newspapers, not in the courts.

Free-rider campaigns have also been conducted against foreign students and temporary residents claiming benefits while in England, but loopholes which allow wealthy British individuals and corporations to avoid paying tax in this country remain open. Asylum seekers have been victims of particularly aggressive policies to avoid free-riding, depriving them of cash benefits, of rights to seek employment and to access mainstream services such as education and in some instances, healthcare. Similar repressive policies have been introduced in the USA and other western countries. Again, almost no restrictions on the freedom to travel, to earn and to receive education and healthcare are put in the way of the affluent elite of the global economy.

We have seen that policies to protect society from the dangerous have often failed to strike a balance between risk concerns and the demands of justice, changing the balance in rules of evidence in favour of the prosecution, introducing provision for lengthy incarceration and post-release surveillance and control, and proposals to allow for incarceration of persons diagnosed as having a Severe Personality Disorder, even without their having committed an offence. The UK appears to be following the USA in turning to forms of civil commitment to avoid judicial resistance to the use of incarceration to prevent future crime, either by means of extended imprisonment after the completion of a sentence for a crime, by an offender who is still regarded as dangerous, or by means of preventive incarceration even without a crime having been committed (Janus, 2000). Mental health legislation, which looks to dangerousness rather to legal values such as proportionality and proof of guilt, may well be increasingly mobilised if judiciaries resist moves to incorporate popular demands for greater protection against dangerousness into penal law because of adherence to legal principles of justice (Freiberg, 2000).

External threats are also responded to ever more vigorously, often with scant regard for principles of justice. International co-operation on crime has led to the sharing of information on individuals across borders through international policing groups and international databases. The European Union has introduced community-wide policing and data-pooling, and has extended its reach into the former Soviet countries such as the Baltic states of Estonia, Lithuania and Latvia. Again, policing priorities have been those of the powerful, with belated attention to crimes such as trafficking of women. Refugees and asylum seekers have been constructed as threats rather than as objects of pity, and have been associated with people-trafficking, crime, disease, and seen as drains on host nations' economies. The word 'refugee' is often accompanied by the adjective 'bogus', and the status of asylum seekers is that of guilty until proven innocent.

As well as crime and migration, threats of terrorism are added to the more traditional threats of war and invasion by hostile states. Threats of wars and incursions have been dealt with through international organisations, through non-aggression pacts, and through balance of arms. At least, this is the case for the wealthy industrialised nations, who have experienced historically unprecedented periods of peace since the Second World War. Provision of security is unequal, and the poorer nations continue to be involved in state-against-state aggression, in civil wars and in colonial wars (Hogg, 2002; Holsti, 1999). The breakup of colonial rule in Africa, and of communist rule in Yugoslavia and the Soviet Union has led to brutal wars (Rwanda, Congo, Angola, Bosnia, Kosovo, Chechnya, Azerbaijan, to name a few); in which the west has sometimes intervened and sometimes stood back and let the brutality continue. All the while in these regions and elsewhere round the globe, the west has fuelled the wars by selling arms.

The threat of terrorism, for most western states, looms larger than the threat of war. Nations which have lived with the threat and reality of terrorism for some time (the UK with the IRA and loyalist terrorism, Spain with ETA, for example) are accustomed to anti-terrorist legislation which suspends many of the rules of law, such as no detention without trial. Even before 11 September 2001, the USA intervened in other countries without United Nations authority, and Israel has disregarded UN resolutions in its dealings with Palestinians. Since 11 September, the USA has enacted anti-terrorist legislation under which people can be declared terrorists or aiders of terrorism on the flimsiest of evidence, and the conditions under which suspected Taliban and Al-Quaida fighters and their supporters are held and may be tried goes against the rule of law of the USA and most other western countries. The suspension of rights for these fighters and suspects, according to Dworkin, is the real threat to American values (Dworkin, 2002).

In the present, liberal concerns with equality of security, equality of freedom, and respect for the rights and dignity of all persons are very far from being met. The politics of risk and safety is a politics of inequality, of lack of respect for freedom and dignity of all, and of lack of regard for established rights and systems of legality.

Conclusion

The threats to justice inherent in contemporary risk society, theoretical risks and practical risks, are not necessarily brought about by the demise of liberalism, or a weakened adherence to liberalism. Punitiveness is, as we have seen, often attributed to neo-liberalism or neo-conservatism, but recent trends in fact also illustrate the weaknesses and unresolved conflicts in liberalism itself. Zero-sum approaches to rights and restrictions violate the 'equal liberty' principle, and the tenor of the times is that some people – the risky – have no rights to liberty. This enhancement of the rights of some by removing the rights of others is hard to avoid if security is taken seriously, and even more so if it is politicised. Balancing rights, giving content to the liberal notion of 'maximum liberty compatible with the equal liberty of all others', is extremely difficult, perhaps almost impossible. The difficulties of obtaining the 'equal liberty' balance are such that the perennially tempting solution is the exclusion of some groups and individuals from the constituency of justice and rights altogether. Privileging the rights of some and denying them to others is much easier than trying to maintain an equilibrium between rights given to all.

Institutions of justice in the liberal democracies were developed to protect people first and foremost against the state. Modern western societies have been successful in establishing constitutional governments in place of absolutist governments, and in establishing bureaucratic systems to entrench and administer the rule of law. So long as citizens saw the dangers they faced as being faced in common, the institutions and utilities of modern governments enjoyed public support, and the consensual mode saw even events like crime as arising from misfortune as much as from wickedness. Offenders were punished, but not for ever, and they were not expelled from society. The problem of protection of offenders against disproportionate or vengeful punishment being dependent on the goodwill of the law-abiding and respectable, was meliorated by the fact that such goodwill was, in the main, present.

Now that individuals are far more conscious – in their daily mental and social routines – of dangers from other individuals than from governments or fates, and now that we inhabit a culture of blame, the goodwill on which liberalism depends is withdrawn. The balancing of rights has gone: the only rights that matter for most people are the safety rights of selves and loved ones. The sense of shared risk, shared responsibility has also gone: we cope with risk by a constant scanning of all with whom we come into contact to see whether or not they pose a threat to our security, and the only way we can operate this scanning is by adopting stereotypes of safe and risky kinds of people.[14]

Liberalism has had little to offer in answering questions about how much security, how little freedom. The principle of equal maximum liberty cannot protect those who are deemed below, or beyond, equality. Mill's celebrated harm principle is another good general maxim, but it does not help us to answer questions of what harms to prioritise; how much curtailment of freedom is justifiable to balance how much harm; how high the probability of harm should be to justify certain restrictions of freedom.

Few would argue with Mill that security is the one essential good, and so it appeals to common sense that basic security rights, the rights to life and possession of one's property, should be safeguarded before all else. But while this may be beyond dispute, as Dworkin argues one cannot proceed from this to saying that the right to life and physical security is everything, all other rights as nothing compared with baseline safety (Dworkin, 1978). If rights to freedom, privacy, non-interference and no punishment without conviction are rights at all, then they are in the same *category* of things as life and property, and therefore must be comparable at least to the extent that they demand to be held in balance. Safety might triumph, but it cannot be not all-conquering if the idea of rights has any purchase.

The most effective way in which competing rights can be unbalanced in this zero-sum way is by putting some people outside the constituency of justice altogether. This again is a persistent feature of liberal theories of justice. All the variants of liberalism distinguish between those who are within the construction of rational, contracting, citizens – those among whom liberty is to be equalised and maximised – and those against whom the just society must defend itself. Children; lunatics; women; slaves; colonial subjects; criminals; the sick and persons of different religion or race are, or have been, to an extent which varies with time and place, judged to be unworthy or unable to carry out the demands of rational co-operation, and so do not share in the rights defended by justice.

Contemporary penal and public safety policies increasingly tend to exclude those defined as dangerous – the risky – rather than temporarily suspend full membership in the moral community. The penal theories mentioned in the previous chapter (most obviously the communicative versions of retributivism, but to a significant extent all of them) assume that the offender is still a member, even though some of his/her rights are temporarily withdrawn. Communications aimed at deterrence or penitence can only be addressed to someone who is rational, who shares some of the values, who feels suspension of fellowship to be a loss – to someone, in other words, who shares at some level a moral language. Penal communication is aimed at influencing choice: the objective is that the offender will choose not to offend again, the potential offender will choose not to offend at all.

Risk management leaves the possibility of choice of good deeds or bad deeds open, but risk control removes the possibility of choice by removing the possibility of action. Whether by incarceration, curfew or exclusion from certain venues, strategies are, as all the 'new penology', 'governmentality' and 'neo-liberalism' commentators note, aimed at managing the possibilities of action rather than attempting to change the offender's moral choices. But if people do not have the opportunity to commit (further) crime, then neither do they have the opportunity to demonstrate by restraint from crime that they have rejoined the moral consensus. Liability to punishment for transgression of the norms of co-operation among members of a society depends on their being able to choose to conform or to deviate from society's norms, and as Matravers remarks, in a slightly different context, those who do not have the possibilities of co-operation, including its benefits, cannot be punished. Society may – rightly or wrongly – do things to them in its own defence, but if they do not share the advantages of co-operation, then whatever is done to or about them cannot be classed as (justified) punishment.[1]

To deprive people of the opportunity of choice of action is to treat them as non-members, beings to whom the normal rules of rational action planning do not apply. Risk assessment databases make up people as amalgams of the various factors they include, and this 'making up people' changes their possibilities of personhood (Hacking, 1986). They are deprived of their rational humanity and become determined creatures of statistical risk-assessment systems; instead of being flesh and blood, inconsistent, unpredictable humans acting out of their own interests and desires, free to change their perceptions of these and their moral cognitive sets at any time in the present and future, they become the predictable embodiment of databases, for whom the behavioural uncertainty of actual choices in actual situations is replaced by the statistical certainties of factorial calculations. Once an offender or a suspect becomes a data-constructed bearer of the characteristics of danger, there is no way back to becoming a rational moral agent; the route from the fortress to the wilderness is one-way.

Risk classification and risk control are, therefore, first and last strategies of inclusion and exclusion, and what is more, they form an impregnable, unchallengeable ordering which leaves some individuals and groups outside of rights, outside of the moral-legal community. Denying rights to those who are recognised as sharing the criteria for rational co-operation is denounced as discrimination or injustice; drawing the boundaries of justice along lines of risk and danger is seen as responsible governance and citizenship.

Risk control strategies throw into sharp relief the perennial questions of whose rights matter; who is to adjudicate rights conflicts and on what basis; who is inside the fortress of justice and who is outside in the wilderness of danger? These questions will be explored in the following chapters.

Notes

[1]Suspension of rights and bodily punishment come together, of course, in the death penalty; the notion of a *human* right, however, is that it is inalienable, it cannot be cancelled. Punishment should, therefore, suspend rather than remove rights, and so as societies have modernised they have tended to dispense with the death penalty, which involves taking away the right to life irrevocably: the right to life cannot be suspended, but must be either maintained or erased altogether. This is discussed further in Chapter 7, below.

[2]McConville et al. (1997); Cohen (1985); Feeley and Simon (1992, 1994); Melossi (2000); Rutherford (1996).

[3]Debates about and critiques of 'new penology' often ask whether penality has now become 'postmodern' (Garland, 1995; Lucken, 1998; Miller, 2001; Pratt, 2000b). There is no

need to assume, however, that 'new' means 'postmodern', and to my mind the descriptions of new penology fit the late-modernity framework rather better than they do a postmodernist frame. Postmodernist perspectives on justice are discussed in Chapter 6, below.

[4]Soothill et al. (2000) also point out that general discussion and also research on sex offending tends not to differentiate types of sexual offences. Their 32-year study of sex offenders' reconviction finds significant differences in both amount of offending and differentiation of offending, depending on the form of sexual offence.

[5]Michael Stone's conviction was subsequently declared unsafe by the Court of Appeal in February 2001, but a retrial was ordered rather than the defendant being finally acquitted. Stone was reconvicted, although no new evidence was offered.

[6]As well as Beck (1992), Douglas (1992), Giddens (1990), Simon (1987), Rose (1996a and 1996b) referred to above, see also Bauman (1989) for a powerful reminder of the potential of modernism to treat people as risks to be eliminated.

[7]Halcrow (1989: 66–108) describes this as 'eating our way to victory'. (The present author remembers very well the sudden embrace of previously unthinkable ideas about probation after a number of leading chief probation officers were entertained at a fashionable Italian restaurant in Chelsea by a Home Office minister.)

[8]Jack Straw, who became Labour Home Secretary after the 1997 election, boasted that the Labour front bench hadn't opposed a criminal justice measure since 1988 (Anderson and Mann, 1997: 269; Sim, 2000: 327).

[9]The authors of a special edition of the journal *Punishment and Society* (2001) use the term 'mass imprisonment'. In the introduction to the edition, Garland (2001: 5) points out that the USA seems likely to reach a record imprisonment rate of 2 million in the year 2001. This is, he says, an unprecedented event in the history of liberal democracy.

[10]The train journey from the town where I live to Manchester goes past an installation which has kept the same name down the decades, although its use has changed. Since the 1960s it has been successively a nationalised coal-mine, a private coal-mine, and is now a private prison.

[11]The American footballer O.J. Simpson was tried and acquitted in October 1995 of the murders of his former wife, Nicole Brown Simpson, and her friend Ronald Goldman. The victim's families were later awarded punitive damages against him in a civil trial. Among the evidence which called Simpson's guilt into question was the fact that a bloodstained glove produced by the prosecution appeared to be too small for his hand.

[12]Whether rights are conditional or inviolable is discussed further in Chapter 7, below.

[13]An experience of my own provides an illustration of the young/old split coming about because of commodification of security. I spent the 1990s living in a row of ex-miners' cottages in the north-east of England, and over the years noticed that as the elderly residents of the row died or moved out and their homes were bought by young professional people, part of the 'gentrification' of the row included fitting burglar alarms, which were installed as standard along with the double glazing and other refurbishments. I received a visit from a burglar-alarm salesman. At the end of his sales pitch, I said 'So the idea is that if I buy one of these systems an opportunist burglar would pass by my cottage and burgle the unalarmed one next door.' 'Yes,' he said, 'that's exactly it', and got his sales contract out. 'But my next-door neighbour is an elderly widow who is probably less well-insured than me, and would undoubtedly be more traumatised by a burglary.' The salesman shook his head at me, and hastily departed.

[14]This scanning through stereotype plainly does not ensure security: the most prolific known serial killer in the UK evaded suspicion for many years and was therefore able to kill so many people precisely because he did not match the usual stereotype – the killer Dr Harold Shipman.

3
The Communitarian Challenge

In late modernity, criminal justice is oriented to public protection and public appeasement rather than to 'doing justice'. 'Community safety' is the discourse in which criminal justice professionals locate their goals, their practices and their ideals. The last chapter explored the *risk/safety* part of the term; this chapter is concerned with *community* – its meaning and importance in present political/philosophical discourse; its relationship with liberal justice.

The discourse of community challenges liberal theories and institutions at two levels. First, there is a challenge at the political level. 'Third Way' politicians such as Tony Blair and Jack Straw in the UK and Bill Clinton in the USA have taken up the arguments of communitarians – the US writer Amitai Etzioni has been particularly influential on English politicians – that liberal societies have emphasised individual rights at the expense of what individuals owe to their communities. The mantra of this political communitarianism is that *rights* come with *responsibilities*.

This communitarian political agenda is frequently referred to as *value communitarianism* because it is inserting community into the social contractarian equation as a source of value. Communities are posited as having moral value in the way that individuals do: communities have rights; individuals have obligations to communities as well as to each other.

The other level at which communitarianism challenges liberalism is philosophical/epistemological. Communitarian philosophers such as MacIntyre, Sandel, Taylor and Walzer reject the Kantian liberal notion of a self prior to its ends. They argue that individuals acquire their identities (their values, their projects, their social roles, their conventions, their hopes and fears) from the communities in which they live their lives. This *constructivist communitarianism* proposes the 'situated self' as a more realistic account of the subject of modernity than the 'unencumbered self' of Kant, Rawls and other deontological liberals.

The most important questions that liberals raise against communitarianism are in two closely related clusters. There are questions of *membership* (what are the boundaries of community, who is included, who is excluded; who can join; can individuals enter and exit voluntarily) and questions of *evaluation* (if all values are constituted through membership of communities, from where would the possibilities of critique, opposition, change, arise).

In this chapter I will examine these communitarian challenges and some possible and actual liberal responses to them. I will look at the practices and institutions that are being developed in the name of community, and look at compromises and safeguards that are emerging from the liberal/communitarian dialogue. My coverage of the communitarian literature will necessarily be selective, dealing with those aspects which have bearing on the central topic of this book – the prospects for justice in the risk society.

The emergence of a politics of community

There are two main themes in the manifesto of political communitarianism. The first asserts the responsibilities individuals have to communities; the second proposes a presumed decline in community as a crucial factor in rising crime rates and other social ills. Both elements identify the competitive, materialistic individualism of late modernity as the key factor in the break-down of community and in people's lack of recognition of their responsibilities towards communities. These themes have been embraced by politicians, and the academics who have propounded them have become the policy 'gurus' of centrists seeking an agenda which is neither the economic nihilism of neo-liberalism nor a return to the social democracy that neo-liberalism displaced. Pre-eminent among the gurus is Etzioni, and his work will be drawn upon as representative of this contemporary political value communitiarianism (1993, 1998).

Before the emergence of this new value communitarianism, 'community' appeared in social theory in nostalgic terms, portrayed as something lost, something left behind by the dialectic of history, something to be regretted but not recaptured. The sociological tradition of Tönnies, Weber and their successors compared unfavourably the *Gesellschaft* modern industrial society with the *Gemeinschaft* pre-modern society. *Gesellschaft* societies are depicted as anonymous, impersonal, with associations entered into temporarily and conditionally, for reasons of personal gain; *Gemeinschaft* societies (of which, of course, none of the nostalgia sociologists has had personal experience) are sentimentally depicted as face-to-face, warm and nurturing, composed of individuals interacting in a multiplicity of intersecting, stable roles, sharing history, values, day-to-day experiences and future prospects. *Gesellschaft* produces atomism; *Gemeinschaft* sustains solidarity (Nisbet, 1962a, 1962b). Etzioni (1998: x,xi) is careful to distinguish himself and those with whom he is allied in the new communitarian movement from this older sociological tradition of Tonnies, Weber and Parsons. He says that theoretically, the point of the new communitarianism is to problematise the relationships between individuals and groups; between responsibility and freedom; between solidarity and autonomy, relationships that the 'loss of community' writing neglects. Politically, new communitarianism sets itself the task of re-establishing community at a factual, institutional level and at a level of values and obligations in today's pluralist, individualist, consumerist society. The core of contemporary political communitarianism is, perhaps, the belief that 'up to a point social order and liberty are mutually sustaining and reinforcing, but that if either is enhanced beyond that point, they become antagonistic and adversarial' (ibid.: xi).

One of the main spurs to this new political communitarianism was the libertarian brand of liberalism that became influential (especially in the USA) in the 1970s and 1980s. This had left-wing and right-wing versions, but essentially it was a resistance to anything but the most minimal government.[1] Whilst right-wing versions concentrated on economic issues, opposing for example anything other than a very low level of taxation, left-wing versions concentrated on social issues – opposing the criminalisation of cannabis; wanting to decriminalise sexual practices hitherto regarded as deviant. Right-wing libertarianism saw the state as having no legitimate role in the redistribution of wealth and opportunity; left-wing libertarianism saw the state as having no role in enforcing conventional morality.

In the USA, where this libertarianism was most robust and widespread, it was played out in a culture with strong commitment to the idea of rights, and so its discursive form was that of guarding against state/community encroachment on individual rights. Initially, then, some of the communitarian argument was directed against the ACLU (American Civil Liberties Union). The issue of free speech posed the question of a conflict between individual rights and community interests particularly keenly. Whether the right to free speech protects speech which incites race hatred; whether freedom of expression extends to allowing the circulation of pornography, were fiercely contested issues (Dworkin, 1978, 1986a; MacKinnon, 1989). These questions also arose in the UK and elsewhere, although they did not present such huge difficulties. The lack of such cultural/ideological attachment to the concept of constitutionally defined specific rights blunted the argument in the UK, while in much of mainland Europe, a notion of public interest has survived in much stronger form than in the English-speaking countries. Moreover, the experience of Nazism in so many countries has made Europeans much more wary of unfettered freedom of expression.

Groups like the Ku Klux Klan in the USA, the National Front and the British National Party in the UK, and their European equivalents undoubtedly pose a dilemma for liberal democracies. Whilst it is easy to proscribe groups whose primary purpose is to perpetrate acts of terrorism, there are numerous groups whose ideas may be offensive to many, but whose primary purpose is, they claim, political: to win elections, not battles. These groups claim that their organisational purpose is to express opinions, to try to gain support, although some believers in the cause might resort to violence. The problems of violence and threat associated with the Klan were dealt with by banning intimidatory paraphernalia – wearing hoods in public places – and acts of violence perpetrated in its name were prosecuted. Similar approaches were followed in Europe: banning the 'military wing' of the IRA; prosecuting followers of left- and right-wing groups for criminal acts and conspiracies; proscribing the wearing of hoods, masks or the display of symbols such as the swastika.

But speaking in public, marching and demonstrating are supposedly rights which mark out a free society. Whereas most of the liberal democracies have no difficulty with enacting legislation to ban incitement to criminal action, expression of distasteful opinion without engaging in or advocating criminal action is a problematic issue for liberals. The liberal ideal is that offensive, intolerant views will be discredited through counter-argument, that 'ventilation' through public debate is a better option than 'festering' through suppression. This is the argument of liberals such as Dworkin (1978).

Through the 1970s and 1980s, some of the fiercest arguments were around the question of 'giving a platform to racists', on the streets, on the television screens, and on university campuses. In the USA denial of opportunities for speech were generally thought unconstitutional, prohibited by the First Amendment. A Supreme Court judgment in 1989 expressed this succinctly:

if there is a bedrock principle underlying the First Amendment, it is that the government may not prohibit the expression of an idea simply because society finds the idea itself offensive or disagreeable.[2]

The only form of speech held not to be protected by the First Amendment was that where words themselves were of an illegal nature: 'lewd, obscene, libellous or profane words, and "fighting words" – those which, by their very utterance inflict injury or tend to incite an immediate breach of the peace' (Gellman, 1991: 362–3).[3]

A similar position emerged in the UK, with certain forms of expression illegal under obscenity, blasphemy and conspiracy laws. This category of proscribed forms of words was extended by the banning of 'incitement to race hatred' under the 1976 Race Relations Act, but there was no general denial of freedom of expression to anti-minority groups or individuals.

The problem had been cast in traditional liberal form as concerning individuals – a speaker with objectionable views might be persuaded by another individual countering with more tolerant and progressive arguments; on the other hand a charismatic speaker might inflame an individual to criminal assault on the person or property of other individuals. Awareness gradually developed that the issue was wider than that a particular speaker or group could incite their listeners to go out and inflict criminal assaults and damage on the objects of hatred and their property: a general climate of intolerance produced more widespread crime and intimidation against ethnic, religious and sexual minorities, and it was realised that their sensibilities should be respected as well as their persons and property protected.

A new genre of 'hate crime' has been introduced to deal with what is perceived as a new and growing problem. While serious acts of violence, and acts such as setting fire to property, are covered by existing criminal laws on homicide, arson, etc., the new concern is with 'low level offending, in some cases at the borderline between expressions of opinion and the perpetration of assault, intimidation, menacing and vandalism' (Jacobs, 1993: 114).

The main legislative response to this problem has been sentence enhancement for offences which target a minority victim.[4] Many of the states in the USA introduced such provisions during the 1980s and 1990s, and a similar provision was included in the 1991 Criminal Justice Act in England and Wales, albeit in a rather hesitant form. Similar sentence enhancement provisions exist in other European countries. This kind of legislation has not generally been thought successful in the USA (Fleisher, 1994; Gellman, 1991; Jacobs, 1993), and although it has not been evaluated systematically in the UK, most community relations groups appear dissatisfied with the outcomes.[5] Two principal objections have been put forward by US critics. First, there is the practical difficulty of assessing motivation, of being sure (to a juridical standard of certainty) that a minority victim was deliberately targeted. Second, there is the difficulty of principle that enhanced sentencing comes, at the very least, undesirably close to punishing mental states rather than actual behaviour.

This brief discussion of 'hate crime' legislation is introduced here to illustrate the point that the liberal response to consciousness of new kinds of harms and claims for protection have characteristically recognised only individual harms, and have found difficulty in recognising the category of harms by individuals against groups. They have also found difficulty in dealing with giving offence rather than causing actual physical harm. These difficulties arise because of the liberal presumption that individual liberties should be restricted only in cases of 'clear and present danger', and that restriction of liberty is always, at best, a necessary evil. More recent debates, however, have proposed the community, as well as individual potential victims, as an entity with claims to protection. Sometimes 'the community' in question is a geographical or political area; at other times it is a religious or ethnic group within an area: the point is that 'the community' has emerged as a moral being with claims to protection from harm.

Examples of this (re-)emergence of community as a moral being include deliberations over whether marches and demonstrations should be allowed that may be offensive to communities in which they are held or through which they pass. Organisers of Orange Order marches in Belfast and Derry are now asked to route them away from mainly Catholic areas; National Front marches may be refused permission to go through black or Asian neighbourhoods; neo-Nazi marches in Europe are kept away from Jewish or other minority neighbourhoods. Where the problem used to be seen solely in terms of the conflict between rights of free expression and association, and the maintenance of peace and order and the prevention of crime, being offensive to a community is now an important consideration.[6] The test for prohibition is, now, not only whether a 'reasonable person' might be incited to hatred, violence or vandalism, but whether a 'reasonable community' would be offended.

As well as gaining rights to consideration which may weigh against traditional individual rights, the new politics has given communities rights to protection such that not only may one-off activities such as marches and demonstrations by groups be banned, but certain individuals may be banned from areas indefinitely. Curfews, exclusion orders, injunctions and informal refusals of entry by, for example, shopping mall security guards, keep certain persons from certain areas at certain times.

The community's status as moral entity, as potential victim, as legitimate claimant for protection, is made clear in the UK's 1998 Crime and Disorder Act.[7] This Act brings together a variety of policy initiatives and trends in the governance of localities and populations, and makes community safety a primary and explicit objective of governmental policy. Individuals may be made subject to curfews, to Anti-Social Behaviour orders, to injunctions and exclusions, because of being identified as troublesome or objectionable. No legal behavioural definition is stipulated to warrant the imposition of these new forms of regulation, and most of the innovations come within civil rather than criminal law, so there is no rigour with regard to standards of proof and rules of evidence. Local authorities, police and members of the public can initiate proceedings. Opposition to the Act came mainly from liberal lawyers, and there has been some reluctance on the part of local authorities to use the provisions of the Act because of concerns about due process and civil rights, but there has been no significant challenge to the idea of the community as an entity to which a duty of protection is owed.

While many of the innovations developed during the 1990s in the name of community safety are illustrative of the changed perspectives on risk discussed in the previous chapter, they also exemplify this new conception of community and communities. Preventive incarceration, risk assessment for parole decisions and similar provisions are aimed at preventing long-recognised forms of harm to individuals; even the newer preventive provisions such as sex offender supervision and notification schemes, and violent offender penalties, envisage harm to (a series of) individuals. But alongside these risk control measures has come a series of measures aimed at communities *qua* communities. Not only protection from offensive demonstrations, but also protection from a wide range of behaviour which is held to affect the quality of life of communities – drinking in public spaces; dog-fouling; littering; failure to keep gardens tidy – these can provoke reactions regardless of whether they are actually reported as having harmed or offended any particular individual. They provoke reaction because they are contrary to a community's idea of itself and because they offend against the sense that individuals owe responsibilities to their communities.

Community as moral resource

Another important strand in new communitarianism's critique of over-emphasis on individual rights is the argument that the centrality of individualism to modernity has led to the decline of community as a moral *resource*. Right-wing communitarian politics laments the decline of values associated with 'traditional' communities; left-wing communitarianism laments the decline of the sense of identity and connectedness which membership of a community provides. Both versions see the replacement of the traditional community by the contemporary network of voluntary role-differentiated associations as decline rather than as progress; both associate the decline with detrimental loss of social control and of social support for individual identity and fulfilment.

Etzioni calls for restoration of community values and community institutions. Value communitarians advocate more emphasis on two-parent families, with parents caring for children themselves and involving themselves in their education and moral training. Extended families, knowing one's neighbours, involvement in community affairs, are all aspects of life which are alleged to have declined, and to be in need of revitalisation. Etzioni suggests that individual material advancement has been pursued at the expense of community involvement and that not only has this resulted in community decline, but it has also failed to yield individual happiness (Etzioni, 1993: 124). This view has become widely shared, although Etzioni's evidence is far from convincing (Crawford, 1996: 251–2).

Communitarian politics sees contemporary western life as a vicious spiral in which community decline leads to lack of informal social control... which leads to a rise in criminal and anti-social behaviour... which leads to further demoralisation and decline of community. Right and left versions of communitarian politics may place different emphasis on individuals and institutions as causes and cures of community decline, with the right blaming the people for their irresponsibility and the left blaming neglect of community facilities and economies, but the differences between the two perspectives are not enormous. Thus Etzioni turns to right-realists such as James Q. Wilson (1983) when considering remedies for crime, and supposedly left-of-centre governments turn to Etzioni for policy ideas.

Community is a moral resource as well as a moral claimant: Etzioni argues that communities have a *suasive* capacity with which to moralise and control their members. A similar claim is at the heart of John Braithwaite's conception of *reintegrative shaming* (1989). Drawing on, among other things, Durkheim's anomie theory, which suggests that suicide rates and other symptoms of social pathology are lower in communities with clear normative boundaries, Braithwaite argues that the anonymity and asociality of modern societies means that people have lost a sense of shame about anti-social behaviour. In close-knit communities, people's own moral willpower is buttressed by fear of feeling ashamed if they behave badly, and fear of bringing shame on those they care about. Social shame depends not only on clear moral rules, but also on the likelihood that our behaviour will be witnessed or learned about by people who know who we are. Braithwaite advocates cultivating processes and institutions that can bring about reintegrative shaming: inculcating a sense of shame for wrongdoing, but without excluding the wrong-doer from the community.[8]

As well as reintegrative shaming, however, communitarian politics has brought forth zero-tolerance policing and full-enforcement criminal justice. The argument here is that it is important to arrest community decline before it is 'too late'. Wilson and Kelling (1982) in their celebrated 'broken windows' article, say that when a neighbourhood overlooks low-level crime and 'incivilities', it gives the impression of being uncared-for, it gives the impression of having ceased to be a viable community. Symptoms of neglect, such as broken windows being left unrepaired, indicate an area that is beyond regeneration. Policing against low-level crime and against incivilities, is therefore important.[9] This policy of vigorous law enforcement against low-level criminality and offensive behaviour has been enthusiastically taken up in several US cities, most famously New York, and also in some parts of the UK, notoriously Cleveland in north-eastern England.

The difference between right and left community strategies lies less in the nature of policies and innovations than in their source. Crawford describes right strategies of community building as 'top-down', whereas left strategies are 'bottom-up' (1997: 97–8). Right-wing communitarian policies such as zero-tolerance policing and arrest-and-charge responses to crimes that might at other times be dealt with by cautions or diverted to health/welfare institutions involve recruiting members of communities to support state agencies in disciplining other members: people become the 'eyes and ears' of the police. Left-wing community strategies support local grass-roots movements and initiatives, such as community associations, credit unions and the like, with policing strategies responsive to local demands.

Community justice

'Community', then, is both means and end in contemporary control discourses (Lacey and Zedner, 1995; Nelken, 1985). Community is what control strategies are intended to restore, and community is simultaneously the resource by which control is to be effected. Both these aspects – means and end – are present in the 'community justice' movement that has become prominent in recent years (Clear and Karp, 1999). Community justice used to signify merely a location outside of the large state carceral institutions, although the boundaries of state institutions and community institutions were not always clear (Cohen, 1979). In some contexts community punishment means non-custodial penalties; in other contexts it can mean local rather than state or federal institutions, such as local jails rather than federal penitentiaries, or local authority secure units rather than central government youth custody centres. Proponents of punishment in the community have placed great emphasis on retaining offenders – especially young offenders – in their communities, arguing that communities should retain care for 'their' young people even if they have committed offences. Another argument for community penalties has been that people get into trouble through being unable to cope in their communities, through lack of opportunities, lack of access to community resources, lack of support networks, and that removing them to institutions would not equip them to deal with the same circumstances when they return.

The new dimension of community as claimant on the justice process, community as an injured party, emerged patchily. For example, some formulations of the rationale for community service, introduced in England and Wales in 1971, included the explicit aim of 'introducing into the penal system a new dimension with an emphasis on reparation to the community' (Home Office, 1970: para. 33). It was only in the 1990s, however, with the blossoming of a better articulated 'community justice' movement and the proliferation of programmes incorporating some or all of its elements, that this community-oriented aspect of criminal justice became prominent. Community justice

> can be thought of as at once a philosophy of justice, a strategy of justice, and a series of justice programs. As a philosophy, community justice is based on its pursuit of a vision of justice recognizing that crime and the problems that result from crime are a central impediment to community quality of life. Thus the community justice approach seeks not only to respond to the criminal event, but also sets as a goal the improvement of quality of community life, especially for communities afflicted by high levels of crime. (Clear and Cadora, 2001: 60–1)

Community justice has emerged as the main hope for penal progressives, with professions such as probation as well as penal reform groups advocating it as the most desirable criminal justice rationale, filling the vacuum left by the decline first of rehabilitation and then of desert (Harding, 2000). It appears to offer a way to pull the valued strands of seemingly contradictory policies together, combining concerns both for crime control and for fairness to offenders (Clear and Karp, 1999). Mid-way between state-centred criminal justice and civil justice which deals with conflicts between individuals, this new philosophy recognises the status of the community as victim, and also as the site of resources for effecting rehabilitation: like other discursive manifestations of community, it is both means and end. It is worth quoting a little more from Clear and Cadora's discussion, which describes the vision of community justice clearly and succinctly:

> The offender's misconduct represents a moral and social offence against the community. The behavior raises questions about the offender's willingness to live within the community according to its prescribed conduct rules and the symbolic claim that one citizen may use others in the community unfairly. Both stand as a challenge to continuing community life and place the offender at odds with the community. The criminal incident in effect suspends the offender's status within the community until a just response to the crime is achieved. (2001: 61)

'A just response' means just for the offender, the actual victim and the community. What the bounds of just responses are for offenders is the least clearly articulated element in community justice (Braithwaite, 1999), although its advocates usually imagine community justice outcomes would be more constructive and humane than the present repressive risk control penalties of state justice. Just responses to victims usually entail reparation for harm done and programmes undertaken by or restrictions placed upon the offender to provide reassurance of future safety; and for communities similar measures of reparation (some form of community service) and rehabilitation (drug addiction treatment, for example) to reduce the likelihood of reoffending.

I do not intend to detail all the projects and policies that have been implemented under the general heading of community justice.[10] The points I wish to highlight here are the community justice movement's emphasis on (1) the offender living according to the community's 'prescribed conduct rules'; (2) the idea of 'suspension from the community'; and (3) the community as source of coercive as well as 'suasive' power.

Community justice typically uses three strategies: community policing, crime prevention, and restorative justice. The common theme of the first two is responsiveness: police priorities and crime prevention projects are to be formulated in response to public demand. Both claim to bring communities together, but in fact they employ tactics of division, tactics centred on the expulsion of difference.

Community policing in practice generally means that in addition to pursuing targets set by governments (whether central or local), police set up community liaison panels, holding local forums where residents are encouraged to bring forward their own problems and priorities. A common theme of these panels is identifying 'incomers', people from outside the area who are thought to be responsible for bringing trouble. People displaced by regeneration schemes in near by neighbourhoods, as well as refugees and immigrants, are 'the usual suspects' here. Similarly, community crime prevention programmes whether police led or local authority led usually include schemes such as neighbourhood watch and CCTV surveillance that encourage residents to look out for the 'suspicious stranger'. Neighbourhoods where the 'normal' residents would be 'outsiders' in respectable neighbourhoods, are written off as beyond regeneration in the broken windows hypothesis, and generally identified as 'dangerous places' (Campbell, 1993), no-go areas, hotbeds and seed-beds of trouble.

In town and city centres, the crime prevention priority is to make the malls and pedestrianised zones safe for shopping (Beck and Willis, 1995). 'Community' in this context means the community of business and of those with spending power, and crime prevention is usually a pick-and-mix of individual businesses protecting their own stock and premises; businesses acting jointly, for example sponsoring CCTV in a shared car park, paying for private security personnel and technology in a mall; and partnerships involving business, local authority and police.

These developments have been analysed and although they have been found to have some beneficial effects on crime levels, they are generally not thought to be generative of 'community' (Bassett, 1996; Crawford, 1997; Hughes, 1998). Concerns voiced about crime prevention schemes include the narrow range of interests served; the lack of democratic accountability; and the privatisation of public space. Schemes are usually labelled 'community', but this generally means a small number of sectional interests. The predominance of business interests has led to crime prevention schemes being described by one critic as corporatism 'masquerading' as communitarianism (Crawford, 1997). Neighbourhood schemes, too, represent the interests of property owners and 'respectable' residents, with the exclusion of the interests of some: for example young people are often targets of exclusion expressed through opposition to student accommodation or accommodation for young single people. 'Safer shopping' and 'inward investment' can entail sweeping the streets 'clean' of people sleeping in doorways; it can mean expulsion of people hanging around in groups. In residential areas crime prevention and improvement of quality of community life may entail restriction of ball games; it can mean the eviction of people with unkempt gardens; it can entail refusal to allow buildings to accommodate asylum seekers, the homeless, ex-offenders or the mentally disordered.

These examples illustrate one way in which space becomes privatised – owners of private spaces come to control access to what were formerly public spaces (the high street; the town square; the open ground between tower blocks; the neighbourhood green; the privately patrolled housing estate). Furthermore, we increasingly do our shopping, visit restaurants and cinemas, not on public high streets but in malls and leisure parks that are privately owned and controlled. These 'intermediate spaces' are private places open to the public, or at least, to those credit-card-bearing sections of the public deemed by the corporations which own the spaces to be 'desirable' (Shearing and Stenning, 1981.)

Accountability is another focus of critique. Community safety and community regeneration schemes replace traditional democratic accountability of elected bodies to voters with accountability between members of partnerships. Businesses can easily come to dominate partnerships because of the perceived need on the part of local authorities to induce them to stay at all costs. In other contexts (especially neighbourhood crime prevention schemes) police usually dominate, partly because they control important information, such as crime statistics, and partly because they have the most clearly defined powers and duties in relation to crime (Gilling, 1993). The interests of 'ordinary' residents may become downgraded, and the interests of the powerless and marginalised are entirely overlooked: there is no accountability at all to them.

Restorative justice is the third strategy of community justice.[11] Again, community appears as claimant, as objective, and as resource. Crime is seen as an injury to the community as well as to the individual victim, and the offender is expected to make reparations to both. Restorative justice is, therefore, a much wider concept than the reparation and mediation schemes which are sometimes seen to be restorative justice (especially in the UK), but which are actually only one element of it. Again, there are excellent accounts of restorative justice that I do not intend to repeat here.[12] My main concern is the way in which community is used as a resource, in restorative justice.

Advocates claim that restorative justice deals more fairly and constructively with offenders and victims than established justice processes, and evaluations generally report high rates of satisfaction about the way both victims and offenders felt enabled to give their version of events. Victims reported feeling they had their harms, and offenders the problems that were associated with the crime, attended to properly (Braithwaite, 1999; Daly, 2002b; Maxwell and Morris, 2001, *inter alia*). But some restorative justice theorists make claims for the effectiveness of restorative justice to prevent reoffending by using the coercive as well as the suasive capacities of communities. In his major review of restorative justice projects, Braithwaite introduces the character of *Uncle Harry*. Restorative justice, Braithwaite argues, can involve a range of people close to the offender who can control his behaviour in situations where formal control agents would not be present. Uncle Harrys can drive a drunken friend or relative home from the pub, or call a taxi; they can recommend them to potential employers; they can drive them to addiction courses; they can visit their homes to ensure that they are in at night; as Braithwaite puts it, 'Uncle Harrys have a more plural range of incapacitative keys they can turn than a prison guard who can turn just one key' (1999: 67).

From the point of view of rights and justice, the difficulty is that such extension of control has no clear limits; this enlistment of community as a resource for incapacitating offenders seems to fit the descriptions of 'blurring the boundaries' between controllers and friends, being free and being under supervision, described by Cohen's 'dispersal of discipline' thesis (Cohen, 1979). If a community is being created through restorative justice processes, there is a danger that it becomes a coercive community rather than community of care as suggested by restorative justice proponents.

In summary, consideration of restorative justice, crime prevention and community policing raises important issues about the nature of 'community' invoked in communitarian ideas about criminal justice (Lacey and Zedner, 1995; Crawford, 1996, 1997). First, 'community' is generally a coalition of interests of some sections of the local society. Community safety schemes usually represent business, housing associations, residents' associations, local authorities and criminal justice agencies, as well as some officially recognised community associations. Police are often the dominant partners. The homeless, young people, minority ethnic persons other than representatives of approved associations, the mentally ill, offenders and addicts are usually absent from consideration. Although crime surveys repeatedly show these excluded groups to be disproportionately the victims of crime – and therefore the very people whom community safety strategies should be in existence to protect – they are the groups who are targeted for capture on CCTV footage, for reporting by neighbourhood watch and neighbourhood patrol schemes (Norris and Armstrong, 1998). These marginalised groups are excluded from public spaces and from 'safe' shopping malls.

Community safety schemes too often operate through prejudice and stereotype, excluding rather than including, configuring towns and cities as ecologies of fear with security personnel operating as boundary patrols making sure that people do not stray beyond the limits of their designated spaces (Davis, 1990). What is being shaped by these strategies is the artificial, sanitised, one-class community of Celebration, Florida[13] rather than diverse, pluralist, tolerant urban communities such as Amsterdam or Barcelona (Van Swaaningen, 1998).

Restorative justice schemes vary in who represents the community, but most schemes envisage involvement of 'communities of care' of victims and offenders – relatives, friends, supporters. Although offenders are allowed to give their accounts of the offending, the purpose of the proceedings is to induce the offender to accept the victim's and community's view of the meaning of the act and the harm occasioned. Whether or not any rehabilitative or retributive measures are imposed, an important feature of restorative justice is communicative, and it is the community's ideas of good behaviour that is the message communicated. Restorative justice is advocated as a more effective means of getting offenders to understand social values; there is no possibility of negotiating 'what happened' as in some earlier abolitionist theories which appear to have been displaced by restorative justice (Hudson, 1998b). Restorative justice fuses the suasive and coercive powers of communities, and it has as yet produced no principled limits on impositions which may be made on offenders, or any account of the rights offenders have in proceedings.[14]

Communitarian objectives in relation to law and order do not appear to be able to deliver on regenerating a spirit of community which is tolerant, inclusive, and which distributes rights to, and resources for, freedom and security equitably (Crawford, 1998). In the risk society, sense of community appears to be a narrow vision, and to be something which is easiest to realise in communities that are already strong and united (Abel, 1995). Crime is a divisive, not a unifying phenomenon, and for a community to come together on crime and disorder involves deciding who to exclude, who to include; who to protect and who to control. Where strong communities do not already exist, 'community' usually springs up in opposition to some perceived threat: rising crime, prostitution, drug dealing, a motorway, a social housing development, a community care facility. The sense of community currently operating is also complicit in refusing certain groups of people access to housing, employment, treatment and leisure as well as branding some of them criminals and undesirables.

Critical communitarianism

The coercive possibilities of communities, together with an understanding that they may embody and enforce the values of certain sections, rather than of all members, raises at least two critical questions for liberals. First, what are the limits to coercive enforcement of community values; second, how can community values be critiqued and opposed?

Communities constantly reveal themselves as repressive. From the narrow social conformism of the tightly knit village to the vigilantism of community hounding of those labelled deviant, communities can enforce a constriction of freedom of choice about how one lives. Communities may express narrow, bigoted and objectionable values – antagonism to refugees and asylum seekers; intolerance of young people; intolerance of lone parents; religious bigotry; and deep-seated racism and sexism. What safeguards do value communitarians offer against excessive enforcement of dominant values, or against rigid, repressive traditionalism? In other words, how do communitarians respond to charges of majoritarianism and value despotism?

Etzioni's communitarianism appears to be pitched at the level of local communities which are subsections of larger, pluralist societies. His communities are neighbourhoods nested within states. He takes seriously the danger of majority tyranny, and of the coercive powers of communities damaging individual freedom too much. Since his communitarianism is rooted in anxiety that the equilibrium between individual rights and responsibilities has tipped too far in favour of individual rights, rather than being opposed to the idea of rights *per se*, he is correspondingly concerned that the balance should not tip too far in the opposite direction. Etzioni has two answers to the problem of coercive communities. The first is that communities should recognise that protection of their traditions, rules and values is limited by the more general principles of liberal justice, principally human rights:

> no community has a right to violate higher-order values, values that we all share as a society, or even humanity. (1993: 37)

His other answer lies in the overlapping pluralism of liberal societies. He explains that although traditional communities may have been homogeneous, authoritarian and repressive, enforcing value conformism on all regardless of inclination, modern communities are not, and could not be, like this because none is the total social milieu of its members:

> contemporary communities tend to be new communities that are part of a pluralistic web of communities. People are, at one and the same time, members of several communities, such as professional, residential and others. They can, and do, use these multi-memberships (as well as a limited, but not trivial, ability to choose one's work and residential communities) to protect themselves from excessive pressure by any one community. (Etzioni, 1998: xiv)

He argues that communities are not only overlapping, but also 'nested', each within a more encompassing one. Local communities are nested within regional or national communities; local religious and ethnic groups are nested within multinational groups (the Catholic church, Islam and Judaism, the Armenian diaspora, etc.); and professionals have allegiances to national and international professional associations. These larger groups are sources of traditions, rules and values that mark out the boundaries of influence of the immediate community. States have laws that are binding on local and regional communities; ethnic and religious groups have rules and traditions to which local members adhere; professions have internationally shared codes of practice.

Putting together these two bounds of community influence – that communities must respect higher-order values and that communities' influence is restricted by their nested, overlapping nature in modern societies – Etzioni's answer to charges of majoritarianism made against communitarians is that (American) modern society is not a simple majoritarian democracy, but a constitutional democracy. Constitutions establish rights and freedoms that majorities cannot abrogate.

Those of us who live in societies without written constitutions will not find much to guarantee our liberties in these assurances. In the UK, without a written constitution, there is little to stand in the way of Parliamentary tyranny. The Human Rights Act (1998) brings the European Convention on Human Rights into domestic jurisdiction, but it took action by the UK Parliament to do this, and it is as yet unclear how much impact it will have in the spheres of crime prevention and punishment of offenders (Henham, 1998; Hudson, 2001). The UK has resisted ratification of the European Charter of Basic Rights and Freedoms, so that the situation of a society such as this being 'nested' in a larger European grouping, alongside mainland European countries with much stronger traditions of rights guaranteed by written constitutions, is having some impact, but not the restraining influence on community coercion that Etzioni's formulation suggests. Nesting within the European community has not, for example, stopped the spread of CCTV without satisfactory definition of its bounds and of people's right to refusal to be filmed; it has not stopped the introduction of provisions for incarceration of persons diagnosed as having Serious Personality Disorder.

Etzioni's second defence against coerciveness of communities is that in contemporary societies we are all members simultaneously of many communities, and therefore none can hold too much power over the individual. This surely generalises the experience of one particular group: the professional elite, and especially the male, white, secular or Protestant professional elite. For them it is true that the extent of their links with family; with the neighbourhood in which they grew up; with the religious/political affinity of their parents; with childhood friends; with region and even nation, is a matter of choice. It is also true that the extent to which they mingle their professional life and other associational commitments such as family, church and leisure is also a matter of choice. But this is certainly not the case for, for example, orthodox Jews, Muslims, Sikhs or Hindus, for whom traditional rules of religion and family culture penetrate areas of life that are more autonomous for white, secular or Anglican citizens. The capacity to manage overlapping group memberships to maximise personal freedom of choice is very different for a white secular male and a female member of an Asian faith community, even though both are members of communities nested within the larger community of a western liberal democracy.

Etzioni's constitutionalism focuses on the old liberal political theory principle of specifying the spheres in which individual rights are protected, and those in which majorities make rules (at either local or national level). This is the familiar public/private distinction, which offers no protection to the freedom of the powerless in what are designated as private spheres (which usually means women and children in domestic settings; ethnic, religious, disabled and other minorities in employment, accommodation and leisure settings). Minority rights are not protected in these non-public realms; on the contrary, progress has been achieved by opening private realms up to the public gaze. The risk then, of course, is that majoritarian opinion will uphold the abuses of power. Change has been very slow in these areas: marital rape has only recently been recognised; domestic violence has only lately been taken seriously; parents hitting their children is still regarded as acceptable in the UK and the USA.

Etzioni (1998) argues that divisions between spheres of majority and individual rule – the public and the private – are backed up by the values held by most Americans. But the location of rule-making is no guarantee of the content of the rules, as the examples above illustrate. Americans and the citizens of other modern liberal societies may indeed, as Etzioni suggests, agree broadly on the boundaries of the public and the private, but this is no guarantee that the rules and customs of both realms will not reflect community values that are, for example, sexist, racist, xenophobic and homophobic. Members may countenance gross inequalities of power and income – among groups within societies; among employees within companies; among partners and children within families. The key question for communitarianism is, then, from where is critique of community values, and therefore the possibility of change, to be derived?

For Etzioni, the answer is from universal standards of rights. Other 'critical communitarians' also see the source of critique, and therefore the ultimate guarantor against oppressiveness of communities, as human rights, which are universalist value systems that transcend community context (Selznick, 2001). For Fraser and Lacey (1993) and Benhabib (1992), communitarianism finds its critique in the universalist value systems of liberalism and feminism. These value systems encompass ideas of rights and liberties at the levels both of *political obligation* and of *identity*, and therefore they can generate problematisation over a range of oppressions: race; gender; sexuality; religious and cultural membership.

Communitarian constructivism

Fraser and Lacey propose a *dialogic communitarianism* which entails permanent critical dialogue between community values and universalist value systems such as human rights and feminism. But this begs the questions of (a) what is the source of these value systems that will provide the critique of a community's values? and (b) how is an individual or a government to choose between competing values, in general or on any particular occasion?

Communitarian constructivism developed in the works of MacIntyre (1981, 1988), Sandel (1982), Taylor (1979, 1985, 1989) and Walzer (1983) attacks not only the primacy of the liberal idea of rights, but also the propositions about the self at the heart of the Kantian strand of liberalism. They take Rawls (1972) as the major contemporary exemplar of this liberalism. These communitarians contest the notion of a self which is prior to its ends; a self which finds its moral rules through independent exercise of reason. This means that they contest deontological liberalism's insistence on the priority of the right over the good; and they also contest the possibility of a universalist viewpoint abstracted from social relationships.[15] Communitarians argue that the liberal view of the self (1) is empty; (2) violates our self-perceptions; (3) ignores our embeddedness in communal practices; (4) ignores our need for communal confirmation of our individual judgments; and (5) pretends to an impossible universality or objectivity (Kymlicka, 1989: 47). The first four criticisms cluster around the alleged *atomism* of the liberal self; the fifth attacks the *meta-ethical foundations* of liberalism (Gardbaum, 1992: 691).

Atomism is a quality that is regularly associated with modern liberalism.[16] In all the forms of social contract theory, the individual enters as a lonely creature, whose relationships with others are those of encroachment and competition. The 'natural' self engages in a Hobbesian war of all against all, and the contract is to cede power to a sovereign in exchange for protection against violation by other people. As liberal political theory developed, the contract between sovereign and people became as important for the limits on sovereign power as for the creation of sovereign power: the freedom of individuals must be protected against abuse of power whether by sovereign tyrants or by sovereign majorities. Other individuals and society as a collective are thus posited by liberalism as constraints on, and sources of danger to, the individual. The liberal self, the inhabitant of crowded modern cities, is thus lonely, beleaguered and fearful. For communitarians, this denies our experiences of kinship, solidarity and connection, and ignores our feeling of lack when these are absent; and it poses an unnecessary and damaging division between self and society.

Liberalism places enormous emphasis on individuals' capacity to choose their own version of the good life, to select their projects and commitments – no values, no beliefs, no associations, no desires are valid unless the individual herself chooses, or at least endorses, them. This freedom from prior commitments is the cornerstone of liberalism. Taylor (1989) describes this as an empty freedom. How, he asks, are we to choose anything at all if we have no prior values by which to assess the choices available? Our projects, he argues, are what make life worthwhile and, moreover, our self is constituted *through* our projects, rather than our projects being chosen by a pre-constituted self.

Sandel and MacIntyre continue the critique of the liberal self, contrasting the *unencumbered self* of Kantian–Rawlsian liberalism with the *embedded self* of Aristotelian republicanism and contemporary communitarianism. The actual person, they argue, has a range of commitments (to family, to neighbours, to society, to religion, to colleagues) which structure their choices and form a bedrock of relationships. A person's range of relationships and the values and traditions of their communities do not smother possibilities of choice of projects and endorsement or rejection of cultural norms, but form what Taylor describes as 'authoritative horizons' within which those choices and endorsements/rejections are made (1989: 157–9).

Put simply, communitarians claim they describe our experiences of life in society more accurately than deontological liberals do. Of course we make choices – of career; of where to live; of whether to spend more time with our family, at work or in solitary leisure pursuits; whether to follow our parents' religion or not; which political party to vote for – as the liberals say, but communitarians claim that we can never do so without consciousness of whether we are following or breaking with family traditions and expectations; whether a relationship is going to be strengthened or put under pressure; whether others whose opinions matter to us will approve or disapprove. Choices are not made in a bubble of atomistic individualism, but from within a web of values, role models and relationships.

Just as we form our values and choose our projects through the possibilities and expectations offered by the rules, roles and relationships in which we are embedded, so, for communitarians, we need these networks to confirm our choices and to reaffirm our sense of ourselves. Communitarians at this point offer what looks very much like a version of interactionist social psychology transposed into philosophical terminology.[17] It points to a need for commonality, a need to feel we are alongside people who think like us, make choices like ours, value the things that we value. We need to feel that we are understood by others, and that others approve our thoughts and deeds. Our sense of ourselves is built up through reflection on the reactions of other people to us. The writing of leading communitarians on identity echoes the social phenomenology of Alfred Schutz, who suggested that a 'reciprocity of perspectives' is necessary for humans to live their lives: to be able to interact with others, it is necessary to assume that another, given the same biography as oneself, would make the same choices as oneself (Schutz and Luckmann, 1974).

On the themes mentioned so far, communitarians are more or less united. They take exception to the 'unencumbered self' of liberalism. They dispute the possibility of making totally free choices, choices unencumbered by socially transmitted values and by a web of existing relationships. Communitarian constructivists (or constitutive communitarians, as they are also labelled) claim that liberals put too high a value on freedom of choice, and give it too high a place in the constitution of human 'being in the world'. For communitarians, our projects, our relationships, our commitments, make us what we are; we are not identified as human by the one thing we have in common, the capacity to choose our projects. Taylor reveals the essential point of difference. Liberals, he explains, elevate the choosing over the choices: it doesn't matter what our projects are, what matters is our capacity to choose them. The self prior to its projects is, for communitarians, an empty self, a bleak abstraction, and thankfully (?) an impossibility.

The value of community

Sandel, Walzer, Taylor and MacIntyre, then, insist that we are 'situated', or 'embedded' rather than 'unencumbered' selves. We choose, but we do not choose completely freely, nor do we choose within a vacuum. We choose within a set of available rules, traditions, roles, values and relationships. For communitarians, this means that these aspects of community have a value in themselves. If these aspects of community are antecedent to individuals' choices, then individuals cannot be the only source of value. And if these elements of community have value, it follows that individuals have obligations towards their communities. The strength of this obligation – in other words how closely constitutive communitarians approach value communitarianism – varies among communitarian theorists.

Taylor's is an example of a communitarian position that is not far from Dworkin and Rawls. He concedes the liberal case that freedom to choose one's own life projects, to pursue one's own idea of the good life, is of the utmost importance, but he then presses the communitarian claim that this high valuation of individual autonomy only arises in a certain kind of society – modern liberal society. Taylor then argues that people therefore have a duty to sustain the culture that promotes those values. This is very close to Dworkin's observations on the need for a certain kind of culture if liberal values are to be protected, and a consequent duty on individuals to protect the liberal cultural structure from 'debasement or decay' (1986a: 230).

Rawls also grants the connection between rules of justice and cultural ideas of the good in his references to a 'thin' theory of the good throughout his theory of justice (1972). In his later work, culminating in *Political Liberalism* (1993a), Rawls re-emphasises the fact that his rules of justice are political rules for a modern pluralist democratic society rather than metaphysical foundations for any possible system of justice. His rules are dependent on an *overlapping consensus* of values of tolerance, respect for physical integrity, and equal respect among the plurality of social groups (Rawls, 1987). He argues that these are consensus values that will be respected regardless of other elements of conflicting concepts of the good, and that these consensus values can generate agreed rules of fair procedure for the settlement of disputes arising from value conflicts, and for ensuring tolerance of a diversity of ways of life within the larger society (Rawls, 1989, 1993a).

The main difference between these liberals who acknowledge the importance of the cultural milieu and those who might be termed 'liberal communitarians', is that for the former, defence of the culture means defence of those values that have arisen within the culture – autonomy and freedom – while for the latter, defence of the culture may mean defending against excessive interpretations of, or adherence to, these liberal values. For liberals, the culture is to be defended insofar as it promotes and protects these values; for communitarians, these values are to be promoted and protected insofar as they serve the culture. This comes down to different positions on the right and the good. For Taylor and Sandel, defending a culture which is seen as having intrinsic value necessitates replacing the liberal, good-neutral and right-prioritising core principle of equal respect, with a more good-positive core principle of *the common good*. The common good proposed here is not a suggested universal, such as happiness or welfare in Utilitarianism, nor is it teleologically defined by some yet-to-be-realised political or religious ideal, such as Marxism or the Hegelian *Zeitgeist*. The common good is empirically derived from the community's way of life.

Sandel's *Liberalism and the Limits of Justice* (1982) is generally regarded as a fairly strongly communitarian text. Sandel insists that the situated self is a better description of human identity than the unencumbered self, and that a politics of the common good should replace the liberal politics of neutral concern between rival conceptions of the good. In the preface to the second edition, however, he is careful to distance himself from some of the stronger versions of value communitarianism. He differentiates two claims which are represented in the Kantian-Rawlsian priority of the right over the good. The first, he says, is the claim that certain rights are so important that they cannot be set aside in the name of general welfare; the second is that the principles of justice that delineate our rights are independent of any particular conception of the good life. Sandel is emphatic that *Liberalism and the Limits of Justice* opposes the second of these claims, but upholds the first (1998: x).

Sandel argues that to claim that whatever a community regards as just at any one time is, therefore, just, makes justice the creature of convention, and deprives the concept of any critical political purchase. At the same time, those liberals who regard justice and rights as independent of, or neutral towards, substantive moral/political/social ideas commit the error that is the mirror-image of conventionalisim, viz., relativism. Rights, for Sandel, are supremely important, but they are justified by the moral importance of the goals they serve.

The argument between liberals and communitarians here is, as so often, debated around the idea of the right to freedom of speech. Sandel (1998: xiv–xvi) looks at the cases for banning or allowing a neo-Nazi rally in the 1950s in Skokie, Illinois, a community with a large number of Holocaust survivors, or civil rights marchers in the segregationist communities of Southern USA in the 1960s. He suggests that value communitarians who believe that rights are only valid if they emerge from the community's prevailing values would ban both marches, whereas liberals who see freedom of speech as independent of the content of any actual speech would allow both. Only, he argues, reference to the nature of the values being promoted (race-hate in the one case, race-equality in the other) can give a basis for distinguishing between them. Equality is one of the most worthy of values, congruent with the deepest moral meanings of our (he means the US) community; race-hate is fundamentally antipathetic to the basic values of that community. Sandel points out that the distinction between the two cases also depends on evaluation of the two local communities: 'The shared memories of the Holocaust survivors deserve a moral defence that the solidarity of the segregationists does not' (ibid.: xv).

Sandel's discussion raises the inevitable question provoked by communitarianism: on what basis are evaluations of different communities made; if values arise in communities, how are communities to be evaluated? He relies on a very vague notion of traditions and ways of life, shared understandings of the common good, but he gives no convincing explanation of how these are to be identified, ranked or assessed. His essential criterion seems to be respect for difference, as his neo-Nazi/civil rights example illustrates. Some of his arguments about the inadequacy of liberalism in dealing with moral conflicts because of its refusal to intervene in questions of the good are sound, and his principle of *deliberative respect* is appealing. He urges that far from bracketing out of the arena of political debate, questions of the good – the deep and difficult questions of religion, sexual morality, etc. as some formulations of liberalism demand (Ackerman, 1980 for example,) – are essential to our identity and to our projects.

> we respect our fellow citizens' moral and religious convictions by engaging, or attending to, them – sometimes by challenging and contesting them, sometimes by listening and learning from them – especially when those convictions bear on important political questions ... the respect of deliberation and engagement affords a more spacious public reason than liberalism allows. It is also a more suitable idea for a pluralist society. To the extent that our moral and religious disagreements reflect the ultimate plurality of human goods, a deliberative mode of respect will better enable us to appreciate the distinctive goods our different lives express. (Sandel, 1982: 217–8)

Sandel gives us no way, ultimately, of deciding these debates, no criteria for determining which views might be worthy or unworthy of support. He shows a preference for respect for difference, but gives no compelling arguments as to why this is intrinsic to the community's values, and resorts to a rather vague and mysterious idea of core meanings and deep values. If there are no judgments to be made, then what is the purpose of dialogue? Why not bracket these difficult issues out? If the point of dialogue is to promote tolerance and understanding, then we are brought back to the liberal position of tolerance and freedom to pursue one's own vision of the good being prior values, independent of any one idea of the good.

Walzer (1983) shares the view of Sandel and Taylor that values arise from the shared meanings and traditions of communities, and are not prior or external to them. He adds a new strand to critique of the Rawlsian theory of justice: not only can there not be universal principles of justice covering all societies, but there can be no single principle of justice that governs the distribution of goods within one society. This is because, he argues, the kinds of goods for which principles of justice are sought to set distributive rules are in themselves very different. Each good – food, health, education, citizenship, security – generates its own distributive principle from its nature and from its meaning in a particular community. The nature and meaning of education in modern western society, for example, is such that a just distribution would give everyone the maximum from which they could benefit. Making everyone have exactly the same would not be just.

Walzer's work illustrates vividly the way that theorising about justice has been dominated by the distributive debate. The goods he considers are more or less the same primary goods as in Rawls's theory. He does, however, consider power, and membership of the community, which are of extreme importance in the present context, but his accounts at these points are vague and unsatisfactory. Like Rawls, Walzer has two principles of distributive justice. He adds to his primary principle of deriving the distributive criteria from the meanings of the goods to be distributed, a second, which is to function as a brake on inequality, in much the same way as Rawls's difference princi- ple. Walzer's second principle is that distributions should be autonomous: 'Every social good or set of goods constitutes, as it were, a distributive sphere in which only certain criteria are appropriate' (Walzer, 1983: 10).

What Walzer is anxious to avoid is *domination* by any one distributive power. Distribution of one good or set of goods should not influence distrib- utions of other goods. In western capitalistic countries, he fears, distribution of money tends to dominate other spheres such as education, health and security; other societies may have different axes of distributive domination, such as membership of the ruling party or religious bloc.

Walzer addresses the question of where critique is to arise, and gives the communitarian answer that it can only arise within a community. Any critique from outside is, he argues, paternalistic or neo-colonial, its ostensible good intention disguising its real effect of ideological domination. At the time of writing his celebrated book, this was a progressive and courageous line to take, particularly for an American academic writing in the shadow of Vietnam, the Cuban blockade, and the still-continuing Cold War. Self-determination was – and is – a cause to be preferred over cultural domination.

In his later writings, however, Walzer concedes that this argument for cul- tural self-determination is present in his earlier work as a universal value (Walzer, 1987, 1994). He puts forward a communitarian basis for it by saying that it is not derived from any universal moral precept but from the observa- tion that cultures do in fact desire cultural independence. Humans are, for Walzer, first and foremost culture-producing creatures who make and inhabit worlds of shared understanding: worlds for which they demand recognition. Other values which may appear to be universal he grounds in similar empir- ical fashion: as well as cultural autonomy, he claims that in all societies indi- viduals desire some degree of personal freedom. That these are desires that occur in all communities is, however, an empirically doubtful proposition (Bellamy, 1998: 161). If a community exists which does not wish to preserve its autonomy, or where members do not appear to crave freedom, we are given no basis by Walzer on which to judge it; nor are we given any basis on which to support or not the individual who strives to be free in a community where the majority does not.[18]

MacIntyre (1985, 1988) brings philosophical constitutive communitarian- ism together with political value communitarianism in ways somewhat simi- lar to Sandel, but with a more thoroughgoing value communitarianism, and with a more developed republican ethic. What appears as the ethics of com- mon good in Sandel becomes the virtue of the good citizen in MacIntyre (1985). He expresses in striking form the disenchantment with modernity which is expressed philosophically and politically by communitarians and described sociologically by theorists such as Beck and Giddens. MacIntyre's argument is that deontological liberalism has failed to provide a firm grounding for morality, and therefore cannot produce either a satisfactory theory of justice, or legitimate ways to assess the justice of institutions. The error, as he sees it, of modernism has been to try to separate morality from substantive spheres of judgment, such as ideas of virtue and aesthetics, and to rob morality of its teleological import. In other words, morality is reduced to a conventionality of following rules because they are rules – not because they are the standards of the virtuous, the heroic, the beautiful, or because they are advancing humankind towards realising its essential nature and purpose.

Modern liberalism, he argues, has failed to provide a rational, secular ethical system. The modern standpoint provides no basis for deciding between conflicting claims because it

> envisages moral debate in terms of a confrontation between incompatible and incommensurate moral premises, a type of choice for which no rational justification can be given ... (1985: 39)

This failure, for MacIntyre, is compounded by the Enlightenment expulsion of teleology. Although the principles of morality and justice are presented as compelling because they are derived from universally shared structures of human reason, the Enlightenment philosophers (Pascal, Hume, Diderot, Kierkegaard as well as Kant)

> reject any teleological view of human nature, any view of man as having an essence which defines his true end. [But] to understand this is to understand why their project of finding a basis for morality had to fail ... Since the whole point of ethics – both as a theoretical and a practical discipline – is to enable man to pass from his present state to his true end. (ibid.: 54)

MacIntyre invokes Nietzsche as the pre-eminent chronicler of the emptiness of modernity, an emptiness that could only be overcome by transcending rather than following rules. MacIntyre's conclusion is that three centuries of moral philosophy have failed to produce 'any coherent rationally defensible statement of a liberal individualist point of view' (1985: 259). Liberalism, he charges, has failed to prove its account of subjectivity; of the individual as ultimate source of value; of freedom and equality as the highest-order values, and it has failed to produce any compelling reason for an individual to act out of enlightened self-interest, let alone out of altruism.

MacIntyre sees no escape from the nihilism of Nietzsche, for whom the will-to-power is all that drives us, unless we renounce the ethical theories of the last three centuries and return to the Aristotelian tradition, in which to act morally is to act out the virtues of humankind's particular mode of being-in-the-world, that of being-in-society. Aristotle was right, Nietzsche wrong, concludes MacIntyre, but to escape the pull of Nietzsche, modern societies need to relinquish the separation of individual and society that is the great, mistaken fissure between the morality of the ancients and the justice of the moderns.

MacIntyre welds the republicanism of ancient philosophy together with contemporary communitarianism: he adopts the idea of civic virtue, the good citizen, from Aristotle, but accompanies this with a communitarian discussion of tradition, values and communities. Like all communitarians, MacIntyre sees values as deriving from membership in communities, and sees no possibility of legitimate critique of a community's values and traditions arising outside of that community.

Internal critique – and conflict between members – of a community, is central to his concept of tradition (ibid.: Chapter 15). A tradition is an institutional sphere embodying modes of thought, a common life that is constituted through continuous argument and conflict. He gives the example of a university (p. 222): its roles and practices will incorporate generations of continuing argument about what the role of a university ought to be. Reasoning and critique allows bearers of the tradition to transcend what has previously been thought.

In *After Virtue* (1985) MacIntyre is primarily concerned with the moral destiny of the human individual, and his discussion of critique and development of traditions and practices within cultures is sketchy. He addresses the problems of rival theories of justice and evaluation of different traditions more fully in *Whose Justice? Which Rationality?* (1988). MacIntyre maintains his belief that theories, institutions and practices only arise within traditions, and can only be understood from within their own tradition. Questions such as the extent of inequality that is within the bounds of social justice; whether past injustices should be compensated; whether legal abortion should be allowed; whether the death penalty is permitted or required; when war is justified, can only be answered by appeal to the theories of justice active in the society where the questions are to be decided. We tend to answer them by appeal to apparently universal ideas such as human rights, individual freedom, human dignity and equal respect, but, insists MacIntyre, these are ideas that have arisen *within* our western tradition.

MacIntyre explains that what he is putting forward is *perspectivism*. He argues that those who criticise his and other communitarian positions on the grounds of lack of a source of critique often conflate perspectivism and relativism. We can judge, he says, whether rules and practices are rational for other traditions as well as our own, but only by immersing ourselves in the cultural precepts, the political and philosophical theories of that tradition.[19] We may, of course, not be able to enter the cultural world as fully as members of the tradition and we must always remember that we will be filtering our encounter through our own cultural preconceptions. What is possible, on MacIntyre's account, is judging what is rational for a tradition, and to a lesser extent, judging the rationality of a tradition. A tradition is rational if it allows for debate, for contestation, internally; if it can engage with other traditions when it comes into contact with them; if it can adapt to changing situations.

But he offers us no possibility of substantive evaluative criteria that are not themselves context derived.

Membership, power and rights

One of the main areas of criticism of liberalism is, as we can see, the low value it puts on community membership. Other people represent threats, encroachments, restrictions in liberalism. On the other hand, communitarians fail to deal adequately with the very real possibility of the repressiveness of communities on the individual's freedom to follow her own beliefs and desires, the freedom that is at the heart of liberalism. Etzioni and Sandel, both strong communitarians in many ways, deny that they are therefore majoritarians, but to date communitarianism has failed to produce satisfactory grounding for safeguards for individuals against repressive majorities. Many of the questions that divide liberals and communitarians cluster around the core issue of *membership*: who is included and who is excluded, and just as importantly, can people enter and exit communities as they wish?

The attractiveness of the unencumbered self proposed by liberalism is the possibility it offers that affiliations, as well as traditions, conventions, moral rules and life projects, can be matters of personal choice. I can accept the costs and benefits of identifying with the community in which I find myself, but I need not. It is probably true, as writers from Sartre to Beck so vividly describe, that this means that the subject of modernity is a 'homeless heart', a hungry soul, yearning simultaneously for belonging and for independence (Bellah et al., 1996).[20] Being-for-oneself is lonely and difficult (Sartre, 1958). As for-ourselves beings we have no one but ourselves to blame if things turn out badly, and we cannot use conventionalism to hide from moral dilemmas. The Nuremberg trials not only established genocide and crimes against humanity as legal categories, they also established that 'following orders' is no defence against accusations of immoral action. Institutions of late modernity – divorce, the nuclear family, the social club – encapsulate this schizophrenic desire to belong and yet to be free; to belong only as long as it pleases me, but to have the comfort and reassurance of a network of given relationships.

The essential difference between liberals and communitarians is not the constitution of the self and the derivation of values, since liberals such as Rawls and Dworkin take for granted that their principles of justice and theories of rights arise within a given cultural tradition (post-Enlightenment modernity) and are needed to solve conflicts arising within a particular form of political society (pluralistic democracy). The essential difference lies in the different accounts in the two philosophical tendencies of the strength and nature of community membership.

Communitarians dislike the liberal notion of a self prior to its ends. They take issue with the various personified representations of this notion, the most prominent example of course being Rawls's individual in the original position. To be fair to the liberal position, one must grant that liberals such as Kant and Rawls did not imagine that anyone was born free of affiliations, in a society not already structured and with established ways of doing things. What Kant and Rawls claimed is that to evaluate individual moral action and the justice of social institutions, it is necessary – and possible – to adopt a distance from the phenomena to be evaluated, and to reflect on whether someone using only the exercise of disinterested reason would endorse them or not. It is this possibility of disinterested reason (an idea close to the critical reflexivity of Beck and Giddens) in the modern subject that means that although, as Heidegger (1973) describes, when we are born we are 'thrown' into an already constituted world, nonetheless the ability to distance, to reflect, to decide whether the conventional way is the way for us, means that we are never fully constituted *by* that world.

Communitarians do have some justification, however, when they charge that liberalism fails to appreciate the value to humans of membership in a specific community. Kymlicka (1989) proposes a solution to liberalism's under-valuation of community. Membership in a cultural community, he suggests, could be recognised as a right. Kymlicka's arguments are developed principally in the context of the demands of minority peoples in North America. He argues that because the struggle for African-American rights in the USA took the form of demand for civil rights equality with white Americans, the more recent movements that call for recognition and protection of different cultural traditions have not been dealt with satisfactorily by leading liberal theorists. But, he argues, this is not to say that liberalism could not consider demands for cultural recognition, and his own work draws mainly on the arguments over the extent of autonomy rights that should be granted to French Canadians and to Canada's aboriginal peoples.

Kymlicka uses Rawls's and Dworkin's arguments for equality of freedoms, rights and resources to mount a powerful case for protecting people's rights of cultural membership. The crucial point, he says, is to recognise a cultural structure as a *structure of choice*, which is important for developing within us the capacity to develop and evaluate meaningful life-plans for ourselves (ibid.: 166). He argues that the demise of minority cultures tends to be imposed (through wars, colonisation, 'ethnic cleansing'), and therefore represents a restriction of choice. Kymlicka insists that the same importance liberals attach to the capacity to exit from a culture should extend to people's capacity to remain within it. Critics of Kymlicka's argument point out that he is asking liberalism to sustain and resource communities which may violate its own important conditions for membership – anyone can join, anyone can leave. He is asking liberal societies to help communities avoid liberalisation of their own ways of life (Beiner, 1992). But the societies which Kymlicka has in mind – Canada, the USA, Australia – do offer members of minority communities the right to live their lives in the majority community. No-one has to live on the reservation. Kymlicka's idea of community membership as a right is helpful, cast as it is as something that individuals should have the opportunity and capacity to choose. It provides one criterion by which communities may be judged: do minority communities provide barriers to leaving; do majority communities provide barriers to joining?

Communitarians have the mirror-image problem to liberals' under-valuation of community membership – how to accord sufficient value to the individual within a cultural community. The communitarian difficulty with individual autonomy could perhaps best be addressed by developing the republican strands within communitarianism. MacIntyre and Sandel both emphasise the role of citizenship: exercising the rights and responsibilities of citizenship is the 'good life' which recognises the essential sociality of humans; its members possessing and exercising the virtues of citizenship is what makes the good community. Critics of communitarianism, however, have generally paid insufficient attention to its republican themes (Gardbaum, 1992: 723 fn).

By replacing the libertarian construction of liberalism's 'negative freedom' as freedom from *interference* with an understanding of freedom as freedom from *domination*, republicanism provides an opening for placing more positive value on relationships with other people, individually and collectively. Republicanism evaluates relationships by their quality, not their quantity or extent. The concept of dominion plays a role similar to happiness or welfare in Utilitarianism, but because it is a concept closely linked to freedom, it offers greater protection for liberty than utility for general welfare can do. Dominion is freedom reformulated as a relational concept, and the idea of promoting dominion offers the possibility of uniting liberalism's concern for choice (it is an idea of freedom) with communitarianism's concern for social responsibility (it concerns relations between members). It also generates critique. Concern for increased dominion, argues Pettit, one of republicanism's principal proponents, means that citizens of the republic will contest rather than conform; the republic will be reflexive, responsive and inclusive. Conflict and contestability, because of their vital role in defending freedom against domination, are given a surer grounding by Pettit than they are by Sandel or MacIntyre (Pettit, 1997: Chapter 6).

Pettit's elaboration of republicanism is mainly concerned to differentiate republican and liberal notions of freedom (Rosati, 2000). It does not specifically engage with communitarianism, and indeed in translating philosophical republicanism into institutional spheres of justice and punishment some republican writers (Braithwaite, for example) appear to ally themselves too unproblematically with community justice. There is a fundamental difference between community justice and republican justice, stemming from the theories in which they are embedded. Republicanism is predicated on the notion of power, whereas communitarianism fails to take adequate account of relationships and structures of power within as well as between communities. Promoting dominion and restoring communities through justice processes may well not always coincide.

Both liberalism and communitarianism have unresolved difficulties with the boundaries of membership. Liberalism poses a problem for non-members in that they have to prove that they have the same capacities of dispassionate reason as members. Women, children, members of minority ethnic groups and of other societies have been deemed to be outside the society of reason, and therefore have not benefited from liberal rights. Members can also be deemed non-reasonable through illness or incapacity, criminal behaviour and so expelled (temporarily or permanently) from the fellowship of reason. Communitarianism has no way of judging different communities, and it has no criteria for deciding when groups are sub-groups of a wider community (and therefore included in the politics of the common good) or when they are rival communities. It has offered no persuasive way of deciding when dissidents and deviants are moving the community forward by enlarging the possibilities that can be accommodated within the tradition, and so helping the community adapt to changing circumstances; or when they are threatening its continuing existence. Just as liberals cannot really expect that groups to whom membership is extended (usually after struggle) will always be content with the established definition of rights, freedoms and duties, so communitarians cannot really expect that co-existing groups will be able to constrain their differences within a harmonious whole.

Where liberalism offers the human heart only a tenuous and always revisable solidarity, communitarianism provides no exit from ascribed communities. If critique can only arise within a tradition, how can we ever withdraw our membership? The range of critique afforded in communitarianism seems too narrow; the range of choice available is like being able to choose between rival sects within a religion, but not being able to abandon religion altogether. The reflexive individual can make choices within from a range of possibilities offered by a community, but 'none of the above' is not an available option.

Conclusion

Liberals and communitarians have made considerable advances towards each other. Dworkin and Rawls have made the cultural embeddedness of their theories of justice much clearer in their later works; Kymlicka has demonstrated a possible way of placing more value on membership of a cultural community than liberalism has done hitherto. For the communitarians, Sandel has made clear his disavowal of majoritarianism; Etzioni acknowledges basic rights as limits on what may be demanded of individuals in the interests of the common good. Selznick (2001) explains his liberal communitarianism as essentially 'fidelity to context'. Concepts such as rights and justice remain important, he confirms, but the task for law and morality is to determine what justice demands *in this context*, what rights are operative *in this context*.

Philosophical understanding of the relationship between self and society, and sociological/political debate on the balance between rights and responsibilities, have no doubt been advanced by the dialogue between liberalism and communitarianism. There will always remain unbridgeable gaps between them, however, because they express different facets of the human situation in the modern world. We long for freedom and we long for community: 'community without freedom is a project as horrifying as freedom without community' (Bauman, 1996: 89). Neither liberalism nor communitarianism, however, pays adequate attention to issues of difference within societies, and neither offers a totally convincing account of the grounds for radical critique of one's own or another community.

Political communitarianism poses considerable dangers to justice because of its rights-and-responsibilities mantra. The difficulty is that in criminal justice, in controlling those identified as risky, the rights and responsibilities are seen flowing in just one direction: towards community. As Reiman puts it:

> Individuals owe obligations to their fellow citizens because their fellow citizens owe obligations to them. Criminal justice focuses on the first and looks away from the second. (Reiman, 1989: 124)

As Reiman says, '*Justice is a two-way street – but criminal justice is a one-way street*' (ibid.: 124, emphasis in the original). Communitarianism, in the version that appears to underpin the policies of present and recent governments in the UK and the USA, certainly sees responsibility as a one-way street.

Notes

[1] See the discussion of Nozick's version of liberalism, in Chapter 1 above.

[2] *Texas vs Johnson*, 491 US, 397–414, 1989.

[3] Supreme Court in *Chaplinsky vs New Hampshire*, US 1942.

[4] Usually this covers racial, ethnic and religious minorities, but in some jurisdictions sexuality and disability are also included.

[5] Personal communications to the present author.

[6] This is not, of course, to deny that concerns for prevention of disorder and crime are no longer seen as important. My argument is that community sensitivity is now present as an additional concern, so that there would be a debate about routing marches and demonstrations through areas where they may give offence even if there were little prospect of crime and disorder. For example, when it is thought that a speaker or lecturer at a university holds racist views which may be offensive to part of the student community, invitations to speak may be withdrawn or they may be dismissed from their posts.

[7] For a full description of the provisions of the Act, with a copy of the Act itself, see Leng et al., 1998.

[8] Braithwaite's ideas are discussed further in the section on community justice, below.

[9]It is arguable, of course, that the best alternative to turning a blind eye to incivilities such as shouting in the street is not zero-tolerance policing, but treatment by health-welfare institutions. A lot of types of behaviour that in previous eras would have been defined and dealt with as problems of mental illness, homelessness and poverty, are now defined and dealt with as crimes. See Hudson, 1993, Chapter 4.

[10]For excellent summaries see Clear and Karp (1999), and Kurki (2000).

[11]A fuller discussion of restorative justice can be found in Chapter 7, below.

[12]See for example, Braithwaite (1999); Crawford and Goodey (2000); Daly and Immarigeon (1998); Kurki, (2000); Marshall (1999); Hudson, J. et al. (1996); Zehr (1990).

[13]Celebration is a 'new town', developed by the Disney Corporation. It screens prospective residents to ensure that townspeople have a guaranteed level of income, that they are orderly and respectable, that there is no chance of living alongside the sorts of people that residents have moved there to get away from.

[14]Although some restorative justice writers are moving in the direction of specifying process rights which should apply (Braithwaite, 1999) and there are some moves to set proportionality as an upper limit to measures which may be imposed, though this is not yet widespread in the restorative justice movement (Cavadino and Dignan, 1996).

[15]There are, of course, differences between these constructivist communitarians on a range of other issues, especially the extent to which they endorse value communitarianism.

[16]The arguments used by communitarians here parallel in many ways the depiction of the citizen of modernity given by Beck (1992), Giddens (1990), etc., discussed in the preceding chapter.

[17]See, for example, Goffman (1959); Laing (1961).

[18]In actual situations, the question is not usually freedom or not, but about the degree of freedom, the degree of cultural autonomy. Globalisation, for example, poses real dilemmas about the balance between how far to embrace a global, Americanised culture which may offer degrees of material advantage, and how far to protect a local culture; and there is always a range of views about the most desirable balance between freedom and security in a society, as discussed in the preceding chapter.

[19]Western critics of other traditions are often accused precisely of lacking this sort of cultural preparation. For example, people encountering laws and customs in African and Arab countries are accused of judging them by western standards, and of condemning them as barbaric or patronising them as quaint without any understanding of the culture in which they are embedded. This attitude has been described as ethnocentric, colonial and orientalist (Said, 1978, 1993).

[20]This is the core theme of existentialist novels such as Sartre's *La Nausée* (1938).

4

Identity and Difference: Feminist and Postmodernist Critiques of Liberalism

Feminist critics of liberalism in theory and in institutional practice occupy much common ground with communitarians. They, like constitutive communitarians, reject the idea of an unencumbered self and insist on the self as socially situated; and they also argue that justice consists as much in recognising responsibilities as in guaranteeing rights, and in acting according to the dictates of love and sympathy as in following normative rules. Although, of course, there are many different feminisms, and much argument and debate among feminists concerned with questions of justice, the preference for the situated over the unencumbered self, and finding shortcomings in liberal approaches to rights, are generally shared.

Most feminist writers on justice, however, worry about the potential for repressiveness in communitarian theories and politics, and about the actual repressiveness of existing communities. As we saw in the preceding chapter, feminists such as Benhabib, Fraser and Lacey are disturbed by the apparent lack of source or opportunity for critique. They are not satisfied with the assurances of, for example, MacIntyre and Taylor, that communities and traditions are compelled towards critique because it is only through critique and constructive response to critique that they can be sufficiently adaptive to survive. Nonetheless, feminists argue, if all values arise within communities, how is it possible for critique which is derived from values not within the compass of already established values to be formulated? Moreover, even if such critique could somehow appear, how could it bring about change? Would the majoritarian logic of community not ensure that minority values, even if listened to respectfully, would be outvoted and disregarded?

On the other hand, if feminists accept the situated self, where can they find their critique? This is the source of one of the major divides in recent feminist writings in political and legal philosophy. For some, only philosophical traditions rooted in universalist values can generate the necessary critical evaluation of existing ideas and institutions of justice, and show the way to reform which is likely to be effective because it is not based on totally alien or unknown traditions. Such theorists acknowledge that these universalist conceptions must be the values of a particular tradition – post-Enlightenment liberalism. They maintain, however, that a universalism which is conscious of its context can provide resources for a critique which can escape the particularistic confines of its community situatedness. Feminist political philosophers holding this position include Seyla Benhabib and Iris Marion Young, and it is their work which is principally drawn on here in discussing these ideas. For them, the key question is what remains of value in the universalist tradition, and how it needs modifying or reconstructing in order to meet the challenges of feminism, communitarianism and postmodernism (Benhabib, 1992; Young, 1990).

For other feminists, the challenge of postmodernism makes an accommodation with liberal universalism more problematic. Postmodernism rejects all attempts to construct general categories of selfhood such as the reasoning chooser of liberalism; for postmodernism, unlike liberal feminism, it is not just that the particular model of the self in question is mistaken, but that any attempt to construct a general, universal selfhood is mistaken. Not only are selves and the values and affinities they embody constituted within societies, they are fragile and transitory, constantly reconstituted by each individual as she moves through her life. Ideas of justice, recognition of its demands, and motives for action are similarly not just derived from living in societies, but are continually constructed and reconstructed through the situations and contexts encountered in that society.

Judith Butler (1990, 1992, 1995) and Drucilla Cornell (1991, 1995a), for example, whilst they, too, value the freedom and autonomy held dear by liberals, and whilst sharing Benhabib's and Young's concern for communitarianism's potential for repression of any values and lifestyles outside a narrow range of consensus and normality, want a more decisive break with Kantian ideas of the self. They and other feminist postmodernists[1] say that critique of community-derived values and institutions will have to manage without the foundational guarantees of universalist philosophy and must restrict itself to historical, social and culturally specific claims rather than general ones (Fraser and Nicholson, 1990). Feminists, in other words, should intervene to remedy social injustice in the here and now, using values and insights acknowledged as being derived from their own lived experience. They should not seek to underpin their critique by appealing to abstractions such as universal structures of reason.

Many of the feminist arguments with liberalism centre on the issue of *identity* and *difference*. Feminist claims to equality sometimes take the form of arguments that women should have equal rights to men because they are the same: women, like men, are rational, purposive beings who value the liberal ideals of freedom and autonomy. At other times, and in other contexts, they take the form of claims that women's different capacities and needs should be given equal recognition to men's and be the basis of equal rights and equal values. For some, the key question is that of recognising the different contexts and occasions when women's identity or their difference needs to be the basis of claims to justice. Martha Minow describes this as 'the dilemma of difference':

> When does treating people differently emphasize their differences and stigmatize them or hinder them on that basis? And when does treating people the same become insensitive to their difference and likely to stigmatize them on that basis? (Minow, 1990: 20)

These themes of claiming identity or celebrating difference are present together in most feminisms, but they have also been more or less central to successive waves of feminist struggle, both theoretical and practical. Equality feminism and difference feminism are sometimes seen as distinguishable phases of feminism – often referred to as 'first wave' and 'second wave' feminism – although as Minow's posing of the dilemma of difference illustrates, this is perhaps an overstated distinction. There may be differences of emphasis, but the divide between identity feminism and difference feminism is some way short of being a dichotomy (Scott, 1988).

What unites feminists is that liberal notions of equality have turned on identity and have repressed, excluded or overlooked difference. What divides feminists is the question of whether a post-liberalism with constructions of equality and justice which can accommodate difference is possible and can be grounded philosophically, or whether such aspirations can only be striven for in an endless series of one-off, discrete political struggles and can be theoretically envisaged only as dreams in an 'imaginary domain' (Cornell, 1995b).

This chapter will review these debates insofar as they are relevant to the theme of justice, looking at feminist engagements with ideas of rights, equality, identity and difference. The discussion will encompass both theoretical and political arguments, as feminism requires. It will mainly be concerned with feminist political philosophy, and some reference will be made to feminist jurisprudence; it is not intended to provide a comprehensive account of either of these literatures, but to draw on feminist contributions to the key concerns of this book.[2]

Liberal feminism

For almost as long as liberalism has been propounded, it has been accompanied by feminist critique. John Stuart Mill (1989) himself saw that liberalism should encompass liberation of women, and Mary Wollstonecraft's *Vindication of the Rights of Woman*, first published in 1792, powerfully challenged women's exclusion from many of the rights being claimed for men by liberal political thinkers (1967). These liberals and their more recent successors do not contest the basic concepts and principles of liberalism, but call for their extension to women. Liberal feminism has been important in advancing the political and social position of women, securing significant gains such as the right to vote; the right to own property; the right to education;

the right to work. Struggles over equal pay and greater representation in Parliament; equality in pensions and tax treatment, continue, and are pursued within the established discourse of rights and equality.

Liberal feminism has used the strategy of taking liberalism at its word, developing a form of internal or 'immanent' critique of law and of theories of justice. Immanent critique takes theories, laws and practices, on their own terms, and then contrasts the reality of their implementation and effects with their expressed principles and ideals (Lacey, 1993: 197). This contrasts with external critique, which takes its principles and values – its critical criteria – from another worldview, such as Marxism or religion. Feminist theories external to liberalism, therefore, might eventually be invoked to explain what is uncovered by immanent critique, but they are not the starting point. Liberal feminists used the powerful intellectual tools of liberalism – belief in the universality of reason; the possibility of human progress; the value of freedom and autonomy; the equality of sentient persons – to critique the achievements of liberalism in securing the benefits of liberal society for only half of the adult population (Baumeister, 2000: 18). Immanent critique reveals that while some kinds of rights are easily extended to excluded groups (the vote, free education), the rights that can be extended unproblematically are limited. It quickly becomes apparent that extending most of the supposedly key rights and freedoms offered by liberal societies (equality of opportunity; equal freedom of expression) to women necessitates rethinking their meaning and mechanics of operation in the light of women's life situation and experiences.

One of the most important areas in which this strategy of immanent critique revealed the limitations of liberalism in delivering rights and freedoms to women, and the difficulties of doing so without rethinking their meaning and restructuring their legal institutionalisation, is that of the distinction between private and public spheres. Liberal political theory has held that the state should regulate public life, but private life should be left alone. The idea of the 'private sphere' is constituted in contrast to the public sphere; the private sphere is a sphere in which the government has no business to interfere. It is conceived as a space to which the individual can retreat from the public realm of regulation, expectations and surveillance: in private, the individual can live as she pleases. In fact, this apparently gender-neutral limitation of the sphere of governmental power disadvantages women by depriving them of the protection of the state in at least two ways. First, because of the general situation that men have more power (financial and physical) than women in private settings, this arrangement in fact means that individuals are left to live as *he* pleases. Women are thus denied equal autonomy. Secondly, this designation of private, domestic settings as spheres which law should not penetrate means that women are denied protection where they are most in danger. Women are in more danger in the home than in the street: statistics for rape, assault and injury repeatedly show that women are at greater risk of being harmed by a partner than by a stranger (Stanko, 1990). Women are thus denied equal protection.

Liberalism's promise of restriction of liberty only to prevent harm to others has therefore been reversed for women. Their liberty has traditionally been limited in various ways, including exclusion from certain professions; restrictions on employment after marriage and inequality of taxation – restrictions which are not remotely connected to harm to others. Yet they have been open to harm themselves through lack of interference in the conduct of those persons most likely to harm them, in the settings where harm is most likely, that is, their husbands and partners, fathers and stepfathers, within the home.

Removal of these unwarranted restrictions and corresponding extension of protection to domestic situations has been recent (the second half of the twentieth century), gradual, hard-won, and is still incomplete. Progress in these respects is a considerable achievement of liberal feminism. Gains were made by direct political campaigns using liberalism's own ideas of fairness, justice and protection from harm, and demanding their application to the excluded half of the population.

Liberal feminists contest the public/private boundary: sometimes the objection is to the place where the boundary is drawn; sometimes it is the whole concept of the boundary. Susan Moller Okin (1989) accepts Rawls's basic framework for establishing just institutions, and accepts that his is a system of public, political morality rather than individual, private ethics. She criticises, however, his lack of consideration of the family, which he regards as part of the private domain and therefore of no concern to a political theory of justice. Okin suggests that if family responsibilities were included in matters to be decided behind the veil of ignorance (where Rawlsian rules would presumably mean that decision-makers would not know whether they were male or female in the actual society, but they would share a rudimentary understanding that the cultural norms of the society included caring for children in families rather than in public institutions), childcare would be more equally shared. This would have implications for the organisation of work outside the home, necessitating the sort of 'family-friendly' provisions for flexible working hours and parental leave that are currently being introduced throughout Europe, in the face of much resistance by employers in the UK and other less progressive countries. There would be consequent changes in the socialisation and education of children, since the gender stereotypes which are correlative with traditional divisions of parental responsibilities would be dysfunctional.

Other critics of the public/private divide point out that it is a false division, since the laws which governments pass in relation to employment, education, taxation, property ownership, etc. shape the form of the family, and influence relationships within it (Roach Anleu, 1992). Olsen (1983), too, has pointed out that the family is a constantly evolving institution, which law continually constitutes and reconstitutes. The division between private and public spheres is more myth than reality (O'Donovan, 1985; Pateman, 1988a); the handicaps suffered by women in the public sphere and lack of protection in the private sphere, which have only recently and patchily been redressed, however, are all too real.

Sexuality is another area which is supposedly 'beyond regulation' in liberal societies. Here again, however, the social contours of sexuality (the age of consent; rules for marriage and divorce; rules of consanguinity in sexual relations; what is 'normal' and what is 'deviant' sexuality) are constructed through law. As cases involving sado-masochism have demonstrated, the fact that sexual acts take place in private, between consenting adults, is not sufficient of itself as a defence or as a guarantee against legal interference. Conversely, until 1991, the fact that one of the parties had *not* consented was no warrant for the law to intervene in the case of forced intercourse with a wife by her husband (marital rape, as this is now acknowledged to be).[3] Until the 1990s, unless there was physical injury, marital sex without consent was regarded simply as a failure of the marital relationship, rather than rape (Barnett, 1998: 260).

Liberal feminism's immanent critique, its use of concepts such as equality and fairness which are at the core of liberal theories of justice, was then, a successful strategy when the rights in question were generally accepted, and when there was strong social support for their extension to women. Women's right to work, their right to education and their right to vote were not only socially progressive moves at the time they were achieved, they were consistent with economic necessity. The right to vote was not solely due to the activities of the Suffragettes; it was also a consequence of the need for women's greater participation in roles outside the home during the First World War. Similarly, the rule that women should surrender their jobs in public services, such as teaching and the Civil Service, upon marriage was jettisoned because of the need for women in these posts whilst men were away fighting in the Second World War. Rights which arise only because of the female role, or which need new interpretations to be extended to women, or which depend on appeals to principle without buttressing by economic advantage, are much harder to win. This intractability reveals the limitations of this liberal approach.

The attractions and limitations of the rights approach are illustrated by campaigns around pornography and sexual harassment mounted by Catherine MacKinnon (1987, 1989, 1991). MacKinnon has tried to empower women by providing legal remedies against these behaviours, by recasting them as rights violations rather than objecting to them as offensive to female sensibilities. She has placed sexual harassment on the agenda of employment rights and pornography on the agenda of civil rights (1987). Her best-known arguments – and those most pertinent for liberal theories of justice – are probably those concerning pornography. Her arguments appeal to the liberal principle that restriction of liberty is legitimate if it is intended to prevent harm.

With Andrea Dworkin, MacKinnon has striven to widen perception of the harm caused by pornography. Usually, debates about whether pornographic material should be allowed to be freely circulated or should be restricted hinge on views about whether the material is likely to stimulate a viewer or reader to commit a sexual act which is illegal, or is deviant according to prevailing social norms. MacKinnon's argument is that as well as some women being harmed by deviant or illegal sexual acts, pornography harms all women by reinforcing sexual conventions which position women as the passive objects of male sexual desire rather than as active sexual subjects, and which underscore sexuality as relationships of domination and subordination, as well as reinforcing the association of sex and violence. MacKinnon and Dworkin have promulgated ordinances in some US states which would give any woman who felt harmed by a pornographic item the right to bring a civil suit against its producers and disseminators.

Some liberals (for example Kymlicka, 1989) have described MacKinnon's arguments about the harmfulness of pornography as providing the best case for its suppression, but even if her view about its harmfulness is correct in general, it would be hard to demonstrate in an individual case. Jackson (1992), whilst affirming the importance of MacKinnon's campaign in widening the scope of thinking about pornography, points out that the effect is cumulatively assimilated into sexual consciousness. As she puts it:

> The problem will be in proving that this month's *Playboy* centrefold precipitated an injury such that a court of law will find the requisite causal link. (Jackson, 1992: 206)

Sexual harassment in the workplace is now more generally accepted as an actionable wrong, but it is still difficult to prove the 'causal link' between particular acts of harassment and women's disadvantages in employment. The situation is analogous to pornography in that the kinds of cases that are likely to be successful are those in which an individual harasser can be shown to have gone beyond the limits of what is currently considered acceptable behaviour, resulting in the complainant having to leave her job, or change to a lower grade in another department to escape the harasser; or cases in which the woman can demonstrate some disadvantage, such as her job performance deteriorating to the point at which she was dismissed or downgraded as a direct result of the harassment. It is much harder to establish that the range of accepted behaviour is itself the problem, not just occasions when it is exceeded; and that women may suffer through group disadvantage because of sexist workplace culture. Thus women continue to have a hard time showing connections between routine sexualised 'banter' and the discrepancies between male and female rates of promotion, and the existence of 'male bastions' in certain kinds of work.

Having taken immanent critique of liberal justice as it affects the lives of women as far as it can go, the conclusion is reached that the obstacle to further gains for women is not merely the limited application and extensiveness of institutionalised rights, or the drawing of the distinction between private and public spheres, but the gendered power relations which are constitutive of these conceptions and institutions, power relations which they in turn sustain. Smart (1989: 139) argues that while it might have been appropriate for early feminists to demand rights, continuation of that demand is now problematic. The rhetoric of rights is now exhausted, she suggests, and may even become detrimental to further improvements in the lives of women. There may well be a 'rights backlash' in certain fields, and there may be violent reactions on the part of some men who try to stop women claiming rights which might alter the gender power balance.

Smart's argument is supported in the case of abortion rights, child custody and access rights, where men are now trying to curb the rights of women to abort the babies or restrict access to the children the men have (biologically at least) fathered. Extensions of maternity leave and other employment rights are making women seem costly to employ. In previous eras, the fact that women might leave to have children made them seem a bad risk for employment at all, and certainly for investment in training and staff development. Now, the possibility that women might keep their jobs but go on leave is one of the factors leading to more and more part-time employment, generally with women working just too few hours to qualify for the employment rights in question.

Rights, equality and identity

Immanent critique of liberalism by 'first wave' feminists concentrated on the gap between ideals of universalism and their expression in the development of democratic societies based on the model of the rights-bearing citizen, and the realisation in practice of these ideals: if women were excluded from rights, then claims of universalism and equality could not be upheld. Such an approach culminates in the realisation that it is not simply a matter of rights not being – as it happens – extended to women, but that the very institutions and concepts set up to bring liberal justice into effect – law, the legal subject, and ideas of rights themselves – are masculine.

When MacKinnon, Kerruish (1991) and other radical feminists point out that law is masculine, and when Smart suggests that the rhetoric of rights is exhausted as far as its potential for progressive change for women is concerned, what they have in mind is that the language and institutionalisation of rights, and the protections rights are constructed to afford, are predicated on the ways that men act in the world. The rights that liberal societies grant are to do with freedom of action in the public sphere: they are the freedoms and protections necessary to pursue the male way of life, protecting individuals' roles in paid employment; in participating in work-based and civic politics; as heads of households, and in owning and passing on their property.

Moreover, justice and law are based on assumptions of rational behaviour that are themselves based on male ideals of the priority of reason over emotion, the value of self-control, detachment and impartiality. Legal notions of proper and improper behaviour, permitted and impermissible action in defence of one's self-interests are based on the idea of what the 'reasonable man' would do or expect in the relevant circumstances; ideas of justice are based on what the reasonable man desires and the conditions necessary for the fulfilment of those desires.[4]

The problem with notions of rights, of equality before the law, and other foundational principles of liberal justice, from a feminist point of view, then, is that the best they can offer to women is to be treated like men. The equality to which women may be admitted is equality with a masculine norm. To claim 'their' rights, to participate in society on an equal footing, to claim equal protection, women have to demonstrate that they are 'the same' as men. If women's claim to equal rights is based on their being the same as men, this means, in fact, that only women who *are* the same in respect of the rights in question will have their rights acknowledged, or will be able to claim legal redress if their rights are violated. So, for example, anti-discrimination laws in employment provide redress only for women who can show that they have the same qualifications and experience as a male who is given a job or promotion in preference to them. An effect of this is that where salary levels are dependent on previous experience, credit may be given for prior employment or military service, but a woman is not usually given credit for domestic responsibilities; in family law, denial of child custody to a woman who could provide an equal standard of living to her erstwhile partner would clearly be discriminatory, but it might be seen as giving due priority to the welfare of the child to award custody to the father in the case of sizeable inequality in the provisions available. So, as MacKinnon argues, law based on the notion of equal rights cannot remedy gender inequalities, and cannot provide justice to women on the downside of inequalities (Jackson, 1992). If 'equality' is taken to mean treating like cases alike, women have to prove their 'alikeness' before they can be treated equally.

What is common ground among feminists working in legal and political philosophy is recognition that this 'maleness' of law comes about not just because the legal and political professions have been dominated by men, but more fundamentally because it builds on categories of rationality and reasonableness that purport to be universal/gender-neutral, but in fact are partial/ masculine. When feminists argue that the liberal subject is not universal but male, this is to say that the male cannot stand for the female and means, of course, that 'second wave' feminists are positing the impossibility of a universal subjectivity. The male voice cannot speak for the female; theories of justice and their political and philosophical underpinnings must accommodate the fact that 'humankind has two bodies, female and male' (Pateman, 1988b: 8). Although feminists generally reject ideas of essential, biologically derived differences in female and male reasoning, 'second wave' feminism sees that the ways in which, down the ages, women and men have experienced the world have led to different subjectivities, in advanced western societies as much as in pre-modern societies:

> Research on gender suggests, among other things, that men and women in contemporary western societies are differently constituted as modern human subjects; that they inhabit, experience, and construct the socio-political world in different, often incommensurable ways; that we are just beginning to perceive and to understand the heretofore suppressed feminine dimensions of public and private life; and that what has passed as a gender neutral vocabulary of reason, morality, cognitive development, autonomy, justice, history, theory, progress, and enlightenment is imbued with masculine meaning. (Di Stefano, 1990: 64)

This passage summarises the main themes of 'difference' feminism. The research to which di Stefano refers encompasses women's participation in fields of employment, education, family and social-political life which continually reveal females to be, in general, less competitive than males; more content to remain with tasks that they know they can do well rather than to keep moving on to new ones; more concerned with emotional aspects of situations. Findings across fields of activity, different countries, different times, reveal disparities in what women and men want and how they think, as well as what they are allowed to be and do. The common theme is that females are found to place more emphasis on relationships with others, in contrast to men's emphasis on individuality. What research also demonstrates time after time, society after society, is that the qualities associated with the male role are the most highly valued. As well as being reflected in pay and social status, this higher valuation of masculine traits is reflected in their position in philosophy itself: the valued characteristics of Enlightenment humanism are the idealised characteristics of generalised masculinity.

One of the best-known studies of female–male difference is psychologist Carol Gilligan's (1982) study of reasoning on questions of law, morality and justice. Gilligan replicated Kohlberg's famous experiments in legal and moral reasoning with mixed-gender and female groups of subjects after observing that Kohlberg's subjects were all male.[5] Kohlberg's developmental approach to moral reasoning proposed six stages of moral development, moving from understanding of fairness based on the reasoner's individual needs (stages one and two, exemplified by the frequent childhood wail of 'it's not fair'); to an understanding of fairness based on entering the shared cultural conventions of what is approved and disapproved (stages three and four); and finally to a rule-following understanding of morality which appeals to principles such as rights, equality, reciprocity (stages five and six). In other words, in Kohlberg's scheme (1981), morality progresses from egotism, to conventionalism, to abstract moral reasoning – this is unfair to me; this is what people in my group approve or disapprove; these are the principles on which moral reasoning must be based.

Kohlberg's account of moral progress is an account of moving from considerations of the concrete to the abstract; from responsibility to rules; from connectedness to separateness. The final stage requires moving to a Kantian position beyond one's web of relationships and responsibilities so that morality is identified with the justice of impartialism. Gilligan's (1982: 24–63) claim is that whilst male moral reasoning can be fitted easily into this developmental model at the stage of conventional morality, but with point-ers towards a growing capacity for principled reasoning, female relational reasoning cannot be fitted in at all. She illustrates her argument by referring to her reworking of the 'Heinz dilemma' with a male and female subject, Jake and Amy. Amy's thinking contains imaginative constructions of the conse-quences for the relationships of either stealing or not stealing the drug, and she contests the premise that the choice is between stealing the drug and letting the wife die. She insists that they should talk until they reach an agree-ment, because neither of these outcomes is supportable.

As well as reworking Kohlberg's experiment, Gilligan conducted three studies: a college-student study which questioned a group of 25 people, first as college students and then five years after graduation; a study involving 29 women considering abortion; and a group of 144 males and females matched for age, education, occupation and social class at nine life-cycle points between ages 6–9 and 60. The questions in the studies concerned experience of moral choices; moral dilemmas, as well as reasoning in hypothetical situ-ations of moral conflict. Gilligan found that her female subjects continued to be concerned with responsibilities towards specific others, and with feelings of general responsibility to do good and relieve harm wherever possible. As she summarises in the words of one of her subjects:

> while Kohlberg's subject worries about people interfering with each other's rights, this woman worries about 'the possibility of omission, of your not helping others when you could help them.' (Gilligan, 1982: 21)

Gilligan describes this different moral orientation as a 'different voice', a female ethic of care distinct from the male logic of justice. She makes clear that the difference she suggests is an empirical finding, not a premise underlying her work; she points out that the association of moral voices with respondents' gender is not absolute; and that there is interplay of these voices within each sex, with convergence marking times of crisis and change. Further, Gilligan makes no claim about the origins of the different moral orientations or their likely distribution in a wider population, across cultures, or through time; and she acknowledges social status and power differences influencing the experi-ences of males and females and the relations between them (ibid.: 2).

In spite of these caveats, Gilligan has been criticised by some feminist legal scholars as exaggerating the distinctiveness of her two suggested voices, especially as they are expressed through law and through popular conceptions of morality (Daly, 1989). She is also criticised by other feminist theorists, especially MacKinnon (1989), who charges that despite her qualifications about the generalisability of her findings, her use of the terms 'masculine' and 'feminine' nonetheless imparts an essentialism to what are, at most, expressions of the moral qualities that women are allowed to embody in patriarchal capitalist societies.

Daly is undoubtedly right in her insistence that law contains elements of both a logic of justice and an ethic of care, or the Portia principle and the Persephone principle as Heidensohn has termed them (Heidensohn, 1986). Sentencing, for example, is said to contain the two elements of justice: a formal element – justice as fairness – which concerns dealing equitably and consistently with offenders, and a substantive element – justice as alterity – which is concerned with doing what is most appropriate in the particular case, and which brings an element of individualisation to sentencing. On the other hand, whilst these two elements of justice are always co-present, it can be observed that from time to time the balance between the two shifts. In recent times the tendency has been for legal justice (particularly criminal justice) to emphasize the rule-following, standard case logic at the expense of providing appropriate help and remedies for individual cases (Hudson, 1993). Structuring and restriction of judicial discretion to promote consistency, the decline of rehabilitation and the spread of mandatory sentences have all moved criminal justice systems in the direction of the logic of justice and away from the ethic of care.[6]

MacKinnon, too, is correct to emphasize so emphatically the fact that women are expected to be caring, to be concerned with relationships, that their 'different voice' is perhaps not so much an expression of a different moral register as the articulation of a narrow range of discursive possibilities open to women on questions of morality. I have given so much attention to Gilligan's work because of her specific focus on moral reasoning, a focus which is quite unusual in that most feminist work in the area of justice and morality tends to be written in more generalised terms about women's separate consciousness or subjectivity rather than recording actual empirical data. It is also important as it is the starting point for many debates and controversies within feminist legal, moral and political writing on the question of difference and identity.

However controversial her formulation of two distinct moral registers, where Gilligan is at one with other 'difference' feminists is in pointing out first, the identity between (what she empirically finds to be) male moral reasoning, and the idealised mode of impartial, abstract reasoning; and second, the assumed dichotomy between ideas of responsibility to specific others, caring, and the importance of relationships, and what is taken to be 'justice' in modern societies.

Characterisation of these modes of moral reasoning as Portia and Persephone connects with the earlier points about 'justice' only being available to women who are already equal to/identical with men. Shakespeare's Portia is, of course, a female character, but she is given a voice because as a lawyer she speaks the male discourse of rules and rights; she wins the case by cleverer deployment of the rules than her male adversary, not by introducing any new, 'feminine' concerns. She wins, not by persuading Shylock of the virtue of mercy, but by showing him that the rules he appeals to cannot give him what he feels to be his due.

Moving from the observation that law is male to the realisation that the concepts on which philosophies of morality and justice are based are also masculine makes it difficult if not impossible not to agree with Smart (1989, 1995) that law is an extremely limited vehicle for bringing about changes in the position of women. With MacKinnon, we can see that we will very soon reach the limit of possibility of extending rights and remedies to women, once we wish to move beyond improving the legal status of those women – white, educated, middle-class women – who have adopted male forms of being in the world. If we wish to extend justice to areas that men cannot experience, such as childbirth, or to categories of women who do not wish, or do not have the opportunity, to be 'like men', then more radical reformulations are called for.

Concepts which purport to be universal are easily revealed to be connected not just with males, but with one group of privileged western males. Enlightenment values and constructions of rule-following, impartial reason are revealed not just as the values and constructions of the male, but as the values and constructions of *power*. The hegemony of the discourse of power persuades us that the powerful are the rational, the enlightened, and the powerless are irrational, savage, incapable of governing themselves and therefore unworthy of autonomy and democratic participation. At a political level, the standpoint of power has no incentive to admit any critique, since this may lead to loss of power: we expect the coloniser to resist the claims of the colonised to self-determination.

Philosophically, Enlightenment constructions of abstract universalism are compelled by what Adorno called a *logic of identity* (I.M. Young, 1990: 98). This logic of identity acknowledges only that which humans have in common; it validates only those aspects of being which are shared by all so that it can cast identity as an essence common to all within the category. The logic of identity does not admit degrees of similarity and difference: one either possesses the characteristics of the reasoning subject or one does not. A series of binary oppositions is thus constructed by the logic of identity, and actual beings are assigned to one or other category: reason/emotion; civilised/barbaric; mature/immature; objective/subjective; moral/immoral; normal/deviant. As Young comments, this construction of binary categories means that instead of placing different subjects within a range, a continuum of similarity, those who have some difference become the absolutely different: 'The irony of the logic of identity is that by seeking to reduce the differently similar to the same, it turns the merely different into the absolutely other' (Young, 1990: 99).

Females, because of being observed as different from males in some respects, are thus seen as absolutely other to males in their total subjectivity. The logic of identity offers no middle ground: women must either be like men, or they must be completely other. The dichotomising logic of identity means that because females are thought to give more importance than males to emotional, affective aspects of situations, they are thereby thought to be incapable of reasoned thought; because women's bodily functions and cycles are seen to structure their lives in ways that men's do not, women are seen as dominated by nature and the body whereas men are creatures of mind and civilisation. (Male) objectivity is posited as the universal moral standpoint because it proceeds through impartial moral reflection; it is the exercise of the essential human capacity, speaking for all and encompassing all in its concerns. Female particularism is categorised as non-moral because it discharges assumed responsibility to a particular individual in a particular situation, thereby privileging that individual and so breaching the impartialist tenet of equal concern for all.

Gilligan's ethic of care has been criticised in this vein, the charge being that particularism always leads to a conventional group ethics, which allows the moral agent to prioritise chosen responsibilities (my family; my neighbour-hood) to the exclusion of others:

> An ethics of care, it may be argued, is ultimately inadequate from a moral point of view for the objects of our care and compassion can never encompass all of mankind [sic] but must always remain particularistic and personal. An ethics of care can thus revert to a conventional group ethics, for which the well-being of the reference group is the essence of morality... An ethics of care yields a non-universalizable group morality. (Blum, 1988: 479)

Blum suggests that care has its place in moral deliberation but must be secondary to impartiality; that in any conflict between the two, impartialism should trump care.[7]

Second-wave feminists have argued persuasively that the potential of liberal ideas of justice based on individualism and impartial rationality, institutionalised through rights, to alter the power relationships of dominance and subordination between males and females or to reflect women's modes of experiencing the world whether by giving distinctive rights and protections or by incorporating women's modes of moral reasoning, is limited. They have, further, demonstrated equally persuasively that this limit is unbreachable because the purportedly universal moral standpoint is the viewpoint of a male, privileged elite who because they are the powerful group have no conflicts or experiences which would lead them to champion any other viewpoint.

A question this poses for feminists is analogous to that faced by communitarians: how can alternative constructions of justice and critiques of existing value systems arise that are more than merely narrow expressions of concern for the immediate group, other than by appealing to universalist values which can transcend group particularism? An important current debate among feminist political and moral philosophers is on this key question of whether Enlightenment ideals of reason and justice are capable of reconstruction to accommodate feminine being-in-the-world, or whether the concept of universalism must be abandoned altogether.

Discourse ethics: the encounter with the concrete other

Second-wave feminists, then, reject the liberal conception of a universal subject – an abstract subject transcending context and the specificity of experience. Recalling Pateman's aphorism that 'humankind has two bodies, female and male' (Pateman, 1988b: 8), this has implications for subjectivity. Since we experience life as embodied selves, not as free-floating reason, this must entail (at least) two different subjectivities. This duality of humankind raises several questions. From the point of view of thinking about justice, the following two are of crucial importance:

1 If the ideal of the universal subject is rejected, does this mean that the entire post-Enlightenment philosophical scheme of which it is the heart must be abandoned?
2 If the ideal of the universal subject is rejected, does this mean that there are two essential subjectivities; or are there other equally profound fissures (such as race and religion), which produce different subjectivities; or must the idea of the subject be abandoned altogether?

These questions have brought feminists into conversation with post-modernists as well as with communitarians, and there has been a series of important exchanges between those persuaded by postmodernism (or post-structuralism, which is usually the preferred term) and those who wish to reconstruct rather than abandon the liberal-modernist project.[8] Feminists who lean towards the post-structuralist position fear that trying to remain within the framework of post-Enlightenment liberal philosophy constrains the freedom for development of feminist ideas and means that in the end concepts will be weighted down by their liberal roots. In Cornell's words, liberal feminists will be unable to think 'beyond the limit' (1992). In political terms, it means that the constructions which produce gendered oppressions may be disturbed, but will not be completely displaced.

On the other hand, those who wish to remain broadly within the framework of liberalism fear that without universalist philosophical underpinnings, political ethics will lapse into the conventionalism of communitarianism, with no source of critique. They wish to retain what they see as the emancipatory drive of modern liberalism, and are suspicious of jettisoning the ideas of subjectivity and justice just at the point at which formerly oppressed groups are beginning to achieve recognition and have their claims to justice heard. Two of the most important writers in this developing tradition are Seyla Benhabib and Iris Marion Young. Both are difference feminists who do not want to throw the 'baby' of reflexive, freedom cherishing liberalism out with the 'bathwater' of the masculine false universalism of the transcendent subject.

In her book *Situating the Self* (1992) Benhabib says that the communitarian challenge to a self constituted prior to its social context; the feminist challenge to the privileging of masculinity in the idea of a universal reasoning subject; and the challenge of postmodernism to the idea of a fixed, determinate self must be taken seriously. In the face of these powerful challenges, she asks, what remains of value in universalist moral and political theories? For Benhabib (1992: 2) the

> now seemingly 'old fashioned' and suspect ideals of universal respect for each person in virtue of their humanity; the moral autonomy of the individual; economic and social justice and equality; democratic participation; the most extensive civil and political liberties compatible with principles of justice; and the formation of solidaristic human associations

continue to be important, therefore the universalistic theories which promote them need reconstruction, not dismantling.

Benhabib finds the main flaw in liberal theory to be the way that the universality of the human capacity to reason, to have needs, to feel pain, and to wish to plan one's life according to one's own precepts has been taken to mean, in the concept of the universal subject, that one voice can speak for all, rather than that all must have a voice. What Benhabib advocates is a form of *interactive universalism* which replaces the *generalised other* of post-Kantian ethics with the *concrete other* of the discourse ethics she espouses.

The counterpoint to the universal subject is the generalised other. Liberal ethics asks us to assume the perspective of the generalised other in our moral thinking. The normative command of neutral impartialism is that no particular other is to be privileged: all others are owed equal respect. For Benhabib as for other difference theorists, the problem with this is that the logic of identity dissolves any difference between self and others, as well as between differently situated others. The 'golden rule' of liberal ethics – do unto others as you would have them do unto you – encapsulates this perfectly. The rule only makes sense if we assume that 'you' and 'others' require the same treatment. If universal subjectivity is grounded upon what people have in common, then any sense of difference is lost. If people are to be accorded respect because of what they have in common, then difference cannot be a basis for respect.

Benhabib cites Ackerman's principle of conversational restraint to illustrate the inadequacy of liberalism to meet the challenges of radically pluralist societies. Ackerman believes that areas of profound disagreement should be left out of political discourse and assigned to a private sphere. But, as Benhabib says, reflecting the continuing feminist critique of the public/private divide:

> All struggles against oppression in the modern world begin by redefining what had previously been considered 'private', non-public and non-political issues as matters of public concern, as issues of justice, as sites of power which need discursive legitimation. (ibid.: 100)

Benhabib's point is that liberal political theory cannot fulfil its great tasks of defending freedom and providing critique of established institutions and values (including its own) unless it attends to the voice of the other. And the abstraction of the universal subject means that the otherness of the other is precisely what is lost behind the veil of ignorance. If it is possible to legislate impartially in the general interest because it is possible to suspend the assumption of a specific social identity, then to have any sense of what would be just or unjust for all entails that in essentials we are all the same; what makes for our individuality is merely ephemeral.

In place of this generalised other, Benhabib proposes that the central figure in political morality – in thinking about justice – should be the *concrete other*. She reverses Ackerman's precept, and says that it is in fact the things that are different that need to be attended to. Things that are held in common are by definition not in dispute, and so it is they that can be bracketed out. The ethical stance is not that of the liberal impartialist speaking with the 'voice from nowhere' (Nagel, 1986), but that of listening attentively to the voice from somewhere very particular. The normative requirement is to be able to assume the perspective of the concrete other. Instead of the exercise of reason by a legislating subject who can represent all because he represents no one, Benhabib calls for a radical deliberative democracy, where issues of justice are settled through real conversations among actual, differently situated others with diverse and conflicting demands and aspirations. The capacities necessary for such procedures are the ability to reverse perspectives (that is to say, to be able to reason from the other's point of view), and the sensitivity to hear the voice of the other (Benhabib, 1992: 8).

This, Benhabib explains, is a universalism based on two principles: (1) the principle of universal moral respect, and (2) the principle of egalitarian reciprocity (ibid.: 29). The first principle means that we respect the right of all beings capable of speech and action to participate in moral discourse, while the second principle calls for participatory institutions to be organized so that all have equal rights to initiate topics, to call for clarification of presuppositions, to challenge assumptions and to make claims.

Benhabib looks to this new procedure of universalism to guard against the two ways in which difference comes to be excluded or repressed. The liberal way rules differences irrelevant, which is unsatisfactory, as we have seen, for those who are thus subsumed under a norm which is not congruent with their experiences, such as women subsumed under a male norm. The communitarian way is to try to enforce similarity, so that people are like us or they are outside the community: there are many examples of the coerced assimilation of ethnic and religious minorities to the dominant culture, with the only option that of exclusion from it.

From communitarianism, Benhabib takes the notion of the situated self, and from feminism she takes the notion of the embodied and gendered self. The self she proposes as a participant in the moral dialogue is, therefore, one who brings with her, her commitments, her values and her social/philosophical tradition. Benhabib's universalism is historically self-conscious; she recognises that the principles of freedom and autonomy which she holds dear, and which provide criteria for critique of actual institutions and actual societies, come from within the normative horizon of modernity.

In Benhabib's version, universality is no longer derived from the attributes of subjects, but is a requirement of procedure. Starting from difference rather than sameness, her interactive universality is no longer 'the ideal consensus of fictitiously defined selves, but the concrete process in politics and morals of the struggle of concrete, embodied selves, striving for autonomy' (ibid.: 153).

While Benhabib's universalism is clearly different in important respects from that of Kant and Rawls, she does share liberalism's prioritisation of the right (following the rules of justice) over the good (pursuing a particular idea of what constitutes the good life). Although her discourse ethics allows specific conceptions of the good to be argued for, she suggests that in any clash between values deriving from a particular version of the good and the core principles of universalist morality (freedom, autonomy, equal respect), the latter should trump the former. Referring to the care ethic as well as to communitarian conventionalism, she describes the principles of universalist morality as operating as constraints within which these values should operate.

Young in *Justice and the Politics of Difference* (1990) shares Benhabib's affirmation of Enlightenment ideals while rejecting the 'logic of identity' involved in the construct of the transcendental subject. As she says:

> Enlightenment ideals of liberty and political equality did and do inspire movements against oppression and domination, whose success has created social values and institutions we would not want to lose. (Young, 1990: 157)

Like Benhabib, Young wants difference to be the starting point of moral conversation and not be bracketed out from it, and like Benhabib she argues that radical pluralism demands a plurivocal communicative ethics where different subjectivities argue and bring their different claims on justice to the debate. Participants in moral discourse do not progress from speaking from their own particular situation to speaking with the disembodied voice of the generalised other; rather they progress from seeing only their own situation and the claims it generates to appreciating the situation and standpoint of concrete others and thus recognition of their claims. Claims are normatively valid, for Young, not if they are the result of exercise of lonely, abstract, impartial reason, but if they can be acknowledged and acted upon without violating the rights of others.

Young opens by contesting the 'distributive paradigm' by which liberal theories are dominated. She argues that this paradigm limits questions of justice to questions of fair distribution. This is certainly true of liberal theories of punishment (see, for example, von Hirsch, 1976) as well as theories of social justice which are focused on the distribution of income and resources. Young charges that the distributive paradigm is inappropriate for thinking about non-material goods such as power and opportunity. Above all, she argues, thinking about rights from within the distributive paradigm is unsatisfactory; thinking of them as possessions to be allocated leads to a zero-sum, self against society mentality in which rights for one are always deprivations for someone else.

For Young, justice should be thought about in terms of oppression and domination. These should be the primary terms for thinking about injustice, and therefore for moving to a more just society. Oppression, she explains, has five aspects: exploitation, powerlessness, marginalization, cultural imperialism, and violence. While she acknowledges that distributive injustices may contribute to or result from these forms of oppression, she states that none is reducible to distribution, and all involve social structures and relations beyond distribution (Young, 1990: 9).

Oppression, she argues, happens to social groups, and liberal theories typically lack a satisfactory conception of groups. Although groups are composed of individuals, they exist prior to individuals; individuals' identities are formed partly through their group membership, and individuals are treated by others on the basis of their group membership. Women; the disabled; members of ethnic, racial and religious groups are reacted to first of all on the basis of their group membership, often at the expense of being treated on the basis of their individual characteristics. As Young points out, only white, Protestant, middle-class males are treated first and foremost as individuals because they are the group who identify others, the norm against whom other groups are measured, and they are not members of a marked group themselves.

Like most difference feminists, Young insists on the relational quality of the terms with which she is concerned. One group is oppressed by another; one group is dominant in society: group membership is a relational attribute. For example, a wheelchair user will only experience herself as disabled if she is trying to negotiate a physical/social space organised from the point of view of non-wheelchair users; children learn to think of themselves as 'black' through the abuse and stigmatisation they receive from white children. Similarly, she explains that rights, though they may be conceived as possessions in liberal theory, in reality are relationships: rights are institutionally embedded rules about what people may do in relation to one another. As Young puts it, 'Rights refer to doing more than having, to social relationships that enable or constrain action' (ibid.: 25).

Justice, for Young as for Benhabib, is a procedural issue rather than a question of distribution. She holds to two universalist values: (1) developing and expressing one's capacities and expressing one's experience; and (2) participating in determining one's actions and the conditions of one's actions. Justice demands that these values are promoted for everyone. These values correspond, Young explains, to two social conditions that define injustice: oppression, the institutional constraints on self-development; and domination, the institutional constraint on self-determination. Young argues that justice demands that all be enabled to participate in society's decision-making to ensure that these values are promoted for themselves, and morality consists in seeking their promotion for (concrete) others. Groups who are oppressed or dominated in the present should have specially privileged rights of representation and participation.

Young's relational understanding of social groups means that the standpoint of the powerful group is not privileged. Like Benhabib, she rejects the *assimilationist* model of group rights. On this model, struggle takes the form of recognition of group identity and then campaigning for 'the same' rights as the dominant group, on the basis that the ways in which the subordinated group is the same as the dominant group are much more significant and legitimate than the ways in which they are different. As Kymlicka (1989) *inter alia*, has noted, this has been the model of civil rights campaigning by African-Americans, and this model has dominated struggles of other groups. As we have seen, it does not serve the needs of women beyond very elementary extensions of rights in the public sphere, and it does not serve the needs of those seeking religious, cultural and other forms of rights and recognition based on their differences from dominant groups.

The problem with the assimilationist model is, of course, that it leaves the definition, specification and institutionalisation of rights and other elements of justice in the hands of the dominant groups; other groups must, in the way MacKinnon describes, demonstrate their worthiness for these same rights on the basis of essential similarity. With Young's relational model, what is at issue is the ways in which groups are oppressed and dominated, so that their definition of the situation – their claim to justice – is the starting point and the dominant group is enjoined to look at the situation of dominance or oppression from the standpoint of the subordinate group.

Young discusses Richard Wasserstrom's defence of the assimilationist ideal, a defence which is generally regarded as one of the clearest and most principled elaborations of the liberal ideal of a society where 'difference makes no difference' (Wasserstrom, 1980). Wasserstrom argues that distinctions of race and sex are arbitrary, and that they perversely and unnecessarily limit the possibilities for those on the downside of such distinctions. Second, he argues that only the assimilationist model yields a clear and unambiguous measure of equality and justice. Whenever social benefits are allocated according to group membership there is injustice; treat everyone according to the same rules and standards is the only just measure. Thirdly, only assimilation can meet the liberal ideal of choice, because it is the only way in which people can act on individual preferences rather than group expectations. For Young, however, this assimilationist model exemplifies the position that offers subordinated groups only the possibility of joining the game after it has begun, after the rules have been set, after the prizes have been allocated; new entrants must prove themselves fit to play the game. The assimilationist model demands no reflexivity on the part of the dominant group, no changing of the rules or modifying the nature of the game.

Young, like Benhabib, rejects communitarianism because it incorporates the assimilationist model. To be accepted as members of the community, entrants must prove themselves to be the same in all essentials, they must prove themselves to be 'one of us'. Community with its firm roots in the logic of identity represses and excludes difference. She contrasts community with the city, which she suggests is an ideal that celebrates difference. The ideal of city life is, she says, difference without exclusion; the excitement of the city is its diversity. Although actual cities may be segregated and may reproduce the oppressions and dominations of communities that do not aspire to diversity, we look to the city to provide experiences of unassimilated otherness. If we enjoy cities, we enjoy restaurants and markets of a range of ethnicities, the street musicians from faraway lands, the opportunity to see foreign films and to join in a cosmopolitan throng. The ideal city provides for encounters with myriad otherness, without violence and without exclusion.

The contingent subject; universalism without guarantees

Although cautioning against labelling a number of writers with extremely significant differences between them with the one term 'postmodernist' or 'post-structuralist' and identifying with them, some feminists believe that there are some key positions which Derrida, Lyotard, Baudrillard and Foucault have in common, and which are close to feminist thinking and central to the development of feminist theory. Both feminism and postmodernism offer profound critiques of modernism and its philosophical underpinnings, although postmodernists have generally come from a starting point of philosophical theory and feminists have generally come from an involvement in practical politics (Fraser and Nicholson, 1990). Judith Butler and Drucilla Cornell are among the most important feminist theorists who are closer to post-structuralists than Benhabib and Young are.

Judith Butler (1990, 1992, 1995) takes issue with Benhabib and the other feminists who want to reconstruct the modernist-liberal framework, over the key questions of subjectivity and of the possibility of a philosophically guaranteed universalist procedural theory of justice. Butler argues that there can be no concepts, principles, theoretical propositions or philosophical foundations which are beyond interrogation. This means that the reconstruction of a universal subjectivity into two or more differentiated subjectivities, and of the transcendental generalised other into the contextualised concrete other does not go far enough because it continues to utilise the constructions 'subject' and 'other' unproblematically. Because it is still operating within the tramlines of modern liberalism, the new subject continues to incorporate an idea of agency prior to its constitution in context and experience, even though the reformulated subjectivity is said to be contextually aware and historically self-conscious. Because it is still operating within the parameters of modern liberalism, the 'different' feminine subjectivity still lapses into a logic of identity, seeking to found itself on what women have in common.

For Butler, the point is neither to confirm nor deny the existence of 'subject Woman', but to ask, of any constituted subjectivity, what is included and excluded, who is empowered and who is oppressed, by this construction. While feminists are united in showing the exclusion of the feminine, of the body, of the emotions, in the masculinist universal subject, so their own constructions can exclude and oppress many femininities. Appeals to cross-cultural female behaviour associated with mothering as the basis for the essential feminine subject (Chodorow, 1978) are susceptible to the same critique as Gilligan's 'other voice' of moral reasoning. Mothering does not define selfhood for all women, and moreover, it could never define a unitary female selfhood (Baumeister, 2000: 21). That is to say, not all women are mothers; further, among those women who are mothers there are many different ways of mothering, and being a mother plays a different role in the self-identity of different women.

Feminists should not, then, construct a female subjectivity on the basis of a supposedly universal female experience such as motherhood (or a gendered division of labour, or sexuality, or anything else). They should not attempt to add into a liberal political framework a set of rights and distributions derived from women's needs as mothers. To do so would impose false generalization on a range of very diverse experiences; and, as Cornell argues, any attempt to assimilate women into the established framework of justice 'as women' allows the state to define what it is to be a woman (Richardson and Sandland, 2000: 11). What feminists should do instead is to interrogate and deconstruct the ways in which law and convention construct motherhood and femininity. We should look at the constructions and stereotypes of the 'good mother', 'bad mother', 'feminine' and 'unfeminine' woman, nice girls and bad girls, which regulate the lives of actual, different, women.

Butler's question of what is excluded by prevalent constructions of female subjectivity leads her to look at the ways in which black women, homosexual women, Muslim women and other groups find themselves faced with constructions of femininity which do not fit with their experiences and understandings of selfhood. Like other feminist writers including hooks (1981), Spelman (1990) and Flax (1995), Butler sees that 'subject Woman' ignores the impact of race, class, religion and sexual orientation on the lives of women and on their identities.

Post-structuralists take very seriously the insight that difference is relational. The implication of this relational, differentiated subjectivity is that it cannot exist prior to experience of social relationships, and it is constantly constituted, reconstituted and nuanced by such experience. In other words, not only can there be no unitary subjectivity, but no individual subjectivity can ever be fixed or completed. Subjectivity is forever contingent on context, relationships and experience; it is work in progress, forever becoming. This is more radical than the 'contextually aware' subject of Benhabib and Young, for although they, like Butler, envision subjectivity as an outcome of a particular cultural context, Benhabib and Young do not have this sense of subjectivity being forever fluid, constantly reformulated. For Butler, not only is there no subject that is pre-legal and pre-discursive, there is no agency prior to the individual's context of commitments, relationships and projects, and although gendered identity and subjectivity are culturally produced, they can never be completely culturally fixed.

As well as deconstructing the concept of the subject, Butler interrogates the ideas of justice, rights and the other universalist terms of liberal political morality. Or rather, she argues that, like the idea of the subject, they can never be beyond interrogation. She agrees that these moral precepts are important ideas and that societies that adopt them are societies that most contemporary feminists would prefer to live in. As well as their being inadequately realised in the sense of women's rights lagging behind men's rights, black citizens' rights lagging behind white citizens', she insists that the terms and ideas themselves contain contradictions and contradictory implications.

In the second of her contributions to the debate with Benhabib, Butler looks at Paul Gilroy's analysis of the narrative of modernism in his 1993 work *The Black Atlantic* (Butler, 1995: 128). Gilroy, she says, demonstrates that the modernist narrative of progressive emancipation both required and instituted slavery, and was a cultural resource in the struggle for its abolition. She endorses this reading of the modernist narrative as both a philosophical/political discourse that produces and reproduces exclusions and oppressions, and as a resource which can be revised, reinterpreted, reformulated to serve specific emancipatory aims. She posits Gilroy's description of modernism as narrative resource as contrasting with Benhabib's use of it as a universalistic system which, by virtue of its universalism, transcends all particularistic communitarian values. Butler allows that it may be politically expedient, in the context of actual, local struggles for emancipation, to argue *as if* ideas of justice, rights and equality were universal, but this is not to accord them the status of actually being transcendental universals. However much value we attach to our most deeply held ideals, we must accept that they, too, are contingent on our cultural and relational situation: we can have only contingent universals, not philosophical guarantees. Again, the difference from Benhabib's situated universals may be one of degree, but it is important. Benhabib asks us to be aware that these moral terms arise in the specific cultural context of modernity; but that nonetheless they have a form, a fixity and therefore a dependability that Butler's perspective of discursive contingency does not allow.

As well as interrogating the constructions of female subjectivity based on supposedly cross-cultural, ahistorical experiences or characteristics, Butler (1990) examines the attractions of psychoanalytic theory, especially Lacanian and post-Lacanian psychoanalysis, for feminists. Juliet Mitchell (1975), Luce Irigaray (1985) and Drucilla Cornell (1995a, 1995b) are among feminist theorists who have drawn on psychoanalytic theory as a source of explanation of the construction of male as subject and female as other. The interest in psychoanalytic theory arises primarily because it is clear that the creation of male as subject, female as Other is not just a matter of rational philosophy or political theory, nor even a matter solely of calculatedly taking and keeping power and dominance. Subjectivity and identity also emerge from the subconscious, from fear, desire and fantasy, and these, of course, are the subject-matter of psychoanalytic theory.

Lacanian and post-Lacanian theories take the need for the male to achieve separation from the mother as a starting point in the development of gender identity. The mother must become an object to the male child, and so as the masculine becomes subject, the female becomes Other. For Lacan, the paternal law is the basis of all kinship relations and cultural traditions: the father is the subject to be identified with; the mother is the forbidden, unknowable Other. Psychoanalytic theory here offers an explanation for the cross-cultural persistence of patriarchy, and a grounding for common experiences of the development of gender identity.

Post-Lacanian theory emphasizes the instability of gender identity because the development of separation, of differentiation of self and other relations into subject–object relations is constantly undermined by desire, residing in the unconscious, for reattachment and for possession of the forbidden. This inherent instability of identity commends itself to post-structuralists as it, too, shows that subjectivity could never be fixed and stable. At the same time, for feminists it emphasizes the centrality of gender to identity, and provides a model of at least some commonality in gender identity development which could ground a commonality to experience as male or female. The emphasis on development of gender identity in psychoanalytic theory reinforces the view of gender as the fundamental divide, so that though it will be mediated by race, class, religion and other biographical differences, gender remains the basic building block of identity.

Butler cautions against treating psychoanalytic theory in any of its versions as a foundational meta-narrative. She does not want to replace Kantianism with Lacanianism or with any other grand theory of the origins of all human subjectivity, the essence of all selfhood, or the causes of all human discontents.

Butler quotes Irigaray's radical reinterpretation of Lacan, which holds that the masculine is grounded not just on separation from the female, but on the *rejection* of all that is female. For Irigaray (1985) it therefore follows not just that female subjectivity must be very different from male, but that the very conception of 'subject' is masculine. Woman is always and only the Other; moreover, this is a complete otherness such that the elements of what is conceived to be subjectivity (identity, autonomy, coherence of the self) cannot be constituted as some sort of feminine counterpart of masculine constructions of these elements. There can be no possibility of different but symmetrical subjectivities because, according to Irigaray, the construct 'subject' entails relations of hierarchy, domination and exclusion: the subject can only recognise itself by contrasting itself with the subordinated, excluded Other.

Butler's approach is similar to that of Foucault (1977, 1978, 1986) in that she is concerned to interrogate historically specific discursive regimes in terms of their power-structuring, their exclusions and their subordinations. Though she allows for no fixed, generalized and coherent subject, she sees that exposing the contingent, constituted, regulatory nature of these constructions of fixity, generality and coherence in subjectivities opens up spaces in which emancipatory politics on behalf of the excluded and repressed can operate (Fraser, 1995a).

Drucilla Cornell (1992, 1995a, 1995b *inter alia*), takes a Derridean line in that she follows a deconstructive rationalist model in her approach to justice, and at the same time incorporates Irigaray's reworking of Lacanian themes in her approach to the question of the subject. Cornell also invokes the moral philosophy of Levinas in her advocacy of a standpoint of *ethical feminism*. In the works of Cornell's which are particularly important here, these strands of linguistic deconstruction, psychoanalytic theory and moral philosophy are woven together in shifting proportions. In her more recent work, she also accommodates a reworked Kantian-Rawlsian approach to the procedures for deciding issues of justice.

One important strand, prominent in *The Philosophy of the Limit* (1992) is the Derridean theme of deconstruction and the play of difference. Deconstruction as method reveals the ways in which ideas always contain traces of their opposites: meaning is ascribed through the use of binary oppositions; we recognise what something is by contrasting it to what it is not. Opposite meanings are like two sides of a coin – they exist only in relation to each other. So we know that light is different from dark; health is different from sickness; good is different from bad, male is different from female. Moreover, these oppositions are hierarchical: one pole of the term is always the preferred state to the other. If we try to take one side of an oppositional pair as far away as we can from its contrasting term, if we try to define it positively for its own qualities rather than invoking that which it is not, we find that we reach a limit such that if we lost all trace of the negative, we would lose the meaning of the positive. So all terms must retain traces of their opposites if they are to remain intelligible, but the vestige remaining means that they can never be fully realised as themselves alone, but must incorporate something of their opposite.

For justice, this means that we know what justice is because we can recognise injustice; and we can identify injustice because we have a conception of justice. So the judge or the legislator can never pass judgments or create laws that do not contain traces of injustice; but conversely the most unjust tyrant, the torturer and the oppressor must recognise that they are behaving unjustly because they have an intuition of justice. Justice, in the real world, can only ever be an aspiration, it can never be fully achieved; but specific injustices will not remain for ever and cannot be fully invisible. Justice may be an aspiration rather than an attainable object, but it is a singularly important aspiration. As a project, justice is fated to remain for ever unfinished, but this does not devalue its significance as a project.

Cornell draws on Derrida's theoretical work such as *Writing and Difference* (1978), and also on his very influential essay on the inevitable gap between 'law' and 'justice', *'Force of Law: The "Mystical Foundation of Authority"'* (1990). Like Benhabib and Young, one of her departure points is Adorno's *Negative Dialectics* (1973), which develops a powerful critique of the logic of identity. Her use of Derrida's placing of difference at the heart of meaning, however, takes Cornell beyond Adorno to a position of radical Otherness, seeing the encounter with an Otherness which can never be fully categorised or dissolved into loci of commonality, at the heart of human existence.

Cornell undertakes an 'ethical reading' of Derrida, enlisting the moral philosophy of Emmanuel Levinas (1969, 1981).[9] Her project is not, like Derrida, to demonstrate the inevitability and inescapability of difference. For her, the key question is, 'What should my response be to the otherness of the Other?' Cornell's project thus becomes essentially that of specifying an ethical relationship to the other, and to this end she adopts Levinas's moral philosophy of alterity. This means that the essential requirement of morality is not to balance the claims of self and other, not to balance impartially between competing claims, but to acknowledge a responsibility towards the Other in every encounter. The essence of justice is in meeting the claims of the Other. Cornell (1991, 1995c) describes her project as developing an ethical feminism, of which the core principle is the establishment of a responsive, non-violent relation to the Other. This response to Otherness can only be approached through an attitude of 'fallibilism' and 'musement', which are Charles Peirce's terms to indicate a mind-set of openness to having all one's ideas about the world called into question (fallibilism) and preparedness to be astonished by the mysteries and varieties of life (musement) (Peirce, 1960). Such an attitude allows for no fixed conception of roles, identities, or versions of the good.

In her more recent work, Cornell has given more attention to the question of the subject. She has come to share Irigaray's view of the impossibility of a feminine subjectivity being constituted within a male-defined social world, because in such a world the female is always-already constituted as object, as Other. Cornell (1995b) says that any female subjectivity, any emancipation for women, any replacement of oppression with justice, could only arise within a feminine *imaginary domain* that could think in different categories, dream different dreams, acknowledge different desires, than the masculine imaginary of modernity. She picks up Lacan's depiction of the female as a lack, suggesting that this lack-of-meaning of the female leaves open the space for construction of feminine subjectivities within the imaginary domain. If, like Irigaray, we reject the notion of the female as the not-male, and agree that the measure of woman can never be reduced to contra-man, and if with Lacan we see that the maleness of our identity constructs leaves woman only as absence, as that-which-is-lacked, then a discursive space is opened which could only be filled from within a feminine imaginary domain.

At the same time, Cornell is also encouraging feminist political theorists into alliance with Rawls. She sees room for the insertion of feminine stand-points behind the veil of ignorance because of the very formalism of Rawls's structure, which presupposes no privileging of any one standpoint. Cornell reaches this accommodation with Rawls through a reinterpretation of Kant; or rather, a move of emphasis from the attributes of the universal subject on the basis of which all reasoning beings are entitled to equal respect, to the inclusivity of the Kantian precept that all persons are entitled to equal free-dom and respect. Coupled with the principle that no conception of the good is to be preferred to any other, Cornell derives a procedural test for just laws and institutions which lies in posing the question, 'Would free and equal people agree to this?' (Richardson and Sandland, 2000: 11–12). She argues that this test ascribes no positions, values or characteristics to 'people', and invites them to evaluate laws and institutions according to their compatibility with people's own projects of 'becoming a person'.

Cornell proposes a test for justice at the political level; an ethics of non-violence and responsibility towards the Other, and an appreciation that our most cherished ideals and aspirations are destined to remain unfulfilled, but are nonetheless supremely important to strive towards. She stresses the importance of being alert to the part played by fantasy, desire, fear and repul-sion in the construction of identities and subjectivities, and the centrality of these projections of the subconscious in the constitution of male as subject, female as Other. Her areas of interrogation are language and imagination, in contrast to Butler's more material concerns with exclusion, suppression and the workings of power.

Like Cornell, Butler stresses the importance of the subconscious and its fears and desires. Butler emphasizes the contingency and indeterminacy of all categories, including categories of subjectivity and of supposedly universal moral and political values. The fact that identities are never fixed, and that therefore there can never be one or more female subjects, does not mean, she insists, that we cannot oppose particular forms of oppression of women. Equally, the fact that 'universals' are in fact historically, geographically and socially situated constructs does not mean that we must abandon them, that we must lapse into relativism, and that we may not in certain situations pragmatically act as if they were 'true universals'. It means that our universals must be legitimated in the sphere of political activism rather than established as philosophical foundations; philosophy cannot provide us with guarantees about the validity of our values and truth-claims, we must content ourselves with 'contingent foundations' that remain open to contest (Butler, 1992).

Butler's analysis implies no normative procedural model for deciding actual questions of justice; Cornell attempts to devise one that is compatible with her ideas on subjectivity, with the openness to deconstruction of everything that can be expressed linguistically, and with the primacy of the ethical relationship with the Other. In one sense, the difference between Butler and Cornell, and Young and Benhabib is not very great, and that distance is reduced by Cornell's move towards accommodation with Rawls. Young and Benhabib do, however, continue to advocate a single procedural basis for deliberating issues of justice – discourse ethics – and are interested primarily in justice in the political sense, calling as they both do for a revived, feminist theorisation of the public sphere. They look to the work of Jürgen Habermas, which will be discussed in the following chapter.

The principal differences between Benhabib/Young and Butler/Cornell lie in their models of identity. Post-structuralist feminists insist on the constant fluidity and perpetual reconstitution of identity, so that the self and other who relate to each other will not bring a fully formulated identity to the encounter: identity, commonality and difference will emerge during the encounter, they are contingent upon the encounter. Benhabib and Young, however, seem to see the formation and acknowledgement of identity as prior to the encounter. Acknowledgement of a specific, differentiated identity, such as African-American, black woman, is the condition for staking claims to justice, the condition for participation in the moral conversation.

Benhabib comments that she finds no bridge between Cornell's specification of the ethical – an individual moral relationship – and the social construct of justice. She says that she shares Cornell's aspiration to a non-violent relationship to the Other and to otherness more generally, but finds this no help in thinking about justice within a society. As Benhabib says:

Justice requires not only nonviolence but also respect for the otherness of the other for whom I feel no affection, in fact for the one whose otherness may be repugnant to me... The difficult legal and political questions begin at the point when we have to define the acceptable, fair, just limits of difference which a social order can or will want to live with. (Benhabib, 1995: 117)

For Benhabib and Young, these limits can only be decided by an inclusive, procedurally universal, institutionalised deliberative process. The ideal result of such deliberation would be consensus, and the deliberation would be about the acceptability of a range of fixed, constituted-in-advance, orders of otherness. Cornell's pragmatic alliance with Rawls and Butler's recognition of contingent universals are intended to ensure that their post-structuralist perspective retains its links with feminist politics and that it does not, in proclaiming the 'death of the subject', undermine the possibility of challenging the masculinist institutions of modernity which remain powerful and entrenched, and which continue to oppress and exclude women of many racial, ethnic and religious groups.

The postmodernists whose critiques and deconstructions post-structural feminists draw upon have had little to say about the advancement of justice. Derrida and Lyotard both affirm the importance of justice as an ideal, saying that even though institutional and philosophical representations of ideas such as justice, rights and equality may be shown to be wanting, the ideals themselves retain their normative force. Foucault has done much to illustrate the repressiveness of the normalising strategies of power in modernity, but has given us little guidance about what to defend and what to reform in maintaining the distance between the operation of power in the western democracies and the operation of power in Gulag societies (Hudson, 1996: 134; Walzer, 1986: 62).

Derrida (1987), in his essay for Nelson Mandela, argues for equality in terms which seem to allow it as a contingent universal. We have no trouble, he says, in recognising inequality and therefore must have absorbed/imagined an ideal of equality. Lyotard, in *The Postmodern Condition* gives a somewhat similar defence of justice, arguing that the idea of determining justice through consensus is outmoded – but it is the idea of consensus that is outmoded, not the idea of justice:

Consensus has become an outmoded and suspect value. But justice as a value is neither outmoded nor suspect. We must thus arrive at an idea and practice of justice that is not linked to that of consensus. (Lyotard, 1984: 66)

There seem, then, to be two key issues which divide difference feminists. First, there is the possibility of theorising and implementing a mode of deliberation that would institute a just society; or whether the most that can be attempted is, following Lyotard, an endless series of small, local struggles between different interest groups. Second, there is the question of the status of gender as an analytically useful and empirically valid category which can accommodate a range of different subject positions within it, or the impossibility of using such a category without colluding in the cultural rigidities, exclusions and oppressions that saturate the concept of the subject.

Feminist legal theory and the problem of essentialism

These reflections on subjectivity and on the masculinity of the conceptual underpinnings of modern liberalism are not merely of abstract theoretical interest for those concerned with justice. As well as revealing masculinism and its effects in spheres of employment, family law, and property law, feminist legal theorists and feminist criminologists have drawn attention to the masculinist nature of criminal justice. The subject of criminal law on whom constructions of criminality, responsibility, culpability, defences and mitigations are predicated is the 'reasonable man'. Even if, in these politically correct days, the term 'reasonable person' is substituted for the more traditional 'reasonable man', such change in terminology has not been accompanied by any change in the way law thinks: the subjectivity at the core of criminal justice is male. It is, moreover, a white, middle-class male subjectivity that is produced and reproduced through the discourse and the practice of criminal law (Lloyd, 1984; Naffine, 1990).

Examples of this masculinism of criminal law conceptions abound, in women's treatment as both offenders and as victims. In cases of women who kill partners by whom they have been abused, defences and mitigations are based on what the reasonable man would do in circumstances of abuse. This means that defences of self-defence and provocation are generally unavailable to women because they tend not to kill instantly in the moment of threat or abuse, but usually await a safer opportunity, such as when the man is asleep. Self-defence is almost unavailable to women in these circumstances, and the idea of 'cumulative provocation', which would reflect the situation in many of the cases, is only very slowly and very patchily becoming accepted. In the UK, women are still receiving life sentences for killing their partners after years of abusive treatment, while men continue to receive short custodial sentences or non-custodial sentences for killing when they discover their partners' infidelity or if they lose control in response to nagging. The maleness of ideas of what provocation is and what is a reasonable response is reflected in these 'nagging and shagging' cases (Cooke, 2001).

Gradually, a wider range of expertise is being allowed in these cases, including evidence from feminists working with abused women. The Lavallee case is important because the judgment by the Canadian Supreme Court recognised the maleness of established understandings of reasonable behaviour, provocation and self-defence (Martin et al., 1991).[10] The Supreme Court judgment describes the paradigm case for self-defence as a one-off, unpremeditated bar-room brawl between two men of equal size; it envisages a brief encounter between strangers, in a public place. Self-defence does not recognise threat in private contexts; it recognises neither gendered violence nor gendered fear (O'Donovan, 1993: 429). This acknowledgement in Canada of the partial, masculinist understandings of defences and mitigations has led to more frequent calling for evidence from a wider range of experts than the usual traditionally qualified psychiatrists, scientists, etc. (Valverde, 1996a). The significance of this Canadian development is that by recognising the fact that courts need special witnesses to interpolate the circumstances and motivations of female actions, the Supreme Court is tacitly acknowledging the maleness of law on which feminist criminologists and legal theorists have insisted (Hudson, 2002a).

Rape is another type of crime that is often quoted to illustrate the maleness of criminal law. Rape is constructed around the concept of the normality of the promiscuous male sex drive, forever alert to opportunities for sexual gratification, and the concept of the female role as manager of male sexuality. This is why consent is the crux of whether intercourse is rape or not, and it also explains the persistence of the idea that it is the woman's sexual history which is relevant and important, not the man's. In other words, the issue in law is not the violence or unpleasantness of the encounter, but whether the woman made her lack of consent unambiguously clear by her behaviour and her self-presentation, or whether the normal, sexually incontinent male could reasonably have imagined at least some degree of consent.

With routine crimes, MacKinnon's observation that only women who are like men will be treated equitably holds true: women who commit crimes for reasons that are readily understandable by male decision-makers (and even female decision-makers operating the masculine constructs of law) will receive proportionate penalties in line with those that men would receive for similar crimes, although these penalties will take no account of the circumstances that they face specifically as women (Hudson, 2002a).

Women who are treated leniently in criminal justice processes pay a high price for such leniency: they are treated as less responsible, less rational than male offenders or other women who are treated more severely. Feminist criminologists have noted paternalism and infantilism in the penal treatment of some women (Edwards, 1984); women are treated not according to the crimes they commit but according to the sort of women they are adjudged to be. A *familial justice* model has been proposed to explain the ways in which perceptions of female offenders as 'good mothers', 'faithful wives and partners' or as bad mothers, promiscuous or feckless, influences sentencing (Eaton, 1986; Worrall, 1990). If women can be presented as victims – of coercive men, of abuse, depression, instability or addictions – they may be dealt with leniently (Daly, 1994). One of the implications of this is that women who because of stereotypes or convention are less able to be presented as victims and/or as acting in a feminine, albeit illegal, manner – black women; unconventionally dressed women; lesbian women; strong, independent women who may be perceived as aggressive or manipulative – are likely to receive more

139

severe penal treatment than those who fit the stereotypes of conventional, victimised femininity. Although the legal category 'diminished responsibility' may be restricted to homicide, in routine cases women can only be accorded any understanding of the individual circumstances surrounding their offending, and accorded any sympathy or meeting of their needs, at the expense of being defined as in some way having diminished responsibility, lesser rationality.

There have been calls to inject more of an ethic of care into criminal justice, as an ingredient of a feminist jurisprudence which would be based on the problem-solving, relational mode of female moral reasoning. Such proposals have been criticised for the same reasons as Gilligan's model on which they are based, a critique which is made sharper by the experience of paternalistic treatment of women as a species of lesser rationality (MacKinnon, 1989: Chapter 13; Smart, 1995: Chapter 10). What is common ground to all proposals, counter-proposals and critiques is that treating women the same as men – as happens when they are dealt with in relation to a dominant, unproblematised male penal norm – is not treating them equally. Equality is not a matter of treating women the same as men, but of treating them appropriately, given their circumstances and their offending patterns. At the level of policy, Pat Carlen calls for a *woman-wise penology*, which has two principles:

1 That the penal regulation of female law-breakers does not increase their oppression *as women* still further.
2 That the penal regulation of law-breaking men does not brutalize them and make them even more violently or ideologically oppressive towards women in the future. (Carlen, 1990: 114)

Neither of these conditions is met in the penal systems of the UK, the USA or other major countries today. Women continue to be imprisoned for routine property offences, regardless of the fact that they pose no physical danger to the public; they are imprisoned regardless of their responsibilities for their children; if they receive community penalties they may have to travel many miles to attend a women's project (Carlen, 1998; Hudson, 2002). Men are sent to institutions which have sexist and racist cultures; the cultures of institutions for young male offenders, in particular, are characterised by militaristic, authoritarian regimes which inculcate brutalised, hard-man personality traits.

Although, then, there is consensus among feminists that a female standpoint needs to be interjected into law, the standpoint of the white, middle-class female cannot be taken to represent all women. Not only are different kinds of women treated differently by courts and criminal justice agencies, but different kinds of women have different demands to make of criminal justice. Again, rape provides a good example. Writing about the USA, Chesney-Lind and Bloom note that taking rape and domestic abuse more seriously has led to the jailing of more men, 'particularly men of color' (1997: 46). Angela Harris points out that black women have a conflicted stance on rape. Black women are even less successful than white women in bringing rape prosecutions.

They are far from the stereotype 'ideal victim', who is white, middle-class, married, raped by a stranger in the street or an intruder in her home, and they are therefore given even less legal protection than are white women. On the other hand, they are aware of the use of rape allegations to oppress black men: the lynchings in the southern states that were the outcome of the miscegenation laws which prohibited any sexual intercourse between black men and white women, not just forced sexual intercourse. Although such laws are gone, black men raping white women are the group most likely to be convicted, and most likely to get maximum penalties. As Harris says:

> the experience of rape for black women includes not only a vulnerability to rape and a lack of legal protection radically different from that experienced by white women, but also a unique ambivalence. Black women have simultaneously acknowledged their own victimization and the victimization of black men by a system that has consistently ignored violence against women while perpetrating it against men. (Harris, 1990: 601)

Harris criticises the prevalent forms of essentialism she finds in much of feminist legal theory, describing them as dominance theories because of the way in which gender is proposed as the key facet of identity, something which women have in common which is more important than any elements of identity which differentiate them. In such essentialist formulations race, class, religion, sexual orientation or any other difference appear as, at best, a 'nuancing' of identity. She discusses MacKinnon as an example of nuanced dominance, citing cases where MacKinnon has admitted to some difficulty in seeing the issues raised both 'for women', and for members of minority communities. Harris also discusses the work of Robin West, who, she says, draws on the common experience of motherhood as defining the self for women, assuming that this produces a selfhood that is different for men and women, but is essentially the same for all women.

Harris explains that in these essentialist conceptions of self, the idea of gender as so strongly primary means that race or other difference can only ever be a qualifying adjective, not a signifier of an important aspect of identity. Discussing writings by 'women of color',[11] Harris notes that they share a sense that the self-identity of 'women of color' is not primarily a female self or a 'colored' self but a both-and self. Black women do not, she explains, see themselves as black females, or female blacks, but as black-and-female: both terms are of equal importance, although in different relational contexts one or other term may take on greater or lesser weight (Harris, 1990: 604).

Conclusion

The beliefs that are shared by feminist critiques of liberal theories and practices of justice who insist on difference are perhaps more important than the beliefs that divide them. All are insistent that one subjectivity cannot stand for all, and all are equally cognisant of the importance of thinking about class, race, religion, sexuality and other facets of difference. Benhabib and Young conduct their analysis at a political level, and they advocate a reinvigorated theorising of the public sphere, and a participatory democracy based on a discourse ethics rather than on the Kantian model of the lonely reflections of legislating reason, speaking as the voice from nowhere. They want to retain the emancipatory, humanitarian impulse of liberalism, and affirm the need for a universalist philosophical framework to guard against recognition of the situatedness of values slipping into a conventionalist, repressive communitarianism.

Butler, Cornell and other post-structuralists offer a more radical critique of the idea of the self in liberalism, rejecting not just the masculinity of post-Enlightenment ideas of selfhood but also the possibility of any stable, unitary, coherent self. They also deny the possibility of universalist guarantees of values such as justice and its components of equality and freedom. At best, we can pragmatically adopt contingent universals, as Butler proposes, and we can seek ways to insert a feminine imaginary into the spaces left unfilled or inadequately filled by philosophical and institutional constructions, as Cornell describes with reference to that of Rawls.

For (criminal) justice, these insights mean that women should not be treated according to a male penal norm, but should be responded to in ways that recognise the specific contexts in which harms occur. Whether as victims or as offenders, women should be responded to in ways that recognise their differences from men, and from each other.

The next chapter will discuss Habermas's theory of communicative rationality and discursive ethics, on which Benhabib and Young draw, and which is compatible with many of the emergent glimpses of 'new' forms of justice.

Notes

[1] The writers discussed here may not label themselves postmodernist, but their ideas are either explicitly derived from, or closely parallel to, those generally designated by the term. Drucilla Cornell explicitly allies herself with post-modernist deconstructionism, particularly with the ideas of Jacques Derrida, in *Beyond Accommodation* (1991), and *The Philosophy of the Limit* (1992), although in other works she does not make her allegiance so clear.

[2] See for example Barnett (1998); Benhabib et al. (1995); Butler and Scott (1992); Fineman and Thomadsen (1991); Nicholson (1990); Richardson and Sandland (2000).

[3] *R v R* [1991] 2 *WLR* 1065, p. 1074, Criminal Appeals, Chief Justice Lord Lane described the immunity to prosecution of husbands for having sexual intercourse with their wives regardless of consent, endorsed by the Criminal Law Revision Committee in 1984, as 'anachronistic and offensive'.

[4] The change of terminological usage in several jurisdictions from 'reasonable man' to 'reasonable person' is superficial; it is more a matter of politically correct language than of reflecting any real change in the construction of legal and political subjectivity.

[5] Kohlberg (1973) devised a series of moral dilemmas to measure moral development in adolescence: his focus was on age rather than gender. The best-known one is 'the Heinz dilemma',

a scenario in which Heinz has a sick wife; he cannot afford to buy drugs that will help her and the local pharmacist refuses to lower the price. The question posed is, 'Should Heinz steal the drug?' This presents a conflict between moral norms (stealing is wrong, but so also is not doing everything possible to save a life). Kohlberg explores the factors mentioned by different respondents, and the logics they appeal to. Instead of questioning same-gender subjects at different ages, Gilligan explored the dilemma with two 11-year-olds, Amy and Jake. Jake's approach is a mathematical weighing up of rules and rights, whereas Amy's thinking is about the continuing relationships between the wife, the pharmacist and Heinz.

[6]There have been specific calls to strengthen the caring Persephone principle within criminal justice (Masters and Smith, 1998). This myth relates the finding of a solution which satisfies Persephone's father, who wants her with him in the underworld, and her mother, who wants her with her on the earth. The solution is for Persephone to return to the underworld for part of each year. Although the myth is used to explain the changing seasons, with the world grieving her absence during winter and blossoming to greet her return in spring, it has also been used to illustrate the principles of relational justice, which seeks to find a solution acceptable to all parties rather than deciding one party to be in the right and the other in the wrong.

[7]This is very much the position in criminal justice. Representations from care discourses (such as social work, and psychiatry) are allowed, but are very much subordinated to juridical discourse, and are only allowed at the discretion of the representatives of juridical discourse (Hudson, 1993: Chapter 6).

[8]Among the most important are *Feminism/Postmodernism* (Nicholson, 1990) and *Feminist Contentions* (Benhabib et al., 1995). Post-structuralism signifies a perspective which rejects the structuralist grand theories such as Marxism, Freudianism and modernism, and is sometimes preferred because post-modernism can signify allegiance to a particular group of writers, among the most prominent of whom are Baudrillard, Derrida and Lyotard.

[9]Levinas's moral philosophy is discussed in Chapter 6, below.

[10]*R. v. Lavallee* [1990] 1 S.C.R. 852.

[11]'Women of color' is a usual and acceptable term in US literature.

Part II
Reaffirming Justice

5
Reaffirming Modernity: Habermas and Discourse Ethics

Those feminists who seek to give difference a central place in theories of justice, but who nonetheless wish to retain the ethical framework of modernism with its core principles of autonomy and equal respect, draw on the work of German political theorist, Jürgen Habermas. Seyla Benhabib and Iris Marion Young, in particular, appropriate his ideas of *discursive rationality* and *discourse ethics*. They do not adopt his ideas uncritically, and have charged that his theory does not manage decisively to break with the Kantian abstract, identical in all relevant respects, person and establish an individual, yet socially situated, flesh-and-blood, gendered and embodied self as the agent and claimant of justice (Benhabib, 1986, 1987; Young, 1990). In one of his most recent works Habermas (1996a) acknowledges the importance of the feminist critiques and tries to demonstrate the extent to which his theoretical framework can accommodate them. In turn, feminist political theorists have reconsidered his work, and although points of criticism remain, Habermas's work is being seen as a highly significant resource for the development of theories and institutions necessary to promote justice in the late-modern period (Fraser, 1992; Johnson, 2001).

Habermas has produced a large volume of work from the 1960s onwards, with several major books as well as substantial articles and interviews. I make no attempt to deal with all this work here, but will concentrate on the themes that are most relevant to my topic of reaffirming and reconstructing 'justice'.[1]

After a brief explanation of Habermas's background influences, the chapter will present and examine his major themes of discursive rationality and discourse ethics, and the principles they yield for establishing just political processes. After consideration of some critiques of this work, his recent work on law will be discussed. This contains his thinking on law, on rights and justice, and his accommodation with an 'ethics of care'. As well as his debates with feminists, and his position *vis-à-vis* communitarianism, we will examine Habermas's engagement with post-structuralists such as Derrida, Foucault and Lyotard. I will consider his remarks on risk society, and make some suggestions concerning the implications of Habermas's theory of discourse ethics for criminal justice. The chapter will conclude by evaluating Habermas's contribution to 'reaffirming justice'.

Background: Habermas and the Frankfurt School

Habermas's work is rooted in the *critical theory* developed within the Institute for Social Research at the University of Frankfurt. The Institute was founded in 1923, in the wake of the defeat of Germany in the First World War and the rise of communism with the Russian Revolution and the establishment of the Soviet Union. In the late 1930s many of the most distinguished members of the Institute fled from Germany, and were offered facilities first of all at Columbia University, and subsequently at other US universities. After the end of the Second World War some chose to remain in the USA. The best known of these to English sociologists is, perhaps, Herbert Marcuse, who developed some of his most widely read critiques of the 'military-industrial complex' and the manipulative nature of the mass media, from the sociology department of the Berkeley Campus of the University of California (Marcuse, 1968).

The leader of this phase of the Frankfurt School was Max Horkheimer. Like other members of the group, he had used the years in the USA to study the rise of fascism in Germany, his studies in prejudice complementing Adorno's *The Authoritarian Personality* (Horkheimer, 1947, 1950; Adorno, 1950). Horkheimer was worried by the closeness to government of American social science, and so returned to Germany. In 1950, with Horkeimer as director and Adorno as assistant director, the Institute reopened in Frankfurt.[2] Habermas joined the Institute as research assistant to Adorno, was Horkheimer's successor as director, and at the time of publication of the English-language version of *Between Facts and Norms*, was emeritus professor of philosophy.

Critical theory is 'critical' in two senses. First, its proponents have engaged in what today is usually known as a 'history of the present': seeking to understand today's trends and conditions, but using a variety of disciplines and methods. It seeks to explain the present, but its goal, its telos, is the attainment of a better future; for critical theory, the role of philosophy and the social sciences is to reveal the present in order to contribute to enhanced emancipation in the future:

> Horkheimer describes critical theory as a theory of the contemporary epoch that is guided by an interest in the future, that is, by an interest in the realization of a truly rational society in which men can make their own history with will and consciousness. (McCarthy, 1976: xi)

This critical history pursues both internal (immanent) and external critique, exploring modern capitalism's failure to live up to its own promises and holding it up to the values of another viewpoint. While the earlier Frankfurt School theorists identified the epoch they sought to understand as capitalism, the external critique was that provided by Marxism. Critical theory could never be simply a branch of Marxism, though, because its critique embraces wider aspects of modernity than those related to its capitalist form, and because of its use of non-Marxian systems of thought. The Institute embraced thinkers from a wide variety of disciplines – philosophy, psychology, sociology, art and literary criticism, law, economics and more – and they worked so as to merge the insights of major systems of thought in their various disciplines. Early critical theorists' writing is notable for its attempts to bring Marx's theories together with the other major contemporaneous system for understanding human behaviour, Freudian psychoanalysis. Frankfurt theorists are also the inheritors of the philosophical tradition of German idealist rationalism, so the intellectual ghosts of Kant and Hegel are never far away.

The unity they bring to this eclectic range of influences and projects is their commitment to critique in the sense of seizing the critical moment, the moment of change, and seeing the potential for both liberation as well as domination in modernity in its various guises (Adorno with Horkheimer, 1973). The essential imperative of critical theory is theoretical and practical political commitment to emancipatory change, and Habermas continually reaffirms his own attachment to the emancipatory motif of Enlightenment thought as well as the emancipatory political drive in Marxist thought: he affirms the Enlightenment goal of emancipation from the authority of conventional thought as well as the Marxist goal of emancipation from material inequality and the oppression of unequal power.

Habermas has witnessed not just the rise of fascism and the horror of the German Holocaust, but also the unfolding of Stalinism within socialism. Where the earlier writers had focused on the dangers of domination and alienation in capitalist societies, Habermas has needed to confront more squarely the fact that the possibilities of totalitarianism are inherent in modernity itself. Horkheimer, Adorno and other members of the mid-century generation sought to reveal to itself a German society which had not acknowledged its role in the Holocaust; for Habermas, the problem he sees raised by reunification and the demise of the Soviet Union is that present-day Germany is overly confident that it has overcome its past.

Like the earlier writers, Habermas explores many contemporary theories and explanatory frameworks, including feminism and post-structuralism. He also engages with Luhman's systems theory, which is much more widely known and influential in Germany than here, and with the ideas of Rawls and Dworkin. He draws considerably on the sociological paradigms of Weber and of Talcott Parsons. Unlike earlier critical theorists, one perspective he does not pay any substantial attention to is psychoanalysis: there is no place for even the most influential of contemporary psychoanalytical theory, that of Lacan, within his theoretical constructions. From the early 1990s, feminist political and moral theory is granted something approaching the status of external critical perspective in his work, analogous to the place of Marxism in the earlier phases of the Frankfurt School.

The second sense of the term 'critical' which is central to the work of the Frankfurt School is Kant's distinction between *critical* and *metaphysical* ideas. A critical concept or idea is one which acknowledges its conditions of possibility – linguistic, cultural, political, historical; a metaphysical or ideological concept represents itself as natural, ahistorical, asocial, unconfined by time and place. In Kant's time, philosophical constructs were represented metaphysically, being advanced as how the world is, emanations of the divine. In our secular times, metaphysical ideas may well not pervade our culture (though significant residues remain), but certain ideas are presented ideologically, as fixed states that cannot be altered, rather than as the outcomes of human choices. An axiom such as 'you can't buck the markets' is an example, representing the market as an invisible, inevitable guiding hand rather than a mechanism of exchange operated by human agents and therefore subject to intervention and change.

Critical theory has, therefore, as its overarching analytic framework, investigation of the 'conditions of possibility' of the area of social life being analysed. Investigations have included the conditions of possibility for the rise of Fascism; media manipulation under advanced capitalism; the conditions of possibility of dialectical reasoning, of aesthetic judgment and – the critical theory work with which penologists are probably most familiar – the conditions of possibility of leniency and severity in punishment (Rusche and Kirchheimer, 1968).

Habermas's project is to investigate the conditions of possibility for arriving at rules and institutions which can deliver and protect justice in a social world which is not only radically pluralist, but which is subject to the Marxist-defined ills of reification and alienation as well as to the populist politics of a media-saturated culture which has lost sight of the idealism of liberal democracy. His project involves analysis of some of the problems of modernity, an analysis which features prominently in his early work, and then the development of a theory for the derivation of moral principles and social rules. This latter phase continues the Kantian-Rawlsian tradition of seeking universally binding rules of procedure.

These works combine philosophical reflection with consideration of the findings and analytic frameworks of the empirical social sciences; they take many earlier Frankfurt School themes as points of departure. The Frankfurt School argument with positivism about the nature of truth[3] provides some of the groundwork for the development of Habermas's discourse principle of procedure, while the work on media and ideology is reflected at many points in his work. In his latest substantial work, Habermas (1996a) looks at law. He sees it, in Durkheimian manner, as the authoritative mechanism for social integration in a secular society, and as protector of rights and freedoms in a society composed of free individuals acting in their own interests. He examines its role and its working in relation to his principles of discourse, within the 'conditions of possibility' analytic framework. The conditions of possibility with which he is concerned are those of law's legitimacy in late modernity.

Habermas has increasingly identified himself as a defender of Enlightenment liberalism. Although, he says, he is not merely an apologist for modernity, since he is all too well aware of its dark sides, he holds that modernity still has 'normatively convincing contents' (Habermas, 1992a: 226). Freedom and equality, he argues, are well worth defending. Fascism and Stalinism have demonstrated the dark sides of modernity, but, after all, we only recognise them in their full horror because of our cultural grounding in the democratic and humanitarian ideals of the Enlightenment.

Modernity, Habermas argues, is necessarily subject to recurrent crises, and because of its aspirations to universalism and its break with conventional authority, it must find solutions to its crises from within its own principles and values: 'it is the first form of society which cannot draw uncritically on the resources of tradition, but is obliged to unfold its fundamental forms from within itself' (Dews, 1992: 31).

If, as has been argued through Part I of this book, modernity's aspiration to justice is in crisis, then Habermas's proposals are highly relevant as resources for dealing with this particular crisis.

The development of discourse ethics: (1) consensus and truth

Across the sciences generally, there has been a move away from a *correspondence* theory of truth, that is, the belief that 'truth' consists in correspondence to a factual state of being, in favour of a *consensus* theory, that 'truth' is a status which is accorded to an idea that achieves a consensus of belief in a relevant community. By the 1960s, the move towards consensus theories had become decisive in the social sciences, and a gulf opened up between positivism, which rests on correspondence of observations to facts, and critical, interpretative social sciences which seek to achieve understandings rather than predictive rules.

Habermas contributed to this debate, and in his earlier phase, represented by *Knowledge and Human Interests* (1971), showed his general allegiance to the critical theory side of the argument. He qualifies this, however, by granting that there might be different kinds of 'truth regimes', and also by wanting to incorporate Popper's principle of the 'falsifiability' of accepted truths. In this early book, Habermas distinguished different kinds of interests human beings have, interests which require their own forms of knowledge. One set of interests is targeted at domination of nature, and another is targeted at human functioning as social-cultural beings. For the first, technical and scientific interests, it is necessary that there is correspondence between ideas and reality (we need to be able to be confident that bridges will be strong enough to carry traffic, aeroplanes can stay up in the sky, etc.). For the other kind of interests, however, the 'practical interest' is in constructing and maintaining intersubjectivity, allowing people to understand each other, enabling them to co-operate, and encouraging them to respond to each other's needs. The knowledge required for the pursuance of this kind of interest is interpretative.

Habermas introduced themes which have remained central to his work, being developed, refined and applied as it has progressed. One prominent theme is the increasing dominance of instrumental rationality over communicative rationality. Habermas characterises the form of rationality which serves the technical interests of humans as 'instrumental rationality' and that which serves the interest of achieving intersubjective understanding as 'communicative rationality'. The result of the dominance of instrumental over communicative rationality is that technical questions are far more prevalent than moral questions; what should be ethical issues are dealt with as though they were technical issues.

One obvious example of this dominance of instrumental over communicative rationality is war. Will it be effective? Will we be able to achieve our objectives? Is there an end-strategy? These are questions far more frequently asked than 'is it morally right?' And we can see the dominance of instrumental rationality in any proposals to introduce new measures to combat threats to safety and reduce risks of crime: 'will it work?' is often the first and only issue raised, with 'is it just?' being asked by very few.

Another theme is the focus on discourse and communication, signalling Habermas's embrace of the 'linguistic turn' in philosophy and the human sciences. Throughout his work, Habermas seeks solutions to his political and ethical questions in interaction through language rather than reflection of reason: it is to structures of language rather than structures of the mind that he looks for the principles of justice.

In *Legitimation Crisis* (1976), Habermas poses the question of how legitimacy is to be secured for the authorities, rules and processes needed to resolve the recurrent crises of modernity. This leads him to investigate the conditions under which a consensus would be valid, and also to incorporate something of Popper's insistence that truth claims should be accessible to testing. Habermas wants to retain a sense of the universality of truth. His questions reflect the concerns of liberals about Utilitarianism and communitarianism: that it should be possible to distinguish valid consensus from simple majoritarianism, and that it should be possible to hold the conventional morality of a particular community to account against principles of morality that have universal validity. As Dews comments, for Habermas, 'it is not the universality of philosophical truth claims which is to be abandoned, but rather their non-fallibilist aspect' (Dews, 1992: 24).

Habermas's answer to the question of what identifies a valid consensus is that consensus is valid if it is arrived at only by 'force of the better argument' rather than any other form of force or domination. This, he argues, is the only condition under which consensus could be a criterion of truth. The issue, then, is to identify conditions of discourse under which one could be confident that the only force to have prevailed is the force of the better argument. Habermas accordingly develops his rules for an *ideal speech situation* which would enable 'the better argument' to prevail. The conditions are that all participants should have an equal chance to speak, to introduce topics, to express attitudes and feelings, to question other participants, to call ideas into question, and to give reasons for or against ideas and proposals.

Such conditions mean that society must be equal and democratic; they mean that 'truth' cannot be separated from 'freedom' and 'justice' (McCarthy, 1976: xvii). The prerequisites for the ideal speech situation are rarely met in actual societies, but the extent of their presence or absence gives an indication of the legitimacy of authority. The less the equality or democracy, the fewer legitimate resources will be available to solve problems faced by modernity.

These ideas on discursive legitimation were revealed in much more fully developed form with publication of the two-volume *Theory of Communicative Action* (1984, 1987). Here, Habermas extends his discussion of undistorted communication to a schema of formal properties of a discourse ethics which will allow rules and procedures to be democratically validated and thus attain legitimacy.

First and foremost, Habermas rejects any dichotomising of truth claims which depend on correspondence to 'real' facts, and truth claims linked to aesthetic or moral reason, which are regarded as expressing opinions. He argues that while correspondence theories of truth cannot readily be extended to moral or aesthetic judgments, such judgments are putting forward truth claims in that they present themselves as statements with which reasonable people would tend to agree; they are intended to convey more than just the view of the speaker. To say that 'murder is wrong' or 'chateau-bottled wine usually tastes nicer than *ordinaire*', is not just to express personal opinion or prejudice; it is not impossible to imagine a rationally founded consensus on such judgments (Outhwaite, 1994: 41). The means of verification or falsification may be different from those employed by the propositional, factual truth claims of instrumental reason, but what Habermas is pointing out is that the categories of 'truth' and 'validity' are invoked in the ethical and evaluative judgments of communicative reason just as they are in those of instrumental reason.

For all types of claims-making statements, their acceptance involves at least four kinds of background condition:

1   that the claim is understandable;
2   that its propositional content is true;
3   that the speaker is sincere in proposing it;
4   that it is proper for the speaker to be making this claim.

In communicative interaction, there needs to be an assumption that the speaker intentionally holds the beliefs she does and follows the rules that she does; there also needs to be an assumption that she can justify them discursively when asked to do so. The truth-finding involved in moral and aesthetic judgments is the determination of whether or not they conform to intuitions, laws, cultural traditions, sincerely held beliefs, experiences and desires of the relevant community. This truth can only be decided discursively, by undominated discourse involving all those affected by the issue in question.

The development of discourse ethics (2): discourse and universality

In *The Theory of Communicative Action* (1984, 1987), Habermas moves beyond establishing his rules for discourse which can justify consensus as a criterion for truth, to putting forward a full-blown discourse ethics. He uses his consensus theory of truth as a model for a theory of justice:

> Justice is nothing material, no determinate value, but a dimension of validity. Just as descriptive norms can be true, in other words express what is the case, so normative sentences can be right and express what we are required to do. (Habermas, 1992b: 249)

Just norms, then, are not defined by qualities such as contributing to the greatest sum of human happiness, but justice is the property which belongs to norms that can achieve rational consensus.

Habermas's discourse ethics involves accepting the conditions of discourse outlined in his earlier work, and also accepting the primacy of communicative over instrumental action. Living in society means engaging in co-operation, providing conditions for co-ordination of actions reflecting shared interests, and agreeing procedures for resolving conflicts between action-plans oriented to individualistic goals. Because intersubjective understanding is the prerequisite for these conditions to be attained, communicative action – action to achieve understanding – is logically as well as ethically prior to instrumental action in modern societies where the conditions of co-operation have to be generated by the members themselves rather than being bequeathed by tradition.

Discourse, as the mode in which communicative action is conducted, yields the criterion for the validity of social rules:

> Only those rules are valid which are, or can be, agreed by all those persons actually or potentially affected by those rules or their side-effects (D).

He then derives a principle of universalization (U) which points beyond the idea of particular norms to more general principles:

> Only those rules or institutions are generalizable that all members of a communication community agree to as representing generalizable interests rather than individualistic claims.

Habermas's principle of universalization is clearly related to those of Rawls and Kant. Like Rawls, he seeks to ensure that universal rules should be in the interests of all members of the community and should not be formed on the basis of self-interest of individuals or groups; like Kant he posits a test of rational generalizability. The principle is also, importantly, different from Kant and Rawls in that it shifts the process of universalization from the individual solitary, reflective reasoner to the community reasoning aloud through discourse:

> The emphasis shifts from what each can will without contradiction to be a universal law to what all can will in agreement to be a universal norm. (McCarthy, 1978: 326)

The core of Kantian universalism is maintained by the centrality of the 'generalizability test' for evaluating substantive rules and norms. Habermas insists that any social norm can be called into question, and that members of society will decide its validity by thinking about its consistency with individuals' intuitive sense of what gives a norm its commanding quality, its 'ought' quality, as White terms it (White, 1988: 38). Habermas says that this is a question of whether the norm being considered incorporates interests that are general throughout society rather than just reflective of the self-interest of the norm proposer or defender. The Kantian examples of promises and contracts serve Habermas as well: one cannot imagine it to be in the interest of all members of society to have a rule that promises mean nothing and contracts can be disregarded without penalty. For Kant, the rule would be logically ungeneralisable because promising would lose meaning and contracts would be worthless and therefore cease to exist; for Habermas, no community could agree the rule because it would never be the case that there would be no members who would not want to give up the certainties and protections of promises and contracts. With Habermas, the test of universalisability shifts from being the Kantian test of *non-contradiction*, to being a test of *communicative agreement* (Benhabib, 1990: 6). Norms and actions are assessed as right or wrong according to whether they accord with rules which promote general interests, whether they can be subsumed under generalizable categories of moral action and conform to general rules and procedures of justice.

This link to generalizability is important for Habermas's distancing from communitarianism. He gives much more attention than Kant does to the social contexts in which people think and act, and his theorisation of the 'lifeworld' is much more developed and central than Rawls's 'thin theory of the good'. Habermas's links to critical theory make him acknowledge fully that participants' communicative competencies are developed within a society; that their moral values and ideas of the good life are formed within a social-cultural context and that these values are brought into discourse with the participants, rather than discarded in the manner of Rawls's original position/ veil of ignorance.

Habermas gives prominence to analysis of the 'life-world' of culture, tradition and social relationships in which the individual is embedded. The theme of the 'colonisation' of this life-world by instrumental reason at the expense of communicative reason which was prominent in his early work is maintained throughout his later phases, and one of his claims for his theory of communicative action is that it is the best framework for understanding the relationships between these forms of reason in the life-world of modernity. Discourse allows the arguments of instrumental and communicative reason to be brought into debate together; discourse can, for example, allow – even require – the discussion of both the practical effectiveness and the ethical dimensions of CCTV, detention of persons with a Severe Personality Disorder, and other risk control strategies.

Allowing for consideration of arguments from different forms of reason and action imperatives, and mandating consideration of the perspectives of all involved or likely to be affected, means that discursive validation will always tend towards possibilities of generalizability. This is because discourse participants must think of all who might be affected, not just those who are making claims in the present. Although norms will be proposed or challenged from within a community, the impetus to generalizability means that they are considered in relation to criteria connected to universalizability. Discourse ethics, therefore, can mediate between the poles of universalism and communitarianism, being more contextually sensitive than the abstract individualism of some forms of liberalism, whilst avoiding the communitarian pitfalls of relativism and the lack of source of critique. Habermas draws on the contextual moral sentiments of actual individuals in actual situations, but shows that communicative, norm-guided action 'has a core which is linked in a conceptually necessary way to certain universal, rational moral standards' (White, 1988: 38).

Habermas's analysis of the life-world does not lead him to propose anything directly comparable to Rawls's list of primary goods. This list, Habermas argues, ties Rawls's theory to a particular variant of the good life (that of modern welfare liberalism), and therefore cannot yield universalist principles of justice. Habermas, like Kant, formulates a procedural theory of justice in which the aspects of good that are relevant aspects of communicative competence, and therefore components of a theory of justice, are only those which are structurally related to the possibility of unconstrained discourse. Political/social structures which endorse *symmetry* (all are to be given equal rights in discourse) and *reciprocity* (all must pay attention to the views and claims of others) are requirements of the ideal speech situation and are therefore universalizable principles of justice. Other elements of the good life are tied to particular communities with their unique traditions and value systems and Habermas argues, like Kant, that justice cannot incorporate these, only provide procedures for adjudication of claims arising from competing ideas of the good life. Discourse ethics, then, differentiates *moral questions* which, under the aspect of universalization or *justice*, can in principle be decided rationally, from *evaluative questions...* which present themselves under their most general aspect as questions of the *good life* and which are accessible to a rational discussion only within the horizon of a historically concrete life form or individual life history. (Habermas, 1982: 251 emphasis in the original)

Although Habermas makes this distinction between principles of justice and conceptions of the good, he nonetheless acknowledges that it is only in certain forms of society that his approach to moral and political questions would have any chance of implementation. He cites modern society 'in its better moments' as providing these preconditions for discourse ethics (Outhwaite, 1994: 57). He also revives the idea of civic republicanism as being the kind of cultural milieu in which discourse ethics would hold sway. In discussing MacIntyre's *After Virtue* (1985), he contrasts the situation of the citizen of alienated phases of modernity with the citizen of the republican metropolis, asking of MacIntyre

Where does he derive his equivalent for what Aristotle could still rely on – I mean the metaphysical pre-eminence of the polis as the model form of life, where human beings, and indeed all human beings who are not barbarians, can realise the telos of a good life? (Habermas, 1992b: 248)

What is necessary for discourse ethics to influence actual rules and institutions, is the existence not just of democratic mechanisms, but also of education and socialisation practices which foster the spirit of republican consciousness and motivate active participation in social affairs – the very opposite of the 'death of the social', the competitive individualism held to characterize late modernity. This cultivation of the republican spirit does not just mean inculcation of an ethos of responsible citizenship, but also respect for the life-worlds of the diversity of groups within the society.

Habermas uses the example of the asylum debate in contemporary Germany to show how lack of these conditions can result in 'democratic will-formation' that is very far from a model of communicative rationality. What he calls the 'second life fiction' of Germany after 1989, 'that we have all become normal again', means, he says, a de-valorisation of the political, industrial and intellectual capital of former East Germany. Rather than a thrust towards liberalisation, this amounts to a 'creative destruction' of the life-world of the east, leading to a defensive hostility in which right-wing violence flourishes (Habermas, 1993).

Assessment and critique

Habermas's work on communicative ethics and discourse is regarded as a significant contribution to political and moral philosophy, and has been described as being as important in the 1980s as Rawls's *Theory of Justice* was in the 1970s (Rasmussen, 1990: 3). Its combination of systematic and detailed analysis of life-worlds of modernity with normative philosophical reflection gives the work both breadth and depth of an impressive, and perhaps somewhat intimidating, scale.

There has, of course, been critique. Much of this concerns the philosophical adequacy of the work, and is not relevant to the questions raised in this book. Some substantive criticisms, however, are extremely relevant and must be reviewed. Habermas has responded to many of his critics, and his more recent works reflect these debates. He has been particularly responsive to criticism of the operability of his theoretical constructs, and to feminist criticisms of the implications of his insistence on a form of Kantian generalizability.

The most frequent doubt raised by sympathetic philosophical critics, however, is of more than technical interest, because it calls into question the validity of the heart of his theory. This is Habermas's assertion of communicative rationality as the core of modernity. Habermas substitutes a theory of language for the theories of mind of earlier philosophies. This mirrors the 'linguistic turn' in the human sciences generally (for example the influence of Saussurean linguistics on structuralist sociology and psychology in the 1960s and 1970s; the language basis of Lacanian psychoanalysis, and of course Wittgenstein's placing of language at the centre of analytic philosophy).

The great advantage of this linguistic base is that it allows Habermas to reconcile the Marxist concern with justice with the post-Nietzschean preoccupation with meaning, thus allowing for a theory of justice that can take account of both autonomy and authenticity (Bernstein, 1995). The difficulty is that Habermas's claims about the communicative basis of modernity, and hence the communicative essence of morality, are made to do a very great deal of work in his theory. Communication, he says, because of its very structure, has as its goal the reaching of intersubjective understanding, and the coordination of individual action plans. The logic of communication is such that there needs to be reciprocity of attention, and is also such that the inexorable pull towards consensus means that claims will be tested against the criterion of generalizability. The consensus-seeking logic of language, Habermas claims, means that discursively agreed norms will transcend particularism, reaching towards universality.

There are several problems with this. Habermas could simply be wrong about the inevitability of communication being oriented to reaching agreement. David Hoy suggests the possibility that Habermas conflates different meanings of 'understanding'. While the word is often used in the sense of 'reaching an understanding', which does imply reaching agreement or at least compromise, it also makes sense to talk of understanding something but not agreeing with, or to, it (Hoy, 1994: 180–8). If reaching agreement is not the inherent logic of communicative action, then Habermas's claims for the derivation of universal moral rules from the properties of discourse are shaken at their foundations.

If Hoy is right, then instrumentality is a part of communicative rationality. Habermas allows a connection between instrumental reason and discourse ethics through his notion of 'strategic action'. This is a form of instrumental reason which enters into discourse and works against the achievement of uncoerced consensus. Strategic action aims to secure domination; that is to say, its goal is to make others act in accordance with the claims of the proponent. The strategic actor is not motivated to modify her claims after hearing the arguments of others. At many points in his argument, Habermas presents strategic action as an impediment to discursive consensus-building, and so one of the goals of discourse is to bring about change from strategic to communicative orientation. This cannot always be achieved, and Habermas does allow for compromise to be reached rather than consensus. He lays down conditions for compromise, however, which involve at least some motivation towards co-operation.[4] Elsewhere, Habermas suggests a role for strategic action in securing enforcement of discursively validated norms, for example, punitive sanctions securing compliance with criminal law.

For penologists, the objection that Habermas's idea of the communicative basis of modernity is made to do too much work, may bring to mind David Garland's caveat on the influence of Foucault on theorising about punishment. Garland argues that since the publication of *Discipline and Punish* (Foucault, 1977), punishment has been seen solely in terms of power. An analysis from the point of view of power has been taken by many to indicate that power is the only point of view from which punishment should be analysed. Looking at something from the point of view of power is not, however, the same as saying that power is the only thing that should be looked at (Garland, 1990: Chapter 7). Similarly, describing modernity from the point of view of communication is illuminating, but this is not the same thing as proposing that communicative rationality is the fundamental core of modernity. Habermas with communication, like Foucault with power, oscillates between using communicative rationality as an explanatory device and positing it as the essence of modernity, the thing to be explained.

It is the Kantian aspects of his thought that have provoked the strongest critique from feminists and from others who are sympathetic to his project of re-affirming Enlightenment ideals, and who share his goal of navigating a path between universalism and communitarianism. These criticisms centre on the formalism of his procedural ethics, and on his invocation of a general rather than a concrete other, both in his accounts of democratic will-formation and of universalism deriving from the generalizability of interests.

One of the most common objections to Habermas's discourse ethics is that it is empty because of its formal proceduralism. That is to say, like Kant's proceduralist principles of justice, it provides only procedures for deciding the justice of social norms, but no guide for actual practical actions or for the substantive content of norms. It is also empty because, like Rawls, it is an 'ideal theory'; discursive validation occurs in an 'ideal speech situation' which, like Rawls's 'original position', could never exist in an actual society. Furthermore, Habermas's theory could be charged with confusing description with principle: it describes what a just society would be like, rather than proposing principles which could bring a just society into being.

The preceding chapter introduced the idea of the *concrete other*, proposed by Benhabib and also adopted by Young as the subject at the centre of their own model of discursive ethics. In her rigorous critique of Habermas's theory of discourse ethics, Benhabib (1986) focuses on both the emptiness and the generalisability requirement, which she sees as inextricably intertwined.

Habermas claims that discursive validation of norms under conditions of undistorted communication will identify people's 'real' interests, and also those interests which are generally held in common and are therefore 'generalizable'. He does not make very clear what he has in mind when he refers to 'generalisable interests'. His desire to avoid tying his theory to a particular community's values precludes him from giving a Rawls-style list, so he describes them in rather vague terms as 'needs which can be communicatively shared'. Pettit (1982: 225) suggests that these include the traditional 'negative freedoms' of liberalism such as freedom from arbitrary arrest, and also 'society-regarding' interests such as desire for a peaceful and cohesive society. These, Pettit explains, are interests which are not competitive: one person's pursuit of them would not interfere with anyone else's pursuit of them and they are therefore compatible with the 'equal freedom' maxim. Security, as conceived in liberal theory, would obviously be a generalizable interest.

The point for Benhabib is that Habermas contrasts these interests with 'particular desires and private satisfactions or interests'. This means that just as much as Kant, Habermas's theory of justice necessitates abstracting everything that is individual, different and concrete, and adopting the voice of the generalised other to articulate 'real' interests rather than responding to needs and claims as directly expressed by the concrete other. Generalizability, according to this argument, inhibits Habermas from completing the move from the monovocal logic of Kant's solitary reasoner to the plurivocal 'real discourse' that Habermas wants to install at the centre of his theory of justice. Generalizability also inhibits him from moving from the negative freedoms of liberalism to the richer model of autonomy that feminist theory and republican theory envisage.

Benhabib argues that Habermas's use of Mead's psychology of the generalised other leads him to assume that the rational individual can recognise and anticipate the real interests of others, so that the just society is one with a system of rights and entitlements that protect those interests which the rational 'I' can identify with. Habermas compounds his incorporation of Mead's standpoint of the generalised other – who must be identical to me because 'I' am part of the generalised other for the 'Other' – by utilising Kohlberg's cognitive psychology which also sees the abstract discussion of rights and entitlements as the most mature stage of moral development. This means that what Habermas excludes is responsiveness to the need interpretations of actual others and solidarity with, rather than repression of, their uniqueness and difference. The standpoint of the generalized other and a politics of rights and entitlements is, of course, exactly the philosophy of liberalism, so by failing adequately to develop the themes of needs interpretation and solidarity, Habermas fails to achieve the significant move forward from traditional liberalism that he seeks.

Benhabib supports Habermas's commitment to discourse ethics, and to the possibility of universalist values which are worth defending and extending, and which can provide critique of communitarian values. She proposes replacement of the standpoint of the generalised other with that of the concrete other, a standpoint which requires participants in discourse to

> view each and every rational being as an individual with a concrete history, identity, and affective-emotional constitution. Our relation to the other is governed by the norm of *complementary reciprocity*: each is entitled to assume from the other forms of behaviour through which the other feels recognized and confirmed as a concrete individual with specific needs, talents and capacities. The norms of our interaction are ... the norms of solidarity, friendship, love and care. (Benhabib, 1986: 341)

Other feminists have also criticised Habermas's rejection of particular individual needs and desires from the domain of justice, objecting that this division of 'generalisable' and 'individual' rests on the public/private distinction that has been so vigorously contested by almost all contemporary feminists (Fraser, 1989). As well as pointing out this dependence on the idea of a private sphere, they argue that Habermas's model of the public sphere remains that of masculinist liberalism: the worldly domain of the male (Fraser, 1989, 1995a). This masculinist error is confirmed by the way in which at many points in his work Habermas describes the rationalisation of life-worlds in terms of the 'erosion' of traditional forms of community and family life.

Other critical themes proposed by feminists centre on Habermas's focus on identity construction through language-mediated interaction, which, they say, cannot capture other important aspects of gender identity formation (Meehan, 1995).

Habermas's theoretical construction is built up from masculinist building blocks. The rationalism of Kant and the subsequent western tradition which identifies 'reason' as a quality which is associated with the male; the cognitive moral psychology of Kohlberg which is entirely based on studies of males; the emphasis given to problems of reification, alienation and exploitation derived from Marxist theories of production demonstrate the masculinism at the heart of his framework. While Habermas claims to displace subject-centred reason by language and displace production by communication as the bases of his theory, he takes over the masculinist conceptual constructions of these older theoretical traditions both in suggesting the problems to be confronted by modernity and specifying the values to be defended by re-affirming modernity.

Law and democracy: Habermas's recent work

An important new body of work appeared in the 1990s, which applies Habermas's communicative theory to the legitimacy of law, and to questions of justice and democracy raised by the disintegration of states and emergence of new national identities in the wake of the defeat of Eastern bloc communism as well as by migration, and the deepening and widening of the European Union. Although he maintains the formulation of principles and procedures of justice elaborated in *The Theory of Communicative Action*, Habermas has more to say about rights, and he has also addressed some of the criticisms made by feminist theorists.

The most influential book of this later period, *Between Facts and Norms* (1996a), was published in German in 1992. This book is part sociology of law, part debates with legal philosophy, and part contribution to democratic theory. The book's question is, 'What grants legitimacy to law?' This question parallels Habermas's earlier questions, 'What grants truth to statements?' and 'What grants rightness to norms?', and of course the answer to the new question is the same: validation through discourse. Again paralleling the structure of his earlier investigation into the necessary relation between truth and justice, he seeks to demonstrate a similar internal connection between the rule of law and democracy:

> The argument developed in *Factizität und Geltung* [Between Facts and Norms] essentially aims to demonstrate that there is a conceptual or internal relation, and not simply a historically contingent association, between the rule of law and democracy. (Habermas, 1996b: 137)

In posing the question of the legitimacy of law, Habermas makes two sociological assumptions. The first, with Durkheim, is that in a modern secular society law is the most authoritative institution for achieving social integration; the second, against Weber, is that law requires something external to itself in order to achieve legitimacy.[5]

Functionally, Habermas sees law as performing the key task of social integration. By 'social integration' he means regulation of systems within society as well as reconciling the different cultural values of individuals and groups. Integration in a factual situation of complexity means ensuring that the systems steered by money and power remain within the normative framework of society; it also means ensuring that this normative framework is capable of enabling individuals to pursue their own, probably very different, goals. Concretely, this means that law should have enforceable rules to secure individuals' compliance with the principle of equal freedom (laws against violation of persons and property), and also enforceable rules which ensure that companies and official organisations conduct their operations in accordance with the moral rules of the society.

Analytically, Habermas sees his task as mediating between a sociology of law which reduces it to power, and a philosophy of law which sees it only in terms of abstract reflections on what law 'ought' to be. Sociological 'disenchantment' with law loses sight of its potential for advancing societies towards justice; the rational reconstructions of law in legal philosophy 'lose touch with the reality of contemporary societies and thus have difficulties in identifying the conditions necessary for the realisation of these principles' (Habermas, 1996a: 43).

Habermas develops a social theory of law, which rests on its location between the 'fact' of social complexity and the 'norm' of justice. Law must at the same time be both a system of rules that can be coercively enforced and a system with a basis in justice that will enable those affected to grant it legitimacy by giving it their rationally willed consent. In traditional societies facticity and normativity were fused, but in secular, pluralist societies a different form of authority is needed to link these domains. If the integrating force is not traditional authority, then it can only be domination by power which disregards normative legitimation (a military dictatorship, for example) or a rule of law normatively legitimated by democratic will.

Habermas argues that the principles that rational citizens will adopt and the procedures by which they will adopt them are inseparable. As in his earlier work, Habermas adopts the Kantian framework for establishment of the basic rights that law must both embody and enforce. Kant's criterion of legitimacy is based on what is often translated as a 'principle of right', a principle which encapsulates the conditions under which it is morally permissible to universalise coercible limits on the behaviour of individuals in pursuing their own ends. He expresses this principle of right, his 'moral conception of the law', *as the sum of those conditions under which the free choice of one person can be conjoined with the free choice of another in accordance with a universal law of freedom.*

Habermas in no way disputes this principle, but he argues that Kant misses the aspect of law which is social reality. Kant, he states, specifies what law would be in order to be just, but fails to consider the way the social reality of law shapes people's actions, their ideas and experiences of what is just. Kant's formulation captures the normative aspect of law, which is its rooting in a universalizable freedom that gives it its claim to legitimacy; but he misses its facticity, the social context in which its coercive aspect will be deployed and in which its claims to legitimacy will be tested. Communicative action theory situates the idealising character of validity claims in concrete social contexts, and therefore a discourse theory of law reflects this facticity–normativity duality of law (Rehg, 1996: xvii).

In formulating his discourse theory of law, Habermas elaborates a system of rights that are necessary to institutionalise the discursive process by which valid laws can be established. These rights will ensure that their application will be in accordance with the 'equal freedom' principle. Rights, for Habermas, are neither properties of individuals as in natural law versions of liberalism, nor articulations of the shared values of communities as in communitarianism, but they are elements of a legal order based on equality and popular sovereignty. The rights Habermas specifies are the rights that 'citizens must confer on each other if they want to legitimately regulate their interactions and life contexts by means of positive law' (1996a: 122). He lists five kinds of basic rights. These are:

1 rights to the greatest possible measure of equal individual liberties;
2 rights associated with membership status;
3 legal 'due process' rights;
4 rights to equal participation in democratic process

He supplements these categories with a fifth category of welfare rights to ensure that the four primary kinds of rights can be effectively and equally utilised (ibid.: 122–3).

Having specified the normative content, the discursive conditions for the possibility of legitimate law, Habermas moves on to analysis of the facticity of law – the institutional apparatus necessary for legislation and implementation. Here, he demonstrates that just as the normative content of law can only be derived and tested in actual social contexts, so the reality of law can only be legitimated normatively.

In the course of developing his arguments about the necessity for democratic process and strict regard for constitutionality, Habermas takes issue with Dworkin's (1986b) theory of the 'Herculean' adjudicator who looks only to law for solutions to difficult cases and pays too little regard to social context, and with Luhmann's systems theory which depicts law as a closed system, completely self-referential ('autopoetic') obeying its own systems imperatives without reference to external discourses (Luhmann, 1985).[6]

Habermas's analysis of the social reality in which law acts moves from looking at law as an institution to looking at the operation of democratic power. Here, too, discursive legitimacy is the alternative to domination. He looks beyond central state power to a 'peripheral' network of associations in which questions can be raised and public opinion formed. Habermas calls for a radical 'deliberative politics' (1996a: Chapter 7) in which citizens' rights to participation are exercised across a range of state representational institutions, community and voluntary associations, campaign groups and social movements.[7] What he puts forward is a 'two-track' model of state and public sphere (Bohman, 1994: 926). This model gives more emphasis to civil society and social movements than existing representational democracy does, but

Habermas also confirms the importance of the high tiers of constitutional democracies (the legislature, the supreme court).

Bringing together his sections on law and on the institutions of political power and public opinion formation, Habermas reaffirms 'rights' and 'popular sovereignty' as the key terms for legitimacy of law. They demonstrate, he says, the necessary and internal relationship between democracy and the rule of law. Law and democratic politics are the systems which co-ordinate individuals' strategic action plans by making them accountable in terms of communicative rationality. Further, both law and democratic politics carry out the task of bringing money and power under regulation by norms mandated by discursive agreement. As in his earlier works, Habermas uses discourse both as an explanation (he gives a proceduralist account of law and politics) and as the fundamental principle of justice (he urges a discourse ethics to ground law and politics).

Does *Between Facts and Norms* meet earlier critiques of Habermas's discourse theory?

In the section on deliberative politics, Habermas pays attention to feminist critiques of his earlier works on the public sphere. He summarises both feminist arguments against the rigid public/private divide and liberal defences against further 'intrusions' of the state into the private realm. Habermas suggests that his discourse theory resolves the problem between them. Using the example of domestic violence, Habermas concedes the feminist argument that such matters have been inaccessible to remedy and have remained out of the spotlight of public censure for too long, but points out that his rules of discourse prescribe that anything may be brought forward, so opening a space for feminists to introduce this and similar topics. To reassure those worried about inroads into privacy, however, he argues that access to discourse is a different matter from the mode of regulation of any of the matters discussed. 'But not everything reserved to the decisions of private persons is withdrawn from public thematisation and protected from criticism'; not everything debated in public is removed from private regulation (Habermas, 1996a: 313). Further, Habermas acknowledges that the dividing line between public and private spheres cannot be drawn once and for all, and suggests that 'boundary disputes' (and he adds pornography and childcare as examples) usually arise as contested needs interpretations in the peripheral networks of opinion formation, gradually becoming acknowledged as recognised interest positions that can be put on to the formal political agenda: it is at this point that change in the manner and locus of regulation can be discussed.

Although he acknowledges feminist claims, Habermas expands his discussion rather than changes his position. While he allows for the public/private divide to change, he nonetheless assumes its continuance. He persists in the language of unreconstructed liberalism, saying that thematisation of private-sphere activities in discourse does not imply any *encroachment* on existing rights and freedoms; that to talk about something is not necessarily the same as *meddling in another's affairs* and confirming that 'Certainly the intimate sphere must be protected from intrusive fears and the critical eyes of strangers' (ibid.: 313, emphasis added).

The final chapter of the book considers different paradigms of law, and here Habermas moves closer to feminist positions (ibid.: Chapter 9). He appears to endorse Iris Young's (1990) critique of both liberal-market and welfare paradigms of law in that they both conceive of 'rights' as possessions to be distributed. He quotes her objection to the dominance of the 'distributive paradigm', and her insistence that rights are relationships and not things. Habermas endorses Young's view that rights are to do with freedom and dignity; they are to guard against forms of subordination, discrimination, and violations of freedom and dignity that restrict people's exercise of their public and private autonomy.

Habermas summarises the radical feminist critique of social-welfare and liberal politics of equality, the core of which is that because these follow existing interpretations of needs and rights, they reinforce gender stereotypes. Regulations and entitlements become part of the problem they are intended to solve. The liberal-market paradigm ignores inequalities; the social-welfare paradigm freezes them in by regarding them as something to be compensated. Habermas cautions against feminists rejecting the idea of rights *per se*; the error, he argues, is to construct rights in these paradigms of law, not the idea of rights in itself. A discursive approach, however, means that public discussions must be held which enable men and women affected by constraints and inequalities to articulate for themselves the ways in which their opportunities to take advantages of individual and public liberties are restricted. He commends Martha Minow's (1990) concept of rights as relationships, which he says are to be negotiated within a community committed to discursive problem-solving.

He also argues that needs, gender roles and identities must be argued discursively rather than interpreted by judges, officials or legislators, conceding Fraser's points that only participants themselves can decide what is of concern to them and that needs interpretation is a matter of contest and 'struggle' (Fraser, 1992: 129; 1989: 161–90). His proceduralist framework of law can never establish new universal understandings of the 'identity of the sexes in a just society', he says, but he claims it can allow for the correction of injustices that are identified through discursive participation of those affected. Attention to gender inequalities is facilitated along with challenges to other inequalities in discursive ethics because:

> it is the privileged agent who is confronted with the choice of either demonstrating to what degree his inequality can be discursively justified

or relying on coercion to defend that inequality...a choice that renounces the claim to moral legitimacy... (White, 1988: 77)

Benhabib's preference for the 'concrete' rather than the 'generalised' other brings the question of consideration of needs together with the question of the uniqueness of the individual 'other'. Habermas discusses her critique, and also the absence of an 'ethic of care' along the lines proposed by Gilligan, taking these objections alongside the criticism that his proceduralist theory of justice provides no guide to action in concrete cases (Habermas, 1992b: 250–2; Benhabib, 1987, 1990).

Habermas's answer to these points is that the formal principles of his theory are concerned with the *grounding* of norms, and that different principles apply to the *application* of norms in individual cases. Discursive processes which rely on generalizability criteria establish that norms are valid and enable the introduction of valid norms, but discourses of application 'concern not the norm's validity but its *appropriate reference to a situation*' (Habermas, 1996b: 217, emphasis in the original). Discourses of application (the adjudication of actual cases) he explains, must take account of the fullest range of features of the case and its context. At the level of application, needs as well as rights are relevant, uniqueness as well as generality is in focus. Habermas adopts Klaus Gunther's 'principle of appropriateness' as the core concept in discourses of application (Gunther, 1993). Habermas claims that once the complementarity of grounding and application is fully appreciated, it becomes clear how discourse ethics does justice to the concerns of Gilligan and Benhabib (Habermas, 1992b: 251).

This explanation of the place of needs in his scheme represents some advance on his previous response. Habermas had previously responded to criticism of the emptiness of his discourse ethics, of its lack of consideration of the good as well as the just and its inattention to the concrete other, by defending his use of Kohlberg's notion (drawn largely from Mead) of the 'ideal' other. This construction, Habermas argues, combines the principle of benevolence with the principle of justice through the principle of equal respect. Kohlberg's theory, Habermas argues, maintains the Kantian insistence that principles of rights and justice cannot be sacrificed to questions of utility, but he says that as Kohlberg describes it, the idea of equal respect means that discursive agreement of norms must consider the consequences of the norms for those concerned: in other words people's well-being cannot be excluded from concern (Habermas, 1990: 42–3). This formulation of the ideal other, however, still leaves interpretation of consequences with the decider/judge; there is no insistence on interpretation of consequences and needs resting with the 'other' who will be affected.

A further problem remains, moreover, with Habermas's separation of discourses of grounding and application. What this does is to leave questions of needs in the secondary sphere of application, and also to confine the concrete other within the same sphere. This gives rights primacy over needs, and leaves the construct of the generalised other untouched as the source of normative validation. Generalizability still holds sway over concreteness.

Although Habermas's position as elaborated in *Between Facts and Norms* and other recent works does not fully meet the objections raised by Benhabib, Fraser and other feminist theorists to his earlier formulations, it must be granted that Habermas has been at some pains to point out that his discourse ethics is compatible with feminist perspectives in legal and political theory. We can see why his theory has aroused much interest among feminists (Johnson, 2001; Meehan, 1995) and why the basic framework of discourse ethics has been taken up by Benhabib and Young. Habermas has not addressed the questions of identity construction in other than a cursory fashion, but these are not his questions and it is unreasonable to expect any one theorist to address all possibly relevant questions.

Other recent works continue to look at deliberative democracy and the grounding of morality, and in these Habermas maintains his prioritisation of the universal over the particular, and rights over needs (Habermas, 1998). Johanna Meehan (2000) quotes Habermas's views on rights versus tradition in the case of migrant workers. Habermas says that the rights of, for example, young Turkish women must be enforced against the will of fathers who appeal to the privileges of their culture, and that generally, individual rights must be enforced against collective claims springing from fundamentalist or nationalistic self-understanding (Habermas, 1996d).[8] Meehan comments that:

> Habermas's clear stance against any toleration of human rights violations seems right and admirable but I am left to wonder about that Turkish girl and her father, and about the tragedy that state intervention in that relation may wreak. Will the father be jailed, the mother left destitute with children she cannot feed, angry and alienated from a daughter still very emotionally attached to her? Does the girl have the resources, economic, psychic and otherwise, to make use of the autonomy which is being protected? Will she be made happier by the increased autonomy thrust upon her? (Meehan, 2000: 47–48)

This passage calls to mind the section on feminist legal essentialism in the preceding chapter. Perhaps Habermas occupies a position in relation to universalism based on western liberalism similar to that which Harris ascribes to MacKinnon, that at best Habermas's view is 'nuanced' by gender and cultural difference just as MacKinnon's view of gender is described as being at best 'nuanced' by race. Meehan's comments raise the possibility that the girl might identify herself as Turkish-and-female, rather than having a 'true' identity in which Turkish is a secondary adjective qualifying the primary noun 'female'. Perhaps her cultural tradition is as important to her as her claim to share in the rights accorded to German women.

What is most revealing in Habermas's quoted statement is that the question of the appropriate norm is decided in advance, for all cases. This shows first of all, the taken-for-grantedness of his prioritisation of the values of western liberalism, and secondly, it calls into question his commitment to the openness of discourses of application. Either he cannot imagine a free and equal society agreeing on a right to cultural identity (such as proposed by Kymlicka) as a basic right, and as such to be balanced on the same scale as the individualistic rights of western liberalism, or else discourses of application do not have the capacity to take into account all considerations and consequently suspend certain norms in particular cases.

Benhabib is not suggesting that the concrete other should be the discursive subject only at the level of discourses of applicability, but that she should be the discursive subject *in toto*. To this end, Benhabib proposes that the principle of universalization (U) in Habermas's scheme be abandoned, and that the discourse principle (D) be the sole principle for validation of norms. This demonstrates that she sees the concrete other as the subjectivity for grounding as well as for applying norms. Habermas says that justice and solidarity are two sides of the same coin (1992b: 252). For Benhabib, as for other 'difference feminists', it is rather that autonomy and solidarity are two faces of the coin of justice.

Legitimacy and the risk society

Habermas ends his discussion of paradigms of law in *Between Facts and Norms* with a section on *crisis theories* (1996a: 427–46). He depicts 'crisis theory' as positing that the constitutional state has become overwhelmed by the burden of demands placed upon it. Possibilities of democratic control are weakened by the complexity as well as the quantity of tasks with which governance is burdened, so that dependence on experts and technocrats reduces the capability for democratic regulation and oversight. Standards of instrumental effectiveness become the only standards by which policies are judged. Such standards may be proper for evaluating the exercise of devolved administrative power, but they displace standards of normative legitimacy which are proper for deciding whether the policies should be introduced, and for ensuring that their operation complies with legal standards and moral values.

Habermas gives only a brief sketch of this crisis in the constitutional state, but in doing so he echoes many of the themes of risk society and governmentality perspectives. For example, he says that the tasks of government are pursued in the context of modernity's development to a stage where it needs but at the same time distrusts expertise, and in which the state itself has lost its formerly 'sacred' status. The state's capability to deal with its foundational task of preventing disorder is doubted and diminished, according to the crisis paradigm, while at the same time ever more new problems arise because of risks associated with science and technology (and, we would now add, because of the need to prevent terrorism).

169

These demands mean that the state is empowered and armed to the point that the *constitutional state* gives way to the *security state*. Protecting rights and liberties in such a state is problematic, and individual legal protection is 'dissolved'. The security state represents a 'transformation of the boundary conditions of constitutional freedom that occurs when a society produces so many security risks that it is able to protect institutional values only by consistently expanding the surveillance apparatus' (ibid.: 433).

Not only does the legislature become more marginalized by the growth of the administrative power of its own executive branches (the police, immigration controls, security services, etc.), but it also must co-operate with organisations and corporations which are beyond legal regulation and are undisturbed by lack of democratic authorisation. The exercise of power, on this account, is unchecked, and in Habermas's own terms, power is exercised only in terms of instrumental reason. Problems are only posed instrumentally (will it work?), and not legally (is it constitutional?), or ethically (is it just?).

Habermas disputes the inevitability of loss of legitimacy and erosion of individual rights described by the crisis paradigm. He argues that if new forms of exercising power in response to risk dissolve the bonds between politics and the realisation of rights, then new forms of democratic regulation must be found. Choices between competing rights (safety versus privacy, for example) must be made, and between competing goals (maximum security or maximum freedom, for example); demands for evaluation of strategies and policies in normative terms still arise: new discursive formations must be formed in order to meet these needs. As Habermas puts it, 'procedural law must be enlisted to build a *legitimation filter* into the decisional processes of an administration still pointed as much as ever towards efficiency' (ibid.: 440 emphasis in the orginal).

No developed framework is presented for this new normative evaluation. Habermas mentions hearings, ombudsmen, quasi-judicial procedures, judicial review – he calls for imagination and experimentation. The point he is making is that risk society cannot give up on the protection of rights and liberties or on guarding the democratic legitimacy and normative validity of the exercise of power. In the security society the gulf between facts and norms, the reality of social complexity and liberal ideals of justice, may be such as to require new forms of regulation and new forums of democratic legitimation. The security state may invent new forms of regulation and legitimation, but it must not be allowed to become extra-constitutional and it must not let efficiency and effectiveness in risk elimination be the only standards that matter.

Habermas's argument with post-structuralism

Most books about theories of punishment contain at least one chapter on Foucault, but not one on Habermas (for example Garland, 1990; Howe, 1994;

Hudson, 1996). This book contains a chapter on Habermas, but not one on Foucault. At its simplest, the reason for this is that Habermas writes about justice without saying much about punishment; Foucault writes about punishment without saying much about justice. What they have in common is that they both place the totalitarian propensities of modernity at the centre of their analyses.

Foucault gives us a method and a vocabulary with which to analyse the workings of power; he encourages us to look at the motives of power and to be wary of 'reforms' and 'benign' technologies which are not always (or not often) what they are represented as being. Foucault's influence is very much present in the chapter on risk in this book. What Foucault does not do, however, is give us any criteria by which to guard against the transformation of the liberal welfare state into the neo-conservative security state. Habermas does not present such a vivid depiction of the workings of power; the section on 'risk society' in *Between Facts and Norms* is sketchy and derivative. The concentration on the state and 'administrative power' scarcely reflects the diversity of security provision, and still less does it reflect the growth of security not just as a technology of power but as a commodity to be bought and sold in the market place (Zedner, 2000: 208–9). On the other hand, Habermas does propose a way of evaluating new moves, by subjecting them to discourse and exposing them to the 'force of the better argument'.

While Foucault offers more descriptive richness, his analysis of punishment in terms of power has been criticized as overly functionalist, concentrating only on the instrumental aspects of punishment (Garland, 1990: Chapter 7; Hudson, 1996: Chapter 7). Habermas, while not having much to offer on empirical description of punishment, does attend to the normative element of the security state and the rule of law, and argues powerfully 'against the degeneration of criminal justice into a state instrument of crime control in which its power-critical dimension is ignored' (Van Swaaningen, 1997: 207). By different routes, both Foucault and Habermas lead towards what the philosopher Ricoeur has called a 'hermeneutics of suspicion', that structures of governance are, at the outset, to be regarded as structures of power and domination (White, 1988: 77).

Foucault and Habermas have different projects concerning reason. Foucault is interested in the *historicity* of reason; Habermas is interested in the *theory* of reason (Hoy, 1994: 146). Habermas sees Foucault, Derrida, Lyotard and other contemporary post-structuralists primarily as followers of Nietzsche who reject Enlightenment belief in the emancipatory potential of reason. He subjects this anti-rational tendency to stern critique in his volume of essays *The Philosophical Discourse of Modernity* (1987). Two of the twelve essays are about Foucault. According to Habermas, Foucault's characterization of the human sciences in his works on madness, punishment and sexuality depicts them and the asylums and prisons of the normalising regime as the monuments to victory of a regulatory reason that no longer subjugates only madness, but also the needs and desires of the individual organism as well as the social body of an entire population. A *gaze* that objectifies and examines, that takes things apart analytically, that monitors and punctuates everything, gains a power that is structurally formative for these institutions. It is the gaze of the rational subject who has lost all merely intuitive bonds with his environment and torn down all the bridges built up of intersubjective agreement, and for whom in his monological isolation, other subjects are only accessible as the objects of nonparticipant observation. (Habermas, 1987: 245)

Habermas sees modernity as an 'unfinished project' (1996c), and casts Foucault, Derrida and the other post-structuralists as abandoning the Enlightenment ideals of freedom and autonomy to a new age of irrationality and conservatism. They all share the goal of displacing Kantian subject-centred reason, but while Habermas seeks to replace this with a reconstructed communicative reason, he charges the post-structuralists with taking subject-centred reason as 'the whole of reason'. While he concurs in seeing subject-centred reason as concerned with dominating an objectified world (including the world of other humans as well as the natural world), Habermas believes that what needs to happen is for this instrumental reason to be subordinated to communicative reason.

Derrida, Lyotard and Foucault, however, do not focus on different forms of reason, but on the boundary between reason and non-reason, between reason and its Other. Post-structuralists draw an opposite conclusion from the logic of language to that of Habermas. Habermas sees the telos, the goal of language as reaching intersubjective understanding and consensus (Dallmyr, 1996: 84). Derrida, Lyotard and Foucault, however, see the telos of language as domination and exclusion. What is excluded by definitions of sanity, legality, respectability and normality – and above all by definitions of reason – is what is to be uncovered by post-structuralist analysis. For Derrida, the attempt to fix meaning in universal concepts and by representing the world through linguistic clarity is a violent metaphysical project. For Lyotard, the emphasis on consensus betokens a similar violent exclusion of those who do not share the consensus; it means exclusion of those who challenge the majority view of the 'better argument'.

The post-structuralist case (drawn on by Butler and Cornell in their arguments discussed in the preceding chapter) is that people must be able to fit the dominant construction of rationality to gain admittance to the counsels of reason. This coercion into meeting the requirements of the rational subject is present in Habermas's format of discursive proceduralism just as much as in earlier formulations of liberal political theory – we have only to recall his rules of discourse, and his conditions for compromise. This is why, post-structuralists argue, the pluralism of modernity, even the modernity of the Habermasian imaginary, can only ever be partial. Modernity relies crucially on drawing distinctions between reason and unreason, and erecting barriers to keep unreason out.

Habermas rejects post-structuralism precisely because it rests on an appeal to the Other of reason. He is quite correct to characterize post-structuralism in this way (Coole, 1996: 221). Reading Habermas, Derrida and Lyotard, how-ever, it is clear that Habermas and the post-structuralists have very different imaginings of the Other. Habermas is, as Coole perceptively remarks, unable to attribute any emancipatory potential to Otherness. Indeed, his work is haunted by the figure of the Nazi (and now the neo-Nazi), and he fears the ever-present danger of the defeat of reason by prejudice, which is exactly the way in which the earlier Frankfurt School writers interpreted the rise of Fascism in 1930s Germany. Habermas's essays on the asylum debate, new con-servatism, fundamentalism and the plight of the young Turkish woman, all reveal his categorisation of alterity, Otherness, as dangerous and destructive.

The shadowy figure of alterity in Derrida and Lyotard, on the other hand, is not so much the irrational, the enemy of reason, as someone who has been denied reason. This denial is conjured up by the need for reason to have an opposite by which it can be defined; this need is imposed by the logic of lan-guage. The slave, the colonial subject, the racially different, the woman, the child, the insane, all the oppressed and excluded, are prefigured in the open-ness to alterity urged by the post-structuralists.

Lyotard and Derrida do not deny the importance of an ideal of justice. They do, however, deny the possibility of Enlightenment, or any alternative, dis-course, providing objective, universal, philosophically grounded criteria by which all theories and practices of justice could be judged. If no external, uni-versal standard of justice or indeed reason can be derived, then all that can be done is interrogation – deconstruction – of one's own linguistically and politically constructed ideas and practices. By examining what is included and what is excluded, what is preferred and what is dominated, through deconstruction of meanings, present injustices can be made visible and become accessible to amelioration.

Much of the schism between Habermas and the post-structuralists – Habermas's (1987, 1996c) fierce critiques; Lyotard's (1984) defence of postmodernism and Derrida's work on justice and on difference (1990, 1978) – reflect divergent perspectives on reason and their opposite envisioning of difference. As well as different ideas on the structure of language, their dis-pute reflects different ideas about the primary functions of language: in Habermas's case, to co-ordinate action; for the postmodernists, to disclose the world. Behind these differences lie two fundamentally divergent ethical orien-tations, involving two distinctive senses of responsibility. For Habermas, the human's prime responsibility is to act in the world in a normatively justified manner; for the postmodernists, primacy is given to the responsibility to be responsive to otherness (Passerin d'Entreves, 1996: 2).

Conclusion: Habermas and criminal justice

Habermas has had little to say about criminal justice. Even in *Between Facts and Norms* he made little differentiation between criminal law and other kinds of law. Nevertheless, readers should by now readily appreciate why Habermas is positioned in this book as a resource for building a criminal justice system that can respond more justly to perceived risks and threats.

Occasionally, it is possible to see something like Habermas's 'practical discourse' at work. In the recent downgrading of cannabis so that the presumption of law is that users will not be arrested and charged but cautioned, with only suppliers likely to be prosecuted, there has been a sense that criminal law enforcement was becoming too distant from social opinion; similar trends are evident in debates about decriminalising the assisting of suicide in 'mercy killing' cases. Yet we can find plenty of examples of laws being introduced or penalties strengthened in response to irrational media-led campaigns based on fear and vengeance. The conducting of politics as a continual election campaign, forever mindful of the reactions of the tabloid press and constantly watchful of opinion polls, brings to mind Habermas's reference to a speech by philosopher Michael Frank, who said that 'the dominant conception of democracy finds expression in the requirement that politics should bow to pressure from the streets' (Habermas, 1993: 59).

Attention to the principles of discourse ethics would lead to a much more rational debate if the necessary policy preparation, in the sense of more information being given and more efforts being made to ensure that those likely to be affected – which would include offenders and those designated as 'at risk' of offending as well as victims and community representatives – were included in debates. Education, community regeneration and reduction of social inequalities would be necessary to bring about anything approaching the 'ideal speech situation' required for rational discursive will-formation.

It seems probable that Habermas would see criminal justice as concerned with application rather than grounding of norms, and perhaps as an area where instrumental rationality rather than communicative rationality would be appropriate. Nevertheless, Habermas's insistence that actions guided by instrumental reason – and punishments oriented to deterrence or incapacitation fit here – should always be accountable to communicative rationality, means that criminal justice strategies should always be able to be defended discursively against criteria of generalizability. This would imply that penal strategies and actual judgments would have to be compatible with higher-order discursively validated ideals such as justice and fairness, safeguards against punishing the innocent, etc. Habermas's description of the operation of discourses of application – that they should consider all aspects of a case, the individual as well as the general, – would also have implications for punishments. It is difficult to see how 'actuarial justice' or the use of mandatory sentences would fit with these requirements.

174

Peter Bal (1996) has also considered the implications of Habermas's discourse ethics for criminal justice. He emphasizes Habermas's two substantive moral principles, justice and solidarity. Justice, he says, stands for equal respect and equal rights for all; solidarity for empathy and care for the well-being of our fellow human beings (Bal, 1996: 74). Bal argues that human rights should be the anchoring point for practical discourses on criminal justice, and that Habermas's principles of justice suggest that due process rights and the right of offenders to be treated as human beings rather than objects in instrumentally strategic processes should be secured in criminal justice systems. He cites de Haan, whose model of criminal justice as claiming redress incorporates Habermas's discursive principle (de Haan, 1990). Bal and de Haan both urge equal participation of all parties, and claim that all perspectives (victim, offender, community) should be included in discourse.

Habermas is important, then, for his reaffirmation of the liberal ideals of rights and equal respect and equal liberty, and for his proposals of a communicative ethics that makes these ideals more defensible in the light of the critiques of traditional theories of justice considered in Part I. Theories and developments in the practice of restorative justice, which take criminal justice in the direction of greater discursive openness, are discussed in Chapter 7, below. The relationship of discursive justice to rights will also be developed further in that chapter.

My estimation of Habermas is that he is right in championing the continuing importance of the ideals of post-Enlightenment modernity. He is also correct in insisting on the necessity for ongoing critique of the values of any specific community, and that such critique must have universalist aspirations. And in a post-metaphysical age, we have to accept the view that modernity must unfold its critique from within itself; critique cannot be grounded in anything other than modernity's own ideals: universalism must be an aspiration, it can never be philosophically 'proven'. Arguments about whether this grounding and this aspiration to universality proceed through rational reconstruction (as with Habermas) or by deconstruction (as with the postmodernists) seem to be to do with the way in which Habermas and the postmodernists conceive the nature and task of philosophy. What they share is the belief (both right and necessary) that societies such as our own must continually hold our own ideals, laws and practices up to scrutiny.

The weaknesses in Habermas's structure, I would argue, stem from his lack of openness to Otherness. Derrida and Lyotard make valid points about domination and exclusion, points which are also made by feminists and remain unanswered by Habermas. This lack of openness to alterity is at the root of his failure to construct the subject of discourse as the concrete rather than the generalised other, and also at the root of his failure to develop a theory which is properly relational. Despite his uncritical reference to Minow's relational model, by his insistence on the equality of all in their communicative capacity prior to their entry into discourse; their similar orientation to communicative rather than strategic action because of the impetus of language, and his preference for consensus as the goal of discourse, Habermas denies himself the possibility of developing a relational model of justice because there is no other to have a discursive relationship with.

Habermas takes us many steps forward, and his work has succeeded in creating new interest in the normative theories of law and democracy. He signposts the path towards constructing a universalism that does not depend on a subject isolated from her social context, and yet gives those – myself included – who want to resist the claims of strong communitarianism a firmer sense of direction. Additionally, Habermas has stimulated a dialogue which has led to development and clarification of ideas such as deliberative democracy, civic republicanism and discursive decision-making which are important resources for revitalised political theory. Habermas's work, then, adds up to an immense contribution to thinking about justice. The linked questions of alterity and relationalism, which in my view remain inadequately encompassed in his work and for which we need to look to the postmodernists and other theorists, are addressed in the remaining chapters.

Notes

[1]Major works by Habermas include *Legitimation Crisis* (1976), *The Theory of Communicative Action*, two volumes (1984 and 1987), *Between Facts and Norms* (1996a) and *The Inclusion of the Other* (1998). Helpful secondary literature includes Deflem (1996) *Habermas, Modernity and Law*; Outhwaite (1994) *Habermas: A Critical Introduction*; Rasmussen (1990) *Reading Habermas*, and White (1988) *The Recent Work of Jürgen Habermas: Reason, Justice and Modernity*.

[2]For a history of this period of the Institute and a critical analysis of the main Frankfurt School work, see Jay (1973).

[3]Connerton (1976: 32–7) provides a good account of this dispute.

[4]Habermas states his conditions for acceptable compromises most clearly in *Between Facts and Norms*. They are that compromises provide for an agreement that '(a) is more advantageous to all than no agreement whatever, (b) excludes free riders who withdraw from cooperation, and (c) excludes exploited parties who contribute more to the cooperative effort than they gain from it. Bargaining processes are tailored for situations in which social power relations cannot be neutralized in the way rational discourses presuppose. The compromises achieved by such bargaining contain a negotiated agreement *(Vereinbarung)* that balances conflicting interests. Whereas a rationally motivated consensus *(Einverständnis)* rests on reasons that convince all the parties *in the same way*, a compromise can be accepted by the different parties each for its own *different* reasons' (Habermas, 1996a: 166).

[5]Weber's sociology of law uses a four-cell scheme which differentiates systems of law as 'formal' and 'substantive', 'rational' and 'irrational'. A formal system reaches judgments only with reference to its own rules; a substantive system appeals to something external, such as religion. Both formal and substantive systems can be rational or irrational. A formal irrational system gives authority internally but does not lay down codes, so that judges make decisions on an *ad hoc* basis, but in conformity with the power they are given by the system; in a formal rational scheme judges must make decisions according to laid-down rules covering the cases they are likely to have to deal with. A substantive rational system will have a code of

rules and penalties which are derived from religion or some similar non-juridical ethic; a substantive irrational system will make decisions by referring to some non-juridical authority (the priesthood, an oracle, for example) each case that comes before it (Cotterell, 1984). Weber characterises formal rational systems as the 'ideal-type' of modern legal systems. Modern societies do tend towards this type, with more emphasis on consistency, reduction of judicial discretion, more mandatory sentences, etc.

[6]Some commentators see criminal justice in the UK and elsewhere as approaching a state of near autopoesis in the 1980s. In the period leading up to the 1991 Criminal Justice Act in England and Wales, the reforms that were enacted were almost all in pursuit of due process goals such as fairness and consistency, rather than to further external (public/political) goals to do with crime control (Bottoms, 1995). In the social context in which the system operates, it is hardly surprising that the legislation and principles of the era were undermined by external pressures (Faulkner, 1996; Hudson, 1995).

[7]The idea of 'deliberative democracy' has generated a volume of secondary literature – see, for example Bohman (1994), Cohen and Rogers (1995), Dryzek (1990) and Fishkin (1991).

[8]Habermas, (1996d)

6
Giving Difference its Due: Discourse and Alterity

We have encountered postmodernism in the two previous chapters. In the chapter on feminist critiques of liberal justice, we discussed the arguments between those 'difference' theorists who maintain some allegiance to liberal theories and ideals (Benhabib and Young) and those feminists who embrace the post-structuralist rejection of fundamental liberal concepts concerning identity and universalist philosophical foundations. The chapter on Habermas concluded with a review of the disagreements between him and postmodernists, especially Lyotard and Derrida. The disputes between Habermas and the postmodernists centre, it was argued, on the treatment of difference. For Habermas, difference is something to be overcome through discourse; for Derrida and Lyotard, difference is what is repressed or expelled by discourse. While Habermas appears to perceive no positive value in difference, for the postmodernists difference is at the core of their ethics. Difference is, therefore, at the heart of postmodernist concerns with justice; for postmodernists the task of justice is that of giving difference its due.

First of all, some explanation of the terms 'post-structuralism' and 'postmodernism'. Post-structuralism is a term used mainly in the social sciences, and signals a rejection of structuralist modes of analysis. Structuralism analyses phenomena – society, personality, language, moral development – as structures in which the relationships between elements are as important as the elements themselves; structures cannot be understood without accounting for these relationships (Piaget, 1971).[1] Many of the most important nineteenth- and twentieth-century theories are structuralist. Marxism, for example, depends on the relationships between capital and labour, bourgeoisie and proletariat, it is a theory of the *relations* of production; Freudianism also depends on the relations between the elements of personality, the ego, id and superego.

In the 1960s and 1970s, structuralism dominated the social sciences. Piaget's and Kohlberg's developmental psychology; Althusser's structuralist Marxism; Lévi-Strauss's structural anthropology, and Chomsky's structural linguistics were highly influential (Piaget, 1977; Kohlberg, 1973; Althusser, 1969, 1976; Lévi-Strauss, 1968; Chomsky, 1964, 1972, 1975). Although much social science retains vestiges of structuralism and work continues to be produced in the structuralist tradition, in sociology, law and psychoanalytic theory many writers have rejected the structuralist paradigm. Structuralism is said to be too closely allied to positivism and functionalism, and also to be too abstract and impersonal.[2]

Postmodernists are post-structuralists too (although some traces of structuralism are discernible in Derrida and Lyotard's reliance on theorising about the nature of language), but as well as rejecting structuralist theoretical forms, they also reject in a much more radical way the presuppositions about the nature of the subject and the nature of reason, on which modernist theories and philosophies (whether structuralist or not) rely. Postmodernism is mainly associated with philosophy and literary criticism, but is becoming more influential within legal theory, history and the social sciences, including criminology.

Postmodernism is a collection of themes rather than a coherent philosophy (Lea, 1998). These themes cohere around questions of language and truth; narratives of history and progress; and identity and subjectivity. Postmodernism rejects the idea of a necessary correspondence between language and that which it purports to describe; it rejects the idea that there can be any 'grand narrative' which reveals the essential character of society, whether this is a progressive narrative such as that of Enlightenment humanism, or a more critical narrative such as Marxism. This means that postmodernists reject linear ideas such as progress, and universal truths or values. Postmodernists also reject the idea of humans having fixed, unitary identities, seeing identity instead as a continuing process of experimentation and self-definition within changing relationships. Postmodernists reject any imposition of a singular, transcendent point of view, and any ascription of stable, singular meanings to acts, events, persons or things.

These denials of the concept of the fixed, essentially identical human subject, of the possibility of unambiguously progressive or regressive developments, of the possibility of philosophically grounded universal "truths" or "values", has led to characterisation of postmodernism as relativistic and nihilistic. If there can be no universal values, if there is not an essential human subject, if no meaning can be established as true in contrast to alternative meanings, then, it may be supposed, terms like morality and justice can have no purchase. Certainly, some postmodernists seem to fit this picture. Those described as 'sceptical' postmodernists seem to offer a gloomy picture of a postmodern age which, having lost faith in the Enlightenment narrative of moral and scientific progress, is an age of fragmentation, social chaos and absence of moral parameters (Rosenau, 1992). Baudrillard is the postmodernist most frequently cited as representative of the 'scepticals'.

In contrast, other postmodernists share the scepticals' critique of the discourse of modernity, but are affirmative of ideals such as justice, freedom and equality. They seek to identify ways of thinking about these ideals which do not lapse into modernist foundationalism, and do not merely put forward a new grand narrative. These affirmative postmodernists seek to recover the ethical dimension of justice, a dimension which has been suppressed by concentration on distributive fairness and formal proceduralism in modernist theories of justice such as Rawls's. They see the separation of justice from ethics as implicated in some of the worst totalitarian excesses of modernist society. The most important of these affirmative postmodernists are Derrida, Lyotard and Bauman.

This chapter is only concerned with the 'affirmatives' (Rosenau, 1992), and it is only concerned with those aspects of their work which are directly relevant to questions of justice.[3] Although they mount a powerful critique of liberalism, they conclude that the ideal of justice remains relevant and important and, far from embracing relativism, one of the convictions expressed and responsibilities accepted is that 'we must decide'. The distinctiveness of affirmative postmodernism is not an embrace or even a resigned acceptance of relativism, but the belief that we must decide and evaluate, 'without criteria' (Lyotard and Thébaud, 1985: 17). The chapter will recapitulate and re-emphasise the postmodernist critique of liberalism, and will then work through themes which appear in affirmative postmodernist writing on morality and justice.

Liberalism and the expulsion of difference

It was pointed out in the preceding chapter that one of the key differences between Habermas, and Derrida and Lyotard, concerns the nature and role of discourse and language. For Habermas, the way to achieve justice and promote emancipation is to bring groups and individuals to discourse. Iris Young, too, seeks the answer to the disempowerment of women, ethnic minorities and other groups who have been excluded from liberal rights and justice, in extending enhanced, specially protected rights to discursive participation; Benhabib suggests discourse as her primary principle of justice, arguing that by itself it provides a better prospect of meeting the claims and needs of the different other than if it is harnessed to Habermas's principle of universalisation.

For Lyotard and Derrida, however, discourse is not a mechanism for realising justice. The imperative of discourse, they argue, is not, as Habermas claims, to reach intersubjective understanding, and they view the possibility of unconstrained consensus or compromise as contrary to the logic of communication through language. They see the telos of discourse as exclusion and domination; further, they see this telos as inescapable because of the logic of language and of modernist reasoning.

Definition and naming depend on differentiation of a thing or a quality from its opposite. We can only recognise things by being able to distinguish them from what they are not; terms have meaning because of the relation with their opposites. Thus the term 'female' would have no meaning if we did not have a sense of male: 'female' only has meaning if we know that beings are differently sexed. Crucially, we only have a sense of the reasonable or rational if we are able to contrast reasonable with unreasonable, rational with irrational persons – and of course dangerous from safe persons, good from bad persons and honest from dishonest persons. If there were no line-drawing between the reasonable and unreasonable, good and bad, safe and risky, then evaluative terms could not come into being with any sense. It is, therefore, necessary that some person or group must always be identified as the negative pole of any quality in question.

Liberalism turns this conceptual/discursive logic into a political logic. The mistake, on this account, of those who seek to extend liberal rights and the privileges of citizenship in a liberal polity to hitherto excluded groups is that they miss this negative imperative of definition. It is not simply by accident or oversight that liberalism has excluded certain persons or groups; exclusion is an integral and unavoidable principle of liberalism because of the categories of thought and language from which it is constructed.

Critics of liberalism have commented on this necessary exclusion in relation to women, concluding like MacKinnon that the best that can be done is to extend rights to women who can be demonstrated to be, in key respects, like men (educated, employed, property-owning, tax-paying). Other critics have shown the compatibility of liberalism and imperialism: identification of other races as irrational 'savages' or as pre-rational 'like children' justifies withholding rights to self-determination and self-government from them.

Gilroy (1993) and Said (1978, 1993) discuss the necessity for liberalism of constructing irrational, uncivilised black and oriental 'others' who are defined by their lack of everything that distinguishes the citizen of the west. They are defined by their lack of human rights; their lack of democratic governance; their adherence to religious law rather than to western formal law; their presumed lack of achievement in 'modern' arts and sciences. The analyses show that the constitution of the otherness of subjugated races serves not only to describe them but also to formulate the narrative of western supremacy, reflecting western culture and reason back to itself exactly as it would like to believe itself to be. These narratives discount the value of non-western cultures, ignoring their richness and hybridity, as Said (1993) points out; and as Lyotard argues, they forget the violence which accompanied the triumph of western modernity (Venn, 1997: 3). This 'forgetting' means that the narrative of the colonised peoples only begins at the point of western intervention; their past is consigned to the invisibility of the repressed and marginalized.

Parallel critiques by postmodernists and by post-colonial theorists such as Gilroy and Stuart Hall point to the linkage of the idea of rights and the repression of people who are excluded from rights. Again, the argument is that discursive logic dictates that for rights to have meaning, to be cognitively as well as politically recognised, there must be groups without rights, so that the difference between rights and non-rights can be appreciated. For Patricia Williams (1991) the 'alchemy of race and rights' can constitute black women as abstract, rights-bearing citizens, it can construct an image of responsible personhood to set against the way that black females are encountered as 'already known' through stereotypes as 'unreliable, untrustworthy, hostile, angry, powerless, irrational, and probably destitute' (p. 147). Speaking the language of rights, buttressed by actually possessing rights, supports Williams's presentation of herself and her acceptance by others as an educated professional, a law professor in fact. Williams also, however, shows that the alchemy of race and rights can produce slavery, a situation in which law constitutes and legitimates the rights of white slave owners. As she says, 'the legal system did not provide blacks, even freed blacks, with structured expectations, promises, or reasonable reliances of any sort' (ibid.: 154).

In the case of slavery, as with other manifestations of imperialism, the relationship between rights is not that of balancing rights held by both parties; the rights relationship is that of rights/no rights. Toni Morrison echoes the postmodernist theme of the necessity for each 'thing' to be defined by contrast to its opposite. She is not at all surprised that the Enlightenment, with its ideal of freedom, accommodated slavery. Rather, she argues, it would be more surprising if it did not, since 'The concept of freedom did not arise in a vacuum. Nothing highlighted freedom – if it did not in fact create it – like slavery' (1993: 38, quoted by Venn, 1997: 13).[4] As with freedom, so with equality: the presence of inequality is necessary for us to envisage equality.

The necessity of the negative Other – a necessity born out of the binary nature of representational language – has, of course, implications for justice beyond the feminist critique of the logic of identity. It is not only that groups (women, black people, foreigners) can only gain access to rights and can only make claims on justice by demonstrating that they are like the dominant groups for whom rights are in place and justice is available, in relevant respects (and of course what are 'relevant respects' will be decided by the dominant group). What the definitional necessity of the negative Other means is that there must always be a group who can be identified as the negative. As one group gains rights another, or a residue of the rights-gaining group, must remain without rights in order to maintain the understanding of what rights are.

We can see this clearly in contemporary attitudes to minority ethnic groups in our society. As we move towards more equal citizenship, new distinctions emerge. Groups who accept the British or American 'way of life' are distinguished from those who do not. Those who see their first loyalty, and describe their primary identity as British are distinguished from those whose primary allegiance and identity remains with their or their family's country of origin. Various tests are introduced to check out these questions of allegiance and origin: accepting western dress conventions, at least at work; the notorious 'cricket test';[5] the more recently suggested qualification of competence in the

English language, even to the extent of speaking English in the home. Adherents of non-Christian religions are divided into the reasonable and the fanatical or fundamentalist; other governments are divided into the democratic and the autocratic, as though there were a dichotomy of democratic/ non-democratic rather than a continuum of more or less democratic; regimes are characterised as pro-western or anti-western, part of the alliance of free nations or part of the 'axis of evil'. And, of course, within western liberal societies themselves, people are characterised as responsible or irresponsible, deserving or undeserving; children are innocent or evil, vulnerable or predatory; women are good mothers or bad mothers, sad or selfish if they are childless. Rights and privileges of liberal citizenship are distributed according to these distinctions, which are endlessly and inevitably constituted and reconstituted.

A highly significant implication of this necessity of the negative Other, indeed an implication which is crucial to the concerns of this book, is that liberalism finds no need to concern itself with justice towards the negative Other. Liberalism is concerned with those who meet the criteria for reasonable citizenship. Liberalism finds no problem in dealing with the negative Other through total denial of rights: as well as slavery, liberalism countenances tyranny over the Other. Despotism is, as Mill states explicitly in the Introduction to *On Liberty*, a legitimate mode of government in dealing with barbarians, provided it is for their own improvement (1963–91). Mill's endorsement of despotic rule for 'barbarians' is not an accidental lapse into racist thinking, a residue of the thinking of the times, thinking which would be unconscionable by liberals today. It is not an accident or a remnant of pre-progressive thinking, but a constitutive principle of liberalism to divide people, at home and abroad, into the civilised and the barbarians (Carty, 1990; Valverde, 1996b).

Although, as Valverde says, the race-specific application of this principle as in slavery and colonialism may no longer be acceptable (though the examples given above of the division of people of other races and nationalities into the acceptable and the non-acceptable throws even this into doubt), it remains the case that governance according to principles of rights and justice is only for those who are accepted as conforming to the defining characteristics of the rational liberal subject. Moreover, as she reminds us, it is not just other people who have to prove themselves acceptable; all of us have to demonstrate that we have suppressed our inherent wellsprings of Otherness – the child within and the savage within – in order to claim the privileges of citizenship.

Acceptance of despotism as the legitimate means of governing barbarians explains why we find no guidance from liberalism on questions of the limits that should be placed on measures taken to protect good citizens against the risky and dangerous – whether the risky and dangerous are within or without society. The barbarian at the gates and the enemy within are necessary constructions, but they have no real existence for us as moral agents with claims upon us. They are constituted only to show us to ourselves, to provide a negative image of what we must be, and the tenets of rights-respecting democratic governance do not apply to them.

The argument that this exclusion of Otherness is a constitutive necessity rather than an accidental oversight or historical remnant is given force by the exclusions in contemporary variants of the liberal approach to justice. Rawls (1972) makes clear that his theory only applies among people already committed to the idea of justice; Habermas's conditions for compromise specify a commitment to communicative reason. Habermas's discussion of the Turkish girl and her father shows the principle of exclusion in operation very clearly. The liberal state will support the young woman who wishes to live by western values; the father who is characterized as traditional and reactionary, not sufficiently respectful of individual autonomy, can claim no support for his values. There is no balancing of claims here, no sense of needing to find a solution that gives her some measure of autonomy yet gives a measure of respect to the father's cultural traditions; liberal discourse works instead to define who is worthy of support and who is not.

The exclusions of the Enlightenment and of subsequent liberalisms, then, are not *exceptions* to liberal universalism: they are *expressions* of the principles of liberalism which limit inclusion within the community of rights and justice to certain characteristics and ways of life (Valverde, 1996b: 363). If the postmodern critique is correct, any attempt to characterize the rational citizen, the subject of justice, the principles of ethical governance, or any such abstraction, must produce its own set of exclusions. It is not simply that the categories of Enlightenment philosophy involve inclusions and exclusions of mind/body, reason/passion, adult/child, male/female, white/black, civilised/savage; it is that the nature of categorisation is such that to define, to bring to discourse, is thereby to create exclusions, to recognise some identities and to repress others.

Postmodernist theorists adopt a methodology of *deconstruction* to reveal the exclusions entailed by the categories of modernist systems of thought. This involves interrogation of laws, constitutions, philosophical writings, literature and other forms of 'text', pushing the words, phrases and ideas to their limits to uncover the oppositions and repressed or expelled meanings that can be excavated.[6] Law is a fruitful source of deconstruction because of its textuality: laws are written as statutes; cases and judgments are recorded, interpreted and reinterpreted, analysed and evaluated.

Deconstruction is associated first and foremost with Derrida. Contrary to criticisms that it has no political import, he and other postmodernists claim that it is political because it reveals the politics of law and philosophy. Deconstruction reveals what has been repressed or marginalized. For example, women's experience has been repressed and marginalized in systems of thought and their legal enactments which are based on a male worldview and valorise masculine qualities and aspirations. Deconstruction of ideas of justice quickly reveals who is denied justice, which forms of behaviour or relationships are not thought to belong to the province of justice (the 'dangerous' mentally disordered person, the Taliban fighter caught in a battle not defined as regular warfare between recognised states, 'private' domestic relationships, for example).

Probing the language of a text reveals the politics of acts of inclusion and exclusion, protection and repression contained in law and philosophy, and destabilizes the claims to authority of these powerful discourses. Deconstruction is destabilising and radically democratic because it denies the authority of the writer (in this very broad sense of text, so that legislators, judges, thinkers and actors are included in this category of 'writer') over the reader. We are all readers and interpreters, and so deconstruction establishes equality in that all readers' interpretations have equal status. Derrida's incorporation of the idea of hermeneutics from Heidegger and Gadamer means that the reader always brings something of their own to the text, so that each and every interpretation exceeds the text; the author cannot encompass all meaning(s) within the text (Ward, 1998: 178–9).

Interrogating the meaning of law, legal interpretation, penal codes, the scope of rights, the extent of political representation, social policies, established 'truths' and 'common sense' is political because the citizens of modern liberal democracies are meant to accept authority rather than question it; we are meant to be trusting and deferential rather than challenging and iconoclastic:

> By asking a continual series of questions, deconstruction seeks to sap the strength of a social structure whose substance lies in the prohibition of asking. (Morrison, 1997: 521)

Law's violence

Derrida frequently uses the words 'violence' and 'force' in describing the necessity for discourse to define through repression and exclusion. The titles of the first two essays in his *Writing and Difference* (1978), the book which did most to bring him to the attention of English-speaking academics, are 'Force and Signification' and 'Violence and Metaphysics'. Writers on law and justice who have drawn on his and other postmodernist work have taken up this theme of violence, commenting that even Marxist and feminist critical legal theorists have neglected the violence – threatened and actual – involved in the operation of law.

Fitzpatrick (1992) works through the theme of the necessity of the negative Other in liberal thought, showing how this necessity applies to law. He argues that the core of modern law is its actual and metaphorical association with racism and imperialism (p. 107). Modern law, he says, is founded on contrasts between 'light' and 'dark', 'civilization' and 'savagery', 'nation' and 'tribe'.

Modern legal systems rest upon the distinction between the legal subject of western liberal societies and 'lesser breeds without the law'.

Fitzpatrick shows that although the order brought about by modern law, both within a state itself and by states acting outside their own territories, is accomplished through violence, the mythology of law denies this violence. There is no triumphalism of conquest accompanying the entrenchment of modern law; rather, we find the creation of a mythical contrast between an orderly state of law and a violent state of nature. The law of nature is depicted as indeed, red in tooth and claw, while the nature of law is depicted as peaceful and fair: without law there is only barbarism, the morality of might is right rather than law's morality of fairness and reason.

It is perhaps no longer controversial that slavery and imperialism were dependent on beliefs and stereotypes about other races, so that their subjugation could be made to seem compatible with the liberal Enlightenment's self-presentation as progressive and emancipatory. Claims that colonial governments were better for people than tribal governments, that conditions on a slave plantation were better than conditions in 'free' Africa, were used to justify colonialism and slavery; the point of postmodernist critique is both that such beliefs depended on western liberalism's general disregard of other cultures, and devaluation of those elements of which it was aware, *and* that this disregard and devaluation were necessary to liberalism's constitution of itself as rational, progressive and freedom-loving. It is also no longer contested that enslavement and subjugation were shaped and enshrined in law: slave-owners' rights; Acts of government for colonial territories; Acts of settlement which gave native American, aboriginal and other indigenous peoples' lands to the conquerors of the new world. The point here is the way that postmodernists bring law to the heart of history, implicating it in the politics of oppression and challenging the myth that it is the bringer of peace and order.

Derrida speaks of the 'force' of law by reminding his readers of the centrality to law of its *enforceability* (1990: 925). He says that this is not merely a secondary or exterior possibility attaching to law but is part of the essence of law. A rule that was not enforceable, that could not be backed up by sanctions if disregarded, would not be called a law, but a custom or norm. Other postmodernists, and those who take postmodernist critiques seriously without becoming fully-fledged members of the movement, draw attention to the violence involved in the everyday operations of modern law, violence that occurs even when it restricts itself to its home territory.

Critical legal theorists and postmodernists who take the idea of the violence of law seriously charge that legal scholarship in recent years has principally been concerned with interpretation of judgments and legal texts – that is to say, with uncovering the principles on which they are based, discussing opinions about constitutionality, changing interpretations according to changing times, etc. – as though law is made and applied only in a context of calmness and reason, and as though judges correspond exactly to the model of the fair, impartial, wise person of law's idealisation of itself (this is the model of the judge to be found, for example, in Dworkin's empire: Dworkin, 1986b). Robert Cover, law professor at Yale University, issued a powerful challenge to the dominance of this interpretation scholarship in American jurisprudence with his essay, 'Violence and the Word' (1986). The article opens with the arresting statement, 'Legal interpretation takes place in a field of pain and death' (1986: 1601).

Cover discusses the founding of the United States through violence (the War of Independence, the defeats of the plains Indians), but goes on to talk about the violence and subjugation involved in everyday practices in criminal courts, in addition to the unusual circumstance of actually dispensing death in capital murder cases. He talks about the dissonance between the fact that the outcome is going to be incarceration or some other restriction of liberty, or demands for money in the form of fines or compensation, and the quiet orderliness of the proceedings, almost like civil courts. As Cover remarks:

> If convicted, the defendant customarily walks – escorted to prolonged confinement, usually without significant disturbance to the civil appearance of the event. It is, of course, grotesque to assume that the civil façade is 'voluntary' except in the sense that it represents the defendant's autonomous recognition of the overwhelming array of violence ranged against him and of the hopelessness of resistance or outcry. (ibid.: 1607)

Cover allows that there are some societies where contrition governs defendants' behaviour more than violence does, but he is of the opinion that 'it is unquestionably the case in the United States that most prisoners walk into prison because they know they will be dragged or beaten into prison if they do not walk' (ibid.: 1607)

Like Foucault, Cover sees that it is the court's physical control over the defendant's body that is at the heart of the criminal process. He tells of realising this in the 1960s when dissent by activist Bobby Seale ended with his being bound and gagged in court (ibid.: 1607 footnote). Today, defendants in the US courts are heavily shackled, and dissent may lead to the defendant being immobilised through activation of a stun belt.

Cover's article concentrates most graphically on control of the defendant's behaviour during the trial, but control of the defendant's body is also the essence of punishment, whether custodial or non-custodial. The court disperses of the body in time and place: the convicted person is ordered to be 'free' or to be in prison for a longer or shorter term; if not imprisoned, a convicted person can be ordered to be at home but under curfew, perhaps electronically monitored, for specified hours; a convicted person may have to report to a probation centre or part-time prison, or they may have to spend a specified number of hours working, where and how they are directed. As Cover says, judges and defendants may well have completely different understandings of the purposes of punishment, the justifications for punishment, the effectiveness of punishment – but they arrive together at the particular act of punishment 'having dominated and having been dominated with violence, respectively' (ibid.: 1609).

Accordingly, the second part of the statement, that interpretation takes place in a field of pain and death, is the stark reminder that 'The judges deal pain and death' (ibid.: 1609).

Sarat and Kearns extend Cover's analysis. It is not just that violence is inscribed on bodies subject to incarceration or execution, they say, it is that suffering is incurred when a welfare mother's benefits are reduced, or when a homeless man is made to 'move along' (Sarat and Kearns, 1991: 210). We could add many more examples, such as the forcible deportation of asylum seekers whose claims are denied; the eviction of tenants if a court rules in favour of a landlord who wants to gain possession; the financial hardship suffered by people whose claims against insurers or pension providers are disallowed. Like Fitzpatrick, Sarat and Kearns describe suppression of the reality of law's violence in favour of a mythology of law as bringer of peace, as: 'law's crowning achievement, namely its reputation as the only alternative to general, barbaric violence when its own violence is a numbing commonplace of everyday life' (ibid.: 211).

Like Cover, they comment on the dominance in legal theory of concern with law's 'reason-giving activities', that is to say, the interpretations, judgements and arguments of judges, rather than concern with the painful effects on individuals that flow from those deliberations.

Sarat and Kearns argue that the mythology of law (to use Fitzpatrick's term) as the antidote to violence diverts attention from the pain inflicted by law and means that what, they say, should be a central challenge to law and to legal theory, namely to explore and respond to the gap between law's rhetoric of exercising reason and the actuality of its extensive and legitimated use of violence against persons, is not taken up. This neglect of the violence of law means that the majesty of law is unchallenged by demonstrations of its monstrousness, and its authority cannot be disturbed by descriptions of its vengeance. Even self-proclaimed radical legal scholars, they assert, while they may explore the contradictory or partisan nature of law, nonetheless remain focused on the rhetorical and ideological aspects of law's power, not the actual violence it commands:

> The horror of modern life, as the critics understand it, is not that the tanks roll or that the executioner's job is done. It is, instead, found in the fact that there is so much consent or so little outright coercion. (ibid.: 259)

The tanks roll and the executioner's job is done, at the command of law. Derrida, Lyotard and other postmodernists are profoundly affected by the experience of the Holocaust, but the lessons they draw are very different from those drawn by Habermas and the members of the Frankfurt School. For post-modernists, the Holocaust does not signify the defeat of reason by prejudice: it is an instantiation of the possibilities of modernity. The Holocaust is an instance (the paradigmatic instance perhaps) of the necessity to create the negative Other and then to expel that Other. The perfect Aryan could only be identified by contrast to the non-Aryan, the Jew; the non-Aryan must be expelled, and the most modern of nations, the nation in whom the Enlightenment ideal was most perfectly embodied in Kant, in Goethe, in Beethoven, produced the most efficient means of expelling the Other – the gas chambers of the 'final solution'.

For Lyotard (1990), the Holocaust shames the claims of modernity to reason and progress. After Auschwitz, he says, there can only be silence: modernity cannot rationalise, it cannot justify (Ward, 1998: 175). The silence of Heidegger, whose *Being and Time* (1973) is reckoned by many to be one of the great works of twentieth-century philosophy, who having joined the Nazi party during the rise of Hitler, refused to condemn the gas chambers after the war, deeply disturbed continental philosophers. For the early Frankfurt School, the Holocaust and its apologists stimulated a search for understanding of the failure, as they saw it, of reason; and as we have seen, for Habermas it stimulated his taking upon himself the task of finding a way to secure reason at the heart of governance. For Lyotard and Derrida, on the other hand, it meant the end to the 'grand narratives' of modernism, and it meant that philosophers, politicians and other defenders of modernism no longer deserved deferential attention (Lyotard, 1988). After Auschwitz, modernity should maintain a shamefaced silence.

The Nazi regime and its deeds were legal. Hitler did not come to power through a *coup d'état*, he was constitutionally elected. Stripping Jews of all the rights of citizenship; restriction of Jews to ghettos; the concentration camps and the 'final solution' with its gas chambers, were all supported by law. A series of laws, regulations and special measures introduced during the 1930s

> robbed Jews of their livelihoods, impoverished and demoralised them, and isolated them from the larger society, in which they had moved freely only a few years earlier. They made Jews socially dead, trans-forming them into subhuman material, weeds to be cleansed from the garden. (Morrison, 1997: 307)

As Morrison describes, Nazism was not only legitimated through specific laws, it was also supported by jurisprudence. In other words, it was not that a rogue faction gained power, and passed laws which were not supported by either the population at large or the legal establishment. The Hitler regime came to power constitutionally, its policies received support from wide sections of the German public, and the legality of their promulgations was underscored by at least some German legal theorists.

Morrison discusses the writings of legal theorist Carl Schmitt, who explained that democracy requires homogeneity, which can only be attained by eliminating heterogeneity (ibid.: 308–10). Schmitt (and Morrison) argues that this is counter to liberalism's belief in the equality of all persons, but we can see that Schmitt's view of the conditions for democracy to operate accords with the logic of identity which liberalism is accused of embodying. Liberal democracy depends on homogeneity and the expulsion of heterogeneity. This can be seen in from its earliest formulations where Mill assumes that all people will value freedom equally, through Rawls's invocation of persons wanting the same primary goods and similarly capable of acting out of respect for justice, to Habermas's discursive community of persons alike in accepting the rules of undominated speech and attuned to the achievement of intersubjective understanding.

Reflecting upon the Holocaust, then, reveals for postmodernists the inability of liberal philosophy to provide secure foundations for justice, and moreover, it shows that the combination of modernity's inescapable desire to expel difference and its unmatched instrumental efficiency, can produce horrific events. It also reveals the lack of identity between law and justice: the treatment of the Jews by the Hitler regime may have been legal but it can by no stretch of the imagination be characterised as just. Such reflection further demonstrates that modernist combinations of values (nationalism, mistrust of Otherness), authoritarian habits of deference and obedience, and the majesty of law to a large extent created by its own rhetoric backed by its force, tend to generate respect for law rather than love of justice.

At the time of writing this chapter (September 2002), we are witnessing another demonstration of the violence of law, and of respect for law rather than care for justice. As I write, the USA is pressing for a 'strong resolution' to be passed by the United Nations Security Council authorising military assault on Iraq if Saddam Hussein, Iraq's president at the time, does not allow inspection of his weapons and weapons manufacturing facilities precisely to the extent and under the conditions stipulated by the US. The governments of the UK, Canada, Germany and many other countries are concerned that the USA may attack even without UN authorisation. Both at government and at popular levels discussion is far more about the necessity for UN approval and acting within a 'framework of international law', than about the justice of the military attack *per se*. Presumably innocent civilians will be killed whether or not any action is backed by international law and UN resolutions, but such 'collateral damage', as it is chillingly called, is apparently acceptable if mandated by law and unacceptable without sanction by law. Of course there are dissenting voices in all countries who oppose attacking Iraq with or without UN legitimation, but these are fewer than the voices to be heard talking about law but not about killing. For most, and certainly for most speaking within official discourse, the tanks may roll and the bombers may bomb, but only at the command of law.

Justice and the ethics of alterity

Lyotard, Derrida and Bauman all insist on the importance of justice; they urge building strongly, quickly and extensively on the ground of justice. They argue against the logic of identity in Enlightenment thought which, as we have seen, they locate as the origin of injustice since it necessarily works to constitute categories of persons who are not owed justice. They argue against foundationalist claims of the narratives of modernity, and contest the universal principles of justice proposed by Rawls, Habermas and other liberals. All ideas, systems and laws are open to challenge and deconstruction, but this is not to be taken as any lack of commitment to justice. Lyotard says that although systems of justice based on ideas such as consensus may be outmoded and suspect, there is nothing outmoded or suspect about the ideal of justice itself (1984: 66); Derrida urges us to be 'juste' with justice, and tells us that deconstruction of the conceptual, theoretical and normative apparatus surrounding justice is 'anything but a neutralization of interest' in justice (1990: 955).

Postmodern critiques – deconstructions – of Enlightenment thought and modern law lead to two precepts of affirmative postmodernism's approach to justice:

First, law and justice can never be identical;

Second, justice involves adopting a stance of ethical openness to difference, to Otherness.

The legality of the Holocaust demonstrates empirically, and conclusively, that law and justice are not the same. In any case, most of us have no problem in recognising the gap between the two ideas because it makes sense to us to speak of unjust laws. Apartheid South Africa's 'pass laws' were widely regarded as unjust not merely with hindsight but when they were in force, as were segregationist laws in the southern states of the USA, and we can all proffer our own more mundane examples of laws we regard as unjust. The gap between law and justice is uncloseable, for the postmodernists, because of the logic of language. If every term must contain a trace of its opposite, then a law which sees itself as the embodiment of justice must necessarily at the same time be an embodiment of injustice.

Derrida discusses this binary necessity in 'Force of law: The "Mystical Foundation of Authority"' (1990), an essay which is quoted by most writers and commentators on postmodernist perspectives on justice, and which is notably drawn on by Cornell (1992) in her own work on justice. He speaks of the co-presence of a term and its opposite – justice/injustice – as an *aporia*, a contradiction that cannot be dissolved or resolved. Law or politics, therefore, cannot resolve or dissolve the distinction between law and justice; law can never bring justice into being and neither, of course, can philosophy. What one can do (and has a responsibility to do) is to expose particular forms of injustice inherent in prevailing theories of justice and their implementation in law and politics. But having corrected those injustices, one has to accept that new forms of injustice will arise, and one has a responsibility to be equally active in their identification.

Justice, for Derrida, is an ideal, an aspiration, which is supremely important and worth striving for constantly and tirelessly, but which can never be finally achieved. He demonstrates the gap between actual law in action and law as it aspires to justice in his essay for Nelson Mandela. Derrida describes Mandela, who at the time of the writing of the essay was still a prisoner and so someone adjudicated as having broken the law, as a *man of the law* (Derrida, 1987: 26). Mandela, Derrida reports, says that he admires the law, but what he admires, Derrida argues, is not the actual law, which benefits white South Africans to the detriment of black South Africans, but the noblest tradition of law, the tradition of remedying identified injustices through successive constitutional enactments from Magna Carta through the US Constitution to the Charter of Liberty promulgated by the African National Congress in 1955 (Mandela himself was a prominent member and principal drafter of the Charter). Mandela, says Derrida, regards the actual constitutional laws of the Republic of South Africa in the apartheid era as a violation of this law; the laws of the Republic are the laws of a *coup de force*, and are unjust.

Mandela serves 'the law', the aspirational law which strives towards justice, rather than 'laws'. Derrida's sense of 'the law' here echoes Kant's 'principle of right' in that it is a fundamental law/principle of equal respect for all. The difference between the Kantian tradition and Derrida is that whereas Kantians such as Rawls and Habermas attempt to describe principles and procedures which can incorporate this supreme law in actual institutions, Derrida sees it as something which will always be unattainable, something which remains just out of reach. For Derrida and for Lyotard, 'the law', or 'principle of right' – justice, in other words – exists as a horizon to be looked towards, a criterion of justice against which existing laws can be measured and held to account.

Derrida and Lyotard both refer to the gap between law and justice arising not only because of the distance between aspiration and reality but also because the nature of law is such that each case must be fitted into a category of cases, whereas the nature of justice is that each case must be responded to in its singularity. They use their motif of the 'force' of law in another sense here, in the sense of the particularity of cases being forced into the generality of rules; the sense they give is of an object being fitted into a box which isn't quite big enough for it.[7] Again, they are not alone in recognising the problem, it is the implications they draw that are new. We saw in the previous chapter that Habermas's response to lack of accommodation to individual circumstances, to the situation of the concrete other, in his discourse model of justice, is to distinguish between discourse rules and rules of application: he is still seeing the solution to the problem of *particularity* in a *general* set of rules.

Postmodernism does not offer an alternative set of rules, but calls for the reintroduction of ethics into questions of justice. Kantian rule-guided reason has to move aside to make room for morality. Morality is based on emotions and so in Kantian, modernist terms it is unreliable, unreasonable, and must be 'tamed' within a cage of rules and procedures. According to Bauman, the expulsion of emotion leads to attenuation even of the exercise of reason; if individual cases are not thought about in their particularity then 'reason' means nothing more than acting according to the rules, and justice or legality resides in the rules given by the legislators and implemented by the enforcers. Following the rules is, of course, the very opposite of the Kantian vision of post-conventional autonomy, a moral order where each person is the authority for her own moral principles and rules.

> Just how much the wager on reason was prompted by the desire to tame and domesticate the otherwise obstreperous moral sentiments through lodging them safely in a straightjacket of formal (or formalizable) rules, is shown by the tendency of the balance between reason and rules to shift constantly to the side of the rules: to the 'deontological' conception of morality according to which in order to know whether the act was morally correct or not... it is enough to know whether the acting was in agreement with the rules prescribed for that sort of action. (Bauman, 1993: 67)

Referring back to his argument in *Modernity and the Holocaust* (1989), Bauman says that the moral proceduralism of modernity makes possible the collective 'moral' participation of individuals in morally outrageous acts.

Bauman argues against proceduralism's making the moral conscience of the actors less important than their obedience to rules, and its separation of the rightness of behaviour from the goodness of its outcome. Nonetheless, he and other postmodernists are as concerned to distinguish themselves from communitarians as from liberals. Communitarians such as MacIntyre want to reinstate morality; Utilitarians want to judge actions by their effectiveness for bringing about good consequences. So what is the difference between communitarian or Utilitarian ethics and postmodern ethics? Or to put the question in another way, how does postmodernism deal with two problems, one familiar and one new? The old problem is, if goodness of outcome is to be the measure, how is the individual to be protected against sacrifice to the general good?; and the new problem is, if action is to be motivated by the agent's moral sentiment, how can it be ensured that the action is right from the point of view of the Other to whom it is directed?

Postmodern ethics addresses these dilemmas by placing the Other, the recipient or target of an action, at the heart of morality. Postmodern ethics is an ethics of alterity, postmodern justice is a justice of alterity rather than a justice of fairness; it is a substantive justice of ethical attention to the Other rather than a procedural justice of distributive fairness.

Derrida, Bauman and Lyotard draw on the work of Emmanuel Levinas for an ethics of alterity.[8] For Levinas, the ethical relationship between 'I' and 'Other' is the basic term of morality. Crucially, this relationship is a face-to-face encounter, unmediated by interpretation or classification. Unlike the liberal ethics based on recognition of similarity between self and others, Levinas's ethics of alterity starts from difference. Liberal ethics is based on the precept that I should treat others in the way I would wish to be treated because actions will affect them in the same ways that they will affect me, and that I can imagine this (empathise) because of the characteristics we have in common. This is the appeal to sameness that Shylock makes with his 'do I not bleed?' speech. In Levinasian ethics, there can be no such knowledge; we must act towards the Other without reaching shared understanding, without any confidence of the effect of the action, without any confidence that this Other would treat me similarly.

Just by being the subject/object of my attention, the Other lodges a moral claim on me; seeing the Other being 'in my face' (to give meaning to a contemporary colloquialism) brings with it a moral responsibility. To Levinas this responsibility is prior to any other kind of relationship: it is pre-social, pre-rational, pre-discursive. The face-to-face relationship is a relationship of 'proximity without cognition' (Trey, 1992: 419).

Levinas's view of ethical conduct being based on acknowledgement of this moral responsibility to alterity is obviously attractive to Derrida, Lyotard and Bauman with their insistence that difference lies at the centre of morality, and that morality needs to be reinserted into conceptions of justice. This is an ethical relationship based on the impossibility as well as undesirability of eradicating difference. In contrast to Habermas, the goal of discursive relations is not to achieve consensus, but to *give difference its due.*

This demand to give difference its due is precisely the demand which postmodern critiques suggest that no version of liberalism can meet. Levinasian ethics addresses what is a problem area even for a theory such as Habermas's discourse model (Trey, 1992) and also, I would argue, for Young, Benhabib and other liberal feminists, however much they may push liberalism to its limits. Even if, like Young, they want to preserve a privileged place in political discourse for previously marginal groups, such groups have to be identifiable and discernible as having some sort of homogeneity within the group, and they have to be, and be recognised as being, capable of participation in the rule-governed discourse of liberal politics. Even if, like Benhabib and Fraser, they insist that groups and individuals are to speak for themselves, putting forward their own versions of their suffering, their needs and their demands, they still have to be able to articulate their claims in ways that can be understood, that seem reasonable, and that can be acknowledged as legitimate. Even if, like Kymlicka, they advocate giving cultural membership the status of a right, so that cultural assimilation is no longer the condition of access to rights, the culture has to be recognisable and recognised *as* culture. In the Levinasian scheme, only the *presence* of the Other is necessary. In the ethics of alterity, the ethical relationship constitutes the Other as the face and myself as the moral agent with an unconditional responsibility towards the face.

In what Bauman (1993: 85) calls 'the most dramatic reversal of principles in modern ethics', Levinas 'accords the Other the priority which was once unquestionably assigned to the self'. The Other does not, however, pay a price for this priority by losing her existence as distinct from the self: the Other in Levinas's scheme is not the self as *alter ego*, nor is she an extension of the self (Douzinas and Warrington, 1994). The Other is logically prior to the self in that the presence of an Other is the precondition of language, because without an Other there is no-one to address; she is the pre-condition of society, because without an Other there is no-one with whom to co-operate or compete; she is the pre-condition of law and politics because without an Other there are no rights to establish, no boundaries to maintain, no conflicts to resolve or interests to balance; she is the pre-condition of the self because without an Other there is no interaction, no call to identify ourselves or to position ourselves. In the ethics of alterity, this foundational priority of the Other is transposed into an ethical priority.

If, however, it is no longer the case that the self is prior and the Other comes to be recognised as deserving of equal respect because of likeness with self, because of being the same as self, it is not the case for Levinas that it is the qualities of the Other that proclaim her as a subject to whom responsibility is owed. If the reversal of priority of the self into priority of the Other means that the ethical relationship is no longer based on qualities of the self, it does not thereby become the case that the ethical relationship derives from the qualities of the Other. Responsibility does not depend on the reasonableness or similarity to self of the Other, nor does it depend on the merits of the case. Responsibility to the Other does not depend on the desert of the Other, or on any rights being earned, rules being kept or services rendered. In the Levinasian ethic, *responsibility does not depend on reciprocity*. Responsibility to Otherness is the beginning, the foundation of the moral relationship, not something that derives from it.

We can see, then, that the ethic of alterity is very different indeed from both communitarianism and Utilitarianism, and that it appears to provide a basis for bringing morality into theories of justice that meets the critiques of these other consequentialist systems. Levinas's ethics of alterity does not demand that the good of the individual Other be weighed against the good of the general citizenry, and it does not require of the Other that she adopt the values of the community in order to have claims on justice. Levinasian ethics is also clearly of interest in thinking about ways of responding justly to those assessed as risk-bearing. According to this ethics, no-one is outside the moral realm. There is no-one whose difference is 'beyond the pale', so intolerably Other that she should not be treated as she requires, and there is no necessity that she should account for her behaviour, her beliefs or her lifestyle in ways comprehensible or acceptable to those to whose attention she has come.

Levinas sees any departure from this ideal of accepting unconditional responsibility for the Other as vacating the moral ground. Any attempt to define, to categorise, to change, to deny, to suppress, is a violation of the moral relationship, and signifies that the encounter has changed from being a moral relationship to being a power relationship. All attempts to constrain alterity are efforts at domination rather than at behaving ethically. This is, of course, exactly what Cornell means when she talks of her ethical feminism as attempting to achieve a non-violent relationship with the Other: Otherness must stake its claims in its own way; it must not be reduced to categories already accommodated within the moral/political community; the moral responsibility towards it is unconditional and boundless. On this account, no-one is beyond morality, no difference negates responsibility.

Society, however, inevitably intrudes upon and disrupts the face-to-face encounter between self and Other and we move, according to Levinas, from an order ruled by morality to an order which is ruled by justice. Levinas says that the existence of a multiplicity of Others, who will have relationships with each other as well as with me, and who will make conflicting demands on me, necessitates the entry of a third party, a judge. When persons come to law as plaintiffs or are brought before it as defendants, they are already in a conflict with at least one other person – a third party is needed to pass judgment on the conflicting claims. Unlike the emotional, wholly engaged and totally responsible attention of the self in the moral relationship, the third party in the political relationship of justice needs to be objective, disinterested, a cool judge who stands at a distance from the parties, outside of the face-to-face relationship of the moral dyad. This entry of the third party (the judge) signals the removal of the conflict from the realm of the personal and places it within the confines of the realm of institutions (Douzinas and Warrington, 1994: 419). Bringing conflicts to adjudication needs the existence of law and politics; it needs a state which can institutionalise a system of justice.

The relationship between morality and justice is not made very clear in Levinas's writings, and it remains for those persuaded by his ethics to elaborate conceptions and processes of justice which could incorporate his ethic of responsibility to Otherness. If, as he says, and as Derrida, Lyotard and Bauman agree, we must have justice, then what would a justice of alterity be like, how would it operate? One clear principle that is central is that there must be a 'deep' equality: if responsibility to the Other is not dependent on reciprocity, desert, or any special characteristics, then all have equal claims. There can be no question of rights being sacrificed because of irresponsible behaviour, or because of being assessed as dangerous or risky. Acceptance of this radical justice of alterity, basing justice on an ethics of responsibility to

Otherness is, Levinas's writing suggests, the only safeguard against repression of the different; it is the only defence against the Holocaust.

Lyotard: justice and the multiplicity of discourses

The question that arises, then, as Levinas acknowledges, is whether an ethics of responsibility can be operationalised as a jurisprudence of alterity. Can the asymmetry of the unconditional responsibility owed to an unmediated, uncategorised and irreducible Otherness be reconciled with the impartial symmetry of equal recognition of competing claims? Can morality be the basis of law, can law be 're-moralised'? Douzinas and Warrington ask:

> What is the relevance of a discourse that claims a pre-ontological and pre-rational status and emphasizes the uniqueness of the face, for a legality that has universalistic pretensions and bases its empire upon the rationality of judgment and the thematization of people and circumstances? If the ethical response is based on the contingent appearance of a face in need, can there be a justice that moves beyond the ethicity of the contingent thus helping the re-ethicalization of the law? Can the ethics of alterity be generalized and thus become the justice of the law? (1994: 416)

Lyotard attempts to deal with some of these issues in *Just Gaming* (Lyotard and Thébaud, 1985) and in *The Différend* (1988). He shares many of Habermas's themes, such as the task of philosophy in relation to the provision of a grounding for justice, and critique of the increasing domination of instrumental rationality. Like Habermas, Lyotard is critical of the transposing of ethical questions into technical questions, referring to this as the dominance of 'performativity' in modern life. What is deemed important in developed modern societies, he says, is not virtue, justice or solidarity, but that systems should perform to maximum effectiveness. Unlike Habermas, however, Lyotard does not suggest that the solution is to establish dominance for communicative rationality over other forms of rationality. Lyotard does suggest that discourse is the process through which the search for justice must operate, but he does not specify any general rules for discourse.

Lyotard's interrogation of philosophy leads him to two basic conclusions which mean that he sees justice and discourse in very different ways from Habermas. The first conclusion he draws, *contra* Habermas, is that a discourse of justice cannot be derived from a discourse of truth. Descriptive or analytic discourses (such as truth) cannot, Lyotard argues, generate moral imperatives; one cannot move from description to prescription (B. Smart, 1999: 139). The second conclusion, entailed by the first, is that it is the task of the philosopher to mediate between discourses rather than to propose one overarching discourse which can provide grounding for beliefs and values and which can legitimate law and politics.

Lyotard's notion of the 'incommensurability' of discourses is important, and it is linked to the postmodern theme of the violence of capturing meaning or feeling by discourse. Fitting one kind of concern into the discursive form of another order of concerns is a signal of injustice. Foster, in a comparison of Habermas's and Lyotard's approaches to justice, gives the example of environmental protection groups being forced to use the language of economic efficiency (Foster, 1999: 88). Habermas would urge that economic rational concerns are not the only issues that need to be taken into account, and he would argue that communicative reason, operating through his rules of discourse, would ensure that the non-instrumental aspects of the issue can be included. For Lyotard, this is not enough: the non-economic concerns may be overwhelmed by the economic, and in any case there can be no real communication between non-equivalent discourses.

It is this non-commensurability of discourses that accounts for Lyotard's insistence on the impossibility of moving from description to prescription. In *Just Gaming*, Lyotard and Thébaud argue that description of society does not yield prescriptions for social policy, because descriptions of what is, and prescriptions of what ought to be, are different orders of reason. Lyotard extends this argument in *The Différend* using the example of unemployment: that two million people are unemployed does not of itself mean that policies to reduce unemployment ought to be implemented (Lyotard, 1988: 108). Such policies may of course be desirable, but this must be argued for in terms of morality, sympathy, solidarity or perhaps economic dysfunction; it does not simply follow automatically from the descriptive statement of fact. Certainly, as we have seen in recent years, economic discourse cannot 'do justice' to the suffering inflicted by unemployment, since arguments can also be made that less than full employment is economically healthy, signalling flexible labour markets and keeping inflation in check. Social oppression, in Lyotard's view, results from the suppression of the heterogeneity of forms of rationality that organise different discourses.[9]

The gap opened up by the non-commensurability of discourses, the loss inevitably sustained if claims can only be put in the terms of a dominant discourse, is called by Lyotard '*le différend*'. Doing justice to the différend (*faire droit au différend*) is the task of justice; the task of justice is to turn the Other from victim to plaintiff (ibid.: 21). If Otherness must speak the language of the dominant self, then it will be silenced; if the only terms which are granted discursive legitimacy are the terms of the dominant discourse, then the claims of the Other will be dismissed as illegitimate.

The task of the philosopher, then, as Lyotard sees it, is not to create a new meta-discourse to reconcile the heterogeneous discourses of a pluralistic social world, but to protect discourses arising in the social world from domination. There is no call to philosophy to provide the principles to guide the institutionalisation of justice; instead there is a duty to make sure that all discourses remain within their boundaries and do not arrogate to themselves objects and domains which are not properly theirs. Justice has no discourse of its own; its mandate is to patrol the discursive boundaries, guarding against domination, because to give difference its due depends upon allowing Otherness to speak its own language.

Lyotard invokes Aristotle's concept of *reflective justice*, which casts the philosopher-judge as having to decide between the rival claims, couched in a multiplicity of voices, jostling for recognition in the ancient *agora*, the market place and forum at the centre of Athenian life. The way the philosopher-judge is to go about her task is explained using the metaphor of the archipelago,[10] with each discourse an island, close to the others and linked to them in various ways, the islands being various sizes and shapes, separated by water, distinct but connected. Lyotard's philosopher-judge launches expeditions from one island to the other, showing to each what is to be found in the other (ibid.: 131). The philosopher is not merely an interpreter, or a travel-writer. She is a reflective judge, creating links and passages between one and the other; often being called on to decide where the territory of one begins and another ends.

For a model of the quality of judgment the philosopher-judge must exercise, Lyotard turns to Kant's third critique, the *Critique of Judgment* (Kant, 1986). Unlike the philosophies of reason which emphasize identity, rule guidance and the derivation of generalizable imperatives, the philosophy of judgment calls to an aesthetic mode of evaluation. Judging the artistic quality of paintings, for example, the viewer/critic/art historian may well be aware of some rules (about proportion, composition, etc.) but judgment does not take the form 'this painting conforms or does not conform to the rules' but 'this painting is beautiful', 'this painting arouses a response', 'this painting reflects the human predicament', or some such singular, emotional opinion. Aesthetic judgments may refer to rules, but they do not depend on rule-following; paintings may be valued because they breach artistic conventions, because they open up new artistic possibilities. Most of all, paintings are judged individually. Even when movements in painting are being considered, the singular is usually distinguished from the general. 'I don't like impressionism much, but Monet's *Garden at Giverny* is beautiful' is a statement that makes sense, even though both speaker and hearer know that Monet is an impressionist painter.

Lyotard's approach to doing justice to the Other, then, is to insist that all claims to justice must speak in their own language – they must not be constrained to translate their grievances into a dominant discourse (law, economics, history, for example); and to insist further that all claims and conflicts must be considered as unique, not as instances of general categories, to be dealt with by application of general rules. Present and past injustices must therefore be able to be heard, and any new representations of justice or any new social rules and practices (new rights, new laws, new definitions of citizenship, new boundaries of public and private, for example) must be challenged to see not only what they exclude, but also what is lost through accommodation to dominant discourse in the making and granting of claims.

The term *paralogism* is introduced to express this commitment to Otherness activated through challenges to existing or emergent constructions (White, 1987–8: 313). Lyotard likens this to the scientific method of continual attempts to disprove established theories: the scientific mode of progress through falsification. This model justifies, even demands, new challenges; it acknowledges that nothing can ever be regarded as 'proven', no 'truth' can ever be established for all time. Because challenge is least likely to come from those with vested interests in established ideas, listening, ensuring discursive facilities, to those outside the establishment is essential. Paralogism not only allows for openness to Otherness, it mandates it.

Lyotard's work, like that of Derrida, calls for a responsibility to Otherness which can only be approached by paying attention to new social movements, to dissidents, to deviants, to the outsider and to the stranger. If there is a core principle, it is that the proliferation of 'small narratives' must be fostered energetically (B. Smart, 1999: 140; White, 1987–8: 314). The role of justice is to protect the discursive boundaries of these small narratives, guarding against their expulsion, and guarding against the loss involved in assimilation.

Commentators on Lyotard's approach to justice, even if generally sympathetic to the idea of justice as responsibility to alterity and to his critique of Habermas's communicative ethics, ask how the limits to, or constraints on, responsiveness to different discourses, openness to radical Otherness, may be determined. After all, Lyotard has said that, even without criteria, we must decide. Incommensurability of discourses does not entail relativism, it does not mean that evaluative and comparative judgments cannot be made.

Lyotard turns to Kant's principle of a 'horizon' of 'reasonable beings', who can exist together. In Lyotard's formulation, this means a horizon of maximum diversity, and the measure of whether an action or law is just or unjust is whether or not it allows the domination of one narrative by another. We are led back, therefore, to the ideal of maximum freedom without constraining the freedom of others: a Kantian ideal, but in Lyotard's envisioning an ideal with the notions of both 'freedom' and 'others' expanded to the maximum.

Conclusion: postmodernism and the possibilities of justice

The writings of Lyotard and Derrida contain no clear prescriptions for a new theory of justice. With its bringing together of a rigorous approach to the philosophy of language and discourse, and a radicalised 'hermeneutics of suspicion' of the Enlightenment categories of reason, its innovative analysis of the 'force of law' and the injunction to ask first and foremost, 'Who is excluded, or repressed, or marginalised?', its advocacy of unceasing search for 'new moves' to challenge existing narratives and foster new ones, and its espousal of an ethics of alterity, affirmative postmodernism points us towards new ideas about justice which can move beyond some of the closures of modern liberalism. Its positive affirmation of justice as an ideal, and the contribution of some important works signalling directions in which to move in thinking of approaches to justice which could meet the challenges of the risk society, explain the inclusion of these postmodernist writers in this reaffirmation part of this book.

Postmodernism looks to the boundaries of liberalism, inviting us to look to 'the limit' and beyond, of our conventional thinking about justice (Cornell, 1992). The great challenge postmodernism poses – and the challenge which is the question of this book – is how are we to do justice to those who are incomprehensibly Other? How do we give a respectful, attentive hearing, accepting our responsibility to respond with justice, to the incomprehensibly outsider narrative, to the stories of those we react to as irrational, bizarre, hostile, perhaps monstrous, and of course risky? To return once again to Habermas's conundrum of the daughter of the Turkish migrant worker, how do we support her right to the life she chooses *and* his yearning for the life of his traditions? How do we avoid deciding for her *or* him; how do we buttress autonomy and at the same time console homesickness; how do we tread the line between the incommensurable discourses of rights and culture?

Bauman (1991) suggests that only a justice based on an ethics of alterity can point the way towards moving beyond contemporary racism and the always lurking, always beckoning dehumanisation of Otherness that facilitated the Holocaust. The 'tolerance' of liberalism gives no guarantees, because of the asymmetry of the relationship of (superior) tolerating self and (inferior) Other to-be-tolerated. Tolerance depends on the disposition of the tolerator, it can be given or withdrawn as the tolerator feels inclined, it acknowledges no responsibility to the tolerated. Only an ethics of alterity which places an unconditional responsibility on those who encounter Otherness goes beyond the contingency of toleration, towards a duty to safeguard the freedom and well-being of the Other.

Lyotard and Derrida both refuse any fixed definition of justice. It has no unchanging nature, no essence; it is beyond definition. Justice is always yet to be achieved; it is imaginable yet beyond knowing; it is unattainable, yet it commands our tireless striving. For both Lyotard and Derrida, 'the desire for justice is a desire for the as-yet-unknown' (B. Smart, 1999: 141).

Although Levinas gives us little more than hints on how his ethics of alterity might be the basis of an approach to justice, his work is clearly important and has stimulated some of the most creative new thinking on justice. In a discussion answering some questions prompted by his writing, he makes clear that 'legal justice is required. We must have a state.' The quality of that legal justice, the nature of the state, he suggests, will depend very much on the prevailing view of the nature of humankind and the kind of relationships one person has with another:

it is very important to know whether the state, society, law and power are required because man is a beast to his neighbour (*homo hominus lupus*) or because I am responsible for my fellow. It is very important to know whether the political order defines man's responsibility or merely restricts his bestiality. (Levinas, in Hand, 1989: 247–8).

Exactly.

Notes

[1] A bicycle is a good example of a structure, in this sense – an assemblage of saddle, wheels, handlebars, etc. would not be 'a bicycle' unless the parts were arranged in the usual way.

[2] The impersonalism of structuralism is particularly associated with Althusser, whose 'theoretical anti-humanism' sees people merely as the bearers of structures. This form of theory is not to be confused with 'structuration theory' formulated by Giddens (1993), which analyses social life in terms of the interaction of social structures which are pre-given to the individual and the individual as active agent.

[3] The most important works in this context are Bauman (1993) *Postmodern Ethics*; Derrida (1990) *'Force of Law: The "Mystical Foundation of Authority"'*; Lyotard and Thébaud (1985) *Just Gaming*, and Lyotard (1988) *The Différend*. Good accounts of these works can be found in Benjamin (1992) *Judging Lyotard*; Boyne and Rattansi (1990) *Postmodernism and Society*; Critchley (1992) *The Ethics of Deconstruction: Derrida and Levinas*; and B. Smart (1999) *Facing Modernity*.

[4] It is worth remembering here that the Athens of Aristotle, which is often invoked by communitarians, and is also invoked by Lyotard, was a society with slavery.

[5] Norman Tebbit, Conservative politician and close ally of prime minister Margaret Thatcher in the 1980s, proposed a 'cricket test' of loyalty to Britain – which team would an Afro-Caribbean or South Asian citizen support if England were playing against the West Indies or India/Pakistan? (Cook, 1993).

[6] Postmodernism is sometimes described as proclaiming that 'all there is text', that representation is all there is of reality. This does not mean, as in the notorious example of Baudrillard's much misunderstood discussion of the reality or otherwise of the Gulf War, that events, actions never happen. What it means is that events and actions are given meaning through language. Humans name events, describe events, participate in events, through language, so that events as well as written documents are 'texts' which are, as it were, brought to life through language. Deconstruction has been likened to a 'restaurant where one can only order the menu' (Berman, 1990, quoted by Lea, 1998: 170). Rather, the point is that one can only order anything by using language, and indeed one can only prepare the dishes on the menu by using language to buy the ingredients, read recipes, instruct kitchen staff.

[7] Putting the pillows and duvet back into a traditional bedding chest when the guests have gone is an example that comes to mind. The bedding always seems too big for the chest, partly because blanket boxes were designed long before duvets became common, at least in the UK, but new or reproduction chests tend to follow the old shape and dimensions.

[8] Levinas's best-known works are *Totality and Infinity: An Essay on Exteriority* (1969); *Otherwise than Being or Beyond Essence* (1981), and *Ethics and Infinity* (1992). Useful collections and readers are Bernasconi and Woods (1988) and Hand (1989).

[9] Lyotard's arguments here echo those of feminists who criticize the expulsion of feeling, body and nature in the modernist discourse of reason.

[10] The connotation Lyotard gives to the word 'archipelago' is somewhat different from Foucault's. Foucault invokes the image of Solzhenitsyn's account of Stalin's 'carceral archipelago'. Lyotard's meaning is closer to the more conventional geographic meaning, denoting a chain of islands, separate but forming a geographical and/or political unit.

7

Doing Justice in the Risk Society

Justice and risk

The starting point for this book was my fear that justice is under threat in the risk society. Demand for security is undermining support for justice. To put this another way, the reduced meaning of security is leading to contraction of the meaning of justice. There is an ever more strident demand for those who threaten our security to be brought to justice, but both 'security' and 'justice' have lost half their traditional connotations. Security has become dominated by the aspect of its meaning which is safety of person and possessions from violation by other people. Being secure in one's freedoms and being secure from government surveillance and restriction, are elements of security which are downgraded. 'Justice' has come to be almost synonymous with punishment, and the aspect of justice that involves taking responsibility for the person who is brought before the court, the Other who is the object on whom state power is brought to bear – justice as alterity – is almost disappearing.

The political problem faced by justice today is encapsulated by Levinas's observation on the different implications of creating social institutions on the basis of dealing with our fellows as threatening beasts or as persons to whom we owe responsibility. Those risk posers with whom state power and public concern is so engaged are not regarded as fellow citizens, essentially the same as lawful citizens, gone wrong but not beyond the reach of moral reasoning and prudential deterrence. In Garland's terms, the range of harms responded to within the framework of criminologies of the self has shrunk and the range of those responded to within the framework of criminologies of the other has expanded (Garland, 1996).

Criminals both within and without the borders of liberal societies are represented and dealt with as *monstruums*: creatures 'whose features are essentially different from ours and shocking to the well-behaved' (Melossi, 2000: 311). These constructions of monstrousness are exemplified by the labelling of street criminals in the USA as *super-predators*, 'the youngest, biggest and baddest generation any society has ever known' (Bennett et al., 1996, quoted by Melossi, 2000: 311). The policy answer to these criminals is the rise of mass imprisonment, the building of life-trashing 'super-max' prisons (Garland, 2001). As Dilulio, one of the authors of the term 'super-predator' puts it, the appropriate policy is 'Let 'Em Rot' (Dilulio, 1994). Another paradigmatic monster is the terrorist, whose grievance warrants no exploration; he or she is presumed immune to normal human emotions such as compassion, and is oblivious to such reasonable objections as the innocence of victims.

These representations create demons who are entirely different from us: their acts are 'impossible to imagine oneself doing, on the edge of human comprehension and empathy' (J. Young, 1999: 114). As Young says, this monstrousness is presented as a quality alien to oneself, a quality possessed by a rogues' gallery of monstrous others. In an age which has seen not only the Holocaust but also ethnic cleansing in late twentieth-century Europe and even thuggish behaviour by British soldiers in Cyprus, the often bizarre and violent forms of sexual desire demonstrate, Young argues, that to accept the binary of normal/monstrous is to deny the monstrousness that lurks in all of us. Acceptance of the binary is also, I would add, to deny the human, the normal, in those we label as monsters.

There are, then, two orders of political challenge that need to be met by those wishing to defend justice in the risk society. First, there is the challenge of de-demonising routine crime, re-establishing that in dealing with burglars, car thieves, muggers and drug dealers we are dealing with people who remain members of our communities. Even crimes we may particularly deplore, such as racial and gendered violence, are reflective of patterns of inclusion and exclusion in our societies (Young, 1999). The second order of challenge is that of dealing with people who are so different that they really do seem to be beyond inclusion in the liberal community. This may be because they are literally outside, coming from other countries; or it may be that they appear to be outside our moral and imaginative community, for example serial killers, paedophiles, 'home grown' terrorists. We should constantly question our boundaries of inclusion and exclusion, but there will always be some who remain excluded from membership and beyond the reach of empathy. We have to find ways of doing justice to these 'outsiders' as well as readmitting some of those we presently classify as outsiders to the status of insiders.

Liberal justice and its critics

We have seen that as well as being undermined by the politics of risk, justice has been challenged by some powerful theoretical adversaries. Communitarians, feminists and postmodernists have found liberal justice wanting in many respects and each of the challengers has exposed important weaknesses in liberalism's capacity to balance individual rights and responsibilities to community; to provide justice appropriate to different identities rather than justice to only those qualities which are male or like the male; or to avoid repression and marginalization of those who do not conform to the characteristics of the self of modern liberal subjectivity.

Liberal theories leave unanswered the question of how much liberty may be curtailed to prevent how much harm, and communitarians fail to answer the question of how much may be demanded of members in support of their community's way of life. Feminist and postmodern theorists have had little concrete to say about how to respond to those who threaten us from within and without our borders. Cornell aspires to a non-violent relationship with the Other; Iris Young has celebrated the heterogeneity of the city where difference is encountered, negotiated and celebrated; Benhabib wonders about the limits of acceptable difference, whether boundaries are those of repugnance or threat. While feminists and post-modernists both refute liberal notions of fixed, unsituated, essentialist identity, they also point to the potential repressiveness of communities towards those who cannot or will not be assimilated into a homogeneous community identity. Where liberal and post-liberal feminists look to liberalism's universalist discourse to provide critique of community values, postmodernists, including postmodern feminists, argue that there can be no philosophically guaranteed universal values. Nonetheless, they too suggest that critique must appeal to an ideal of universalism. Both Judith Butler (1992) and Richard Rorty (1989) espouse the idea of *contingent universals*. They suggest that we should pragmatically adopt ideas such as freedom and equality 'as if' they were universally shared values in order to have standards by which to evaluate our own and other societies and also to derive codes both for our treatment of others and for making claims for our own treatment.

Liberal and communitarian perspectives on criminal justice reflect the logic of identity and the criterion of membership of their philosophical/political background theories. They only consider justice within the society, and only among those who are similar in 'relevant respects'.[1] Both liberal desert theories and communitarian/republican punishment theories assume that penalties derive their possibilities of effectiveness from the fact that criminals can understand the message of community morality and that they will be motivated to avoid the hard treatment of punishment just like any other citizen. Desert theories also justify punishment on the Rawlsian grounds that a desert-based sanctioning system is what all people in the original position would opt for; that even the most disadvantaged are better off in a society governed by the rule of law and therefore the rational part of their will (the part criminals and non-criminals have in common) must want the laws to be upheld. Republican criminal justice depends on identity logic with the idea that a (moderate and constructive) sanctioning system contributes to the enhancement of dominion and that dominion is of equal value to all (Braithwaite and Pettit, 1990).

Theories of justice have not been greatly concerned with questions of risk: liberal theories have been dominated by questions of distribution and post-liberal theories have been dominated by questions of identity (Fraser, 1995b). Nancy Fraser argues that the politics of identity has moved too far away from a politics of justice, with the danger that all difference and all identities are valued equally and are valued indiscriminately (Fraser, 1997). The problem, for Fraser, is that questions of identity have been separated from questions of oppression and inequality, leading to a relativist stance which lacks the ability to respond appropriately to varieties of difference.

Fraser suggests that there are at least three types of difference. Some differences are qualities which have been under-valued but which are desirable and should be more generalized (for example, 'female' caring qualities should be generalised to men); some differences are merely expressions of human diversity which should be acknowledged and enjoyed, whereas others, such as violence and racism, are pathologies which should as far as possible be eradicated. This differentiation of difference seems to provide an opening for a criminal justice which is predicated on difference rather than identity.

From the various critiques of liberal justice there emerge some conditions which justice must satisfy if it is to meet the overlapping demands of communitarian, feminist and postmodern critiques. Justice must be:

- relational – it must take account of relationships between individuals, groups and communities;
- discursive – it must allow claims and counter-claims, critiques and defences of existing values to be weighed against each other in undominated discourse;
- plurivocal – it must recognise and hear the different voices of the plurality of identities and social groups that must have their claims met and find ways of living together, in radically pluralist contemporary societies;
- rights regarding – justice involves defending the rights of individuals and of communities;
- reflective – justice must flow from consideration of the particulars of the individual case rather than subsuming unique circumstances under general categories.

The principle of justice which is at the heart of all the perspectives and theories, the primary point of overlap, is the principle of *equal respect*. This is the *sine qua non* of justice, the one moral imperative common to all conceptions of justice (Reiman, 1990: 123–4).

The previous two chapters explored approaches to justice which attempted to meet these requirements proposed in the critiques of liberalism discussed in Part I. Habermas's discourse theory proposes a procedural model which could meet most of these demands. The affirmative postmodernism of Derrida and Lyotard does not offer a procedural model but does put forward principles and hints towards ways of escaping the liberal closure of justice at the boundaries of community. Postmodern approaches also take seriously the last requirement, that justice should be reflective, that it should address cases in their uniqueness, rather than determining correct outcomes by reference to general rules (Ferrara, 1999). In the next section, modes of criminal justice which approximate to Habermas's discursive justice will be reviewed. This will be followed by a discussion on human rights, which looks towards the Levinasian ideals of responsibility without reciprocity incorporated in post-modernist works. The chapter, and the book, will close with some remarks on balancing risks and rights: these remarks are motivated by the ideal of equal respect.

Discourse and community

The importance of keeping in view the 'situatedness' of individuals within their community is common to most critiques of liberalism, and it is a point which 'reconstructed' liberalism has accepted. Community justice is therefore an idea whose time has come. Community justice was introduced in Chapter 3, and reservations were expressed about its three aspects – community polic-ing, crime prevention and restorative justice. Nonetheless, it is acknowledged that community justice has emerged as the main hope for penal progressives. I return here to restorative justice, exploring some of the conditions under which it could meet the requirements of justice and could contribute to de-demonisation, re-humanisation, of offenders.

I have been anxious, together with other sympathetic doubters, that restorative justice as practised to date has shown insufficient regard for offenders' interests and moral status.[2] It shares with other consequentialist approaches the danger of using offenders as means rather than ends because of its emphasis on reparation to victims and communities (Walgrave, 2002).

Restorative justice aims to provide reparation to victims without subscrib-ing to the vengeful tendency of much recent criminal justice policy and prac-tice, whereby what is good for victims must be painful to offenders (Hudson, 2002b; McEvoy et al., 2002). It aims to provide restoration to the victim and the community while at the same time making constructive demands on offenders that will offer them the possibility of reintegration into the com-munity they have harmed by their crime. Early theoretical advocates of restorative justice proposed it as a move away from punishments that could be harmful to offenders, introducing instead a form of responding to harm that concentrates on restoring fractured relationships between offenders, victims and communities (Van Ness, 1993; Zehr, 1990). Inspiration was drawn from religious communities, aboriginal first nation groups whose justice tra-ditions emphasised restoring relationships and whose punishment practices were designed to be inclusive rather than exclusive.

Restorative justice fulfils the discursive condition outlined by Benhabib and Habermas. Its processes are meetings or conferences in which victims, offenders and (in some models) community representatives offer their accounts of what has happened and what should be done to make amends and to reduce the likelihood of future offending. At its best, this means that victims and offenders are able to give their accounts in their own terms, and be supported by families, friends or other supporters (communities of care). They can tell of the harm suffered, the reasons for the offence, the fear caused in the community – victims and offenders are revealed to each other as real people and communities have a presence as entities that can be harmed (Hudson, 2002b).

For victims, the justice aspiration of turning them into claimants may be approximated. This is the claim made by Hulsman (1986) in relation to serious sexual offences, including rape. Victims, he says, are empowered by having the opportunity to recount the harm done to them in their own words, encouraged and reassured by their own chosen supporters. Similar claims of empowerment are made for restorative justice in relation to racial violence and domestic violence (Hudson, 1998b; Morris and Gelsthorpe, 2000). Care needs to be taken to avoid recreating the oppression of the crime relation: offenders must not be able to intimidate victims by interrupting with forceful interjections of their own version of events or by dehumanising victims through denial of harm or by blaming the victim.

On the other hand, conferences or meetings, if they are to live up to the restorative justice ideal, should take care that offenders are not dominated by other participants. Concerns have been expressed about police-led models, where police may intimidate, where they may lean on young and inexperienced offenders to admit to offences for which there is no substantial evidence or to give evidence about other young people (Braithwaite, 1999; R. Young, 2001). The most comprehensive and wide-ranging evaluation of restorative justice schemes published to date concludes that safeguards for offenders against intimidatory procedures or disproportionate outcomes are inadequate because there is, in most societies, little articulation of offenders' rights generally (Braithwaite, 1999).

The problems connected with restorative justice arise if it is conceived too much as the justice of any one party, whether this is the victim, the offender or the community. While it would not be accurate to see restorative justice simply as part of the victim movement (Kurki, 2000), it is certainly true that one of the main arguments of its proponents has been that formal criminal justice processes marginalise victims, allowing them a limited role as witnesses rather than a central role as claimants. Restorative justice is victim-centred, or at the very least it is victim-sensitive (Wright, 2002).

While criminal justice should certainly be victim-sensitive, the extent to which – and even more, the ways in which – it should be victim-centred, is debatable. Some restorative justice schemes give victims a veto on proposals about reparation and programmes to reduce reoffending, or a veto on the continuance of proceedings, and some schemes prohibit persons whose attitudes may be unacceptable to victims, from participating as supporters for offenders. Some restorative justice advocates come close to saying that they are not concerned with what happens to offenders since their overriding purpose is to provide redress to victims; others come close to saying that they do not need to justify their impositions on offenders because the outcome of restorative justice is not 'punishment', but something else (Dignan, 2002; Walgrave, 2002).

Conversely, restorative justice may be weighted too heavily towards offenders. Along with the desire to make criminal justice more victim-centred, one of the main impulses behind the movement has been to intro-duce more constructive, less exclusionary responses to offending; restorative justice is inspired by the wish to take crime seriously without adding to the relentless penal inflation of recent years. Restorative justice is often seen, by its proponents and its critics, as a form of diversion from formal criminal jus-tice. Police cautioning schemes for juveniles, conferences and meetings instead of formal court proceedings, are intended to divert those who have admitted their offences, out of the criminal justice system with its stigmatis-ing, exclusionary consequences.

Seeing restorative justice as diversion has prompted opposition to its use for a range of acts and actors beyond a narrow range of young offenders committing routine offences. Debate has been particularly intense about the use of restorative justice for domestic violence, with opponents arguing that this is yet another attempt to divert violence against women from the justice system (Lewis et al., 2001). Commenting on sexual assault cases in her eval-uation of South Australia's restorative justice programme for juveniles, Daly (2002a) states that in such cases the objective cannot be diversion. She explains that in these kinds of cases criminal justice processes need to make very strong statements that what has been done is a 'wrong' as well as a 'harm'; that it offends against the moral values of society as well as causing injury to an individual. One of the objections made to the use of restorative justice for domestic violence is that this aspect of public wrong is dissolved within a 'logic of mediation', which recasts the offence as a relationship dif-ficulty (Cobb, 1997). The demand is for effective justice, by which is meant effective in censuring the wrong as well as effective in providing redress and reducing the likelihood of further offending by the perpetrator in the case being dealt with (Hudson, 2002c).

Restorative justice may emphasize reparation to the community rather than either providing redress for victims or assisting reintegration of offenders. 'Restorative cautioning' schemes in England and elsewhere prompted this concern.[3] In these programmes, young people who admit to an offence may receive a police caution rather than being prosecuted in a formal court. The caution is administered in a process which has many of the features of restorative justice: parents or other supporters may be present; they are encouraged to give their account of the offence and the reasons for it; victims may participate but do not necessarily do so; there may be commu-nity representatives present or the community interest may be represented by police. As well as receiving the caution, the young person may be required to undertake some measure of work to make amends to the community, as well as apologising to the victim. The concern is that this 'cautioning plus' imposes penalties without due process. In the years since the schemes were introduced greater care has been taken to ensure that young people taking part would otherwise have been prosecuted rather than receiving a simple caution or having no action taken, and to ensure that impositions are not disproportionate to the harm done.

There are unresolved debates about the role of community in restorative justice: what is the community; how can it be represented; what are its interests (Crawford and Newburn, 2002); and about the respective interests and appropriate responsibilities of community and state (Ashworth, 2002a). Vigorous debates also continue about the extent to which restorative justice ought to incorporate the standards of formal justice and the extent to which the values of retributive criminal justice and restorative justice are compatible (Cavadino and Dignan, 1996; von Hirsch et al., 2002; Zedner, 1994).

It remains to be seen whether restorative justice becomes incorporated into criminal justice as a procedure for dealing with certain offences and offenders allocated to it by the formal system, the first storey of an 'enforcement pyramid' with the usual range of punitive or incapacitative sanctions available for those unsuitable for or unresponsive to restorative measures (Braithwaite, 1999; Ashworth, 2002a), or whether it will become a 'replacement discourse', gradually supplanting formal criminal justice.

Where restorative justice in practice approximates to the ideals of its theorists, it incorporates the principles that justice should be discursive; that it should be responsive to the circumstances of the particular case rather than subsuming individual acts and actors under general classes, and that it should allow a plurality of voices within the discourse. As Braithwaite and Young report in their reviews of restorative justice projects, many schemes make great efforts to guard against domination by any of the parties, and whatever disagreements there may be about the effectiveness of restorative justice in bringing about 'restoration' of victims and offenders to each other, there seems to be general agreement among evaluators that it gains high approval rates among both victims and offenders for providing them with the opportunity to have their say, to be listened to respectfully and to be dealt with fairly (Daly, 2002b).

As well as by approximating as nearly as possible to Habermas's undominated, thematically open ideal speech situation striving for intersubjective understanding, restorative justice can best avoid the potential problems of using either victims or offenders, or even communities, as means rather than ends, by adopting a 'deep' relationalism. Although restorative justice theorists talk about restoring relationships rather than inflicting retributive punishments, there is little by way of in-depth exploration of relationalism in restorative justice theory or expression of relationalism in restorative justice practice. The only relationship which is brought into play is the victim's and offender's relationship with each other as parties to the crime. Relationships of either to the community or to the wider society are not examined: the parties are allotted roles as parties to the crime rather than being seen as involved in a complex web of relationships of responsibilities, opportunities and pressures. The parties locked in their crime relationship can be decontextualised from society, so that the dense relationalism implied by the construct of the situated self is absent from most restorative justice formulations.

Norrie (2000) elaborates a properly relational theory of criminal justice. He examines both the Kantian notion of individual responsibility based on the idea of a rational, freely choosing subject and its opposite, the determinist model of human subjectivity which sees actions as arising from social structure. While he rejects both models standing alone in their strongest forms, he points to an element of truth in both. Norrie adopts Bhaskar's theory of *entity relationalism*, which conceives of identity in terms of a dialectical relationship between individual agency and social structure (Bhaskar, 1993). As a theory of action, Bhaskar's theory is similar in many ways to Giddens's structuration theory, which sees individual agency operating within a social structural context; as a theory of identity it comes close to providing an operational interpretation of Benhabib's version of situated identity which incorporates both individual agency and social constitution.

Norrie argues that criminal justice in liberal societies rests on too strong a form of Kantian free-willing individual responsibility, and so has insufficient capacity to respond to the circumstances and motives of individual, differently situated offenders.[4] He also engages with proponents of communitarian perspectives on criminal justice, paying particular attention to the work of Duff, a primary theorist of the communitarian approach. Norrie argues that Duff's failure to incorporate a dialectical relational view of responsibility leaves him with only the equally unsatisfactory alternatives of remaining within the framework of Kantian individual responsibility, which gives the community the possible roles only of victim/claimant or resource–as in much restorative justice theory and practice to date–or of adopting a social determinist approach. The social determinist model would contradict Duff's communicative ideal of criminal justice, which depends on seeing the offender as someone who can appreciate the wrongness of her offence, who can accept the legitimacy of sanctions, and – crucially – who can change. While Norrie's criticisms may be valid for the works of Duff's on which he principally draws (Duff, 1993a, 1993b, 1996), in more recent work Duff has developed a fuller relational approach.

Through a series of articles culminating in the book *Punishment, Communication and Community*, Duff has reflected on the relationships between offenders, communities and the state (1998a, 1998b, 2001). He explains that his model of punishment and his inclusion of community as an interested party with claims on justice presupposes the existence of a liberal state, with moral values to a large extent shared. The preconditions for justified punishment are that the state represents community values, and that the offender being punished has not only committed an offence, but is also a member of the community. By being a member, Duff means that the offender must not be excluded from the rights and privileges of membership either because of prejudice or discrimination, or because of circumstances such as extreme poverty. If these preconditions do not exist, then the state has no right to punish; if they do exist, then there is a right to punish, and the objective of punishment should be reintegration into the community. Duff allows that either or both state and community may be implicated in the causes of the crime as well as being victims of it, and that either or both may have responsibilities to the offender to remedy exclusion, as well as having claims to redress from the offender.

Duff's justice is very close to the best ideals of restorative justice, but he sketches a relationship between restorative justice (or other forms of community justice) and formal state criminal justice that is distinctive. Where restorative justice allots criminal justice the role of big stick, Duff proposes a regulatory role. The role of formal courts is, he says, to ensure that community justice remains within the parameters of liberal rule of law: the harm principle and due process. Formal criminal justice must ensure that there is no penalisation without a crime being committed and that measures should reflect harm done rather than harm anticipated. Formal courts must stand behind community justice to guarantee the rights of offenders as well as to provide a deterrent or incapacitative big stick.

These reflections on restorative justice and the relational theories of Norrie and Duff point towards the limits of the kinds of discursive justice proposed by Benhabib and Habermas. The limits are those of the social, moral and discursive community. These theories of justice and punishment are operable within the liberal community; they are models for dealing with comprehensible harms inflicted by fellow-citizens. Community justice (in common with other forms of criminal justice) has limits of legitimacy: as Duff argues persuasively, states and communities cannot legitimately punish those whom they exclude from the privileges of membership. Discursive justice has limits of shared understandings: although consensus as desired by Habermas or the acknowledgement of the perspective of the other which is the aspiration of restorative justice may be rare, for discourse to proceed there must be at least some comprehension of the other's point of view. Does restorative justice reach its limits if there are two different and unreconcilable perspectives, his and hers for example (Finstadt, 1990)? How can community or state conceive the appropriate penalty if the offence is one which most of us cannot imagine either as victim or offender, if there is not the slightest sense that in the same circumstances we might feel pressured to do the same? In the international community, how can citizens of liberal democracies imagine what it can be like totally to despair of the possibility of peaceful change; how can those of us raised to value autonomy conceive of the effects of a culture or cult which instils group loyalty or obedience to commands rather than encouraging independent, reflective decision-making?

Discursive justice – whether restorative justice or formal criminal justice reconstructed to give voice to victims and offenders, witnesses and advisers representing a wider range of standpoints – may be able to help ameliorate the first problem I suggested faces risk society, the demonisation of fellow members of society who perpetrate routine harms which, even though they are condemned, can be comprehended. It is difficult to see, however, how it can secure justice for those whom, for whatever reason and in whatever way, we do not recognise as our fellows. To do justice to the ultra-Other, we need to put rights at the centre of our models of justice.

The importance of human rights

Most of the theories and theorists considered have discussed the importance of rights. Whilst some (communitarians) argue that in liberalism rights have been overemphasised at the expense of duties, and others (feminists) point to the limitations of rights as a political discourse for improving the position of women, they do not deny the importance of the existence of rights. Some liberals argue for the extension of rights to include welfare rights and/or cultural rights, while others warn against extending the concept of rights beyond protection of liberalism's negative freedoms (Ignatieff, 2001). There are arguments about whether rights should be universalised, or whether attempts at universalisation are manifestations of western cultural imperialism. Habermas, Benhabib and Iris Young put rights at the centre of their models of justice, and while it has been argued that postmodernism is incompatible with human rights either as a theoretical construction or as a basis for political action (Salter, 1996), in fact the work of Bauman, Derrida and Lyotard rests on a radical conception of rights that makes it possible to fulfil the responsibility we must accept towards the Other. Human rights has become, it seems clear, the major normative discourse of the present era (Cohen, 1993).

There are several good texts dealing with the history of human rights legislation; human rights in both domestic and international law and politics; philosophical arguments and debates.[5] I am concerned here primarily with two issues: to whom are rights owed, and under what circumstances, if any, may they be suspended?

Human rights: conditional or inalienable

The various declarations and conventions specify conditions or reasons for suspensions of the rights they proclaim. These are generally reasons of specific harm or threat to the same rights of others, and also reasons of national security or emergency. It would seem, therefore, that rights, although they may be described as human rights or fundamental freedoms, are conditional.

213

In that sense, the post-1945 generation of rights legislated in the aftermath of the Second World War is little advance on the old declarations of classical liberalism. There is, however, a change of emphasis which is important in establishing the limits to encroachment on human rights which may legitimately be made in the cause of national security.

The eighteenth-century rights charters, such as the American Declaration of Independence and subsequent Bill of Rights, were aimed at laying down frameworks of government. The core of these declarations is to establish democratic governance; the rights are granted by the people themselves through the democratic principle of government-by-the-people. Although the Declaration begins with a Kantian-style reflective statement of fundamental equality, the key issue is popular sovereignty.[6]

The new generation of human rights legislation, however, is designed to protect individuals from the worst things that others may do to them, whether those others are governments, individuals acting in the name of governments, or individuals acting in their own interests. Where the eighteenth-century declarations express hope for a modern era free from ancient tyrannies, the twentieth-century declarations express despair at the depredations human has wrought on fellow human in the modern era.

Although Article 1 of the Universal Declaration of Human Rights (1948) also expresses the Kantian belief in equality and freedom for all, the preamble is sombre:

> Whereas disregard and contempt for human rights have resulted in barbarous acts which have outraged the conscience of mankind...

a stark contrast with the ringing faith of the preamble to the American Declaration of Independence of 1789 that:

> We hold these truths to be self-evident, that all men are created equal, that they are endowed by their Creator with certain unalienable Rights, that among these are Life, Liberty and the Pursuit of Happiness.

After the Second World War, a 'juridical revolution' in rights sought to protect individual human rights from abuse by governments as well as by individuals (Gutman, 2001: viii). The judgment of the Nuremberg Tribunal in 1946 had established that individuals could be found guilty of war crimes and crimes against humanity, and provided for punishment of individuals for violations of international law. Punishment of the vanquished by a tribunal of victors is not difficult to achieve; what has proved far less easy is providing a means for individuals to gain redress for rights violations by governments. The various regional charters, such as the European Convention for Human Rights and Fundamental Freedoms (1953), the American Convention on Human Rights (1969) and the African Charter on Human Rights and People's Rights (1981), are examples of legal instruments introduced to secure rights and provide remedies for individuals within continents or groups of countries.

There have also been many conventions, protocols and declarations aimed at protecting the rights of vulnerable groups – asylum seekers, women, children, religious or racial minorities – and preventing particular sorts of rights violations: torture or the death penalty, for example. Some countries have introduced charters to settle particular rights questions: for example the Canadian Charter of Rights and Freedoms (1982) deals with cultural and language rights of the French-speaking population, as well as with land rights and other political and civil rights of first nation peoples.

While some of the rights contained in national and regional charters are specific to the rights claims in those countries, it follows from the legality and the extent of popular support, acquiescence or denial of the Holocaust (Horwitz, 1992) that, post-1945, the juridical revolution was undertaken to ensure that fundamental human rights would not be suspended (derogated) by governments. How, then, is the balance to be struck between rights and risks?

Ashworth suggests that the European Convention on Human Rights establishes a hierarchy of rights, differentiated according to the permissibility of their derogation (Ashworth, 2002b). At the top of the hierarchy are rights which are *non-derogable*, rights which must be upheld in all circumstances and must never be suspended for public interest reasons. These are the right to life; the right not to be subjected to torture or to inhuman or degrading treatment; the right not to be subjected to forced labour, and the right not to be subjected to retrospective criminal law or penalties. The second level of *strong* rights includes the right to fair trial, and the rights to liberty and security of the person. These rights are not absolute and may be rescinded on occasion, but Ashworth argues that they should be limited only under the most pressing circumstances and that their suspension requires very powerful justification. Third-level rights may be suspended or curtailed when necessary for national security, or when they interfere with the rights of other persons or groups. These third level rights include the right to freedom of expression, the right to freedom of thought and religion, the right to freedom of assembly and association, and the right to respect for private life.

Some commentators suggest that these third-tier rights are best regarded as civil rights rather than human rights. One reason for this is that they are rights which are culturally variable, at least in their interpretation (Parekh, 2000). Another is that they allow the extension of rights claims to such a degree that the moral force of rights discourse may be weakened (Ignatieff, 2001). These writers argue the need to distinguish a core of fundamental human rights which is common to formulations in all cultures, an *overlapping consensus* which marks them out as 'moral rights', values which are at the base of every cultural and religious code of ethics (Perry, 1998). These rights do not derive from and should not be suspended by governments.

This restricted core of rights expresses a 'minimal universalism' and properly represents those aspects of humanity which are common to all of us as members of the species, but it does not impose a culturally specific, western set of rights on non-western societies (Parekh, 2000). The universalism of these core rights is such that they will be defended by members of a culture against others who challenge and flout them. For example, Islamic and Hindu rights groups protest against repression of women, use of torture and mutilation, expectations of ritual suicide by widows, as perversions of their own culture.

The post-war juridical revolution in human rights and its interpretation by progressive liberals such as Ashworth, Ignatieff and Parekh mark a significant advance in dealing with protection of the most fundamental human rights. Adherence to the idea that certain rights are non-derogable, they obtain in all circumstances – that they are inalienable – is, however, by no means widespread, and is certainly not immune to being undermined by risk politics. Terrorist attacks and the instability of world politics since 1989 have given new cogency to the old debating question of the 'ticking bomb'. The question is this: if a captured terrorist knows the location of a bomb primed to go off in a crowded place, is it permissible to torture him to make him reveal the location? An even more morally tricky variant of the question is whether it is morally acceptable to kill an innocent loved one of the terrorist in order to learn the location of the ticking bomb.

The ticking bomb dilemma is discussed by Perry, who sets the view that some rights should be absolute against the argument that it is surely permissible to sacrifice one life to save many (Perry, 1998: 88–106). Perry cites a case before the Supreme Court of Israel involving a Palestinian detainee believed to have information which could save lives by preventing terror attacks in Israel. The lawyers for the government argued that no 'enlightened nation would agree that hundreds of people should lose their lives because of a rule saying torture is forbidden under any circumstances'; the human rights lawyer putting the case against torture was accused of taking an 'immoral and extreme' position (ibid.: 94).

The best-known articulation of the 'never under any circumstances' position is that by Finnis, who links together the ideas of human rights and natural rights (Finnis, 1980). Finnis argues that it can never be right to kill or torture one person to save others because the killing or torture and the saving are different and discrete events: the saving of life is not 'part of the act' of killing or torture. The killing or torture has no consequences other than death or mutilation; the good consequences (saving of innocent lives) are derived from other acts by other people (the tortured, telling the location) not from the acts of the torturers. Finnis depends on an understanding of consequences that is normally thought of as direct consequences, and his argument rests on bracketing together acts and their direct consequences, rather than putting acts together with direct and indirect consequences. This is a much stronger argument for absolute prohibition of intentionally harmful acts such as killing and torture than the more frequently heard argument that the bad consequences of such acts are immediate and certain while the good consequences hoped for are distant and uncertain. Finnis depends not on thinking that the person who is tortured or whose loved one is killed might harden her heart still further, think she has nothing left to lose, and become even more adamant in her refusal to reveal the location of the bomb, but on this principle of the discreteness of acts and consequences, so for him the consequences of one act cannot be justified by another act.

In the Israeli case and in the investigation of Taliban and Al-Quaida fighters in the USA, we find lawyers generally known for defending human rights arguing that torture is permissible in the extreme circumstances these nations face. It is difficult to see how the argument to torture in these instances can be based on the idea that one life or the physical integrity of one person should be sacrificed in order to save a greater number of lives, because both Israel and the USA have gone to great lengths to repatriate prisoners, recover bodies and mount rescue missions on the basis that no one Israeli or American life should ever be sacrificed. Justification depends on either the community condition – we are only required to protect the rights of members of our own community – or the desert condition – some people deserve to have their rights protected more than others do. These actual rather than hypothetical instances demonstrate that even the small core of fundamental or moral rights is not by any means always and everywhere regarded as inalienable.

The 'sacrificing one for many' argument begs the obvious question of how many: should one life be sacrificed or one person tortured only to save hundreds, or would two be enough to justify using one person as means rather than end? This quantitative question arises in less dramatic instances than death or torture. It is raised by the policy of incarcerating persistent offenders on the argument that increased imprisonment can be defended on crime reduction grounds. This policy is often defended in terms of how many crimes can be saved for each high-rate offender incarcerated, and arguments often take the form of debating the numbers rather than the morality of the policy (Zimring and Hawkins, 1995).

It is generally accepted that punishment is consistent with human rights, on the grounds that if rights are to be taken seriously, then sanctions against violations must be available (Martin, 1993, Chapter 9). As well as avoiding cruel and unusual punishments, rights-regarding penal systems are usually thought to be systems where penalties are proportionate to harm done, and where penalties are to be inflicted only after proper conviction in a fair trial. The extent to which due process rights (Ashworth's second tier) may be lifted in the interests of security is contentious. Nowhere has the line been firmly drawn, and in most countries due process rights and public interest derogations are the subject of constant arguments between government and judiciary.

While it is unwise to generalise, it is fair to say that in states where there is experience of occupation, civil war or human rights abuses by governments, rights are more vigorously defended than in states where populations have not had these experiences. One example of this is the United Kingdom, which has gone further in suspension of rights during the Northern Ireland 'troubles' than have, for example, Spain and Germany in dealing with their internal terrorists.[7] Until recently, the USA has been an exception to this generalisation. The USA has been reluctant to introduce wide measures of surveillance and to suspend due process rights because of traditional opposition to 'big government'. This reluctance was apparent in 1995 in the aftermath of the Oklahoma bombings, when people became aware of the threat posed by right-wing paramilitary groups but still did not want greater government intrusion and control; public opinion swung towards greater security activism after the events of 11 September 2001.

What is happening now in most western countries, and what is not warranted by human rights philosophy or jurisprudence, is increasing derogation of second- and third-tier rights for prevention of routine crimes. It is made clear by progressive liberals that these rights should not be suspended except in case of national emergency; that suspensions should be clearly and specifically justified, and that suspensions should be temporary. There is a blurring of the distinction between second-tier rights and third-tier rights, in other words between human rights and civil rights. There is also blurring of the distinction between social problem and national emergency, social utility and vital national security. Terms like 'war on crime' and politicisation of crime rates as exceptional or forms of crime as new and unprecedented, blur this distinction between problem and emergency, utility and security. The result is weakening of adherence even to first-tier rights as well as preference for more intrusive safety and crime prevention strategies at the more or less permanent expense of second- and third-tier rights.

If second-tier rights should only be suspended for real national emergencies, and then only for temporary periods, it is only third-tier rights that may be withheld for more routine public interest reasons. It is with these third-tier civil rights that real conflicts can arise, and most would agree that is permissible (sometimes even desirable) to deny these rights – to free speech, free assembly, privacy, respect for family life – if their exercise on specific occasions risks violation of higher-level rights. This formula justifies denial of free speech and free assembly if they are exercised in calling for actions against minorities which would violate their life, liberty or property; it justifies infringing privacy rights to prevent crime; it justifies violating private family life to prevent abuse of women or children.

Because these third-tier rights are, nonetheless, *rights*, as Dworkin explains, it may well be that rights to freedom from abuse or violation of property rank higher than rights to privacy or freedom of assembly, but it cannot be that the rights to be curtailed count for nothing (Dworkin, 1978). On each occasion a right is to be removed or curtailed, the case must be argued and the right be curtailed for the least time possible and be restricted as little as possible – there should not be blanket derogations. Ashworth is entirely right that core, first-tier rights should be non-derogable, and that second- and third-tier rights should only be derogated under very pressing circumstances. The risk to be countered should be urgent and demonstrable. Higher-order rights should never be suspended or restricted to ensure lower-order rights, and second-tier rights should never be suspended where suspension of third-tier rights would be effective.

So far, this discussion of conditionality or inalienability has looked at the derogation of specific rights in specific circumstances; the question remains of who should have rights. This is perhaps the prior and crucial question: we have seen that what purport to be derogations because of circumstances (such as torture or detention without trial in the face of terrorist threats) often depend on ideas about the limits of states' responsibilities for upholding rights of non-citizens, and of deserving and undeserving persons. The rights most often denied by governments are those of people outside rights-bearing categories.

Prisoners, in most countries, are denied the right to vote, and their rights to family life, freedom of religion and expression, and to privacy, are upheld patchily around the world.[8] The rights of offenders and the rights of victims and potential victims often conflict, and the weight given to each varies with time and place. Preventive sentencing is the clearest example of violation of offenders' rights not to be deprived of liberty other than for a crime of which they have been properly convicted (rather than a crime which they may commit in the future).[9] In a society which is more preoccupied with risks than rights, this protection is held as of much less importance than protecting the rights of potential victims not to be harmed. The standard argument is that offenders' rights lose weight in relation to potential victims' rights with each offence: repeat offending makes the probability of future harm much higher. A rights argument would insist that preventive detention would only be permissible for a repeat offender who had damaged the basic interests of other citizens (life, liberty, integrity of the person), calculated on a scale of harm such as the *living standard* proposed by von Hirsch and Jareborg (1991). This would allow for detention of torturers, even if they were not the architects of the regime of torture but functionaries in the system (Cohen, 1993). It would also allow for the detention of perpetrators of repeated assaults, but would not allow for the detention of persistent minor property offenders.[10]

As well as probability rather than possibility of harms which would have profound impact on the life-quality of potential victims, there is another condition that should be satisfied before resort to preventive incarceration. This is that harm reduction measures short of detention have been tried and have failed. States should not detain persons beyond the term proportionate to the harm inflicted by the conviction offence without making strenuous efforts at rehabilitation. Liberal scholarship on rights and rehabilitation is most often directed at prisoners' rights not to be forced to participate in rehabilitation

219

programmes because of sanctions such as loss of parole or remission consequent on non-participation (von Hirsch, 1976; Hudson, 1987). For the mentally disordered, too, the issue is usually posed as the patient's right to refuse treatment as against the public's right to protection.

If the issue is reformulated so that what is at stake is that the offender/patient's rights to enjoyment of human rights and civil liberties must be combined with protection of similar rights and liberties for victims and potential victims which might be jeopardised by the liberty of the offender/patient, then we arrive at a right to treatment or rehabilitation. The way to square the circle is to offer the offender/patient the help or treatment necessary for them to be able to exercise their rights and enjoy their freedom without harming others. Only after appropriate measures have been made fully available and have either failed or been refused should restrictions of offenders/patients be imposed, and these restrictions should follow the minimum restraint criterion entailed by the principle of least infringement of rights. In every decision about the liberty of an individual offender/patient the least infringement test should be applied; in every harm prevention policy innovation a rights audit should be carried out to ensure that the policy makes as few inroads into rights as possible and does not curtail rights at a higher level than necessary or permissible.

Thinking about rehabilitation brings us back to the need for discursiveness and attention to cases in their particularity: rehabilitative efforts must be tailored to the needs of the individual and the circumstances of the harm, rather than selected from a small range of approved programmes. It is not surprising that one of the most imaginative innovations in balancing rights and risks along the lines suggested above takes place in Canada. Canada is by no means immune to international trends towards increased repression in the name of security and increased imprisonment in the name of protection of the public from crime (Mandel, 1994). On the other hand, it seems to have a more entrenched rights culture than many other countries (including the UK), and it was one of the pioneers of restorative justice. The innovation is *befriending circles* for released sex offenders: a group of people volunteer to act as befrienders for a sex offender, and individually and collectively spend time with the person, sharing a variety of social activities as well as being available for the offender to talk to about circumstances associated with their offending. Experience with befriending circles so far has demonstrated them to be at least as effective as more repressive measures of post-release control, so there is no loss of public protection but a significant increase in the offenders' enjoyment of citizenship (Silverman and Wilson, 2002).

Defending human rights: rights, discourse and community

The Holocaust demonstrated both the necessity of formalised human rights and their fragility (Ignatieff, 2001: 81). This terrible event showed that legal inscription of rights and prosecution of human rights violations are imperative, as there will always be brutality and dehumanisation of persons by their fellows. Ignatieff quotes Shklar's phrase that human rights are prompted by a 'liberalism of fear' (ibid.: 80; Shklar, 1998). The fear that prompted twentieth-century human rights juridical activism was fear of governments, and people acting in the name of governments, unleashing barbarities on individuals and groups. This fear has been heightened by successive waves of gross barbarities across the world. Genocide and systematic rape in Rwanda and Bosnia; mass killings and forced labour in Cambodia; forced labour and imprisonment in China, Burma and many other nations show that we cannot regard the Holocaust as a unique event and we cannot be confident in saying 'never again'.

By the end of the twentieth-century, however, a new liberalism of fear had gripped western nations, this time a fear of strangers from both within and without their own borders (Furedi, 2002). Rights to fair trial, rights to privacy, rights to proportionate penalties, rights to asylum and free movement of peoples are being curtailed because of fear of crime, fear of terrorism, fear of dilution of cultural identity, and fear of economic pressures.

So how can rights best be defended? Lukes looks at five types of society in what he calls 'thought experiments': neither utopias nor dystopias but ideal types of societies well known to us (Lukes, 1993). One of his societies is *pro-letaria*, the socialist society which acknowledges no need of rights because the equalities and oppressions they regulate are presumed to have withered away. The other four are variants of liberal society. Rights are unsafe in *util-itaria*, Lukes says, quoting Bentham's pronouncement that 'there is no right which, when the abolition of it is beneficial to society, should not be abolished' (ibid.: 28). *Communitaria* is very similar to utilitaria, in that individual rights are not held to be of greater importance than the good of the community; in particular, rights will not be upheld when to do so would threaten the values and traditions of the community. Moreover, rights are said by communitarians such as MacIntyre to derive from the community and so to be local and specific in character.[11] Utilitarianism and communitarianism deny the very meaning and purpose of rights, Lukes argues. Rights, he correctly says, are restraints on what may be done in the interest of society or community; they are ideas which invoke abstraction from, and therefore allow critique of, spe-cific and local practices; they presuppose certain permanent existential facts about human beings that are not culturally and locally specific.

Turning to two types of liberal society which appear to take rights seri-ously, Lukes points out that in *libertaria* only a narrow set of rights is defended, and also that no-one ever transcends concern for their own or their family's interests. *Egalitaria* is a promised land for human rights, where all will be given equal opportunities for full exercise of rights. Lukes argues that egalitaria is probably unattainable and perhaps should be accepted as unat-tainable, since attempts to implement egalitarian ideals beyond a certain point turn into denials of freedom. For Lukes, human rights is that certain point. He describes human rights as a liberal/egalitarian plateau: a plateau which, he exhorts, needs to be defended.

In the same volume of essays, Rawls reiterates what I will call the *rights stop* of liberalism, the stop which reveals how easily liberalism slides into communitarianism. Rawls gives the old, American constitution, version of rights, saying that rights express standards for

> well-ordered political institutions for all peoples who belong, *as members in good standing*, to a just political society of peoples. (Rawls, 1993b: 68, emphasis added)

Rights apply, according to Rawls, between

> responsible and co-operating members of society who can recognize and act in accordance with their moral duties and expectations. (ibid.: 69)

This rights-stop shows why liberal rights are so easily set aside in the interests of social utility, and why the gap between communitarianism, Utilitarianism, and 'straight' liberalism is so narrow. Offenders, suspects, asylum seekers, dissidents and other such groups are not 'in good standing', and some, such as terror suspects and foreign criminals, will not be of any standing at all. Yet these are the very people rights are needed to protect. Rawls's description of rights does not go beyond civil rights to human rights.

Human rights are needed to prevent stripping people of the status of 'good standing'. Hannah Arendt famously and chillingly describes how the Nazis' stripping the Jews' attributes of good standing as citizens revealed how little (mere) common humanity commands our pity and our humane dealing (Arendt, 1973). We need human rights to protect those persons who are – for whatever reason – beyond our empathy and beyond our recognition as fellow-citizens of good standing.

This view of human rights as the necessary mechanism for securing decent treatment for those who are unable to obtain such dealing through respect, sympathy or fellow feeling is shared by Dworkin, Ignatieff and others who see legally enforceable rights as the way to guard against the inhumane proclivities of human kind. Rorty, on the other hand, has a different approach to the problem of how to secure decent treatment for those who are beyond sympathy or respect. Echoing Lukes's point about the self-interested narrowness of liberal concern, he asks

> ... why should I care about a stranger, a person who is no kin to me, a person whose habits I find disgusting?

and the answer, he says, is not to be found in moral philosophy or law but in

> ... the sort of long, sad, sentimental journey which begins 'Because this is what it is like to be in her situation – to be far from home, among

strangers,' or 'Because she might become your daughter-in-law', or 'Because her mother would grieve for her.' (Rorty, 1993: 133)

Rorty argues that it is no use starting appeals for humane dealing on the basis of common humanity, because most humans do not found their sense of themselves on commonness with others but on *not* being certain kinds of humans. Most of us want to think of ourselves, he says, as being a good sort of human – not a criminal, not a terrorist, not a scrounger. The more people are impoverished and at risk, he says, the more their self-respect depends on not being as bad as other sorts of people, and the more dangerous people's situation, the less they have time for concern about persons with whom they do not identify. The way to ensure human rights is, he argues, a 'progress of sentiment', a progress which consists in an increasing ability to see the similarities between others and ourselves as outweighing the differences. Rorty stresses that the similarities he has in mind are not the abstractions of an essential human nature, but the everyday similarities of caring for our parents or children, and grieving when they are hurt (ibid.: 129).[12]

Defending human rights in the risk society demands challenging dehumanisation of anyone. Whatever their crime, no person is devoid of humanity, and labels such as 'evil', 'animal' and 'super-predator' which define people entirely by their wrongdoing should be contested. The universalism of human rights is a vital counter-discourse to the utilitarianism of risk society. While the content of human rights may be a minimalist core of overlapping cross-cultural values, the reach of human rights could not be more extensive: all persons, not just members of one's own community, not just members in good standing in any community, have rights that each of us is morally obliged to uphold.

Defending human rights in this universalist rather than narrowly communitarian mode means adopting the Levinasian principle of responsibility before reciprocity: the fact that people's actions, beliefs or attitudes are reprehensible or beyond my comprehension does not mean that I do not have the responsibility strenuously to defend their rights. This means that all must have access to discourse, and that processes for dealing with rights and harms must be open to outsiders' stories as well as insiders' stories. As Lyotard puts it, the universalism of human rights is 'the right of universal access to discourse: the silencing of a human being, even if that being has committed a heinous crime, is an irredeemable wrong' (Lyotard, 1993: 144).

Beyond the core of fundamental human rights, rights and wrongs can never be static. New rights concerned with identity and entitlement have been an important part of struggles for justice in the late twentieth-century (Fraser, 1995b), whilst passionate advocacy has led to gradual recognition of 'new' wrongs such as genocide, and acknowledgement of violations particular to women, such as systematic rape, forced motherhood, forced prostitution.

These were not mentioned in the catalogue of 'acts that outraged the conscience of the world' in 1948, but they are now recognised as being of such a category, and so are included in the hearings following crimes against humanity in Rwanda, Bosnia and Kosovo (MacKinnon, 1993). Denial must be challenged at every level, from housing estates suffering endless incidents of crime and disorder to groups suffering gross human rights violations. Discourse must bring forward full acknowledgement of wrongs, but it must not deny the rights of the wrongdoer, the suspect, the different or the dislikeable.

Discourse does not mean straining towards consensus, it does not mean dissolving wrongness into relationship difficulties. Discourse as a process of justice means that all claims must be listened to respectfully and that denial either of wrongs done or of the humanity of the wronged and the wrongdoers is ruled out: the culture of denial in all its forms must always and everywhere be challenged (Cohen, 2000). The appropriate response to wrongs may be punishment, it may be compensation; it should always be acknowledgement, it should never be vengeance, but it may rarely be forgiveness (Minow, 1998). Discourse brings the ethical voice into justice, because it establishes communication. Discussing the handling of torture allegations by South Africa's Truth and Reconciliation Commission, Christodoulidis contrasts the negation of communication which torture imposes – the torturer cannot allow himself to be moved by the cries of pain of the victim – with the re-establishing of communication in the hearings (Christodoulidis, 2000). The torturer is not interested in the victim as a human, a person with passions and beliefs, loved ones and interests. He may not even be interested in whether or not the victim has done that of which he is accused: all he cares about is extracting more information, names and places (Gaete, 1996). Discursive justice re-establishes the communication which the torturer has refused.

Taking rights seriously means taking risks seriously because it means providing for the full enjoyment of rights and preventing infringements. This may entail punishment or control of those who threaten others' enjoyment of rights. On the other hand, rights impose restrictions on what may be done in response to actual or anticipated harm. Returning to the problem of the ticking bomb, we must reject the idea that the only alternatives are violating the fundamental rights of the kidnapped terrorist suspect, or doing nothing and thereby failing to protect the same rights to life and bodily integrity of the potential victims. The rights balance approach would insist that while there are some things one may not do in pursuit of public safety, one must do something. Rather than wasting time deliberating the constitutionality of torture or killing, getting together a group of moral philosophers and lawyers to settle the argument, all state resources should be put into immediate action to find the bomb by other means.

The currently fashionable coupling of rights and responsibilities, the communitarian strand in much social and penal policy, threatens justice because of its incompatibility with the idea of human rights. To apply conditions as to who may enjoy rights – be they terrorists or routine criminals – is to turn away from the understanding of human rights as universal and inalienable that is the legacy of the Holocaust. The fearfulness of risk society is leading western societies to respond to dangers in ways that undermine the basic values of liberal societies, values honed to guard against the dangers of repression and inhumanity as well as to express commitment to democratic governance (Dworkin, 2002). A doctrine of fundamental rights, with some regarded as inviolable and no human being regarded as outside the moral community of rights, is the necessary counterweight to a discursive mode of hearing of harms, providing redress, and trying to reduce the likelihood of future harm.

A Levinasian uncoupling of rights and responsibilities is needed to restore security and justice to their full meanings. Justice entails openness of discourse for claiming redress for harm done and for promulgating policies to prevent future harms, balanced by strong commitment to universal, inalienable, human rights. This is the equilibrium of justice in the risk society.

Notes

[1] See Matravers (2000) for an excellent discussion of punishment in the context of political philosophy.

[2] See von Hirsch et al. (2002) for a debate between restorative justice advocates, desert theorists, and some who stand between the two positions.

[3] See R. Young (2001) for a review of the best-known of the English schemes, the programme run by Thames Valley police.

[4] This is an argument I have also made, in the context of law's inability to give proper consideration to deprivation and restriction of choices. The problem, I have argued, is law's emphasis on agency and its lack of understanding of choice, leading to a conflation of 'responsibility' and 'culpability' (Hudson, 1999, 2000).

[5] See, for example, Brownlie and Goodwin-Gill (2002); Dunne and Wheeler (1999); Evans (1998); Janis et al. (2000); Shute and Hurley (1993); Smith (2002); Steiner and Alston (2000); Wadham and Mountfield (2002).

[6] This is why incorporation of international conventions is difficult in the US: they do not emanate from the will of the American people. Ignatieff argues that this explains the difference between European and Canadian attitudes to the death penalty and those in the US. For Europeans and Canadians, the death penalty is a contravention of the right to life (Article 3 in the Universal Declaration of Human Rights), but for the US it is an expression of the will of the people, and as such could only be abolished through the US electoral process (Ignatieff, 2001: 14).

[7] The 'Diplock' courts which tried cases without juries, and internment of suspected members of the IRA and proscribed Loyalist organisations imposed detention without conviction in a properly constituted court of law.

[8] A recent judgment by the Canadian Supreme Court holds that the disenfranchisement of prisoners is unconstitutional because it is incompatible with the Canadian Charter of Rights and Freedoms (*Soave v. Canada* [Chief Electoral Officer], 2002 SCC 68.)

[9] This is discussed in Chapter 2, above.

[10]Preventive detention is not concerned with the perpetrators of gross violations of human rights or the most serious crimes against the person: these warrant lengthy detention on desert grounds.

[11]The USA's attitude to the death penalty discussed above is perhaps an example of Lukes's sketch of the position of rights in communitaria.

[12]Parekh makes a similar point in relation to the mad or mentally handicapped – they too, he says, are sons, daughters, parents, friends of normal human beings to whom they are deeply bonded (Parekh, 2000: 131).

References

Abel, R. (1995) 'Contested communities', *Journal of Law and Society*, 22: 113–26

Ackerman, B.A. (1980) *Social Justice in the Liberal State*, New Haven, Conn.: Yale University Press

Acton, H.B. (1970) *Kant's Moral Philosophy*, London: Macmillan

Adorno, T.W. (1950) with E. Frenkel-Brunswick, D.J. Levinson and R.N. Sanford, *The Authoritarian Personality*, New York: Harper

Adorno, T.W. (1973) with M. Horkheimer, *The Dialectic of the Enlightenment*, trans. J. Cumming, London: Allen Lane

Adorno, T.W. (1973) *Negative Dialectics*, New York: Continuum

Althusser, L. (1969) *For Marx*, trans. B.R Bennett, London: Allen Lane

Althusser, L. (1976) *Essays in Self-Criticism*, trans. G. Lock, London: New Left Books

American Friends Service Committee (1972) *Struggle for Justice*, New York: Hill and Wang

Anderson, P. and Mann, N. (1997) *Safety First: The Making of New Labour*, London: Granta

Arendt, H. (1973) *The Origins of Totalitarianism*, New York: Harcourt and Brace

Ashworth, A. (2002a) 'Responsibilities, rights and restorative justice', *British Journal of Criminology*, 42, 3: 578–95

Ashworth, A. (2002b) *Human Rights, Serious Crime and Criminal Procedure*, The Hamlyn Lectures, London: Sweet and Maxwell

Austin, J. and Krisberg, B. (1981) 'Wider, stronger and different nets: the dialectics of criminal justice reform', *Journal of Research in Crime and Delinquency*, 18, 1: 165–96

Bal, P. (1996) 'Discourse ethics and human rights in criminal procedure', in M. Deflem, ed. *Habermas, Modernity and Law*, London: Sage

Barnett, H. (1998) *Introduction to Feminist Jurisprudence*, London: Cavendish Publishing

Barry, B. (1965) *Political Argument*, London: Routledge and Kegan Paul

Barry, B. (1973) *The Liberal Theory of Justice*, Oxford: Oxford University Press

Barry, B. (1995) *A Treatise on Social Justice Vol. 11 Justice as Impartiality*, Oxford: Clarendon Press

Bassett, K. (1996) 'Partnerships, business and urban politics: new forms of urban governance', *Urban Studies*, 33, 3: 539–55

Bauman, Z. (1987) *Legislators and Interpreters: On Modernity, Post-Modernity and Intellectuals*, Cambridge: Polity Press

Bauman, Z. (1989) *Modernity and the Holocaust*, Cambridge: Polity Press

Bauman, Z. (1991) *Modernity and Ambivalence*, Cambridge: Polity Press

Bauman, Z. (1993) *Postmodern Ethics*, Oxford: Blackwell

Bauman, Z. (1996) 'On communitarians and human freedom: or, how to square the circle', *Theory, Culture and Society* 13, 2: 79–90

Bauman, Z. (2001) 'Social Issues of Law and Order', *British Journal of Criminology*, 40, 2: 205–21

Baumeister, A. (2000) *Liberalism and the Politics of Difference*, Edinburgh: Edinburgh University Press

Beccaria, C. (1999) 'On Crimes and Punishments', in D. Williams, ed. *The Enlightenment*, Cambridge: Cambridge University Press, pp. 439–70

Beck, A. and Willis, A. (1995) *Crime and Security: Managing the Risk to Safe Shopping*, Leicester: Perpetuity Press

Beck, U. (1992) *Risk Society: Towards a New Modernism*, London: Sage

Beck, U., Giddens, A. and Lash, S. (1994) *Reflexive Modernization: Politics, Tradition and Aesthetics in the Modern Social Order*, Cambridge: Polity Press

Beiner, R. (1992) *What's the Matter with Liberalism?* Berkeley: University of California Press

Bellah, R.N., Masden, R., Sullivan, W.M., Swindler, A. and Tipton, S.M. (1996) *Habits of the Heart - Individualism and Commitment in American Life*, New York: University of California Press

Bellamy, R. (1998) 'Justice in the community: Walzer on pluralism, justice and equality', in D. Boucher and P. Kelly, eds, *Social Justice: From Hume to Walzer*, London: Routledge

Bellamy, R. (2000) *Rethinking Liberalism*, London: Pinter

Benhabib, S. (1986) *Critique, Norm and Utopia*, New York: Columbia University Press

Benhabib, S. (1987) 'The generalized and the concrete other', in S. Benhabib and D. Cornell, eds, *Feminism as Critique*, London: Polity Press, pp. 77–96

Benhabib, S. (1990) 'In the shadow of Aristotle and Hegel: communicative ethics and current controversies in practical philosophy' in M. Kelly, ed. *Hermeneutics and Critical Theory in Ethics and Politics*, Cambridge, Mass.: MIT Press

Benhabib, S. (1992) *Situating the Self: Gender, Community and Postmodernism in Contemporary Ethics*, Cambridge: Polity Press

Benhabib, S. (1995) 'Subjectivity, historiography and politics', in S. Benhabib, D. Cornell and N. Fraser, eds, *Feminist Contentions*, London: Routledge

Benhabib, S., Butler, J., Cornell, D. and Fraser, N., eds. (1995) *Feminist Contentions*, London Routledge

Benjamin, A., ed. (1992) *Judging Lyotard*, London: Routledge

Bennett, W.J., DiIulio, J.B. Jr., and Walters, J.P. (1996) *Body Count: Moral Poverty ... And How to Win America's War Against Crime and Drugs*, New York: Simon and Schuster

Bentham, J. (1970) *An Introduction to the Principles of Morals and Legislation*, ed. J.H. Burns and H.L.A. Hart, London: Methuen (first published 1789)

Berlin, I. (1969) *Four Essays on Liberty*, Oxford: Oxford University Press

Berman, R. (1990) 'Troping to Pretoria: the rise and fall of deconstruction', *Telos*, 85 (Fall): 4–6

Bernasconi, R. and Woods, D. (1988) *The Provocation of Levinas: Rethinking the Other*, London: Routledge

Bernstein, J.M. (1995) *Recovering Ethical Life: Jürgen Habermas and the future of Critical Theory*, London: Routledge

Bhaskar, R. (1993) *Dialectic: the Pulse of Freedom*, London: Verso

Blum, L.A. (1988) 'Gilligan and Kohlberg: implications for moral theory', *Ethics*, 98: 47–91

Body-Gendrot, S. (2000) *The Social Control of Cities*, Oxford: Gendrot

Bohman, J. (1994) 'Review essay: Complexity, pluralism and the constitutional state: on Habermas's *Faktizitat und Geltung*', *Law and Society Review*, 28, 4: 897–930

Bottoms, A.E. (1995) 'The Philosophy and politics of punishment and sentencing', in C.R.V. Clarkson and R. Morgan, eds, *The Politics of Sentencing Reform*, Oxford: Clarendon Press

Bottoms, A.E. and Brownsword, R. (1983) 'Dangerousness and rights', in J. Hinton, ed. *Dangerousness: Problems of Assessment and Prediction*, London: Allen and Unwin

Bowling, B. (1999) *Violent Racism: Victimisation, Policing and Social Context*, revised edition, Oxford: Oxford University Press

Boyne, R. and Rattansi, A., eds. (1990) *Postmodernism and Society*, London: Macmillan

Braithwaite, J. (1989) *Crime, Shame and Reintegration*, Cambridge: Cambridge University Press

Braithwaite, J. (1999) 'Restorative justice: assessing optimistic and pessimistic accounts', in M. Tonry, ed. *Crime and Justice: A Review of Research*, vol. 25, Chicago: University of Chicago Press, pp. 1–127

Braithwaite, J. and Pettit, P. (1990) *Not Just Deserts: A Republican Theory of Criminal Justice*, Oxford: Clarendon Press

Brindle, D. (2000) 'Detention law "an abuse of rights" ', the *Guardian*, 26 May, p. 11

Brownlee, I. (1998) 'New Labour – new penology? Punitive rhetoric and the limits of managerialism in criminal justice policy', *Journal of Law and Society*, 25, 3: 313–35

Brownlie, I. and Goodwin-Gill, G.S. (2002) *Basic Documents on Human Rights*, 4th edition, Oxford: Oxford University Press

Burchell, G., Gordon, C. and Miller, P. eds. (1991) *The Foucault Effect: Studies in Governmentality*, Chicago: University of Chicago Press

Butler, J. (1990) *Gender Trouble: Feminism and the Subversion of Identity*, New York and London: Routledge

Butler, J. (1992) 'Contingent foundations: Feminism and the question of postmodernism', in J. Butler and J.W. Scott, eds. *Feminists Theorize the Political*, London: Routledge

Butler, J. (1995) 'For a careful reading', in S. Benhabib, J. Butler, D. Cornell and N. Fraser, eds, *Feminist Contentions*, London: Routledge

Butler, J. and Scott, J.W. (1992) *Feminists Theorize the Political*, London: Routledge

Campbell, B. (1993) *Goliath: Britain's Dangerous Places*, London: Methuen

Carlen, P. (1990) *Alternatives to Women's Imprisonment*, Milton Keynes: Open University Press

Carlen, P. (1998) *Sledgehammer: Women's Imprisonment at the Millennium*, Basingstoke: Macmillan

Carrington, F. (1983) *Crime and Justice: A Conservative Strategy*, Washington, DC: The Heritage Foundation

Carty, A. (1990) 'Introduction: Post-modern law', in A. Carty, ed. *Post-Modern Law: Enlightenment, Revolution and the Death of Man*, Edinburgh: Edinburgh University Press

Castel, R. (1991) 'From dangerousness to risk', in G. Burchell, C. Gordon and P. Miller, eds, *The Foucault Effect: Studies in Governmentality*, Chicago: University of Chicago Press

Cavadino, M. and Dignan, J. (1996) 'Reparation, retribution and rights', *International Review of Victimology*, 4: 233–53

Cavadino. M. and Dignan, J. (1997) *The Penal System: An Introduction*, 2nd edition, London: Sage

Chesney-Lind, M. and Bloom, B. (1997) 'Feminist criminology: thinking about women and crime', in B.D. MacLean and D. Milanovic, eds, *Thinking Critically About Crime*, Vancouver: Collective Press

Chodorow, N. (1978) *The Reproduction of Mothering: Psychoanalysis and the Sociology of Gender*, Berkeley, Calif.: Berkeley University Press

Chomsky, N. (1964) *Current Issues in Linguistic Theory*, The Hague: Mouton

Chomsky, N. (1972) *Studies on Semantics in Generative Grammar*, The Hague: Mouton

Chomsky, N. (1975) *The Logical Structure of Linguistic Theory*, New York: Plenum Press

Christie, N. (1993) *Crime Control as Industry: Towards Gulags Western Style?* London: Routledge

Christodoulidis, E. (2000) 'Truth and reconciliation as risks', *Social and Legal Studies*, 9, 2: 179–204

Clear, T. and Cadora, E. (2001) 'Risk and community practice', in K. Stenson and R.R. Sullivan, eds, *Crime, Risk and Justice: The Politics of Crime Control in Liberal Democracies*, Cullompton: Willan Publishing

Clear, T.R. and Karp, D.R. (1999) *The Community Justice Ideal: Preventing Crime and Achieving Justice*, Chicago: Westview Press

Cobb, S. (1997) 'The domestication of violence in mediation', *Law and Society Review*, 31: 397–440

Cohen, J. and Rogers, J. (1995) *Democracy and Association*, London: Verso

Cohen, S. (1979) 'The punitive city: notes on the dispersal of social control', *Contemporary Crises*, 3: 339–63

Cohen, S. (1985) *Visions of Social Control: Crime, Punishment and Classification*, Cambridge: Polity Press

Cohen, S. (1993) 'Human rights and crimes of the state: the culture of denial', *Australia and New Zealand Journal of Criminology*, 26: 9–15

Cohen, S. (2000) *States of Denial: Knowing About Atrocities and Suffering*, Cambridge: Polity Press

Connerton, P. (1976) *Critical Sociology*, Harmondsworth: Penguin

Cook, D. (1989) *Rich Law, Poor Law*, Milton Keyes: Open University press

Cook, D. (1993) 'Racism, citizenship and exclusion', in D. Cook and B. Hudson, eds, *Racism and Criminology*, London: Sage

Cooke, R. (2001) 'Snap decisions', the *Guardian*, 30 October: 8

Coole, D. (1996) 'Habermas and the question of alterity', in M. Passerim d'Entreves and S. Benhabib, eds. *Habermas and the Unfinished Project of Modernity*, Cambridge: Polity Press

Cornell, D. (1991) *Beyond Accommodation: Ethical Feminism, Deconstruction and the Law*, London: Routledge

Cornell, D. (1992) *The Philosophy of the Limit*, New York: Routledge

Cornell, D. (1995a) 'Rethinking the time of feminism', in S. Benhabib, J. Butler, D. Cornell, and N. Fraser, *Feminist Contentions*, London: Routledge

Cornell, D. (1995b) *The Imaginary Domain*, London: Routledge

Cornell, D. (1995c) 'What is ethical feminism?' in S. Benhabib et al., op. cit.

Cotterell, R. (1984) *The Sociology of Law: An Introduction*, London: Butterworths

Cover, R. (1986) 'Violence and the word', *Yale Law Journal*, 95: 160–29

Crawford, A. (1996) 'The spirit of community: rights, responsibilities and the communitarian agenda', *Journal of Law and Society*, 23, 2: 24–62

Crawford, A. (1997) *The Local Governance of Crime*, Oxford: Clarendon Press

Crawford, A. (1998) 'Community safety and the quest for security: holding back the dynamics of social exclusion', *Policy Studies*, 19, 34: 237–53

Crawford, A. and Goodey, J., eds. (2000) *Integrating a Victim Perspective within Criminal Justice*, Aldershot: Ashgate

Crawford, A. and Newburn, T. (2002) 'Recent developments in restorative justice for young people in england and wales: community participation and representation', *British Journal of Criminology*, 42, 3: 476–95

Critchley, S. (1992) *The Ethics of Deconstruction: Derrida and Levinas*, Oxford: Blackwell

Crook, S. (1999) 'Ordering risks', in D. Lupton, ed. *Risk and Sociocultural Theory*, Cambridge: Cambridge University Press

Dallmyr, F. (1996) 'The discourse of modernity: Hegel, Nietzsche, Heidegger and Habermas', in M. Passerim d'Entreves and S. Benhabib, eds, *Habermas and the Unfinished Project of Modernity*, Cambridge: Polity Press

Daly, K. (1989) 'Criminal justice ideologies and practices in different voices: some feminist questions about justice', *International Journal of the Sociology of law*, 17: 1–18

Daly, K. (1994) *Gender, Crime and Punishment,* New Haven, Conn: Yale University Press

Daly, K. (2002a) 'Sexual assault and restorative justice', in H. Strang and J. Braithwaite, eds. *Restorative Justice and Family Violence*, Melbourne: Cambridge University Press

Daly, K. (2000b) 'Restorative justice: the real story', *Punishment and Society*, 4, 1: 55–79

Daly, K. and Immarigeon, R. (1998) 'The past, present and future of restorative justice: some critical reflections', *Contemporary Justice Review*, 1, 1: 21–45

Damico, A., ed. (1986) *Liberals and Liberalism*, Totowa, NJ: Rowman and Littlefield

Davis, M. (1990) *City of Quartz*, Berkeley: University of California Press

Deflem, M. (1996) ed. *Habermas, Modernity and Law*, London: Sage

De Haan, W. (1990) *The Politics of Redress: Crime, Punishment and Penal Abolition*, London: Unwin Hyman

Derrida, J. (1978) *Writing and Difference*, trans. Alan Bass, London: Routledge and Kegan Paul

Derrida, J. (1987) 'The laws of reflection: Nelson Mandela, in admiration', in J. Derrida and M. Thili, eds, *For Nelson Mandela*, New York: Seaver Books

Derrida, J. (1990) 'Force of law: the "Mystical Foundation of Authority"', *Cardozo Law Review*, 11: 919–1045

Dershowitz, A.M. (1997) *Reasonable Doubt: The Criminal Justice System and the O.J. Simpson Case*, New York: Touchstone

Dews, P. (1992) 'Editor's Introduction', in P. Dews, ed. *Autonomy and Solidarity: Interviews with Jürgen Habermas*, revised edition, London: Verso

Dignan, J. (2002) 'Restorative justice: limiting principles', in A. von Hirsch, J. Roberts, A.E. Bottoms, K. Roach and M. Schiff, eds. *Restorative Justice and Criminal Justice: Competing or Reconcilable Paradigms?* Oxford: Hart Publishing

Dilulio, J.J. (1994) 'Let 'em rot', *Wall Street Journal*, 26 January: 1714.

D Istefano, C. (1990) 'Dilemmas of difference: feminism, modernity and postmodernism', in L. Nicholson, ed. *Feminism/Postmodernism*, London: Routledge

Douglas, M. (1966) *Purity and Danger: An Analysis of Conceptions of Purity and Taboo*, London: Routledge and Kegan Paul

Douglas, M. (1992) *Risk and Blame: Essays in Cultural Theory*, London: Routledge

Douglas, M. and Wildavsky, A. (1982) *Risk and Culture: An Essay on the Selection of Technological and Environmental Dangers*, Berkeley: University of California Press

Douzinas, C. and Warrington, R. (1994) 'The face of justice: a jurisprudence of alterity', *Social and Legal Studies*, 3, 3: 405–26

Dryzek, J. (1990) *Discursive Democracy: Politics, Policy and Political Science*, New York: Cambridge University Press

Duff, R.A. (1986) *Trials and Punishment*, Cambridge: Cambridge University Press

Duff, R.A. (1993a) *Intention, Agency and Criminal Liability*, Oxford: Blackwell

Duff, R.A. (1993b) 'Choice, character and criminal liability', *Law and Philosophy:* (12) 345

Duff, R.A. (1996) 'Penal communications: recent work in the philosophy of punishment', in M. Tonry, ed. *Crime and Justice: A Review of Research*, vol. 20, pp. 97, Chicago: University of Chicago Press

Duff, R.A. (1998a) 'Law, language and community: some preconditions of criminal liability', *Oxford Journal of Legal Studies*, (18) 189–206

Duff, R.A. (1998b) 'Inclusion and exclusion: citizens, subjects and outlaws', *Current Legal Problems*, 51: 24–66

Duff, R.A. (2001) *Punishment, Communication and Community*, Oxford: Oxford University Press

Dunne, T. and Wheeler, N.J., eds. (1999) *Human Rights in Global Politics*, Cambridge: Cambridge University Press

Dworkin, R. (1978) *Taking Rights Seriously*, Cambridge, Mass: Harvard University Press

Dworkin, R. (1986 a) *A Matter of Principle*, Oxford: Clarendon Press

Dworkin, R. (1986b) *Law's Empire*, London: Fontana

Dworkin, R. (2002) 'The real threat to US values', the *Guardian*, Saturday Review, 9 March: 3

Eaton, M. (1986) *Justice for Women? Family, Court and Social Control*, Milton Keynes: Open University Press

Edwards, S. (1984) *Women on Trial*, Manchester: Manchester University Press

Ericson, R. and Carriere, K. (1994) 'The fragmentation of criminology', in D. Nelken, ed. *The Futures of Criminology*, London: Sage

Etzioni, A. (1993) *The Spirit of Community: Rights, Responsibilities and the Communitarian Agenda*, New York: Simon and Schuster

Etzioni, A., ed. (1998) *The Essential Communitarian Reader*, New York: Rowman and Littlefield

Evans, J., ed. (1998) *Human Rights Fifty Years On: A Reappraisal*, Manchester: Manchester University Press

Ewald, F. (1991) 'Insurance and Risk', in G. Burchell et al., op. cit.

Farrington, D.P. (1997) 'Human development and criminal careers', in M. Maguire, R. Morgan and R. Reiner, eds. *The Oxford Handbook of Criminology*, 2nd edition, Oxford: Clarendon Press

Faulkner, D. (1996) *Darkness and Light: Justice, Crime and Management for Today*, London: Howard League for Penal Reform

Feeley, M. and Simon, J. (1992) 'The new penology: notes on the emerging strategy of communications and its implications', *Criminology*, 30: 449–74

Feeley, M. and Simon, J. (1994) 'Actuarial justice: the emerging new criminal Law', in D. Nelken, ed. *The Futures of Criminology*, London: Sage

Ferrara, A. (1999) *Justice and Judgment: The Rise and the Prospect of the Judgment Model in Contemporary Political Philosophy*, London: Sage

Fineman, M.A. and Thomadsen, N.S. (1991) *At the Boundaries of Law: Feminism and Legal Theory*, London: Routledge

Finnis, J. (1980) *Natural Law and Natural Rights,* Oxford: Clarendon Press

Finstadt, L. (1990) 'Sexual offenders out of prison: principles for a realistic utopia', *International Journal of the Sociology of Law*, 18: 157

Fishkin, J. (1991) *Deliberative Democracy*, New Haven, Conn: Yale University Press

Fitzpatrick, P. (1992) *The Mythology of Modern Law*, London: Routledge

Flax, J. (1995) 'Race, gender and the ethics of difference', *Political Theory*, 23, 3: 500–10

Fleisher, M. (1994) 'Down the passage which we should not take: the folly of hate crime legislation', *Journal of Law and Policy*, 2: 1–54

Foster, R. (1999) 'Strategies of justice: the project of philosophy in Lyotard and Habermas', *Philosophy and Social Criticism*, 25, 2: 87–13

Foucault, M. (1977) *Discipline and Punish: The Birth of the Prison*, London: Allen Lane

Foucault, M. (1978) *The History of Sexuality, Vol. I: An Introduction*, trans. R. Hurley, New York: Random House

Foucault, M. (1986) *The History of Sexuality, Vol. II: The Use of Pleasure*, trans. R. Hurley, New York: Random House

Foucault, M. (1991) 'Governmentality', in G. Burchell et al., eds. op. cit

Fraser, E. and Lacey, N. (1993) *The Politics of Community: A Feminist Critique of the Liberal–Communitarion Debate*, Hemel Hempstead: Harvester-Wheatsheaf

Fraser, N. (1989) 'Struggle over needs: outline of a socialist-feminist critical theory of late capitalist culture', in N. Fraser, ed. *Unruly Practices: Power, Discourse and Gender in Contemporary Social Theory*, Minneapolis: University of Minneapolis Press

Fraser, N. (1992) 'Rethinking the public sphere: a contribution to the critique of actually existing democracies', in C. Calhoun, ed. *Habermas and the Public Sphere*, Cambridge, Mass: MIT Press

Fraser, N. (1995a) 'Pragmatism, feminism and the linguistic turn', in S. Benhabib et al., eds, op. cit.

Fraser, N. (1995b) 'From redistribution to recognition? Dilemmas of justice in a post-socialist age', *New Left Review*, 212: 68–94

Fraser, N. (1997) *Justice Interruptus: Critical Reflections on the Post-Socialist Condition*, New York: Routledge

Fraser, N. and Nicholson, L. (1990) 'Social criticism without philosophy: an encounter between feminism and post-modernism', in L. Nicholson, ed. *Feminism/Postmodernism*, London: Routledge

Freiberg, A. (2000) 'Guerillas in our midst? Judicial responses to governing the dangerous', in M. Brown and J. Pratt, eds. *Dangerous Offenders: Punishment and Social Order*, London: Routledge

Furedi, F. (2002) *Culture of Fear: Risk-taking and the Morality of Low Expectation*, London: Continuum

Gaete, R. (1996) 'A Torturer's Tale', *International Journal for the Semiotics of Law*, 27: 305–14

Gamble, A. (1988) *The Free Economy and the Strong State: The Politics of Thatcherism*, London: Macmillan

Gardbaum, S.A. (1992) 'Law, politics and the claims of community', *Michigan Law Review*, 90: 685–760

Garland, D. (1990) *Punishment and Modern Society: A Study in Social Theory*, Oxford: Clarendon Press

Garland, D. (1995) 'Penal modernism and post-modernism', in T.G. Blomberg and S. Cohen, eds. *Punishment and Social Control*, New York: Aldine de Gruyter

Garland, D. (1996) 'The limits of the sovereign state: strategies of crime control in contemporary society', *British Journal of Criminology*, 36, 4: 445–70

Garland, D. (1997) "Governmentality" and the problem of crime: Foucault, criminology, sociology', *Theoretical Criminology*, 1, 2: 173–214

Garland, D. (2000) 'The culture of high crime societies: some preconditions of recent "law and order" policies', *British Journal of Criminology*, 40, 3: 347–75

Garland, D. (2001) 'Introduction: The meaning of mass imprisonment', in D. Garland, ed. *Mass Imprisonment: Social Causes and Consequences*, London: Sage

Garland, D. and Sparks, R. (2000) 'Criminology, social theory and the challenge of our times', *British Journal of Criminology*, 40, 2: 189–204

Gellman, S. (1991) 'Sticks and stones can put you in jail, but can words increase your sentence? Constitutional and policy dilemmas of ethnic intimidation laws', 39 *UCLA Law Review*, 39: 333–96

Gendreau, P., Little, T. and Goggin, C. (1996) 'A meta-analysis of the predictors of adult offender recidivism: what works? *Criminology*, 34, 4: 575–608

Giddens, A. (1990) *The Consequences of Modernity*, Cambridge: Polity Press

Giddens, A. (1993) *New Rules of Sociological Method*, 2nd edition, Cambridge: Polity Press (first published 1976, Hutchinson)

Giddens, A. (1999) 'Risk and Responsibility', *Modern Law Review*, 62, 1–10

Gilligan, C. (1982) *In a Different Voice*, Cambridge, Mass: Harvard University Press

Gilling, D. (1993) 'Crime prevention discourses and the multi-agency approach', *International Journal of the Sociology of Law*, 21: 145–57

Gilroy, P. (1993) *The Black Atlantic*, Cambridge, Mass: Harvard University Press

Goffman, E. (1959) *The Presentation of Self in Everyday Life*, New York: Doubleday Anchor

Gray, J. (1983) *Mill on Liberty: A Defence*, London: Routledge and Kegan Paul

Gray, J. (1995) *Liberalism*, 2nd edition, Buckingham: Open University Press

Greene, J. (1998) *Getting Tough on Crime: The History and Political Context of Sentencing Reform Developments Leading to the Passing of the 1994 Crime Act*, New York: Soros Foundation

Gunther, K. (1993) *The Sense of Appropriateness: Application Discourses in Morality and Law*, trans. J. Farell, Albany, NY: State University of New York Press

Gutman, A. (1980) *Liberal Equality*, Cambridge: Cambridge University Press

Gutman, A. (2001) 'Introduction', in M. Ignatieff, *Human Rights as Politics and Idolatry*, Princteon: Princeton University Press

Habermas, J. (1971) *Knowledge and Human Interests*, trans. J. Shapiro, Boston: Beacon Press

Habermas, J. (1976) *Legitimation Crisis*, trans. T. McCarthy, London: Heinemann

Habermas, J. (1982) 'Reply to my critics', in J. Thompson and D. Held, eds. *Habermas: Critical Debates*, Cambridge, Mass: MIT press

Habermas, J. (1984, 1987) *The Theory of Communicative Action*, vol. 1, and vol. 2, trans. T. McCarthy, Cambridge: Polity Press

Habermas, J. (1987) *The Philosophical Discourse of Modernity: Twelve Lectures*, trans. F.G. Lawrence, Cambridge: Polity Press

Habermas, J. (1988) 'Law and morality', in S.M. McMurrin, ed. *The Tanner Lectures on Human Values*, vol. 8, Salt Lake City: University of Utah Press

Habermas, J. (1990) 'Justice and solidarity: on the discussion concerning "Stage 6" ', in M. Kelly, ed. *Hermeneutics and Critical Theory in Ethics and Politics*, Cambridge, Mass: MIT Press

Habermas, J. (1992a) 'On morality, law, civil disobedience and modernity', in P. Dews, ed. *Autonomy and Solidarity: Interviews with Jürgen Habermas*, revised edition, London: Verso

Habermas, J. (1992b) 'Discourse, ethics, law and sittichkeit', in P. Dews ed. *Autonomy and Solidarity: Interviews with Jürgen Habermas* revised edition, London: Verso

Habermas, J. (1993) 'The second life fiction of the Federal Republic: we have become normal again', *New Left Review*, 197: 58–66

Habermas, J. (1996a) *Between Facts and Norms*, trans. W. Rehg, Cambridge: Polity Press (first published in German, 1992)

Habermas, J. (1996b) 'Postscript to *Between Facts and Norms*'. In M. Deflem, ed. *Habermas, Modernity and Law*, London: Sage

Habermas, J. (1996c) ' "Modernity: An Unfinished Project": lecture on receiving the Adorno Prize, City of Frankfurt, September 1980', trans. N. Walker, in M. Passerin d'Entreves and S. Benhabib eds. *Habermas and the Unfinished Project of Modernity*, Cambridge: Polity Press

Habermas, J. (1996d) 'Reply to symposium participants', *Cardozo Law Review*, 17: 1477–557

Habermas, J. (1998) *The Inclusion of the Other: Studies in Political Theory*, ed. Ciaran Cronin and Pablo de Grieff, Cambridge, Mass: MIT Press

Hacking, I. (1986) 'Making up people', in T.C. Heller, M. Sosna and D.E. Wellerby, eds. *Reconstructing Individualism: Autonomy, Individuality and the Self in Western Thought*, Stanford, Calif.: Stanford University Press

Halcrow, M. (1989) *Keith Joseph: A Single Mind*, Basingstoke: Macmillan

Hall, S. (1980) *Drifting into a Law and Order Society*, London: Cobden Trust

Hand, S. (1989) ed. *The Levinas Reader*, Oxford: Basil Blackwell

Hannah-Moffat, K. (2002) 'Governing through need: the hybridisation of risk and need in penality'. Paper presented at Law and Society Association Annual Meetings, Vancouver, 29 May–1 June

Harding, J. (2000) 'A community justice dimension to effective probation practice', *Howard Journal*, 39: 132–49

Hare, R.D. (2002) 'Psychopathy and risk for recidivism and violence', in N. Gray, J. Laing and L. Noaks, eds. *Criminal Justice, Mental Health and the Politics of Risk*, London: Cavendish Publishing

Harris, A.P. (1990) 'Race and essentialism in feminist legal theory', *Stanford Law Review*, 42: 581–616

Hart, H.L.A. (1968) *Punishment and Responsibility*, Oxford: Oxford University Press

Hayek, F.A. (1960) *The Constitution of Liberty*, London: Routledge and Kegan Paul

Heidegger, M. (1973) *Being and Time*, trans. J. Macquarrie and E. Robinson, Oxford: Basil Blackwell (first published in German, 1927)

Heidensohn, F. (1986) 'Models of justice: Portia or Persephone? Some thoughts on equality, fairness and gender in the field of criminal justice', *International Journal of Sociology of Law*, 14: 287–98

Henham, R. (1998) 'Human rights, due process and sentencing', *British Journal of Criminology*, 38, 4: 592–610

Hesseling, R.B.P. (1994) 'Displacement: a review of the empirical literature', in R.V. Clarke, ed. *Crime Prevention Studies, 3*, Monsey, N.Y.: Willow Tree Press

Hobbes, T. (1991) *Leviathan*, ed. R. Tuck, Cambridge: Cambridge University Press (first published 1651).

Hobhouse, L.T. (1964) *Liberalism*, London: Oxford University Press

Hogg, R. (2002) 'Criminology beyond the nation state: global conflicts, human rights and the new world order', in K. Carrington and R. Hogg, eds., *Critical Criminology: Issues, Debates, Challenges*, Cullompton: Willan Publishing

Holsti, K. (1999) 'The coming chaos? Armed conflict in the world's periphery', in T. Paul and J. Hall, eds. *International Order and the Future of World Politics*, Cambridge: Cambridge University Press

Home Office (1970) *Advisory Council on the Penal System [The Wootton Report]*, London: HMSO

hooks, b. (1981) *Ain't I a Woman*, London: Pluto Press

Hood, R., Shute, S., Feilzer, M. and Wilcox, A. (2002) 'Sex offenders emerging from long-term imprisonment: a study of their long-term reconviction rates and of parole board members' judgement of their risk, *British Journal of Criminology*, 42, 2: 371–394

Hope, T. (2000) 'Inequality and the clubbing of private security', in T. Hope and R. Sparks, eds. *Crime, Risk and Insecurity*, London: Routledge

Hope, T. and Sparks, R., eds. (2000) *Crime, Risk and Insecurity*, London: Routledge

Horkheimer, M. (1947) *Eclipse of Reason*, New York: Oxford University Press

Horkheimer, M. (1950) 'The lessons of Fascism', in H. Cantril, ed. *Tensions that Cause Wars*, Urbana: University of Illinois Press

Horkheimer, M. (1968) *Kritische Theorie*, ed. Alfred Schmidt, Frankfurt: S. Fischer Verlag

Horwitz, G. (1992) *In the Shadow of Death: Living Outside the Gates of Mauthausen*, New York: The Free Press

Howe, A. (1994) *Punish and Critique: A Feminist Analysis of Penality*, London: Routledge

Hoy, D.C. (1994) 'Conflicting conceptions of critique: Foucault versus Habermas', in D. Couzens Hoy and T. McCarthy, eds. *Critical Theory*, Oxford: Blackwell

Hudson, B.A. (1987) *Justice through Punishment: A Critique of the 'Justice Model' of Corrections*, London: Macmillan

Hudson, B.A. (1993) *Penal Policy and Social Justice*, Basingstoke: Macmillan

Hudson, B.A. (1995) 'Beyond proportionate punishment: difficult cases and the 1991 Criminal Justice Act', *Crime, Law and Social Change*, 22: 59–78

Hudson, B.A. (1996) *Understanding Justice: An Introduction to Ideas, Perspectives and Controversies in Modern Penal Theory*, Buckingham: Open University Press

Hudson, B. (1998a) 'Punishment and governance', *Social and Legal Studies*, 7, 4: 553–60

Hudson, B. (1998b) 'Restorative justice: the challenge of sexual and racial violence', *Journal of Law and Society*, 25, 2: 237–256

Hudson, B. (1999) 'Punishment, poverty and responsibility: the case for a hardship defence', *Social and Legal Studies*, 8, 4: 583–91

Hudson, B. (2000) 'Punishing the poor: dilemmas of justice and difference', in W.C. Heffernan and J. Kleinig, eds. *From Social Justice to Criminal Justice*, New York: Oxford University Press

Hudson, B. (2001) 'Punishment, rights and difference', in K. Stenson and R.R. Sullivan eds. *Crime, Risk and Justice: The Politics of Crime Control in Liberal Democracies*, Cullompton: William Publishing

Hudson, B. (2002a) 'Gender issues in penal policy and penal theory', in P. Carlen, ed. *Women and Punishment: The Struggle for Justice*, Cullompton: Willan Publishing

Hudson, B. (2002b) 'Victims and Offenders', in A. von Hirsch et al., op. cit.

Hudson, B. (2002c) 'Restorative justice and gendered violence: diversion or effective justice? *British Journal of Criminology*, 42, 3: 616–34

Hudson, J., Morris, A., Maxwell, G. and Galway, B., eds. (1996) *Family Group Conferences: Perspectives on Policy and Practice*, Monsey, N.Y.: Criminal Justice Press

Hughes, G. (1998) *Understanding Crime Prevention*, Milton Keynes: Open University Press

Hulsman, L. (1986) 'Critical criminology and the concept of crime', in H. Bianchi and R. van Swaaningen, eds. *Abolitionism: Towards a Non-Repressive Approach to Crime*, Amsterdam: The Free Press

Hume, D. (1955) *Enquiry Concerning Human Understanding* ed. C.W. Hendel, New York: Oxford University Press

Hume, D. (1957) *Enquiry Concerning the Principles of Morals*, ed. C.W. Hendel, New York: Oxford University Press (first published 1758)

Hume, D. (1978) *A Treatise of Human Nature*, ed. L.A. Selby-Bigge, Oxford: Clarendon Press (first published in 1739)

Ignatieff, M. (2001) *Human Rights as Politics and Idolatry*, ed. A. Gutman, Princeton: Princeton University Press

Irigaray, L. (1985) *Speculum of the Other Woman*, trans. G. Gill, Ithaca, NY: Cornell University Press

Jackson, E. (1992) 'Catherine MacKinnon and feminist jurisprudence: a critical appraisal', *Journal of Law and Society*, 19, 2: 195–213

Jacobs, J.B. (1993) 'The emergence and implications of american hate crime jurisprudence', *Israeli Yearbook on Human Rights*, 22: 113–39, Netherlands: Martinus Nijhoff

Janis, M.W., Kay, R. and Bradley, R. (2000) *European Human Rights Law: Text and Materials*, 2nd edition, Oxford: Oxford University Press

Janus, E. (2000) 'Civil commitment as social control: managing the risk of sexual violence', in M. Brown and J. Pratt, eds. *Dangerous Offenders: Punishment and Social Control*, London: Routledge

Jay, M. (1973) *The Dialectical Imagination: A History of the Frankfurt School and the Institute of Social Research 1923–950*, London: Heinemann

Johnson, H. and Sacco, V. (1995) 'Researching violence against women: Statistics Canada's national survey, *Canadian Journal of Criminology*, 37, 3: 281–304

Johnson, P. (2001) 'Distorted communications: feminism's dispute with Habermas', *Philosophy and Social Criticism*, 27, 1: 39–62

Kant, I. (1965a) *The Metaphysical Elements of Justice*, trans. J. Ladd, Indianapolis: Bobbs-Merrill (first published 1797)

Kant, I. (1965b) *Critique of Practical Reason*, trans. L.W. Beck, Indianapolis: Bobbs-Merrill (first published 1788)

Kant, I. (1986) *Critique of Judgment*, trans. James Creed Meredith, Oxford: Clarendon (first published 1790)

Kant, I. (1996) 'A Definition of Justice from *The Metaphysical Elements of Justice*', in J. Westphal, ed. *Justice*, Indianapolis: Hacket

Keith, M. (1991) 'Policing a perplexed society: no-go areas and the mystification of police–black conflict', in E. Cashmore and E. McLaughlin, eds. *Out of Order? Policing Black People*, London: Routledge

Kelly, P. (1990) *Utilitarianism and Distributive Justice: Jeremy Bentham and the Civil Law*, Oxford: Oxford University Press

Kemshall, H. and Maguire, M. (2002) 'Public protection, partnership and risk penality: the multi-agency risk management of sexual and violent offenders', in N. Gray, J. Laing and

L. Noaks eds. *Criminal Justice, Mental Health and the Politics of Risk*, London: Cavendish Publishing

Kerruish, V. (1991) *Jurisprudence as Ideology*, London: Routledge

Kohlberg, L. (1973) *Collected Papers on Moral Development and Moral Education*, Cambridge, Mass: Moral Education Research Foundation, Harvard University

Kohlberg, L. (1981) *The Philosophy of Moral Development*, San Francisco: Harper and Row

Kurki, L. (2000) 'Restorative and community justice in the United States', in M. Tonry, ed. *Crime and Justice: A Review of Research*, vol. 26 Chicago: University of Chicago Press

Kymlicka, W. (1989) *Liberalism, Community and Culture*, Oxford: Clarendon Press

Lacey, N. (1988) *State Punishment: Political Principles and Community Values*, London: Routledge

Lacey, N. (1993) 'Closure and critique in feminist jurisprudence: transcending the dichotomy, or a foot in both camps', in A. Norrie, ed. *Closure and Critique: New Directions in Legal Theory*, Edinburgh: Edinburgh University Press

Lacey, N. and Zedner, L. (1995) 'Discourses of community in criminal justice', *Journal of Law and Society*, 22: 301–24

Laing, R.D. (1961) *The Self and Others*, London: Tavistock

Lea, J. (1998) 'Criminology and postmodernity', in P. Walton and J. Young, eds. *The New Criminology Revisited*, Basingstoke: Macmillan

Leacock, V. and Sparks, R. (2002) 'Riskiness and at-risk-ness: some ambiguous features of the current penal landscape', in N. Gray, J. Laing and L. Noaks, eds. *Criminal Justice, Mental Health and the Politics of Risk*, London: Cavendish Publishing

Leng, R., Taylor, R. and Wasik, M. (1998) *Blackstone's Guide to the Crime and Disorder Act, 1998*, London: Blackstone

Levinas, E. (1969) *Totality and Infinity: An Essay on Exteriority*, trans. A. Lingis, Pittsburgh: Duquesne University Press

Levinas, E. (1981) *Otherwise Than Being or Beyond Essence, trans.* A. Lingis, The Hague: Martinus Nijhoff

Levinas, E. (1989) 'Ideology and Idealism', in S., Hand, ed. *The Levinas Reader*, Oxford: Blackwell

Levinas, E. (1992) *Ethics and Infinity*, Pittsburgh: Duquesne University Press

Lévi-Strauss, C. (1968) *Structural Anthropology*, London: Allen Lane

Lewis, R., Dobash, R.E., Dobash, R.P. and Cavanagh, K. (2001) 'Law's progressive potential: the value of engagement with the law for domestic violence', *Social and Legal Studies*, 10, 1: 105–30

Lianos, M. with Douglas, M. (2000) 'Dangerization and the end of deviance: the institutional environment', *British Journal of Criminology*, 40, 2: 26–78

Lloyd, G. (1984) *The Man of Reason: Male and Female in Western Philosophy*, London: Methuen

Locke, J. (1967) *Two Treatises of Government*, ed. P. Lazlett Cambridge: Cambridge University Press

Lucken, K. (1998) 'Contemporary penal trends: modern or postmodern?' *British Journal of Criminology*, 38, 1: 106–23

Luhmann, N. (1985) *A Sociological Theory of Law*, trans. E. King and M. Albrow, London: Routledge and Kegan Paul

Lukes, S. (1993) 'Five fables about human rights', in S. Shute and S. Hurley, eds, *On Human Rights: The Oxford Amnesty Lectures 1993*, New York: Basic Books

Lyotard, J.-F. (1984) *The Postmodern Condition: A Report on Knowledge*, trans. G. Bennington and B. Massumi, Manchester: Manchester University Press

Lyotard, J.-F. (1988) *The Différend: Phrases in Dispute*, Manchester: Manchester University Press

Lyotard, J.-F. (1990) *Heidegger and the 'Jews'*, Minneapolis: Minnesota University Press

Lyotard, J.-F. (1993) 'The other's right, in S. Shute and S. Hurley, eds, *On Human Rights: The Oxford Amnesty Lecture 1993*, New York: Basic Books

Lyotard, J.-F. and Thébaud, J.-L. (1985) *Just Gaming*, Manchester: Manchester University Press

McCarthy, T. (1976) 'Translator's Introduction', in J. Habermas, *Legitimation Crisis*, trans. T. McCarthy, London: Heinemann

McCarthy, T. (1978) *The Critical Theory of Jürgen Habermas*, Cambridge: Polity Press

McConville, M. Sanders, A. and Leng, R. (1997) 'Descriptive or critical sociology: the choice is yours', *British Journal of Criminology*, 37, 3: 347–58

McEvoy, K., Mika, H. and Hudson, B. (2002) 'Introduction: practice, performance and prospects for restorative justice', *British Journal of Criminology*, special edition on Restorative Justice, 42, 3: 469–75

MacIntyre, A. (1985) *After Virtue: A Study in Moral Theory*, London: Duckworth

MacIntyre, A. (1988) *Whose Justice? Which Rationality?* London: Duckworth

MacKinnon, C.A. (1987) *Feminism Unmodified: Discourses on Life and Law*, Boston, Mass: Harvard University Press

MacKinnon, C.A. (1989) *Toward a Feminist Theory of the State*, Cambridge, Mass: Harvard University Press

MacKinnon, C.A. (1991) 'Reflections on sex equality under law', *Yale Law Journal*, 100: 1281–328

MacKinnon, C.A. (1993) 'Crimes of war, crimes of peace', in S. Shute and S. Hurley, eds, op. cit.

Madriz, E. (1997) 'Images of criminals and victims: a study on women's fear and social control', *Gender and Society*, 11: 342–56

Maffesoli, M. (1996) *The Time of the Tribes*, London: Sage

Mandel, M. (1994) *The Charter of Rights and the Legalization of Politics in Canada*, revised edition, Toronto: Thompson Education Publishing

Marcuse, H. (1968) *One-Dimensional Man: Studies in the Ideology of Advanced Industrial Societies*, Boston: Beacon Press

Marshall, P. (1997) *The Prevalence of Convictions for Sexual Offending in England and Wales*, Research Findings, number 55, London: Home Office, Research and Statistics Directorate

Marshall, T.F. (1999) *Restorative Justice: An Overview*, London: Home Office, Research and Statistics Directorate

Martin, R. (1993) *A System of Rights*, Oxford: Clarendon Press

Martin, D. MacCrimmon, M., Grant, I. and Boyle, C. (1991) 'A forum on lavallee v. R.: women and self-defence', *British Columbia Law Review*, 25: 23

Marx, G. (1988) *Under Cover: Police Surveillance in America*, Berkeley: University of California Press

Masters, G. and Smith, D. (1988) 'Portia and Persephone revisited: thinking about feeling in criminal justice', *Theoretical Criminology*, 2, 1: 5–28

Matravers, M. (2000) *Justice and Punishment*, Oxford: Oxford University Press

Maxwell, G. and Morris, A. (2001) 'Putting restorative justice into practice for adult offenders', *Howard Journal of Criminal Justice*, 40, 1: 55–69

Meehan, J., ed. (1995) *Feminists Read Habermas: Gendering the Subject of Discourse*, New York: Routledge

Meehan, J. (2000) 'Feminism and Habermas's discourse ethics', *Philosophy and Social Criticism*, 26, 3: 39–52

Melossi, D. (2000) 'Social theory and changing representations of the criminal', *British Journal of Criminology*, 40, 2: 296–320

Mendus, S. (1989) *Toleration and the Limits of Liberalism*, Basingstoke: Macmillan

Merry, S. (1981) *Urban Danger: Life in a Neighbourhood of Strangers*, Philadelphia: Temple University Press

Mill, J.S. (1963–91) *The Collected Works of John Stuart Mill*, ed. J. Robson, Toronto: University of Toronto Press: *Utilitarianism*, vol. 10 (1969) and *On Liberty*, vol. 19 (1977)

Mill, J.S. (1989) *The Subjugation of Women*, (first published 1869) Cambridge: University of Cambridge Press

Miller, L. (2001) 'Looking for postmodernism in all the wrong places: implementing a new penology', *British Journal of Criminology*, 41, 1: 168–84

Miller, P. and Rose, N. (1990) 'Governing economic life', *Economy and Society*, 19: 1–27

Minow, M. (1990) *Making All the Difference: Inclusion, Exclusion and American Law*, Ithaca, N.Y.: Cornell University Press

Minow, M. (1998) *Between Vengeance and Forgiveness: Facing History after Genocide and Mass Violence*, Boston: Beacon Press

Mirlees-Black, C., Mayhew, P. and Percy, A. (1996) *The 1996 British Crime Survey*, London: HMSO

Mitchell, J. (1975) *Psychoanalysis and Feminism*, Harmondsworth: Penguin

Moller Okin, S. (1989) *Justice, Gender and the Family*, New York: Basic Books

Montesquieu, C.L. de Secondath baron de (1989) *The Spirit of Laws*, ed. and trans. A.M. Cohler, B.C. Miller and H.S. Stone, Cambridge: Cambridge University Press

Moore, G.E. (1903) *Principia Ethica*, Cambridge: Cambridge University Press

Morgan, R. (2000) 'The Utilitarian justification of torture', *Punishment and Society*, 2, 2: 181–96

Morris, L. (1994) *Dangerous Classes: The Underclass and Social Citizenship*, London: Routledge

Morris, N. (1982) *Madness and the Criminal Law*, Chicago: University of Chicago Press, Chapter 5.

Morris, A. and Gelsthorpe, L. (2000) 'Re-visioning men's violence against female partners', *Howard Journal*, 39, 4: 412–28

Morrison, T. (1993) *Playing in the Dark. Whiteness and the Literary Imagination*, New York: Vintage Books

Morrison, W. (1997) *Jurisprudence: From the Greeks to Post-Modernism*, London: Cavendish

Murphy, G. (1987) 'Does Kant Have a theory of punishment?' *Columbia Law Review*, 87: 509–32

Murphy, J.G. (1973) 'Marxism and retribution', *Philosophy and Public Affairs*, 2: 217–43

Murphy, J.G. (2000) 'Two cheers for vindictiveness', *Punishment and Society*, 2, 2: 131–44

Murray, C. (1984) *Losing Ground–American Social Policy 1950–1980*, New York: Basic Books

Naffine, N. (1990) *Law and the Sexes*, Sydney: Allen and Unwin

Nagel, T. (1986) *The View from Nowhere*, Oxford: Oxford University Press

Nelken, D. (1985) 'Community involvement in crime control', *Current Legal Problems*, 38: 239–267

Nicholson, L. (1990) ed. *Feminism/Postmodernism* London: Routledge

Nisbet, R.A. (1962a) *The Quest for Community*, New York: Oxford University Press

Nisbet, R.A. (1962b) *The Sociological Tradition*, New York: Basic Books

Norrie, A. (2000) *Punishment and Responsibility: A Relational Critique*, Oxford: Oxford University Press

Norris, C. and Armstrong, G. (1998) 'The suspicious eye', *Criminal Justice Matters*, 33, Autumn: 10–11

Norris, C., Armstrong, G. and Moran, J., eds. (1998) *Surveillance, Closed Circuit Television and Social Control*, Aldershot: Ashgate

Nozick, R. (1974) *Anarchy, State and Utopia*, New York: Basic Books

O'Connor, D.J. (1964) 'Locke', in D.J. O'Connor, ed. *A Critical History of Western Philosophy*, New York: The Free Press of Glencoe, pp. 253-74

O'Donovan, K. (1985) *Sexual Divisions in Law*, London: Weidenfeld and Nicholson

O'Donovan, K. (1993) 'Law's knowledge: the judge, the expert, the battered woman, and her syndrome', *Journal of Law and Society*, 20, 4: 427-37

Olsen, F. (1983) 'The family and the market: a study of ideology and legal reform', *Harvard Law Review*, 96: 1497

O'Malley, P. (1992) 'Risk, power and crime prevention', *Economy and Society*, 21: 252-75

O'Malley, P. (1998) 'Introduction', in P. O'Malley, ed. *Crime and the Risk Society*, Aldershot: Ashgate

O'Malley, P. (1999) 'Volatile and contradictory punishment', *Theoretical Criminology*, 3, 2: 175-96

O'Malley, P. (2000) 'Risk societies and the government of crime', in M. Brown and J. Pratt, eds. *Dangerous Offenders: Punishment and Social Order*, London: Routledge

O'Malley, P. (2001) 'Risk, crime and prudentialism revisited', in K. Stenson and R.R. Sullivan, eds. op. cit.

Outhwaite, W. (1994) *Habermas: A Critical Introduction*, Cambridge: Polity Press

Packer, H. (1969) *The Limits of the Criminal Sanction*, Stanford, Calif: Stanford University Press

Palmer, R.E. (1969) *Hermeneutics*, Evanston: Northwestern University Press

Parekh, B. (2000) *Rethinking Multiculturalism*, Basingstoke: Macmillan

Pasquino, P. (1991) 'Criminology: the birth of a special knowledge', in G. Burchell et al., eds. op. cit

Passerin d'Entreves, M. (1996) 'Introduction' in M. Passerin d'Entreves and S. Benhabib, eds. *Habermas and the Unfinished project of Modernity*, Cambridge: Polity Press

Pateman, C. (1988a) *The Sexual Contract*, Cambridge: Polity Press

Pateman, C. (1988b) 'The theoretical subversiveness of feminism', in C. Pateman and S. Grosz, eds, *Feminist Challenges*, Sydney: Allen and Unwin

Pearson, G. (1983) *Hooligan: A History of Respectable Fears*, London: Macmillan

Pease, K. (2002) 'Crime reduction', in M. Maguire, R. Morgan and R. Reiner, eds, *The Oxford Handbook of Criminology*, 3rd edition, Oxford University Press

Peirce, C. (1960) *The Collected Papers of Charles Sanders Pierce*, vols 1 and 2, ed. C. Hartshorne and P. Weiss, Cambridge, Mass: Harvard University Press

Perry, M.J. (1998) *The Idea of Human Rights: Four Inquiries*, Oxford: Oxford University Press

Pettit, P. (1980) *Judging Justice*, London: Routledge and Kegan Paul

Pettit, P. (1982) 'Habermas on truth and justice', *Royal Institute of Philosophy Lecture Series*, Cambridge: University of Cambridge Press, pp. 207-28

Pettit, P. (1997) *Republicanism: A Theory of Freedom and Government*, Oxford: Clarendon Press

Piaget, J. (1971) *Structuralism*, trans. C. Maschler, London: Routledge and Kegan Paul

Piaget, J. (1977) *The Moral Judgement of the Child*, Harmondsworth: Penguin

Popper, K. (1945) *The Open Society and its Enemies*, London: Routledge and Kegan Paul

Pratt, J. (1995) 'Dangerousness, risk and technologies of power', *Australia and New Zealand Journal of Criminology*, 28: 3-31

Pratt, J. (1996) 'Governing the dangerous: an historical view of dangerous offender legislation', *Social and Legal Studies*, 5, 1: 21-36

Pratt, J. (1998) *Governing the Dangerous*, Sydney: Federation Press

Pratt, J. (2000a) 'Dangerousness and modern society', in M. Brown and J. Pratt, eds, *Dangerous Offenders: Punishment and Social Order* London: Routledge

Pratt, J. (2000b) 'The return of wheelbarrow man; or the arrival of postmodern penality *British Journal of Criminology*, 40, 1: 127-45

Pritchard, H.A. (1949) *Moral Obligation,* Oxford: Clarendon Press

Punishment and Society (January 2001) 3, 1: Special issue on Mass Imprisonment in the USA

Rasmussen, D. (1990) *Reading Habermas,* Oxford: Blackwell

Rawls, J. (1972) *A Theory of Justice,* Oxford: Oxford University Press

Rawls, J. (1987) 'The idea of overlapping consensus', *Oxford Journal of Legal Studies,* 7: 1–25

Rawls, J. (1989) 'The domain of the political and overlapping consensus', *New York University Law Review,* 64: 233–55

Rawls, J. (1993a) *Political Liberalism,* New York: Columbia University Press

Rawls, J. (1993b) 'The law of peoples' in S. Shute and S. Hurley, eds, *On Human Rights: The Oxford Amnesty Lectures 1993.* New York: Basic Books

Raz, J. (1986) *The Morality of Freedom,* Oxford: Clarendon Press

Rehg, W. (1996) "Translator's Introduction" in J. Habermas, *Between Facts and Norms* trans. William Rehg, Cambridge: Polity Press

Reiman, J. (1989) *The Rich Get Richer and the Poor Get Prison: Ideology, Class and Criminal Justice,* 3rd edition, New York: Macmillan

Reiman, J. (1990) *Justice and Modern Moral Philosophy,* New Haven, Conn: Yale University Press

Richardson, J. and Sandland, R., eds. (2000) *Feminist Perspectives on Law and Theory,* London: Cavendish

Riley, J. (1998) 'Mill on justice', in D. Boucher and P. Kelly, eds. *Social Justice: From Hume to Walzer,* London: Routledge

Roach Anleu, S. (1992) 'Critiquing the law: themes and dilemmas in Anglo-American feminist legal theory', *Journal of Law and Society,* 19, 4: 423–40

Rorty, R. (1989) *Contingency, Irony and Solidarity,* Cambridge: Cambridge University Press

Rorty, R. (1993) 'Human rights, rationality and sentimentality', in S. Shute and S. Hurley, eds. *On Human Rights: The Oxford Amnesty Lectures 1993,* New York: Basic Books

Rosati, M. (2000) 'Freedom from domination: the republican revival', *Philosophy and Social Criticism,* 26, 3: 83–8

Rose, N. (1996a) 'Governing "advanced" liberal democracies', in A. Barry, T. Osborne and N. Rose, eds. *Foucault and Political Reason,* London: UCL Press

Rose, N. (1996b) 'The death of the "social"? Refiguring the territory of government', *Economy and Society,* 26, 4: 327–46

Rose, N. (2000) 'Government and Control', *British Journal of Criminology,* 40, 2: 321–339

Rosenau, P.M. (1992) *Post-Modernism and the Social Sciences: Insights, Inroads and Intrusions,* Princeton, NJ: Princeton University Press

Ross, W.D. (1930) *The Right and the Good,* Oxford: Clarendon Press

Rotman, E. (1990) *Beyond Punishment: A New View on the Rehabilitation of Criminal Offenders,* New York: Greenwood Press

Rusche, G. and Kirchheimer, O. (1968) *Punishment and Social Structure,* New York: Russell and Russell

Rutherford, A. (1996) *Criminal Policy and the Eliminative Ideal,* inaugural lecture, Institute of Criminal Justice, University of Southampton

Sagoff, M. (1982) 'On markets for risk', *Maryland Law Review,* 41: 755–83

Said, E. (1978) *Orientalism,* London: Routledge and Kegan Paul

Said, E. (1993) *Culture and Imperialism,* London: Chatto and Windus

Salter, M. (1996) 'The impossibility of human rights within a postmodern account of law and justice', *Journal of Civil Liberties,* 1: 29–66

Sandel, M. (1982) *Liberalism and the Limits of Justice,* Cambridge: Cambridge University Press, second edition 1998

Sarat, A. (1997) 'Vengeance, victims and the identities of law', *Social and Legal Studies,* 6, 2: 163–90

Sarat, A. and Kearns, T.R. (1991) 'A journey through forgetting: toward a jurisprudence of violence', in A. Sarat and T.R. Kearns, eds. *The Fate of Law*, Ann Arbor: University of Michigan Press

Sartre, J.P. (1938) *La Nausée*, published in English as *Nausea*, trans. R. Baldick (1965), Harmondsworth: Penguin

Sartre, J.P. (1958) *Being and Nothingness*, trans. H.E. Barnes, London: Methuen

Sasson, T. (2000) 'William Horton's long shadow: "punitiveness" and "managerialism" in the penal politics of Massachusetts, 1988-1999',in T. Hope and R. Sparks, eds. op. cit.

Schutz, A. and Luckmann, T. (1974) *The Structures of the Life-World*, trans. R.M. Zaner and H. Tristram Engelhardt Jr., London: Heinemann

Scott, J.W. (1988) 'Deconstructing equality-versus-difference', *Feminist Studies*, 14, 1: 33-50

Scraton, P., ed. (1987) *Law, Order and the Authoritarian State*, Milton Keynes: Open University Press

Selznick, P. (2001) 'Rights in their place'. Paper presented to the Law and Society Association (USA) Annual Meetings, Central European University, Budapest, 4-7 July

Sen, A. and Williams, B., eds. (1982) *Utilitarianism and Beyond*, Cambridge: Cambridge University Press

Sennett, R. (1992) *The Conscience of the Eye*, New York: W.W. Norton

Shapiro, I. (1986) *The Evolution of Rights in Liberal Theory*, Cambridge: Cambridge University Press

Shearing, C. and Stenning, P. (1981) 'Private security: its growth and implications', in M. Tonry and N. Morris, eds, *Crime and Justice: An Annual Review of Research*, Chicago: University of Chicago Press

Shklar, J.N. (1998) 'The liberalism of fear', in S. Hoffman, ed. *Political Thought and Political Thinkers*, Chicago: University of Chicago Press

Short, J. (1990) 'Hazards, risks and enterprise: approaches to science, law and social policy', *Law and Society Review*, 24: 179-98

Shute, S. and Hurley, S., eds. (1993) *On Human Rights: The Oxford Amnesty Lectures 1993*, New York: Basic Books

Sidgwick, H. (1907) *The Methods of Ethics*, 7th edition, London: Macmillan

Silverman, S. and Wilson, D. (2002) *Innocence Betrayed: Paedophilia, the Media and Society*, Cambridge: Polity Press

Sim, J. (2000) 'Against the punitive wind: Stuart Hall, the state and the great moving right show', in P. Gilroy, L. Grossberg and A. McRobbie, eds. *Without Guarantees: In Honour of Stuart Hall*, London: Verso

Simon, J. (1987) 'The emergence of a risk society: insurance, law and the state', *Socialist Review*, 95: 6-89

Simon, J. (1998) 'Managing the monstrous: sex offenders and the new penology', *Psychology, Public Policy and Law*, 4, 1: 1-16

Simon, J. (2001) 'Entitlement to cruelty: neo-liberalism and the punitive mentality in the United States', in K. Stenson and R.R. Sullivan, eds. op. cit.

Smart, B. (1999) *Facing Modernity: Ambivalence, Reflexivity and Morality*, London: Sage

Smart, C. (1989) *Feminism and the Power of Law*, London: Routledge

Smart, C. (1995) *Law, Crime and Sexuality*, London: Sage

Smith, R. (2002) *Textbook on International Human Rights*, Oxford: Oxford University Press

Soothill, K., Francis, T.S., Sanderson, B. and Ackerley, E. (2000) 'Sex offenders: specialists, generalists - or both?' *British Journal of Criminology*, 40: 56-67

Spelman, E. (1990) *Inessential Woman: Problems of Exclusion in Feminist Thought*, London: The Women's Press

Spierenburg, P. (1984) *The Spectacle of Suffering*, Cambridge: Cambridge University Press

Stanko, E.A. (1990) *Everyday Violence: How Women and Men Experience Physical and Sexual Violence*, London: Pandora

Stanko, E.A. (1997) 'Safety talk: conceptualising women's risk assessment as a "technology of the soul" ', *Theoretical Criminology*, 1, 4: 490–9

Stanko, E.A. (2000) 'Naturalising danger: women, fear and personal safety', in M. Brown and J. Pratt, eds. *Dangerous Offenders: Punishment and Social Order*, London: Routledge

Steiner, H.J. and Alston, P. (2000) *International Human Rights in Context*, 2nd edition, Oxford: Oxford University Press

Stenson, K. (1998) 'Displacing social policy through crime control', in S. Hanninen, ed. *Displacement of Social Policies*, Jyväskylä: SoPhi Publications

Stenson, K. (1999) 'Crime control, governmentality and sovereignty', in R. Smandych, ed. *Governable Places: Readings in Governmentality and Crime Control*, Aldershot: Dartmouth

Stenson, K. and Sullivan, R., eds. (2001) *Crime, Risk and Justice: The Politics of Crime Control in Liberal Democracies*, Cullompton: Willan Publishing

Sullivan, R.R. (2001) 'The schizophrenic state: neo-liberal criminal justice', in K. Stenson and R. Sullivan, eds, op. cit.

Taylor, C. (1979) *Hegel and Modern Society*, Cambridge: Cambridge University Press

Taylor, C. (1985) *Philosophical Papers: Vol. 2 Philosophy and the Human Sciences*, Cambridge: Cambridge University Press

Taylor, C. (1989) *Sources of the Self: The Making of the Modern Identity*, Cambridge: Cambridge University Press

Tonry, M. (2001) 'Unthought thoughts: the influence of changing sensibilities on penal policies', *Punishment and Society*, 3, 1: 167–82

Travis, A. (2000) 'Computer to score chance of criminals reoffending', the *Guardian*, 18 August

Trey, G.A. (1992) 'Communicative ethics in the face of alterity: Habermas, Levinas and the problem of post-conventional universalism', *Praxis International*, 11, 4: 412–27

Valverde, M. (1996a) 'Social facticity and the law: a social expert's eyewitness account of law', *Social and Legal Studies*, 5, 2: 201–8

Valverde, M. (1996b) 'Despotism and ethical liberal governance', *Economy and Society*, 25, 3: 357–72

Van Ness, D.W. (1993) 'New wine and old wineskins: four challenges of restorative justice', *Criminal Law Forum*, 4: 251–76

Van Swaaningen, R. (1997) *Critical Criminology: Visions from Europe*, London: Sage

Van Swaaningen, R. (1998) 'Tolerance or zero tolerance: is that the question?' Paper presented at the American Society of Criminology Annual Meetings, Washington DC, 1–14 November

Venn, C. (1997) 'Beyond enlightenment? After the subject of foucault, who comes?' *Theory, Culture and Society*, 14, 3: 28

von Hirsch, A. (1976) *Doing Justice: The Choice of Punishments*, New York: Hill and Wang

von Hirsch, A. (1985) *Past or Future Crimes: Deservedness and Dangerousness in the Punishment of Crimes*, Manchester: Manchester University Press

von Hirsch, A. (1993) *Censure and Sanctions*, Oxford: Clarendon Press

von Hirsch, A. and Jareborg, N. (1991) 'Gauging criminal harm: a living-standard analysis', *Oxford Journal of Legal Studies*, 1, 1: 1–38

von Hirsch, A., Roberts, J., Bottoms, A.E., Roach, K. and Schiff, M., eds (2002) *Restorative Justice and Criminal Justice: Competing or Reconcilable Paradigms*, Oxford: Hart Publishing

Wacquant, L. (2001) 'Deadly symbiosis: when ghetto and prison meet and merge', *Punishment and Society*, 3, 1: 95–34

Wadham, J. and Mountfield, H. (2002) *Blackstone's Guide to the Human Rights Act, 1998*, 3rd edition, Oxford: Blackstone Press

Walgrave, L. (2002) 'Restoration and punishment: duet or duel', in A. von Hirsch et al., eds. op. cit.

Walker, N. (1991) *Why Punish?* Oxford: Oxford University Press

Walklate, S. (1997) 'Risk and criminal victimisation: a modernist dilemma?' *British Journal of Criminology*, 37, 1: 35–46

Walzer, M. (1983) *Spheres of Justice: A Defence of Pluralism and Equality*, Oxford: Martin Robertson

Walzer, M. (1986) 'The politics of Michel Foucault', in D. Couzens Hoy, ed. *Foucault: A Critical Reader* Oxford: Basil Blackwell

Walzer, M. (1987) *Interpretation and Social Criticism*, Cambridge, Mass: Harvard University Press

Walzer, M. (1994) *Thick and Thin: Moral Argument at Home and Abroad*, Notre Dame: University of Notre Dame Press

Ward, I. (1998) *An Introduction to Critical Legal Theory*, London: Cavendish

Wasserstrom, R. (1980) 'On racism and sexism', in R. Wasserstrom ed. *Philosophy and Social Issues*, Notre Dame: Notre Dame University Press

Westphal, J., ed. (1996) *Justice*, Indianapolis: Hackett

White, S.K. (1987-8) 'Justice and the Postmodern Problematic', *Praxis International*, 7, 3-4: 306–19

White, S.K. (1988) *The Recent Work of Jürgen Habermas: Reason, Justice and Modernity*, Cambridge: Cambridge University Press

Wildavsky, A. (1979) 'No risk is the highest risk of all', *American Scientist*, 67, Jan/Feb: 32

Williams, D., ed. (1999) *The Enlightenment*, Cambridge: Cambridge University Press

Williams, P. (1991) *The Alchemy of Race and Rights*, Cambridge, Mass: Harvard University Press

Wilson, J.Q. (1983) *Thinking About Crime*, 2nd edition, New York: Basic Books

Wilson, J.Q. and Kelling, G. (1982) 'Broken windows: the police and community safety', *Atlantic Monthly*, March: 29–38

Wollstonecraft, M. (1967) *A Vindication of the Rights of Woman*, New York: W.W. Norton (first published 1792)

Worrall, A. (1990) *Offending Women: Female Lawbreakers and the Criminal Justice System*, London: Routledge

Wright, M. (2002) 'The court as last resort: victim-sensitive, community-based responses to crime', *British Journal of Criminology*, 42, 3: 654–67

Young, I.M. (1990) *Justice and the Politics of Difference*, Princeton, N.J.: Princeton University Press

Young, J. (1999) *The Exclusive Society*, London: Sage

Young, R. (2001) 'Just cops doing "shameful" business: police-led restorative justice and the lessons of research', in A. Morris and G. Maxwell, eds, *Restorative Justice for Juveniles*, Oxford: Hart Publishing

Zedner, L. (1994) 'Reparation and retribution: are they reconcilable?' *Modern Law Review*, 57: 228–50

Zedner, L. (2000) 'The pursuit of security', in T. Hope and R. Sparks, eds, op. cit

Zehr, H. (1990) *Changing Lenses: A New Focus for Crime and Justice*, Scottsdale, PA.: Herald Press

Zimring, F.E. (2001) 'Imprisonment rates and the new politics of criminal punishment', *Punishment and Society*, 3, 1: 161–6

Zimring, F.E. and Hawkins, G. (1995) *Incapacitation: Penal Confinement and the Restraint of Crime*, New York: Oxford University Press

Index